New Labour in Government

New Labour in Government

Edited by

Steve Ludlam

and

Martin J. Smith

palgrave

Published by
PALGRAVE
Houndmills, Basingstoke, Hampshire RG21 6XS and
175 Fifth Avenue, New York, N. Y. 10010
Companies and representatives throughout the world

PALGRAVE is the new global academic imprint of
St. Martin's Press LLC Scholarly and Reference Division and
Palgrave Publishers Ltd (formerly Macmillan Press Ltd).

Outside North America
ISBN 0–333–76100–6 hardcover
ISBN 0–333–76101–4 paperback

Inside North America
ISBN 0–333–76100–6 cloth

This book is printed on paper suitable for recycling and made from fully managed and sustained forest sources.

A catalogue record for this book is available from the British Library.

Library of Congress Cataloging-in-Publication Data
New Labour in government / edited by Steve Ludlam and Martin J. Smith.
    p. cm
    Includes bibliographical references and index.
    ISBN 0–333–76100–6 cloth
    1. Labour Party (Great Britain) 2. Great Britain—Politics and government—
    —1997—I. Ludlam, Steve, 1951– II. Smith, Martin J. (Martin John), 1961–

JN1129 .L32 N46 2000
324.24107—dc21   00–042245

10   9   8   7   6   5   4   3   2
09   08   07   06   05   04   03   02   01

Printed in China

In memory of
Gerald David Smith
1935–99

Contents

List of Tables, Boxes and Figures   ix

Preface   xi

Notes on Contributors   xii

List of Abbreviations   xv

1 The Making of New Labour   1
   Steve Ludlam

2 New Labour and the Electorate   32
   Charles Pattie

3 New Labour's Third Way and European   55
   Social Democracy
   Ben Clift

4 New Labour and the Party: Members
   and Organization   73
   Patrick Seyd and Paul Whiteley

5 New Labour's Parliamentarians   92
   Philip Cowley, Darren Darcy and Colin Mellors

6 New Labour and the Unions: the End of
   the Contentious Alliance?   111
   Steve Ludlam

7 The Hand of History: New Labour,
   News Management and Governance   130
   Bob Franklin

8 New Labour, the Constitution and Reforming the State   145
   David Richards and Martin J. Smith

9 Labour's New Economics   167
   Andrew Gamble and Gavin Kelly

vii

10 **New Labour and Education,
    Education, Education**   184
    Colin McCaig

11 **New Labour and Welfare**   202
    Claire Annesley

12 **New Labour's Foreign and Defence Policy: External
    Support Structures and Domestic Politics**   219
    Jim Buller

13 **Interpreting New Labour: Constraints,
    Dilemmas and Political Agency**   234
    Michael Kenny and Martin J. Smith

14 **Conclusion: the Complexity of New Labour**   256
    Martin J. Smith

Guide to Further Reading   268

References   274

Index   301

List of Tables, Boxes and Figures

Tables

2.1 Per cent Labour vote by class, 1992–97   38

2.2 Per cent Labour vote by housing tenure, 1964–97   40

2.3 Attitudes on economic policy, 1964–97   42

2.4 Perceived party image, 1964–97   45

2.5 Attitudes towards business and trade
     union power, 1964–97   46

2.6 The impact of 1997 constituency campaigning, 1992–97   49

2.7 Components of electoral bias, 1950–97   51

4.1 Members' perceptions of the
     Labour party's image in 1989 and 1997   85

4.2 Members' perceptions of who the
     Labour party represents in 1989 and 1997   86

4.3 Members' perceptions of the Labour
     leader in 1989 and 1997   87

4.4 Members' perceptions of their
     influence in the party, 1989 and 1997   87

4.5 Members' views about party
     organization and strategy in 1997   88

5.1 Occupational backgrounds of Labour MPs, 1945–97   94

5.2 Selected occupational backgrounds of
     Labour MPs, 1945–97   95

5.3 Educational backgrounds of Labour MPs, 1945–97   97

5.4 Educational backgrounds of PLP in 1997   98

5.5 Gender balance within the PLP, 1945–97   100

5.6   Rebellions by government MPs in
first sessions, 1945–97   105

5.7   Changes in the attitudes of the PLP, 1992–98   108

5.8   Relationship between first and other sessions, 1945–92   109

8.1   Task forces set up by Labour government, 1997   152

Boxes

1.1   Labour in government and opposition, 1945–79   4

1.2   Labour in the wilderness, 1979–97   8

1.3   Labour's policy modernization, 1983–97   16

Figures

2.1   Labour votes and MPs, 1900–97   33

2.2   Average scores, tax vs. spending dimension   42

2.3   Average scores, jobs vs. prices dimension   43

2.4   Average scores, nationalization vs. privatization dimension 44

4.1   Labour party membership   83

8.1   The reconstituted state under the Conservatives   148

8.2   The reconstituted state under Labour   165

Preface

We resisted the temptation to rush into print with a volume of this kind, in the belief that important judgements could not be made until the content and implications became clear of such key New Labour initiatives as the internal party reform package Partnership into Power, the Employment Relations Act, the key constitutional reform measures, and not least the direction of economic and social policy once the self-denying ordinance was lifted that froze public spending for two years at levels decreed by the outgoing Tory government. New Labour's careful pre-election depression of expectations and limitation of pledges made this all the more necessary. We are confident that this collection will be much more useful to students of British and Labour politics as a result.

The authors of the chapters that follow are all actively researching the subjects about which they have written here, and we are grateful to them for their contributions and for incorporating the results of recent research where appropriate. We have tried to balance the content so that it covers the key questions posed by the phenomenon of New Labour, both as a party and as a government. There are, inevitably, gaps in coverage, many of which will hopefully be filled by the tide of work on New Labour that will doubtless engulf us before very long.

In coordinating the efforts of numerous colleagues in what has become an occasionally manic profession, we have been greatly assisted by the unfailingly constructive and timely interventions of Steven Kennedy at the publishers, and the humbling rapidity and accuracy with which Keith Povey turns around typescripts. We are as grateful as ever to our partners and children for their affection and patience. Finally, the book is dedicated to Martin Smith's father, who died during the final stages of the book's completion. He would undoubtedly have disagreed with the interpretation of Blair that is developed in this book but he would have been interested in the final product.

STEVE LUDLAM
MARTIN J. SMITH

Notes on Contributors

Claire Annesley is Lecturer in European Politics in the Department of Government at Manchester University. Between 1998 and 2000 she was Researcher in the Political Economy Research Centre, University of Sheffield, on an EU-funded project on 'Comparative Social Inclusion Policies: Towards a New European Social Model'.

Jim Buller is a Lecturer in Politics at the University of York. His interest include Britian's relations with the EU. His publications include *National Statecraft and European Integration: The Conservative Government and the European Union, 1979–97* (2000).

Ben Clift is completing doctoral research at the University of Sheffield on the French Socialist Party. His research interests and publications are on globalization and European Social Democracy.

Philip Cowley is Lecturer in Politics at the University of Hull, and Deputy Director of the Centre for Legislative Studies. His publications include *Conscience and Parliament* (editor, 1998), and the *British Elections* and *Parties Review* (co-editor, 1998, 1999), as well as articles in a range of journals.

Darren Darcy is a researcher in the Department of European Studies, University of Bradford. His current research interest is the socio-economic background of MPs. His recent publications are on the remuneration of MPs.

Bob Franklin is Professor of Media Communications in the Department of Sociological Studies at the University of Sheffield. He is co-editor of *Journalism Studies*. Recent books include: *Social Policy, the Media and Misrepresentation* (1999); *Making The Local News; Local Journalism In Context* (1998); *Newszak and News Media* (1997); *and, Packaging Politics; Political Communications in Britain's Media Democracy* (1994).

Andrew Gamble is Professor of Politics, and Director of the Political Economy Research Centre, University of Sheffield. His principal research interests are state theory and comparative political economy. His recent publications include *Hayek: The Iron Cage of Liberty* (1996), *Regionalism and World Order* (co-editor) (Macmillan, 1996), *Stakeholder Capitalism* (co-editor) (Macmillan, 1997).

Gavin Kelly recently completed a Ph.D. in the Political Economy Research Centre, University of Sheffield, and is Senior Research Fellow, Institute for Public Policy Research. His publications include *Stakeholder Capitalism* (co-editor) (Macmillan, 1997).

Michael Kenny is Reader in Politics, University of Sheffield. His publications include *The First New Left, 1956–62* (1995), *Western Political Thought: An Annotated Bibliography of Writings in English Since 1945* (co-author) (1995), and *The New Politics: Political Ideas and Social Movements* (forthcoming).

Steve Ludlam is Lecturer in Politics, University of Sheffield. He is convenor of the Political Studies Association's specialist Labour Movements Group. His publications include *Contemporary British Conservatism* (co-editor, 1996) and *British Elections and Parties Review* (co-editor, 1997).

Colin McCaig recently completed a Ph.D. on New Labour's education policy at the University of Sheffield. He is Research Associate, Department for Educational Studies, University of Sheffield.

Colin Mellors is Professor of Political Science at the University of Bradford, where he is also Senior Pro-Vice Chancellor. His interests include political recruitment, coalitional behaviour, and local and regional government. Besides his standard work, *The British MP* (1978), his publications include *Local Government in the Community* (1987) and *Political Parties and Coalitions in European Local Government* (1988).

Charles Pattie is Reader in Geography, University of Sheffield. He has published widely on electoral geography, party campaigning, and devolution. His most recent, co-authored, book is *The Boundary Commission* (1999).

David Richards is a Lecturer in Politics at the University of Liverpool. His research interests include reform of the civil service. He is conducting an ESRC project on Labour and Whitehall. His publications include *The Civil Service Under the Conservatives*.

Patrick Seyd is Professor of Politics, University of Sheffield, and co-director of the Centre for the Study of Political Parties. His publications include *The Rise and Fall of the Labour Left* (1987), *Labour's Grass Roots: The Politics of Party Membership* (co-author) (1992), and *True Blues: The Politics of Conservative Party Membership* (co-author) (1994).

Martin J. Smith is Professor of Politics, University of Sheffield. He is currently directing an ESRC project on Labour and Whitehall. His publications include *The Changing Labour Party* (co-editor) (1992), *Contemporary British Conservatism* (co-editor) (1996), and *The Core Executive in Britain* (1999).

Paul Whiteley is Professor of Politics, University of Sheffield, director of the ESRC Democracy and Participation Programme, and co-director of the Centre for the Study of Political Parties. His publications include *The Labour Party in Crisis* (Methuen, 1983), *Labour's Grass Roots: The Politics of Party Membership* (co-author) (1992), and *True Blues: The Politics of Conservative Party Membership* (co-author) (1994).

List of Abbreviations

AEEU	Amalgamated Engineering and Electrical Union
AWS	All Women Shortlists
BES	British Election Study
CBI	Confederation of British Industry
CCTC	Childcare Tax Credit
CLP	Constituency Labour Party
CPAG	Child Poverty Action Group
CSJ	Commission on Social Justice
CSR	Comprehensive Spending Review
CTC	City Technical College
CVCP	Committee for Vice Chancellors and Principals
DfEE	Department for Education and Employment
DTI	Department of Trade and Industry
ECB	European Central Bank
EMU	European Monetary Union
ERM	European Exchange Rate Mechanism
EAZ	Education Action Zone
EITC	Earned Income Tax Credit (America)
EPOP	Elections Public Opinion and Parties Group
FBU	Fire Brigades Union
FPP	'First past the post'
FOI	Freedom of Information Act
GCHQ	Government Communications Head Quarters
GICS	Government Information and Communications Service
GM	Grant-Maintained
GPMU	Graphical, Paper and Media Union
HAZ	Health Action Zone
HECS	Higher Education Contribution Scheme (Australia)
IMF	International Monetary Fund
IPPR	Institute for Public Policy Research
ITB	Industry Training Board
JSA	Job Seekers' Allowance
LEA	Local Education Authority
LMS	Local Management Schools
MEP	Member of European Parliament
MPC	Monetary Policy Committee
MSF	Manufacturing, Science, Finance

NAIRU	Non-Accelerating Inflation Rate of Unemployment
NATO	North Atlantic Treaty Organization
NEC	National Executive Committee
NGO	Non-Governmental Organization
NUM	National Union of Mineworkers
OECD	Organization for Economic Co-operation and Development
OFSTED	Office for Standards in Education
OMOV	One Member One Vote
PFI	Private Finance Initiative
PSOE	Partido Socialista Obrero Español
PS	Parti Socialiste
PvdA	Partij van der Arbeid
RDAs	Regional Development Agencies
RMT	National Union of Rail, Maritime and Transport Workers
SALT	Strategic Arms Limitations Talks
SAP	Socialdemokratiska Arbeter Partiet
SCU	Strategic Communications Unit
SDP	Social Democratic Party
SERPS	State Earnings-Related Pension Scheme
SEU	Social Exclusion Unit
SPD	Socialdemokratische Partei Deutschlands
TECs	Training and Enterprise Councils
THES	*Times Higher Education Supplement*
TIGMOO	'This Great Movement of Ours'
TGWU	Transport and General Workers Union
TUC	Trades Union Congress
TVEI	Technical and Vocational Education Initiative
WEU	Western European Union
WFTC	Working Families Tax Credit
WTO	World Trade Organization

1

The Making of New Labour

STEVE LUDLAM

On May Day 1997, the British Labour Party emerged from a very long dark tunnel into the blindingly unfamiliar light of one of the most stunning election victories of the twentieth century. Pundits were left grasping for ever more cataclysmic metaphors. One academic commentator listed 19 political records set in the election, of which 12 related to Labour gains or Conservative losses. Labour's swing and its gains in seats were new post-war records: its total number of seats and its majority at Westminster were its largest ever and broke British records set in the extreme political conditions of the 1935 election (King, 1998). In one sense, of course, Labour had achieved none of these feats. The party, as Tony Blair immediately reassured his new electorate, had been elected as New Labour, and would now govern as New Labour, a formulation he quickly restated in 1999 when mid-term electoral setbacks led to calls for a reorientation on Labour's traditional core voters. 'No self-respecting critical analyst or commentator' as Colin Hay has recently observed, 'can possibly but shiver at the proliferation of entities, processes, institutions, theories, disciplines and now parties to which the ubiquitous prefix "new" has been appended in recent years.' (Hay, 1999, 1) In the marketing of New Labour – since the slogan 'New Labour, New Britain' first appeared above the party's conference platform in 1994, such entities have proliferated at a bewildering rate. In his 1995 party conference address, Blair is said to have used the 'new' word 59 times, of which 16 were appended to Labour – but the 's' word, socialism, only once (Seyd, 1998).

A major difficulty for early analysts of New Labour was judging how far its newness was merely a rebranding exercise to reclaim lost voters. Tory strategists were unable to decide whether to portray New Labour as masking the leftist, red 'devil eyes' of Tory election posters, or as a diluted Thatcherism better delivered by those who owned the trade mark. Socialists and social democrats debated along similar lines. Was New Labour diluted social democracy, owing more than it cared to admit to the right wing of Old Labour (Anderson and Mann, 1997)? Was it masking a fatalistic Thatcherism, resigned to globalized political impotence and the reactionary spirit of a dumbed-down electorate (Hall, 1995)? Or was it, indeed, a new political 'paradigm' (Brivati, 1997), a visionary 'radical centre' negotiating the shifting sands of electoral opinion (Fielding, 1997b), and what would later be branded a 'third way' of delivering economic growth and social justice (Giddens, 1998)? Labour's members had mostly accepted that the party had to pitch its appeal to the voters of 'middle England' if it was to secure a parliamentary majority. Many, after 1 May 1997, hoped to discover that Blair's careful depression of the expectations of Labour's core voters and members, and his repeated reassurance of his target 'Tory switchers', had been the tactical genius of a leader determined, by stealth if necessary, to redress the balance of power and wealth driven so relentlessly in favour of business and the affluent by Margaret Thatcher and John Major. Critics wondered how any meaningful redistribution of wealth could take place given the undertakings to stick to Major's public spending cuts, and the promise not to restore the higher rates of income tax whose removal by the Tories had done so much to widen income inequalities. Would, as John Lloyd, a journalist ally of Blair put it after the election (*New Statesman*, 26 September 1997), ministers have to 'be seen to care like socialists while really cutting like Conservatives'?

Only New Labour's record in office would answer such questions, and reveal just how new it really was, as a political party, as a policymaking government, and as the bearer of political ideas. A central objective of this book is to provide students of New Labour with a broad-ranging assessment of that record in relation to the main areas of economic, social, educational, foreign and constitutional policy. Beyond this, it addresses the crucial question of the nature and components of New Labour's electoral triumph, and whether it can deliver the second term of office Blair so desperately wants and considers how best to interpret the theory and practice of 'Blairism' and how Blair's Third Way relates to social democratic strategies in continental Europe. One of New Labour's many mantras has insisted that Britain could not be renewed until the party itself was. So the book addresses the party's internal reforms, and the characteristics of its New Labour membership, the composition and behaviour of its parliamentarians, and its awkward partnership with Labour's historic allies in the trade union movement. One of the many academic mantras on the subject of past Labour governments has voiced disappointment that they have been 'in office, but not in power', that radicalism in opposition has been crushed in office by the bureaucratic embrace of the Whitehall establishment. Two chapters address aspects of New Labour's drive to exercise power in office: its reconstruction inside government of its media management machinery, and the contradictions between its attempts to reform the machinery of the state – to practise joined-up government – and its programme of decentralizing constitutional reform.

This introductory chapter has several purposes. First, in asserting its novelty, New Labour has constructed a history of Old Labour which, as several students of Labour have pointed out, is highly contentious (Shaw, 1996, 206–29; D. Coates, 1996). One of the consequences of Labour's long wilderness years after 1979 is that most students reading this book have no personal recollection of Old Labour in office. This chapter therefore offers a very potted account of post-war Old Labour, not in an attempt to do full credit to Labour's achievements or failures, but in a way that hopefully helps explain the invention of New Labour (key events since 1945 are listed in Boxes 1.1 and 1.2). Secondly, the chapter discusses the process of Labour's 'modernization' between 1983 and 1994, and the main lines of academic argument about it. Finally, it outlines questions about the character of New Labour that the authors of this volume have been asked, where their subject matter permits, to address, and summarizes the structure of the volume.

From State Planning to Unbelieving Monetarism

First, then, what have been the longer-term features of Labour's post-war record that produced the circumstances out of which the drive to transform the party into New Labour emerged in the mid-1980s? To state the obvious, Labour is a deeply parliamentarist party, an orientation profoundly influenced by the legislative supremacy in the British state of the Westminster Parliament. Even its most radical leftwing leaders have insisted on Westminster's 'revolutionary quality' and the accompanying 'hope of bringing about social transformations' by winning a majority in it (Bevan, 1952, 100). Labour's strategy for social change has been almost exclusively legislative, and given Parliament's supremacy, this has meant, centrally, a national electoral strategy. Hence New Labour's origins lay first and foremost in Labour's four successive election defeats after 1974, and thus in the failure of the party's political strategies before, and immediately after, the 1979 defeat. When veteran politicians suggest that elections are won

4

BOX 1.1   *Labour in government and opposition, 1945–79*

1945–51 Government

Clement Attlee's Labour government nationalizes coal, gas, water, electricity, railways, airlines, road haulage, Bank of England, iron and steel; creates National Health Service, launches National Insurance; carries out wartime coalition commitments to universal free secondary education, and full employment as key aim of economic policy.

1947 Fuel and sterling crises, followed by Chancellor Stafford Cripps's austerity regime. 'Consolidators' call for end to nationalizations. Michael Foot and others issue *Keep Left* manifesto repudiating Cold War foreign policy, renouncing atomic weapons, calling for central economic planning.

1948 'Bonfire' of wartime economic controls, Keynesian demand management ('budget judgement') gradually adopted in preference to central planning.

1949 Founding member NATO, decision to build British atom bomb. Post-war sterling crises culminate in devaluation.

1950 Korean War entry prompts rearmament spending.

1951 Aneuran Bevan and Harold Wilson resign in protest at impact of military spending on public service budgets (NHS prescription charges introduced by Chancellor Hugh Gaitskell).

1951–63 Opposition

Early period characterized by controversies between Bevanite left (and *Tribune*) and 'revisionist' right (and *Socialist Commentary*) over economic and foreign policy, notably public ownership and nuclear arms race.

1955 Attlee resigns, Gaitskell elected leader, defeating Bevan 166:70. Bevan briefly expelled from PLP.

1956 Tony Crosland's revisionist classic *Future of Socialism* published, arguing capitalism fundamentally changed, public ownership a mainly redundant means, not an end in itself; focus of socialists should be social equality. Gaitskell leads Labour opposition to Suez invasion. Bevan elected party treasurer.

1957 Party conference adopts *Industry and Society* modifying nationalization stance and endorsing mixed economy. Bevan repudiates unilateral disarmament, *rapprochement* with Gaitskell.

1959 After losing third successive election, revisionist responses include break link with unions, drop nationalization, and change name

→

BOX 1.1 *Continued*

of party, to appeal to middle-class voters. Bevan elected deputy leader unopposed.

1960 Conference rejects Gaitskell's attempt to scrap Clause IV commitment to common ownership. Union votes carry unilateral disarmament policy. Bevan dies. Wilson challenges Gaitskell for leadership, loses 157:81.

1961 Conference drops unilateralism again after Campaign for Democratic Socialism campaign by revisionists.

1963 Gaitskell dies, Wilson elected leader, defeating rightwing George Brown 144:103.

1964–70 Government

Immediate decision not to devalue pound or reduce world military role leads to deflationary domestic economic policy that undermines 1965 National Plan, alienates unions cooperating in wage restraint (from 1965), and damages public service programmes, generating dissent on the left. Supply-side reforms include industrial reorganization, redundancy payments, and promoting technology.

1965 Comprehensive secondary school system launched by Crosland.

1965 Labour government support for US war in Vietnam alienates many, especially young, party members, in spite of Wilson's refusal to send regular troops.

1966 Tribune Group of leftwing MPs formed.

1967 First Labour attempt at EEC entry blocked by De Gaulle.

1967 Devaluation of pound, Chancellor James Callaghan resigns; withdrawal from military bases 'East of Suez'. Abortion and homosexuality decriminalized.

1968 Prescription charges abolished in 1965, reintroduced. Raising of school-leaving age to 16 postponed.

1969 White Paper *In Place of Strife* proposes legal sanctions against unofficial strikes, TUC rejects, dropped after six months of bitter division. Open University launched.

1970–74 Opposition

1971–3 Social Contract between party and TUC developed, covering industrial relations, economic and social policy, and implying union cooperation in wage restraint.

1971 Pro-EEC Labour MPs led by deputy leader Roy Jenkins rebel against '3-line Whip', enabling Heath government to proceed with entry.

BOX 1.1   *Continued*

1972 Decision to hold national referendum on EEC membership if Labour re-elected leads Jenkins to resign as deputy leader.

1971/2 and 1973/4 winter miners' strikes against Heath government wage limits, both victorious.

1973 *Labour's Programme 1973* advocates radical extension of state economic planning and control of private sector.

1974–79 Government

1974 Price controls, food and rent subsidies, and pension increases introduced.

1975 EEC referendum, 2:1 vote to stay in, anti-EEC leader Tony Benn moved from Department of Industry, interventionist industrial strategy heavily diluted.

1975 World oil price increases push annual inflation above 24 per cent, placing severe pressure on sterling. Under social contract unions agree, with employment secretary Michael Foot, policy shift from real wage freeze 1974–75 to real wage cuts 1975–78. New industrial relations and equal pay legislation helps unions to record membership figures.

1975 Chancellor Denis Healey announces first of series of public spending cuts and deflationary budgets even as unemployment rises above 1 million, removes inflation-proofing from public sector budgets, but speculative pressure on pound continues throughout 1975 and 1976.

1976 Wilson retires, James Callaghan elected leader, defeated Roy Jenkins resigns to become President of European Commission; Foot elected deputy leader. Leftwing discontent grows, many rebellions by Tribune Group MPs, especially Neil Kinnock. *Labour's Programme 1976* published, politically aligned with the left's alternative economic strategy'. By-election losses leave Labour without overall majority. Further sterling crisis, IMF loan negotiations begin.

1977 IMF deal endorses Healey's deflationary strategy, grants loan in return for further spending cuts. Leading revisionist in Cabinet, Crosland, thinks deal 'mad' but inevitable. Pound recovers, reflationary budgets for rest of parliament. Lib–Lab Pact agreed for one year, overcoming Labour's loss of majority. Party activists intensify campaign to increase control over PLP. Rightwing Manifesto Group of MPs launched.

BOX 1.1 *Continued*

1978 State Earnings-Related Pension Scheme (SERPS) introduced. Lib–Lab Pact ends. Majority union support for wage controls collapses, followed by 'Winter of Discontent'.
1979 Universal child benefit introduced. Following sabotage of devolution legislation by Labour MP, government collapses.
For extensive chronologies, see Harmer, 1999.

and lost overwhelmingly on personal economic issues (Hattersley, 1997b, 379), they are asserting what political scientists have sought to demonstrate throughout the post-war era (Butler and Stokes, 1969; Sanders, 1995, 1996). Between 1959 and 1983, throughout the quarter of a century of economic policy crises that followed the Tories' 'never had it so good' years, no government was re-elected to serve two full terms of office, and the volatility of the electorate became the prime target of electoral analysis, So how did Labour's post-war management of the economy contribute to its electoral difficulties and the political crises that triggered its transformation into New Labour?

Throughout the post-war period, political economists of the left, right and centre have pointed to the enormous costs and constraints imposed by the maintenance of the world financial and military role of the UK in the Western alliance (Gamble, 1994; Brittan, 1969; Manser, 1971; Schonfield, 1958). Among analysts concerned with the political consequences, both those highly critical of post-war Labour governments' records (Miliband, 1973; Coates, 1975, 1980; Howell, 1980; Ponting, 1990), and those who have sought to revise such pessimistic assessments (Tiratsoo, 1991; Coopey, Fielding and Tiratsoo, 1993), have drawn attention to the economic and political constraints of holding office in an economically vulnerable, and ideologically conservative, imperial state. A recent survey that endorses neither critical nor revisionist assessments nevertheless insists that it is, above all, Labour's 'traditionalism', the influence on it of an 'established and highly traditional national culture', that characterizes its political trajectory, rather than, even, the collectivism which is said to distinguish it from both domestic opponents and from European social democrats (Shaw, 1996, ix). This traditionalism, Eric Shaw argues, imparted a 'global mind set' to Labour's conduct of government, a prioritizing of the world role that constrained and ultimately wrecked its attempt – the centrepiece of its electoral strategy – to carry through a programme of Keynesian social democracy in post-war Britain: to secure growth and employment by managing demand in the national economy, in order to fund a progressive

BOX 1.2   *Labour in the wilderness, 1979–97*

1979 Tony Benn quits Shadow Cabinet to assume leadership of extra-parliamentary left. Conference agrees automatic reselection of MPs.

1980 Conference agrees new leadership electoral college giving votes to constituency parties and unions. Callaghan resigns to trigger election under old system (MPs only voting), Healey unexpectedly defeated by Foot.

1981 Special conference gives unions 40 per cent of votes, constituencies (CLPs) and MPs 30 per cent each in electoral college; 4 ex-Cabinet ministers led by Jenkins form Social Democratic Party, 29 Labour MPs join. Solidarity Group launched by Roy Hattersley, John Smith and others to organize rightwingers not deserting. Benn challenges Healey for deputy leadership under new rules; emerging 'soft' left led by Kinnock abandons Benn, Healey wins by 50.4 per cent to 49.6 per cent.

1982 Union–party 'Peace of Bishops Stortford' ends constitutional crisis. Foot backs Falklands War. 'Hard' left MPs break with Tribune Group, forming (Socialist) Campaign Group.

1983 Election manifesto based on left policies adopted since 1979 (see Box 1.3). Labour slumps to lowest share of vote (27.6 per cent) since 1918, just 2 per cent ahead of SDP/Liberal Alliance. Foot and Healey resign, leader and deputy leader 'dream ticket' of Tribunite Kinnock and Solidarity Group's Hattersley elected ('hard' left candidate Eric Heffer wins 6 per cent of votes). Expulsions of leaders and supporters of marxist *Militant* newspaper begin. Policy modernization begins (see Box 1.3).

1984 Conference defeats Kinnock's first attempt to introduce one member one vote (OMOV) in selection of MPs. Miners' strike begins, party leadership withholds unqualified support.

1985 Miners' strike defeated. Kinnock disowns leftwing council leaders defying Tory budget cuts in Liverpool and Lambeth. New media and communications machinery established under Peter Mandelson.

1986 Red rose replaces red flag as party's symbol.

1987 Election defeat, nevertheless restores Labour as main opposition party (31 per cent to Alliance parties' 23 per cent). Unions limited to 40 per cent of vote in selection of MPs.

1988 Benn challenge for leadership crushed 89 per cent to 11 per cent. OMOV obligatory for CLPs in future leadership elections.

1989 Policy Review results published as *Meet the Challenge, Make the Change.*

BOX 1.2 *Continued*

1990 Agreement to reduce union share of party conference vote from 90 per cent to 70 per cent. National Policy Forum established, weakening conference, increasing leadership control of policy. OMOV obligatory for CLP seats on NEC, and selection/reselection of MPs.

1992 Election defeat, Kinnock and Hattersley resign, John Smith elected leader with 91 per cent of vote, Margaret Beckett elected deputy leader. Smith launches Commission on Social Justice.

1993 OMOV in MP selection, and leadership elections (reformed to one third each for MPs, unions, and constituencies); monolithic union block votes 'abolished'; union conference vote share to drop to 70 per cent, later to 40 per cent. Benn loses executive (NEC) seat.

1994 Death of John Smith. Tony Blair elected leader on 57 per cent of vote after Gordon Brown withdraws, John Prescott elected deputy leader. 'New Labour, New Britain' platform slogan at party conference popularizes New Labour label.

1995 Clause IV abolished at special conference, by 2 to 1 after membership referendum approves Blair's alternative; Arthur Scargill resigns to launch Socialist Labour Party. Blair ends union financial sponsorship of MPs, drops union conference vote share to 49 per cent.

1996 Launch of *Partnership in Power* reforms adopted in 1997: unions lose majority on reconstituted NEC, gets 30 of 175 seats on revamped National Policy Forum; Policy Commissions take over formulation of party policy under small Joint Policy Committee chaired by Blair, effectively ending traditional policymaking domination by NEC and annual conference.

For extensive chronologies, see Harmer, 1999.

redistribution of wealth and opportunity through an improved, universal, welfare state. While some have warned against exaggerating the primacy of exchange rate policy in this process (J. Tomlinson, 1997), and others against the Labour tradition of demonizing foreign agencies in such accounts (Ludlam, 1992), the central significance of Britain's external political and economic relationships to any account of Labour's post-war dilemmas is beyond question.

Before the war Labour assumed that it would inherit the management of one of the world's richest economies and most powerful imperial states, with all the implied potential for funding progressive social and economic programmes. The industrial and financial dislocation caused by the war, above all in its international financial and trading position, however, left

Clement Attlee's 1945 Labour government facing an economic crisis of unprecedented proportions (Cairncross, 1992; Glynn and Booth, 1996). It nevertheless, on a scale unparalleled in British parliamentary history, rapidly carried through a massive programme of reforming social and economic legislation (Box 1.1). It also set the economic policy framework for its successors, in which three features stand out. First, it moved steadily away from wartime direct planning controls to demand management through the 'budget judgement', in other words, to a Keynesian economic policy regime. This more liberal approach reflected an unwillingness, once manifesto commitments were fulfilled, to widen the scope of state ownership; Labour's 'mixed economy' combined a strategic public sector with a predominantly private sector. Secondly, partly in return for financial assistance, Labour locked Britain into the new US-dominated international system of liberal financial mechanisms, crucially fixed currency exchange rates and progressive liberalization of world finance and trade. Thirdly, in order to address the balance of payments problem, defend the sterling exchange rate, and maintain military commitments as the Cold, and 'hot' Korean Wars began, a regime of austerity in domestic policy was operated from 1947.

In the decades that followed, how did these constraints affect Labour's political success? Britain's economy was, and remains, unusually 'open', a large proportion of its trade international. It became, as the post-war decades passed, one of the weaker industrial economies, producing a long debate on Britain's relative decline (Gamble, 1994; D. Coates, 1994; D. Coates and J. Hillard, 1995). Relative decline in an open economy inevitably undermined sterling's 'fixed' exchange rate, especially after changes in 1958 resulting from conditions of US loans to Attlee's government: sterling finally became freely convertible into other currencies; and remaining import controls were abolished (A. Jay, 1985). A crucial factor was the impact of government overseas military expenditure on the British balance of payments. Britain's post-war recovery had been remarkable, described as Europe's first economic miracle (Blank, 1977). Its balance of payments surplus in private trade was healthy throughout the period, and, as Manser demonstrated, the deficits which triggered sterling crises would not have occurred, other things being equal, but for the costs of the world role (Manser, 1971). Of course, Britain had internal economic problems to resolve, but their resolution was obstructed by the impact of a foreign economic policy consensus often overlooked in discussion of the concept of post-war consensus (Kerr, 1999).

Until 1972, then, when sterling was 'floated', the fixed exchange rate system had the following effect when the balance of payments position looked weak. Holders of sterling knew that a British government could rectify a payments deficit either by devaluing the pound, to make exports more competitive and discourage imports, or by deflating the domestic economy, to reduce imports and encourage exports as the home market shrank. For holders of sterling, sitting tight risked the losses of overnight devaluation. Selling sterling was almost risk-free: if Britain devalued, they could buy back more pounds than they started with; if not, losses were confined to currency dealers' fees. Currency holders, not surprisingly, chose not to run the risk, and bought other currencies until a 'run on the pound' produced a government response. Conservative governments invariably chose to deflate. In the 1940s and 1960s, Labour governments deflated until, unable to defend the currency any longer, they were forced to devalue. Although the sterling crises of 1975–6 took place after fixed exchange rates had collapsed worldwide, sterling remained a world currency, and similar pressures engulfed Labour. Now markets responded to inflation rates accelerated by oil price increases, and, as neo-liberal economics challenged Keynesianism, to concerns over public spending. Most importantly, the US had decided to restabilize the Western monetary system through the International Monetary Fund (United States Senate, 1977; Bernstein, 1983). After two years of increasingly desperate deflationary measures to maintain market confidence in sterling, Labour was forced to apply in 1976 for the IMF's 'seal of good housekeeping' (Ludlam, 1992).

Two further points about Labour's deflationary history need emphasis here. First, the scale: the key packages were not the fine tunings of 'stop-go' demand management, but traumatic changes of direction. In the late 1940s, the scale was less striking than the impact of the bread and potato rationing that even the war years had avoided. The deflation of 1966, though, just a year after the launch of Labour's National Plan, was, in the words of a rightwing Cabinet minister, a 'complete *volte-face* in policy' and 'the biggest deflationary package ever' (Stewart, 1978, 73). Labour's deflationary packages between 1975 and 1977 produced 'the largest cuts in real public expenditure that have occurred in the last fifty years' (Artis and Cobham, 1991, 73). Two leftwing Cabinet diarists noted, after deflationary measures in 1975, 'I despair of the Labour Government as a force for transformation', and, 'I see no reason for the existence of a Labour Government' (Benn, 1989, 416; Castle, 1980, 463). Secondly, Labour's desperation to avoid devaluation in the 1960s was inseparable from its commitment to the Atlantic Alliance in the Cold War, as studies based on US government sources are revealing (Dobson, 1988; Ponting, 1990). Similarly, Labour's struggle to sustain sterling in 1975/6 reflected the concern expressed by the US National Security Commission that a financial default by Britain constituted 'the greatest single threat to the Western world' (Fay and Young, 1978). Labour felt obliged to accept IMF loan conditions and the advice of the under-secretary of the US Treasury to cut public spending to 'get your people back on the reservation' (Whitehead, 1986, 185).

So, leaving aside for the purposes of this narrative the arguments about whether Labour had any alternative in these crises, what were their general effects on Labour's political fortunes? First, deflation undermined key policy undertakings, damaging voters' confidence and generating internal party dissent that further weakened the party's image. Labour's distinctive industrial policies in the 1960s and 1970s, whatever their inherent limitations, were shackled by the deflationary defence of sterling. These policies helped lessen party tensions that had simmered since the 1940s when 'consolidators' opposed further nationalizations and Bevanites demanded more, and throughout the 1950s when Tony Crosland's 'revisionist' *Future of Socialism* insisted that post-war managed capitalism made further state ownership irrelevant to achieving social equality (A. Crosland, 1956). After Hugh Gaitskell's controversial failure to drop the party's constitutional commitment to common ownership (Clause IV), Harold Wilson's 'indicative' planning regime offered an alternative that both sides could support – it was interventionist, but it did not include a shopping list of nationalizations. The collapse of the 1965 National Plan, its growth targets wrecked by deflationary measures to defend sterling in 1966, infuriated the left. It also led eventually to the resignation from the Cabinet of right-wing deputy leader George Brown, whose new Department of Economic Affairs had been humiliated. In the 1970s, deflation made it impossible for the centrepiece of Labour's industrial strategy, the National Enterprise Board, to finance its interventionist role.

Defending Britain's world role similarly undermined social policy objectives, as deflationary packages postponed and cancelled planned improvements in public services. The conflicting commitments produced the resignations of Aneuran Bevan and Wilson from Attlee's Cabinet over the impact of military spending on social programmes (the introduction of prescription charges was the trigger); Wilson's symbolic sacrifice in the 1960s of free prescriptions and the promised raising of the school-leaving age; and the unprecedented cutbacks in public service programmes in the 1970s. Each time, such cuts prompted parliamentary and party rebellions, and sometimes mass protests led by Labour-affiliated unions. After the social policy triumphs of the beleagured Attlee government, disappointment over Labour's impact on social inequality in the 1960s and 1970s was intense, and carefully catalogued by the moderate Fabian Society

(Townsend and Bosanquet, 1972; Bosanquet and Townsend, 1980). Worse, Labour's ultimate social policy, full employment, fell victim to deflation, above all in the 1974–7 period when, time and again Labour introduced budgets designed to increase unemployment when it was already rising (Ludlam, 1992). From 1975, the unemployment rate topped a million for the rest of Labour's term of office, to the embarrassment of ministers, the fury of activists and unions, and the misery of those directly affected.

Deflation also undermined the context of economic growth and social progress within which Labour's union allies agreed, in the 1940s, 1960s and 1970s, to enforce wage restraint. Whatever the surrounding rhetoric of planning, a 'planned growth of incomes', and union participation in 'corporatist' planning institutions, incomes policies were invariably introduced as emergency responses to sterling crises, in the form of freezes, zero norms and, from 1975, of the most dramatic real wage cuts ever experienced by the British labour movement. In the 1960s the results were Cabinet resignations and, when wage policy failed, Labour's attempt to introduce legal sanctions against strikers which failed ignominiously as the TUC, the parliamentary party and much of the Cabinet rebelled. In the 1970s, the Social Contract incomes policy, having been faithfully policed by the TUC for four years, disintegrated in the 'Winter of Discontent'. It was not just falling real wages but also the failure of the promised compensatory improvements in the 'social wage' of public services that finished off the Social Contract (Ludlam, 1995). And falling real wages were exacerbated by another effect of deflation that the Tories would exploit ruthlessly. In the absence of the dividend of economic growth providing a politically painless, redistributable pot of public funds, Labour increased income tax rates such that, by the end of the 1960s, a manual worker who had paid little or no income tax in the 1950s saw a fifth of their pay packet taken in stoppages, and by the crises of the mid-1970s, a third. The combination of higher taxes, declining public services and falling real wages explains much of Labour's loss of working-class votes from 1979 to Thatcher's promises of tax cuts, no incomes policy, and frugality with the public purse.

The rise of 'Thatcherism' was inextricably linked to the final key effect on Labour's electoral fortunes of its long struggle to balance the pressures of maintaining Britain's world role, generating national economic success, and securing more egalitarian social policies. As the limitations of social democracy in one country became all too apparent in the international conditions of the mid-1970s, Labour's 'revisionist' project foundered. As a US Senate report noted of the 1976 IMF negotiations:

the decisions required of the British Government were profoundly political ... behind the technical financial decisions lay fundamental differences over the appropriate balance between the private and public sectors, the priority between capital accumulation and social welfare, the relative weight to be given to incentives and equality... What was at issue was the future shape of the political economy of Great Britain. (United States Senate, 1977, 11–12)

Crosland, the Cabinet's leading Keynesian revisionist, already appalled at the effect of Labour's cutbacks on popular attitudes towards the welfare state, thought the IMF deal madness. He forced Treasury officials and Prime Minister James Callaghan to admit that cuts were being made not for economic reasons, but to restore the elusive 'confidence' of financial markets (S. Crosland, 1982). But he and his supporters agreed to the terms to save a Labour government that, though it went down in 1979 fighting for its non-monetarist incomes policy, nevertheless introduced the language and instruments of monetarism into British public policy, and did so well before the IMF deal (D. Smith, 1987; Ludlam, 1992). When, after the long post-war boom, Keynesian deficit financing finally became necessary to maintain full employment and the welfare state, Labour's Keynesians were unable to carry it through. In defence of sterling and Britain's world role, they appeared to have sacrificed Labour's distinctive industrial policies, much of its social reform programme, and its relationship with the unions that founded the party. As Shaw has succinctly put it, 'Just as the IMF loan marked the disintegration of Keynesianism as the governing economic doctrine so too the Winter of Discontent signified the collapse of corporatism. Without these two pillars, revisionist social democracy fell to pieces' (Shaw, 1994, 7).

From Unbelieving Monetarism to Believing Neo-liberalism?

The immediate consequences are well known: a Conservative government elected on a platform of outright opposition the 'post-war consensus', Keynesian economic policy, the 'mixed economy', the full employment commitment, the 'nanny' welfare state, and union participation in tripartite policymaking (Gamble, 1988). Inside a Labour Party bitterly divided after the 1979 defeat, an activist revolt, supported by some senior figures, including Tony Benn, and by significant union 'block votes', forced constitutional controls on the parliamentary leadership (automatic reselection of MPs and a wider franchise for electing the leader) in the belief that this would help prevent future policy retreats.

The same revolt committed Labour to a radical policy programme (Box 1.3). Years of dispute over economic and foreign policy erupted again, with a dispirited and divided centre-right defeated by a leftwing programme of new nationalizations, massive public expenditure, withdrawal from the EEC, and a non-nuclear defence policy (Seyd, 1987). The left argued that, given the political will to pursue an 'alternative economic strategy', Labour governments could recapture strategic control from international capital. The expected resistance to such a national political economy – a siege economy according to Labour's social democrats – could, it was hoped, be countered by new forms of industrial democracy policing planning agreements between companies and the state (Wickham-Jones, 1996). Weakened by desertions to the Social Democratic Party launched in 1981 by defeated 'revisionists', Labour's new platform, and Michael Foot's brief leadership, were crushed at the 1983 election. In less than five years, both of Labour's principal post-war policy approaches had been rejected by the electorate: the mixed economy Keynesian, corporatist and atlanticist, social democratic approach; and the more radical democratic socialist platform of state-led economic development and anti-capitalist foreign policy. The electorate, much changed socially since 1945, apparently preferred the radical individualism, the neo-liberal economic policy, and the social intolerance of Thatcherism.

What analysts saw as a multiple crisis for Labour (Whiteley, 1983; Shaw, 1994), had worsened between 1979 and 1983. Its electoral crisis deepened, from its worst result for 50 years to its worst ever. Its ideological crisis deepened and was exacerbated rather than relieved by the formation of the rival SDP, intensified rather than attenuated by the policy reforms driven by the party's left wing which, for once in its history, had the support of just enough union block votes to carry the party conference on a range of issues (Minkin, 1992). And the party's organizational crisis deepened in every respect: it was, its new general secretary discovered in 1982, effectively bankrupt (Mortimer, 1998); its membership had hit post-war lows, membership activism fell even more sharply (Whiteley, 1983); the authority and legitimacy of its organizational structures, and its leadership, had been shattered by the constitutional crisis over reselection and electing the leader (Shaw, 1994). The prolonged process of reconstructing Labour as an electable 'catch-all' political party began under the leadership 'dream ticket' of Neil Kinnock and Roy Hattersley, respectively leading members of the leftwing Tribune and rightwing Solidarity groups of MPs. In his declaration of New Labour faith at the party conference in 1995, Blair, praising Kinnock, recalled that, '1983 was, for me, a watershed. New Labour was born then' (Blair, 1995).

The crucial element of the party's electoral crisis was the loss of working-class votes, which had two components. First, the percentage of the electorate conventionally defined as working-class fell from 60 in 1964

BOX 1.3 *Labour's policy modernization, 1983–97*

1983 and 1987 Manifestos	*1989 Policy Review*	*1992 Manifesto*	*1997 Manifesto*
Economic strategy 1983: Massive publicly funded expansion programme (1983 £11bn, 1987 £6bn). National Economic Assessment. price, and exchange Import, controls, job subsidies. 1987: National Economic Summit, and Assessment Reduce unemployment by 1 million in two years. No import, price, and exchange controls.	'We are clear that the control of inflation must be a major priority'. Public spending limited to what 'country can afford'. No import or price controls. No target for reducing unemployment. Supply-side strategy, training to improve competitiveness, attract private investment into 'public investment consortium' projects.	National Recovery Programme, National Investment Bank, National Economic Assessment, 'Invest-ment Decade for Britian', 'direct invest-ment … to create thousands of new jobs', 'work programme, with training 'bringing down unemployment immediately'.	'We accept the global economy as a reality and reject … isolationism'. Match Tory 2.5 per cent or less inflation target. Reform Bank of England to free monetary policy 'from short-term political manipulation'. Public spending 'Golden Rule': only borrow to invest, not for current expenditure, over the economic cycle. For two years, accept Conservative spending limits. 'Ministers will be required to save before they can spend'. Windfall tax on utilities to fund welfare-to-work for 250,000 under-25s with no option of 'life on full benefit'.

Public ownership			
1983: Reverse privatizations with limited compensation, buy into in pharmaceuticals, electronics, building materials. 1987: Social ownership of basic public utilities, convert private shares into securities with guaranteed dividends.	'The great utilities should be publicly owned', but no renationalization requiring 'substantial resources'. Convert privatized utilities into public interest companies by buying 'golden share' at market rates.	'Public control' of Grid (electricity) and water industry, private finance of high-speed rail network.	No renationalizations: 'Government and industry must work together to achieve key objectives aimed at enhancing the dynamism of the market, not undermining it'. 'In the utility industries we will promote competition wherever possible. Where competition is not an effective discipline … we will pursue tough, efficient regulation'.
Taxation			
1983: Shift burden to better off. Wealth tax on richest 100,000. Remove National Insurance ceiling. Reverse Tory tax cuts, using revenue for job creation. 1987: reverse tax cuts of richest 5 per cent, wealth tax on top richest 1 per cent.	'Fair tax' policy. Scrap National Insurance ceiling, but no return to 'the high marginal rates of the past'. No wealth tax. More tax bands, starting at 20 per cent rising to maximum of 50 per cent.	Basic income tax rate to remain at 25 per cent, 40 per cent band retained, introduce 50 per cent top rate. Scrap National Insurance ceiling.	'There will be no increase in the basic or top rates of income tax'. Aim for 10p starting rate Cut VAT on fuel to 5 per cent. 'Although crude and universal council tax capping should go, we will retain reserve powers to control excessive council tax rises'.

BOX 1.3 *Continued*

1983 and 1987 Manifestos	*1989 Policy Review*	*1992 Manifesto*	*1997 Manifesto*
Industry 1983: Compulsory planning agreements, state control of prices, credit, and investment (National Investment Bank), create new science-based industries. 1987: new Ministry of Science and Technology.	Public–private collaboration and partnership; revamp Department of Trade and Industry to encourage enterprise, invest in advanced technologies.	Limited investment incentives. Place pension funds in hands of workers. Compulsory training levy on employers. £300m 'Skills for the 90s' fund.	'We see healthy profits as an essential motor of a dynamic market economy, and believe they depend on quality products, innovative entrepreneurs and skilled employees'. 'A reformed and tougher competition law'. 'Reinvigorate the Private Finance Initiative'. 'new University for Industry, 'lifelong learning'.
Trade unions 1983: Repeal all Tory employment laws, 'discuss' national minimum wage, 50 per cent TU representation on pension boards, radical extension of	Switch of emphasis from collective to individual rights, Charter of Rights for Employees, including right to TU membership and activity. Restoration of limited	'Fair framework of law … no return to the trade union legislation of the 1970s', ballots for strikes, elections, no mass or flying picketing.	'The key elements of the trade union legislation of the 1980s will stay on ballots, picketing and industrial action.' Union recognition 'where a

industrial democracy. 1987: Replace Tory laws with legal rights of representation and bargaining (no industrial democracy). Retain strike and executive election ballots. National minimum wage.	secondary action, keep ballots before strikes and for election of union executives. National minimum wage at 50 per cent of median wage (£2.80 at 1989 prices).	National minimum wage at £3.40 per hour.	majority of the relevant workforce vote in a ballot for the union to represent them'. National minimum wage set 'according to the economic circumstances of the time'. 'A flexible labour market that serves employers and employees alike'.

Welfare

1983: Increase Child Benefit and pensions, restore link pensions/prices/earnings and extend to all benefits. Increase Child Benefit and pensions, restore link pensions/prices/earnings.	'Significant and generous increase in Child Benefit', 'immediate and substantial increase in the basic pension', restore link pensions/prices/earnings.	NHS £1bn additional funding commitment, scrap 'internal market'. Increase Child Benefit and pensions, restore link pensions/prices/earnings	'We will raise spending on the NHS in real terms every year.' Scrap internal NHS market, 1987: spend savings on reducing waiting lists by 100,000 'Retain universal Child Benefit where it is universal today – from birth to age 16'. Basic state pension to be increased 'at least in line with prices' (not earnings) as 'foundation of pension provision' Second, private

BOX 1.3   *Continued*

1983 and 1987 Manifestos	*1989 Policy Review*	*1992 Manifesto*	*1997 Manifesto*
			'stakeholder' pensions to ensure adequate standard of living. Modernize taxes and benefits relationship to promote work incentives.
Education 1983: maximum class size 30, abolish assisted places scheme, 'prohibit all forms of academic selection', universal right to nursery provision. 1987: 'provision for smaller classes' School Standards Council, abolish assisted places, universal right to nursery provision at age 3.	'Reduce class sizes' but no limit set, Education Standards Council, 'value added' measures of school performance, end selection, return Technology Colleges and Grant-Maintained schools to LEA control, 'phaseout' assisted places, 'encourage' private and LA nursery provision.	£600m increase in spending. Reduce school class size to maximum 30. Universal nursery provision in decade, Education Standards Commission. Return opted-out schools to LEA control, end all selection at age11 Scrap student loans, introduce full-grant system	'We will raise the proportion of national income spent on education'. Maximum class sizes of 30 for 5 to 7 year-olds, funded by phasing out assisted places scheme Close 'failing schools', Education Action Zones to attack low standards, and 'remove teachers who cannot do the job.' 'nursery education guaranteed for all 4 year-olds'

Constitution

1983: Freedom of Information Act, abolish Lords, Security Act to control secret services, Elected Scottish assembly with domestic legislative powers 1987: Arts Council for Wales. No specific mention Lords, Freedom of Information Act.	Abolish Lords, no Bill of Rights ('would not provide the protection which we regard as necessary'), Freedom of Information Act, elected Scottish assembly with domestic legislative powers, regional assemblies, Wales under review	Charter of Rights, bill of rights, devolution including English regions, replace Lords with elected second chamber, fixed-term parliaments, encourage debate on electoral reform, Freedom of Information Act. Smith promises referendum on electoral reform.	'Labour will never force the abolition of good schools' Grant-maintained schools 'will prosper'. Student maintenance costs to be repaid by graduates on an income-related basis'. Abolish hereditory votes in Lords. 'We have no plans to replace the monarchy'. Referendum on 'proportional alternative' to Commons electoral system Devolution to Scotland and Wales Directly elected London mayor; regional referendums on directly elected regional government' Incorporate European Convention on Human Rights. Freedom of Information Act.

BOX 1.3 *Continued*			
1983 and 1987 Manifestos	*1989 Policy Review*	*1992 Manifesto*	*1997 Manifesto*
Europe 1983: Withdrawal from EC within lifetime of Parliament. 1987: 'Work constructively in EC but reject EC interference in Labour's programme for national recovery.	No withdrawal, facilitate co-operation, keep national veto and improve Westminster scrutiny. EMS too 'deflationary', no membership of ERM unless linked to co-ordinated EC-wide growth policy Acceptance of Social Charter.	Unqualified support for Social Chapter, 'active part' in EMU negotiations, reform Common Agricultural Policy, press enlargement of EC 'promote Britain out of the European second division'.	'Our vision of Europe is of independent nations' 'Retention of the national veto over key matters of interest.' Press enlargement. Completion of the single market, [single currency] 'the people would have to say "Yes" in a referendum'. Reform Common Agricultural Policy. Sign Social Chapter, 'promote employability and flexibility, not high social costs'.

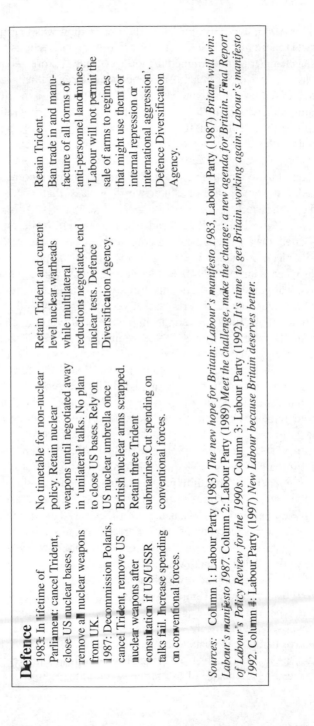

Defence

1983: In lifetime of Parliament: cancel Trident, close US nuclear bases, remove all nuclear weapons from UK. 1987: Decommission Polaris, cancel Trident, remove US nuclear weapons after consultation if US/USSR talks fail. Increase spending on conventional forces.	No timetable for non-nuclear policy. Retain nuclear weapons until negotiated away in 'unilateral' talks. No plan to close US bases. Rely on US nuclear umbrella once British nuclear arms scrapped. Retain three Trident submarines.Cut spending on conventional forces.	Retain Trident and current level nuclear warheads while multilateral reductions negotiated, end nuclear tests. Defence Diversification Agency.	Retain Trident. Ban trade in and manufacture of all forms of anti-personnel landmines. 'Labour will not permit the sale of arms to regimes that might use them for internal repression or international aggression'. Defence Diversification Agency.

Sources: Column 1: Labour Party (1983) *The new hope for Britain: Labour's manifesto 1983*, Labour Party (1987) *Britain will win: Labour's manifesto 1987.* Column 2: Labour Party (1989) *Meet the challenge, make the change: a new agenda for Britain. Final Report of Labour's Policy Review for the 1990s.* Column 3: Labour Party (1992) *It's time to get Britain working again: Labour's manifesto 1992.* Column 4: Labour Party (1997) *New Labour because Britain deserves better.*

to 47 in 1983, and to 38 by 1997; the implication was that unless Labour attracted more middle-class votes, it could not win elections (Heath, 1999). Social change had undermined the left's critique – expressed after the 1955 election defeat in an attack on Mandelson's grandfather – of, 'the great Morrison fallacy ... that you have to gear your policy to the floating voter – to aim somewhere in the no-man's land of a dead liberalism which is imagined to lie between Tory and Labour' (cited in Fielding, 1997a, 45). Secondly, the composition and attitudes of the working class seemed to be changing. The apparent attraction of Thatcher's promises to cut taxes, sell council houses, constrain trade unionism and abjure incomes policies was linked to the emergence of a 'new working class' that owned houses, lived in the south, worked in the private sector and was less likely to join unions (Crewe, 1991; Heath, Jowell and Curtice, 1991). While attitude surveys suggested that Thatcherism's ideological appeal was declining (Crewe, 1988), election studies insisted that the Tories' 'popular capitalism' won them votes (Garrett, 1994). Academic specialists asked whether electoral 'class dealignment' was a merely 'relative' phenomenon, reflecting demographic change and Labour's loss of popularity across all classes, or was 'absolute', signalling the permanent desertion of working-class votes from Labour (Denver and Hands, 1992; Heath, Jowell and Curtice, 1994). The analyses suggested two possible Labour responses: either exploit the weaknesses of Thatcherism's ideological appeal, limit the reform of policy and concentrate on improving Labour's credibility; or concede the strength of 'popular capitalism' and extensively revise Labour's platform. The longer Labour remained in opposition, the stronger the attraction of the second strategy grew.

A 'new strategic thinking', against which all programmatic or organizational initiatives were judged, dominated the struggle for electability. The key components of this thinking were, first, a model of electoral behaviour that required a focus on the images of the party and its leader, and on voters' policy preferences – focusing after the 1987 defeat on issues of trust, economic competence, and fear of increased taxation. Secondly, the party's policy platform was to be repositioned to maximize votes, particulary those of the skilled manual workers and routine white collar workers (C1/C2 voters) who were apparently embracing 'popular capitalism' and rejecting collectivism. Thirdly, campaigning should focus on setting the agenda of party political debate, and therefore, fourthly, targeting leadership-led TV exposure, and, fifthly, deploying the mass psychology of marketing and advertising specialists as effectively as possible (Shaw, 1994, 156–8). Shaw's pioneering analysis has since been confirmed in great detail by one of the leading advocates of this strategy (Gould, 1998a).

Success in this strategy required high levels of party discipline and leadership authority, objectives facilitated by developments that began before 1983. First, the left – openly from the time of Benn's 1981 challenge for the deputy leadership – divided, roughly, into 'soft' and 'hard' components. Kinnock himself had led soft left opposition to Benn's candidature, the bitterness caused intensified by the narrowness of Benn's defeat (Box 1.2). The left also divided over the expulsions of members associated with the marxist paper, *Militant*, part of Kinnock's attack on left-led local Labour councils. Secondly, the party's right wing recovered some cohesion once the question of who was deserting to the SDP was settled, and began to remove leftwingers from the National Executive Committee (NEC) and other key posts. Indeed, by the 1983 election, the centre-right majority could have rewritten much of the left's manifesto, an opportunity cynically declined to ensure that electoral defeat discredited the whole of the left's policies (Hattersley, 1996). And, thirdly, in 1982 key unions, including some shifting their support from 'Bennism' to the 'soft left', arranged a 'Peace of Bishops Stortford': the left would not mount further leadership challenges, and the right would not reverse the recent constitutional changes (A. Taylor, 1987). A follow-up conference arranged union funding to end the party's financial crisis.

Kinnock knew he needed instruments of party control that no Labour leader had ever possessed, and that acquiring such instruments was difficult in a party where 'authority over the constitution is vested in the Conference, where the NEC is elected annually and matches the federal nature of the party and ... the Shadow Cabinet is not within the gift of the Leader's appointment' (Kinnock, 1994, 536). The party's 'federal nature' refers to union block votes, which Kinnock tried to reform in 1984 by introducing one member one vote (OMOV in party jargon). He failed at first, defeated by union votes. But, through systematic meetings with union leaders, Kinnock found that, 'I could guarantee before every meeting what would happen' (Kinnock, 1994, 550). According to one friendly account, 'a phalanx of Kinnock loyalists from the unions' ensured from an early stage in the modernization process that nothing embarrassing emerged from NEC sub-committees (Hughes and Wintour, 1990, 12). Kinnock's project was further protected from 'hard' left attack by 'the evaporation of the difference between the so-called soft left and what used to be called the right' (Kinnock, 1994, 549; cf Lent and Sowemimo, 1996).

During the first phase of Kinnock's 'new realism', policy change was slow, as Box 1.3 demonstrates, but saw the construction of new instruments of control through new joint policy committees successfully deployed from 1984 to circumvent traditional policymaking channels (Kinnock, 1994).

A crucial component of the 'new realism' was distancing the party from trade unionism, precisely as Thatcher attacked unions most fiercely. This was never more apparent than during the miners' strike of 1984/5, when Kinnock was condemned, not least by Labour's national chairman, for denying the miners unconditional support and for attacking the NUM leadership at the 1985 party conference (Heffer, 1986). For Kinnock the strike was 'a lost year' delaying modernization (Kinnock, 1994, 542). From 1985, under the new director of campaigns and communications, Peter Mandelson, advised by Philip Gould's shadow communications agency, the centralization of policy presentation ran in parallel with the transformation of policymaking, giving shape to the implementation of the 'new strategic thinking'. Shaw has summarized the key procedural innovations of Kinnock's modernization as follows: the inner parliamentary leadership took all key decisions; the party's extra-parliamentary institutions were subordinated to the Shadow Cabinet; 'policy-making [was] driven primarily by strategic positioning requirements, with vote-getting as the Party's core function'; and the narrowing of the role of lower-level party bodies to routine work and 'vote-gathering', with limited policymaking inputs (Shaw, 1994, 221). Whether such developments, combined with step-by-step introduction of OMOV (Box 1.2), were 'empowering the membership' (Seyd and Whiteley, 1992, 33) or 'disempowering activism' (Leys and Panitch, 1997, 214), they created a framework, after the 1987 defeat, for a more radical transformation of policy. And this transformation could be undertaken with widespread support among activists and members generally, and not, contrary to the conventional wisdom, in the face of a large gap between the attitudes of these two categories of membership (Seyd and Whiteley, 1992b).

With the SDP/Liberal Alliance challenge defeated in 1987, Kinnock could launch the Policy Review process, employing a number of techniques that New Labour would later develop: leadership tours discussing proposals with invited audiences; direct policy input by non-members and individual members; policy review groups outside the NEC sub-committee structure, with memberships determined by Kinnock's office, which in turn was directly represented on every group and worked to briefs from his chiefs of staff; and presentation to the party conference of policy statements that could not be amended (G. Taylor, 1997). A central purpose of the Policy Review was to formulate new manifesto positions to improve the party's image and appeal to the lost voters the party had to reclaim. The policy reforms intended to attract media attention were those, 'in which the party could be seen to be dropping the main policies which had proven to be electoral negatives: punitive levels of personal tax, extended nationalization, the restoration of union rights, and above all unilateralism' (Hughes and Wintour, 1990, 205; see Box 1.3). Crucially, after the electoral success of Thatcher's neo-liberalism, *Meet the Challenge, Make the Change* (Labour Party, 1989) was interpreted as endorsing the market mechanism, abandoning public ownership, dropping Keynesian macro-economic instruments and objectives, including full employment, in favour of an anti-inflationary framework based on monetary stability (Shaw, 1994). For the hard left, 'To cut a long story short, this is the Thatcherisation of the Labour Party' (Benn, 1994b, 546).

Academic analysis of the Review broadly followed the lines of party debate chronicled by both leftwing and rightwing observers (Heffernan and Marqusee, 1992; Hughes and Wintour, 1990). Some saw it as an accommodation to 'Thatcherism', the 'politics of catch up', and evidence that Labour had ceased even to be a social democratic party (Hay, 1994, 1999; Heffernan, 1996, 1999). Others argued that it constituted, rather, a new attempt, postponed by the left's brief ascendancy, to perform the overdue modernization of Labour's platform previously attempted by the revisionists of the 1950s (M.J. Smith, 1994; also T. Jones, 1996).

At several levels, the resulting antithesis between accommodationist and neo-revisionist interpretations of the Policy Review is potentially misleading. First, Thatcherism may not have been such a radical change of direction at all, but rather a more triumphalist version of the policy shift that Labour's 1974–79 government initiated, as it adopted an 'unbelieving monetarism' in response to economic pressures. From this perspective Kinnock's modernization, and by extension Blair's, look more like a delayed response to the dilemmas that confronted Wilson and Callaghan. In this sense Box 1.3 captures the scale of the modernizers' task, rather than its longer term, historical character. Secondly, focusing on the Policy Review can obscure the modernization process that Kinnock had undertaken between 1983 and 1987 when the foundations were laid and at least partly built on (Shaw, 1994; Box 1.3). Thirdly, how could modernizers not take into account recent economic, social and political factors, exactly as Crosland had in the 1950s? Whether such factors were the result of an allegedly Thatcherite 'hegemonic project' or of a more general policy shift initiated under Labour, they were real political phenomena that a party seeking election could not ignore. One response to the Hay/Smith debate, which was not, in its detail, as black and white as some commentary suggests, was thus to argue that the Review represented 'neither a series of concessions to Thatcherism nor a simple process of modernization', but an attempt by Labour to 'recast its social democratic commitments' (Wickham-Jones, 1995a, 701; cf Seyd, 1993). This recasting heavily featured Labour's adaptation of the neo-liberal, supply-side economic policy emphasis, that would later characterize New Labour's approach (N. Thompson, 1996).

Finally, the domestic policy focus of the arguments diverts attention from important international factors that influenced Kinnock's direction. In France, Mitterrand's experiment with a policy similar to the left's 'alternative economic strategy' failed spectacularly. The attitude of European social democrats towards the EEC's development was becoming more positive. And the Reagan–Gorbachev summit at Rekyavik in 1986, and its aftermath, added a diplomatic rationale to the electoral imperative of abandoning unilateral nuclear disarmament.

Many enthusiasts for modernization saw the Review as the triumphant foundation of a New Model Party. But not all of them: Philip Gould argues that, 'the policy review was fundamentally a missed opportunity for which we paid a heavy price in 1992. Labour was changing too little and too slowly' (Gould, 1998a, 90). Others share this view of the limitations of Kinnock's project, especially in the areas of union involvement in the party, related commitments to forms of tripartite economic management and public ownership, and, crucially, over personal taxation and public expenditure. Gould argues that Kinnock failed to impose his authority across the range of the Review's concerns, with the result that, after the brief triumph of the 1989 European Parliament election, 'until the 1992 election the Kinnock project went into decline' (Gould, 1998a, 98). Kinnock has partly accepted such criticism, but argues that a more 'progressive lunge' risked undermining the consensus he had carefully constructed (Kinnock, 1994, 545). In the view of some leading modernizers, even electoral defeat in 1992 failed to provide the necessary impetus to further policy reform. 'Ultra-modernizers' were frustrated by John Smith's cautious 'one more heave' strategy of letting Conservative unpopularity win the next election for Labour. Smith, though, did take party and policy modernization forward in two key areas.

First, the union link question was revived, when Kinnock's media managers commissioned research to show that Labour lost in 1992, 'because it was still the party of the winter of discontent; union influence; strikes and inflation; disarmament, Benn and Scargill' (Gould, 1998a, 158). A review group on the union link was established by John Smith, who expressed no radical views on abolishing the institutional link (Blair, in the group, supported abolition). Three crucial proposals were adopted. The unions' percentage share of the party conference vote was cut to 70, to fall to 49 as individual party membership increased, and the monolithic block vote was abolished (a union's delegates would each hold an equal share of its total vote). In leadership elections, the union vote was cut to a third, to be cast for candidates in proportion to the results of membership ballots. Finally, a modified OMOV system for parliamentary candidate selection was finally passed at the 1993 party conference, after a dramatic last-minute abstention by a union mandated to vote against.

Kinnock's Policy Review had been described as semi-revisionist in the Croslandite sense, in that it, 'accepted one half of the revisionist equation – capitalism – but not the second half – radicalism for social justice' (M.J. Smith, 1992, 27). Now, secondly, Smith established a Commission on Social Justice whose membership included both Labour, Liberal Democrat, business and academic figures. Its extensive report performed useful functions for the modernizers. It restated forcefully the early twentieth-century 'New Liberal' insistence that social justice was a precondition of economic success, a more readily marketable appeal to 'Tory switchers' than Croslandite egalitarianism. More directly, it placed a large question mark over welfare universalism by suggesting the targeting of both the last great non-means-tested benefits: child benefit, and state pension provision (Townsend, 1995). The latter, the report accepted, would never again be generous enough to actually live on, suggesting a supplementary benefit for those unable to afford to finance a second, private pension misleadingly dubbed a 'universal second pension' (Commission on Social Justice, 1994, 277). Blair's government would pursue both retreats from universalism.

The New Labour project that is popularly dated from Blair's succession to the Labour leadership in 1994 thus followed a long period of modernization of the party's ideology, organization and policy. This longer process was rooted in the failure of Labour's post-war programme of reforming social democracy to sustain electoral success in the face of the financial, industrial and political problems arising from the decline of the British empire; of the collapse of the long world boom in the inflationary chaos of the 1970s; and of the changes in electoral behaviour related to these developments and to the transformation of British industrial society that eradicated, often brutally, much of the labour movement's industrial base. Such experiences, as much as the legacy of Thatcherism, account for the high profile of New Labour themes like anti-statism in economic and social policy; the priority of counter-inflation over employment policy; hostility to trade union activism; and mobilizing private sector funding, rather than personal taxes, to fund public service investment. Historical change, on the other hand, has liberated New Labour in office from two of the most debilitating factors that constrained its precedessors. Sterling is no longer a world currency whose fortunes could ruin a Labour Chancellor overnight, balance of payments deficits no longer newsworthy. And, however strongly

New Labour is committed to US foreign and military policy, the Cold War in which the party could be cynically portrayed to the electorate as being weak-willed – or even on the wrong side – is over.

About this Volume

It has not been the purpose of this chapter to pre-empt those that follow by surveying the literature on New Labour, but the point needs to be made that the debate largely follows the pattern set by the analysis of Kinnock's modernization. One perspective develops the 'accommodation to Thatcherism' analysis (Hay, 1999), accusing New Labour of offering a new 'variant of authoritarian populism' (Hall, 1998). Others, whether supportively noting a long revisionist tradition (T. Jones, 1996), or critically noting a long tradition of the party's 'bourgeois modernizers' responding to the demands of capital (D. Coates, 1996), have insisted on the significance of historical precedents. Yet others have portrayed, in Wickham-Jones's earlier terms, a 'distinctive social democratic politics' (1995a), often characterized as 'post-Thatcherite' (Driver and Martell, 1998). These debates have been accompanied by disputes, not least within Labour's own right wing, about whether the 'third way' represents an unprincipled abandonment of egalitarianism (Hattersley, 1997a,b, 384–5); or a daring rescue of the social democratic project that had appeared dead and buried in the 1980s (G. Brown, 1999; Mandelson and Liddle, 1996), the creation of a 'modernised social democracy' as Blair himself has insisted (Blair, 1998c).

This is not, as readers will soon note, a volume whose editors have imposed any particular perspective on their contributors' interpretation of this New Labour project. The authors of the chapters that follow were asked, however, insofar as their subject matter permitted, briefly to place New Labour in the context of Labour's post-war history, and to incorporate comment on how much New Labour, both before and after May Day 1997, owes to 'Old' Labour, how much to the legacy of the governments of Margaret Thatcher and John Major, and how much to the modernization process under Neil Kinnock and John Smith between 1983 and 1994.

The book is set out as follows. Charles Pattie identifies the components of the electoral coalition that brought New Labour into office, and considers whether they can deliver a second term. Ben Clift unpacks key elements of Labour's Third Way to judge how far they place the party in the camp of European social democracy. Patrick Seyd and Paul Whiteley assess the reforms of New Labour's internal democracy, and reveal the attitudes of the party's mass membership. Philip Cowley, Darren Darcy and Colin Mellors measure the socio-economic composition of New Labour's parliamentarians, and challenge the conventional wisdom that the backbenches are unusually quiescent. Chapter 6 assesses the state of the historic labour alliance of party and trade unions and asks whether it has a future. Bob Franklin unravels New Labour's relentless drive to 'Millbankize' government media relations and discusses the implications for democracy. Martin Smith and David Richards survey New Labour's attempt to reform the machinery of the core executive it inherited, and the parallel but often contradictory drive to reform the British constitution. Andrew Gamble and Gavin Kelly analyse New Labour's economic strategy, and discern crucial social democratic features that lie beyond a neo-liberal consensus. Claire Annesley contrasts pessimistic accounts of New Labour's welfare reforms with a more optimistic view that looks forward to the eradication of social exclusion and the reconstruction of a welfare consensus. Colin McCaig evaluates New Labour's attempt to reconceptualize comprehensive education to attract the support of its individualistic and aspirational electoral bases. Jim Buller analyses New Labour's statecraft in foreign policy, identifying traditional elements and evaluating new concerns such as the much-discussed 'ethical dimension'. Michael Kenny and Martin Smith reassess the variety of interpretations of 'Blairism' and New Labour, and insist on the need for multidimensional judgement. In the light of the findings of the book, Martin Smith concludes by reconsidering the degree of New Labour's novelty, and the radical potential of Blair's project.

Finally, one slightly ludicrous side-effect of Labour's rebranding has been a politico-grammatical dispute in the Labour press over how to write New Labour (the form used by Blair). The *New Statesman* prefers a noncommital, lower case, new Labour; *Tribune* a sceptical, lower case, 'new' Labour; the left Labour MPs' *Socialist Campaign Group News* a sceptical, upper case, 'New' Labour. The Labour Party of course remains, in its constitution, the Labour Party, but in this volume we have used the form New Labour to refer, as party leaders do, to the informally rebranded party image projected since 1994 under Blair's leadership.

2

New Labour and the Electorate

CHARLES PATTIE

From the foreshortened perspective of the start of the twenty-first century, Labour's relationship with the electorate looks very successful. In its early years, it returned only a handful of MPs. But in the 1997 election, the 10 per cent swing from Conservative to Labour, and Labour's 176-seat majority, were post-war records. Furthermore, Labour's honeymoon was unusually long-lasting. In 1999 – despite mid-term reverses in local, Scottish, Welsh and European elections – national opinion polls put Labour well ahead, while the Conservatives showed few signs of recovery. As it faced the new millennium, Labour was undisputed king of the British political jungle. But how did it get there? This chapter traces Labour's shifting relationship with the electorate, first outlining the record, then analysing the changing anatomy of Labour's vote.

Charting Labour's Electoral Record

The perspective above suggests unbroken advance, but closer inspection reveals less sure-footed progress (Figure 2.1). During the twentieth century, Labour was the main party of government after only 9 of 26 elections, and in office for just 22 years. On only three occasions (1945, 1966, 1997) has the party won a comfortable Commons majority. Post-war, Labour has suffered two prolonged periods in opposition, with serious question marks over its ability ever to win another election.

After 1918, Labour gradually eclipsed the Liberal Party. But after the short-lived minority government of 1923, and the 1931 disintegration of Ramsay MacDonald's second minority government, the 1945 result was an unprecedented success. The electorate rejected parties associated with

FIGURE 2.1   *Labour votes and MPs, 1900–97*

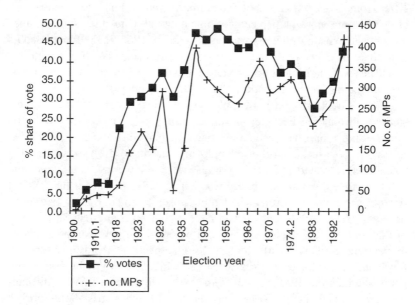

pre-war failures, giving Labour its first landslide victory, a 146-seat majority on 48 per cent of the vote. Clement Attlee's became one of the great
reforming governments of the century, launching the modern welfare state
and setting the public policy agenda for over thirty years. Labour's reforms,
especially the National Health Service, achieved wide popularity, forcing
the Conservatives to adapt, but not securing electoral ascendancy. The late
1940s were also marked by economic austerity, and in the 1950 election
Labour's majority fell to 5 seats. Labour lost in 1951, despite a larger vote
share than in 1945, and more votes than the Conservatives. Labour's first
post-war spell of prolonged opposition began. The Conservatives benefited
from economic growth and rising living standards and increased their
majority in 1955 and 1959, enjoying an unprecedented run of three victories. Analysts began to ask whether social change had consigned Labour to
permanent opposition (Abrams *et al.*, 1960).

The Natural Party of Government

The Conservatives, though, fell prey to a mixture of scandal and relative
economic decline. Harold Macmillan's replacement, Alec Douglas-Home,
was seen as an electoral liability compared to the media-wise and folksy

new Labour leader, Harold Wilson. However, the polls tell a different story. After Home's accession, Labour's lead narrowed and its 1964 victory was close. Labour won 44 per cent of the national vote, the Conservatives 43 per cent. Wilson's majority was just 4 seats. In 1966, Labour increased its vote share by 3 per cent, and its majority to 100 seats. With two victories under his belt, and four Labour victories out of seven post-war elections, Wilson seemed to have made Labour 'the natural party of government' (cited A. Jay, 1966, 390). But Wilson quickly encountered difficulties: sterling devaluation became unavoidable in 1967, and conflict with the unions and more bad economic news damaged Labour's credibility. In 1968 Labour lost control of many local authorities. Even so, as the 1970 election approached, Labour's ratings were recovering, and economic news improved. A Labour victory was expected, so defeat for the 'natural party of government' was a considerable upset. Even so, Labour had made progress. Before 1945, Labour had never achieved more than 38 per cent of the vote. Between 1945 and 1970, its vote share never dropped below 43 per cent in the two-party contest. In retrospect, 1970 was a watershed: it was the last of the post-war elections in which the two main parties routinely shared around 90 per cent of the vote. Mounting economic difficulties undermined the post-war consensus, as Keynesian policies proved ineffective against mounting unemployment, inflation and union unrest (Gamble, 1994). Voters deserted to third parties which, during the 1970s, regularly took around a quarter of votes.

Although it won in February 1974, Labour polled fewer votes than the Conservatives, and owed its haul of seats to the electoral system. Labour's vote slumped below 40 per cent for the first time since 1935, and it failed to achieve an overall Commons majority. Its position improved slightly at the October 1974 election, but its vote remained below 40 per cent, and its small overall majority had evaporated by the middle of the Parliament, forcing reliance on the Liberals and other minor parties.

In the teeth of continuing economic troubles, Labour in government began the move away from Keynesianism towards a monetarist strategy and cutting state spending, and faced mounting opposition. Party activists objected to the abandonment of manifesto commitments and calls for greater intra-party accountability grew (Kogan and Kogan, 1982). The Social Contract with the unions faltered as inflation cut real earnings. The nationalist parties, crucial to Labour's survival by 1978, lost faith in its commitment to devolution. And the Conservative party was recovering under Margaret Thatcher, who moved the party rightward, blaming economic problems on the post-war consensus and demanding strict adherence to monetarism and free market disciplines. Furthermore, social change eroded

Labour's working-class power base. Nevertheless, it was not obvious that Labour would lose the next election. In an autumn 1978 election, widely anticipated, James Callaghan might just have won. But over the winter of 1978–9, the government's position unravelled. The 'winter of discontent' stoked public resentment against both unions and government, producing images used repeatedly by Conservative propagandists, in future elections, as a warning against re-electing Labour. When Labour's devolution proposals for Scotland and Wales collapsed, it lost a vote of confidence in March 1979, and lost the resulting election.

Wilderness Years

As in 1945, 1979 was a landmark election. The new administration quickly pursued its monetarist agenda, abandoning the social democratic consensus. Labour entered opposition divided and demoralized. For a while, Labour was able to gloss over its difficulties, as Conservative popularity plummeted in the face of recession and rapidly rising unemployment. Labour's ratings soared, peaking at around 50 per cent in 1980. But the internal strife led in 1981 to the defection of 13 rightwing MPs to the SDP, later joined by 13 more (Crewe and King, 1995). Briefly, the SDP-Liberal Alliance seemed likely to 'break the mould' of British politics, passing both main parties in the polls. Labour, deeply divided, swung further to the left and its poll ratings fell steeply (Whiteley, 1983; Seyd, 1987). The Conservatives' popularity improved dramatically, as victory in the Falklands and signs of economic recovery took effect (Sanders *et al.*, 1987; Clarke *et al.*, 1990). These factors, with the electoral opposition divided and Labour still feuding, gave the Conservatives victory in 1983 (though their vote share barely changed).

For Labour, the election was a near disaster. After a shambolic campaign, its vote share dipped to 28 per cent, the lowest since 1918, and it was almost eclipsed as the main opposition party when the Liberal-SDP Alliance vote came within 2 per cent of Labour's. Britain's electoral system saved Labour, whose concentrated support in northern, urban and mining areas created safe seats, enabling the party to retain 209 seats. Alliance support was more evenly spread: they took only 23 seats. The severe blow of 1983 forced a rethink. Neil Kinnock, the new leader, embarked on an attempt to bring the party back to the centre, targeting groups like Militant, dropping some of the radical manifesto commitments, and modernizing communications strategy (Shaw, 1994). But Labour lost the 1987 election despite a slick and professional campaign.

Its vote recovered somewhat, but at 31 per cent, was still one of its worst performances. The Conservatives' vote, buoyed up by the effects of economic recovery, again remained virtually unchanged.

In some respects, the 1987 defeat was a greater blow than 1983. In 1987, following Thatcher's Westland crisis, Labour's strong mid-term polls, and its professionalized campaigning, some had hoped for a Labour victory. The defeat was a double blow: Labour had not yet regained enough voters' trust, and now the Conservatives had a further term to consolidate their programme. The political landscape had been transformed since 1979. Following the 1984–5 miners' strike, and legislation aimed at curbing their power, unions were cowed. Many nationalized industries and key public utilities were privatized. Low direct taxation became part of voters' expectations. Like the Conservatives after 1945, Labour after 1987 faced the probability that some accommodation with the new dispensation was a precondition of re-election. Crucially, this meant losing the party's 'tax and spend' image. Labour launched a root-and-branch re-evaluation of its platform, and party management was centralized. It was helped by the acrimonious collapse of the Alliance after 1987, but mainly, in the 1987–92 Parliament, by growing discontent with the Conservatives, whose attempts to slow the economy down plunged the affluent south-east into recession. Homeowners were trapped in negative equity, some blaming and deserting the Conservatives (Pattie *et al.*, 1995a). The poll tax proved highly unpopular, and splits over Europe began to erupt. Thatcher's leadership style became an electoral asset for Labour, which won its first country-wide ballot victory since 1974 in the 1989 European elections.

1992 and After

Conservative electoral fears precipitated a leadership election in 1990, and Thatcher was replaced by the more emollient figure of John Major. The poll tax was abandoned, and Conservative fortunes revived. Until the 1992 election, the parties ran neck-and-neck, many expecting a Conservative defeat, if not necessarily an outright Labour victory. Despite recession, Major created a sufficient sense of economic well-being to win (Sanders, 1991). The campaign was close-fought. In another professional Labour campaign, a 'shadow budget' was presented to lay remaining fears that Labour would tax and spend profligately. But the strategy backfired amid Conservative claims that Labour planned a tax 'double whammy'. Labour was bitterly disappointed. Again, the Conservatives' vote share hardly changed. Again, Labour's grew, but at 35 per cent remained low by postwar standards. The year 1992 should have been a good year for Labour, with economic recession facing a government which had recently been deeply unpopular, and was divided over Europe. If Labour could not win under these circumstances, when could it?

With the economy beginning to recover, the Conservatives could take credit for rising affluence before the next election. The Conservatives' electoral record since 1979 had been remarkable: no party since the mass franchise had won four successive elections, or remained in office for so long. As in the late 1950s, some questioned whether Labour ever could win (A. King, 1992; Heath *et al.*, 1994). But two unforseeable factors transformed the 1992 Parliament. First, membership of the European Exchange Rate Mechanism (ERM) collapsed in September 1992. Almost overnight, the Conservatives lost their reputation as economic managers (Sanders, 1996). Their ratings plummeted to below 30 per cent, staying there for much of the rest of the Parliament in spite of economic recovery. The ERM crisis highlighted Conservative divisions over Europe, further damaging the Conservatives' standing (Ludlam, 1996; Evans, 1998). The second factor was Labour's transformation. Kinnock's successor, John Smith, died suddenly in 1994. Tony Blair, elected to Parliament in 1983, was free of associations with past Labour governments, and strongly associated with party modernizers. He took the party further towards the centre, in both substantive policy and 'symbolic politics'. The reform of Clause IV marked Blair's ascendancy, indicating that Labour had broken with its past, and become 'New Labour'. Blair also returned to the campaign arts of focus groups and spindoctors which had fallen out of favour under Smith. New Labour built a formidable reputation for its campaigning and news management.

New Labour's support surged to between 45 and 50 per cent almost until the 1997 election, but memories of 1992 made senior strategists sceptical about such figures (Gould, 1998b). In the event, the result surpassed their most optimistic hopes: Labour's biggest ever majority, and the largest majority of any post-war government, on one of the largest electoral swings of modern times. The Conservatives suffered their worst defeat since 1906 in terms of seats, since 1832 on vote share. But it is worth noting that Labour's vote, at 43 per cent, had only recovered to 1970 levels – and Labour had lost that election. The landslide was a consequence of the quirky nature of first-past-the-post.

The Changing Anatomy of Labour Voting

What factors explain Labour's shifting relationship with the electorate: success in the 1960s, failure in the 1980s, and back to success in 1997?

The Social Bases of Labour Support

Labour's electoral base has been remade in recent years, from something resembling a classic 'mass party' with a large membership, support based on particular socio-economic groups, to something closer to a 'catch-all party', much more leadership-focused, less reliant on particular socio-economic groups (Kirchheimer, 1966; Katz and Mair, 1995). In Britain, the class cleavage has generally been seen as the most important in twentieth-century politics (Pulzer, 1967). For most of Labour's history, it has, as its name implies, been associated with one side of that cleavage. It was established by the trades unions as the party of the working classes, of labour.

Class cleavage was never absolute, however. A sizeable number of working-class voters voted for the party of property and capital, the Conservatives (McKenzie and Silver, 1968). Without them, the Conservatives would have been unable to win an election after the extension of the franchise. In the 1960s, though, class remained crucial; with a large working class, and more voters growing up in Labour-voting households, Labour's electoral future looked secure (Butler and Stokes, 1969). In the 1960s, between 65 and 70 per cent of manual workers voted Labour, compared to only around 17 per cent of those in professional and managerial jobs (Table 2.1). The Alford Index measures class voting by subtracting the percentage of non-manual workers voting Labour from the percentage of manual workers voting Labour. In the 1960s it measured around 42, indicating quite strong class cleavage (Dalton, 1996). But the 1960s

TABLE 2.1   *Per cent Labour vote by class, 1992–97*

	Professionals and managers %	Intermediate workers %	Manual workers %	Alford index
1964	16.0	27.7	65.6	42
1966	18.0	33.4	69.5	43
1970	24.3	32.7	57.1	33
Feb 1974	18.8	30.3	57.0	35
Oct 1974	18.5	32.6	58.2	32
1979	20.9	27.5	50.7	27
1983	13.1	19.4	42.6	25
1987	17.4	21.4	43.7	25
1992	19.0	26.1	49.6	27
1997	38.5	43.1	60.2	22

Source: British Election Study.

represented a high point for class voting. An influential 1960s study of manual car workers provided evidence for the coming shift (Goldthorpe *et al.*, 1968). Most intended to vote Labour. Older workers, who remembered the inter-war depression, saw Labour as their 'natural' party, voting out of class loyalty. Younger workers, who started work during the long post-war boom, would vote Labour so long as it delivered rising living standards.

Given this increasing instrumentalism, Labour was poorly placed to deal with economic recession when it came. Political failure in the 1970s was reflected in the decline of partisan dealignment, voters' long-term attachments to parties (Crewe and Särlvik, 1983); as well as of class dealignment, the weakening of class as a guide to voting (Franklin, 1985). Labour's share of the working-class vote fell from almost 70 per cent in 1966 to 57 per cent in 1970 and 1974 (Table 2.1). Furthermore, it was losing ground among its strongest supporters. In 1964, 65 per cent of trades unionists voted Labour, by 1979 only 50 per cent did so, in 1983 just 38 per cent. Skilled manual workers, especially in the south, abandoned Labour for the Conservatives in the late 1970s and early 1980s (Johnston *et al.*, 1988; Pattie and Johnston, 1996a). Class cleavage weakened: the Alford index dropped almost continuously between 1970 and 1987, rising slightly in 1992 (Table 2.1). Class still had an influence: half the working class voted Labour in 1992, compared to only one in five professionals. But, methodological counter-arguments notwithstanding, class was much less important than before (Heath *et al.*, 1985; Crewe, 1986; Dunleavy, 1987).

Related factors also undermined Labour's position after 1970. First, it did not compensate by attracting middle-class voters, only around 20 per cent of professionals and managers voting Labour in the 1960s and 1970s, even fewer in the 1980s. Second, it faced a tide of social change, the manual working class declining as a proportion of the working population, from 58 per cent in 1971 to 44 per cent twenty years later. Labour was not only losing support in its core class, its core class was also shrinking. Third, while the proportion of trades unionists in the electorate had grown between 1964 and 1979, from 25 to 30 per cent of respondents to the British Election Study (BES), after 1979 unions lost membership, through mass unemployment and anti-union legislation. By 1992, only 20 per cent of BES respondents were union members.

A fourth social factor was continuing embourgoisement; more affluent working-class voters aspired to middle-class lifestyles. This process, noted above as one explanation for Labour's 1959 defeat, continued even in the recessions of the 1970s and 1980s. Rising ownership of cars and other 'luxury' consumer goods was one marker. More significant was homeownership: in 1964, only 48 per cent of the electorate were home-owners; by 1992 the figure was 72 per cent. More manual workers bought homes, especially after Thatcher gave council tenants the 'right to buy' (Hamnett, 1999; Garrett, 1994). Homeowners are more likely to vote Conservative than Labour (Table 2.2). Ownership now cut across class: compared to working-class council tenants, working-class homeowners were more inclined to vote Conservative (Dunleavy, 1979).

Labour's electoral decline was thus linked to changes in its social base. But there was nothing absolutely inevitable about the link. The Conservatives had seen their ties with their traditional electoral base weaken since the 1960s, although social change had generally worked in their favour (Pattie and Johnston, 1996a). But they reacted by attracting skilled manual work-ers in the south. To recover, Labour had to do the same. It had to make the transition from mass to catch-all party, winning back lost working-class votes, but moving beyond them since, by 1997, the working class was too small to deliver a Labour victory by itself. Much of Blair's strategy after 1994 was designed to reassure the middle classes. It seems to have worked spectacularly well. In the 1997 landslide, Labour's working-class vote recovered virtually to 1960s levels: 60 per cent of manual workers voted for the party (Table 2.1), as did 48 per cent of council tenants (Table 2.2). But even more striking was Labour's dramatically improved middle-class vote, the highest since 1964. Almost 40 per cent of professional and man-agerial workers voted New Labour. As a consequence, the 1997 election was one of the least class-aligned of modern times in Britain, with an Alford Index of only 22. Fully 44 per cent of homeowners voted Labour.

TABLE 2.2   *Per cent Labour vote by housing tenure, 1964–97*

	Home-owners %	Council tenants %	Private tenants %
1964	29.9	70.2	54.0
1970	36.2	59.8	63.6
Feb 1974	27.7	63.6	42.6
Oct 1974	29.6	65.3	43.3
1979	26.7	59.6	38.9
1983	19.0	55.0	27.1
1987	22.7	58.3	35.4
1992	26.5	34.8	39.0
1997	44.2	71.6	48.3

Source: British Election Study.

In 1997, Labour broke out of its shrinking ghetto. But how did it manage this in 1997, while not at earlier elections? The following sections consider possible factors.

Changing Attitudes?

A cornerstone of the theory of democratic elections is that voters select the party which most closely reflects their views and interests. Downs's (1957) economic theory of democracy suggests policy convergence as parties chase the median voter. Parties which move away from median political attitudes should lose votes. This might suggest that, between the late 1960s and early 1990s, public opinion on major policies diverged from what Labour seemed to stand for. Labour's success in 1997 should, equally, have been an outcome of its move back into the centre. There is certainly considerable evidence to suggest that 'issue voting' increased as class voting declined (Crewe and Särlvik, 1983; Rose and McAllister, 1990; Heath *et al.*, 1985). But does this account for Labour's changing fortunes?

Two major axes of opinion can be identified in the British electorate (Heath *et al.*, 1985; Evans *et al.*, 1996): a left–right axis covering issues such as economic growth, public spending, taxation, and an authoritarian–libertarian axis covering issues like law and order and permissiveness. The British Election Studies have asked questions on these dimensions since the 1960s. Responses to three left–right questions suggest some truth in the analysis above (Table 2.3). The state's economic role was a major post-war battleground, with Labour advocating nationalization of some industries, against Conservatives opposition. Thatcher's privatizations forced Labour largely to abandon public ownership, but attitudes to nationalization remain a left–right barometer. During the 1970s, opinion moved to the right as the proportion wanting further nationalization halved between 1974 and 1979, while support for privatization increased substantially. Support for redistribution of wealth fell, less dramatically, by over 10 per cent between 1974 and 1987. In both cases, however, support for leftwing positions grew again after 1987, as Labour's electoral standing improved. It is hard to disentangle cause and effect: did Labour's vote improve because voters moved leftward, or did voters move to the left because Labour looked more electable? But the correlation is relatively clear, and the link to actual political events seems sensible: later privatizations were less popular than earlier ones, damaging the Conservatives.

But while this suggests that attitude change helped Labour, the picture is not clear cut. Despite Thatcherite arguments, for instance, the main

TABLE 2.3   *Attitudes on economic policy, 1964–97*

	Nationalization vs. privatization		Govt should spend to get rid of poverty		Income and wealth should be redistributed	
	nationalize %	privatize %	should %	should not %	should %	should not %
1964	28.5	20.7				
1966	28.9	22.4				
Feb 1974	28.4	24.8				
Oct 1974	32.2	21.9	87.0	6.6	56.2	28.1
1979	16.9	40.0	83.5	8.6	55.2	28.3
1983	17.5	43.0	85.7	11.2	47.5	37.3
1987	17.1	31.9	87.9	7.5	43.9	36.2
1992	23.7	24.0	92.8	4.8	48.2	31.5
1997	27.9	14.5	91.8	4.7	60.8	20.9

Source: BES.

FIGURE 2.2   *Average scores, tax vs. spending dimension*

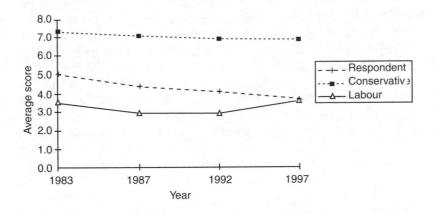

Source: BES.

structures of the post-war consensus, like the NHS, remained popular.
Throughout the period since 1974, large majorities felt government should
spend more to eradicate poverty, even when Labour was most unpopular
(Table 2.3). Considerable evidence suggests that public opinion moved
to the right during the late 1970s, as Labour's popularity fell. Thatcher rode
that wave in 1979, but did not then effect the sea-change in attitudes she
hoped for. If anything, attitudes moved against her government, despite
her election victories (Crewe, 1988; Pattie and Johnston, 1996a; Heath

et al., 1991). We can see this more clearly by comparing where individuals place themselves on particular issues with where they place the parties.

Since 1983, BES surveys have carried 'thermometer' questions asking respondents to place both themselves and the main parties on an 11-point scale between two polar positions (1983 scales have been recoded for comparability). Figures 2.2 to 2.4 show, over time, the respondents' average scores, and the average perceptions of Labour and Conservative positions. The most leftwing position scores one, the most rightwing, eleven, and six is the mid-point. Throughout the 1980s and 1990s the Conservatives argued strongly for limited public spending and low taxes, and branded Labour as the party of high spending and taxes. After 1983 Labour tried to lose its high tax image, and retreated from public spending commitments. Not surprisingly, Labour was perceived as being on the left, and the Conservatives on the right, with voters in between (Figure 2.2). But two features are noteworthy. First, respondents were always slightly left of centre, even in the 'high Thatcherism' years, and, if anything, were closer to Labour's perceived position. Second, over time, as Crewe (1988) indicated, the electorate moved leftward. After 1992, Labour was perceived as moving rightwards, and voters' views converged with what they perceived of as Labour views. Similar and, if anything, starker patterns are evident in Figure 2.3, which shows average scores on the unemployment-inflation trade-off. The leftward drift is again evident on state ownership, as is Labour's perceived shift to the centre (Figure 2.4). In 1983, the average voter was right of centre, favouring more privatization. By 1997, the situation had reversed, the average voter was almost exactly in the centre, much closer to Labour's position.

FIGURE 2.3   *Average scores, jobs vs. prices dimension*

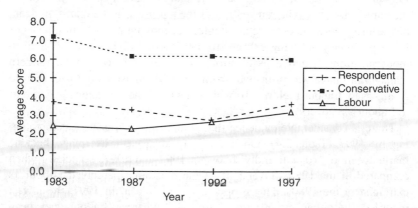

FIGURE 2.4   *Average scores, nationalization vs. privatization dimension*

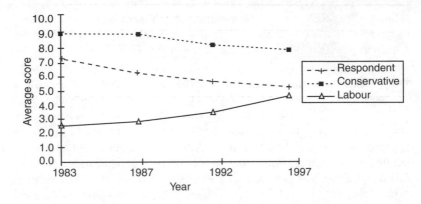

Source: BES.

Such evidence suggests that Labour's victory in 1997 partly reflected its policy movement towards the average voter. However, this cannot entirely account for Labour's changing support. Even in its worst years, public opinion was closer to Labour, but Labour lost elections. Issue voting is important, but cannot fully explain why Labour did so badly in the 1980s (Heath *et al.*, 1985).

Changing Images

Labour modernizers saw image and presentation as important elements in the party's armoury. The reinvention of the party was more than skin deep, but surface appearances were not neglected: moving away from images of fiscal profligacy, leftwing extremism and internal division was crucial to modernization. Negative associations were downplayed, and a modern managerial image was projected, from Peter Mandelson's red rose logo to Blair's New Labour rhetoric. To what extent did these changes play a part in Labour's recovery?

There is considerable evidence that voters saw Labour as less threatening by 1997 (Table 2.4). On a range of measures, its image became markedly more 'voter friendly' between 1992 and 1997, especially when compared to the 1980s. Over half of the electorate perceived Labour as extremist in the 1980s. This dropped to 16 per cent in 1997, the lowest recorded by either main party. Similarly, whereas Labour had been perceived as representing sectional working-class interests, by 1997 only

TABLE 2.4 *Perceived party image, 1964–97*

	% of respondents who perceive				
	a great deal of difference between Labour and Conservative	Labour as		Conservatives as	
		extreme	good for one class	extreme	good for one class
1964	48.0				
1966	43.7				
1970	33.0				
Feb 1974	33.8	44.0	45.3	44.9	65.2
Oct 1974	39.5	54.6	50.4	47.5	65.3
1979	47.6				
1983	83.6	57.4	61.4	54.7	62.1
1987	84.6	57.2	64.4	54.0	62.1
1992	56.1	31.3	56.5	31.0	56.2
1997	33.3	16.4	19.4	36.4	68.9

Source: BES.

19 per cent believed this. In other words, even among non-Labour voters, substantial proportions no longer saw the party in threatening terms. Meanwhile, the Conservatives retained their reputation for sectionalism and extremism among a large group of voters.

Furthermore, Labour was no longer damaged by its association with trade unionism. Between the late 1960s and the collapse of the 1984/5 miners' strike, unions became unpopular, widely perceived as too powerful (Table 2.5). The 'winter of discontent' repeatedly featured in Conservative election propaganda. But, ironically, Conservative anti-union legislation, combined, after 1992, with Labour's arms-length relationship with the unions, effectively neutralized the 'union issue'. Whereas in 1979, 81 per cent of voters thought unions too powerful, by 1997 this dropped to 23 per cent. Perceptions of business power moved in the other direction: by 1997, almost 80 per cent thought business too powerful.

Labour's 1997 success was clearly associated with a radical improvement in public perceptions of the party. But it is harder to blame its failures in the 1980s simply on negative image, when similarly sized proportions saw the Conservatives in the same negative terms but still elected them (Table 2.4). Extremism and sectionalism in themselves were not enough to damage a party. Other sorts of image and perception also played a part.

Perhaps the most important have been perceptions of government competence, especially in economic management. Conservative hegemony after 1979 was largely built on a reputation for competent economic

TABLE 2.5   *Attitudes towards business and trade union power, 1964–97*

| | % saying unions/business have too much power | |
	Unions	Business
1964	62.4	64.8
1966	71.4	63.1
1970	73.1	54.7
Oct 1974	80.9	61.5
1979	81.1	60.3
1983	73.3	68.3
1987	45.4	31.7
1992	32.9	72.8
1997	23.3	78.5

Source: BES.

management, and on the related 'feel good factor' (Sanders *et al.*, 1987; Pattie and Johnston, 1995). But the 1992 ERM crisis destroyed this reputation. Before the crisis, the Conservatives routinely outscored Labour on economic management; afterwards the situation reversed (Sanders, 1995). Voters apparently felt that the economic recovery under way in 1997 was taking place despite Conservative policy, not because of it. In any case, the feelgood factor did not trickle down to everyone. While 40 per cent of voters in 1997 felt the national economy had improved over the previous year, only 25 per cent felt personally more prosperous.

On top of this, the Conservatives were split on Europe, and wracked by sleaze allegations. Taken together, all these factors contributed to a collapse in the Conservatives' image. At the same time, New Labour was concentrating on looking like a government-in-waiting. Voters agreed. In 1987, 94 per cent of BES respondents had felt the Conservatives were capable of strong government, while only 36 per cent felt the same about Labour. The gap was marginally narrower in 1992, but by 1997, it had reversed: 28 per cent thought the Conservatives would make a strong government, 88 per cent thought Labour would.

The image of party leaders also has electoral effects. In 1992, Major was seen as an asset, while Kinnock was not (Crewe and King, 1994; Clarke and Stewart, 1995). Only 14 per cent of voters saw Thatcher as 'caring' in 1983, but 60 per cent thought she was decisive, 72 per cent that she stuck to her principles. While 46 per cent of the 1983 electorate saw Michael Foot as caring, only 7 per cent thought him decisive, and only a quarter that he stuck to his principles. Conservative difficulties after 1992 reflected leadership perceptions. When BES respondents in 1997 were asked to rate party leaders on an 11-point scale (0 indicating strong dislike), Major averaged 4.6; Blair averaged 6.4. Blair also appealed to the desire for a caring but tough leader: 90 per cent in 1997 thought him caring, 87 per cent thought him decisive, 79 per cent thought him principled, and 88 per cent thought he would listen to reason. Critically, 93 per cent thought he would make a good prime minister, compared to only 45 per cent for Major. Even more important, there is good evidence to suggest that the 'Blair effect' itself was a contributor to Labour's improvement between 1992 and 1997. Clarke *et al.* (1998) show that Blair's election as leader gave a significant and long-lasting boost to Labour's already strong standing in the opinion polls. Labour might well have won in 1997 without him, so damaged were the Conservatives. But he was crucial to the scale of victory.

Campaigning

A vital weapon in Labour's armoury was its campaign machinery. Election campaigning has become progressively more professionalized since the war, as the parties have responded to the changing media coverage of politics (Scammel, 1995; Kavanagh, 1995). In particular, the growth of television has necessitated new thinking on presentation, leading to greater national control of campaigning and communications strategy.

Labour's changing relationship with the media has been widely discussed (Chapter 7; Shaw, 1994). After the disastrous 1983 result, the national campaign machinery was overhauled. News management and image became much more important. By 1997, Labour's national campaign was very tightly managed (Gould, 1998b; Kavanagh, 1997; Norris, 1997a). American-style rapid rebuttal tactics were employed (via the Excalibur computer system) to neutralize negative comment. Spindoctors and focus groups became part of the party's campaign vocabulary. Labour was fighting a tightly focused, media-oriented campaign in which all main players stayed resolutely 'on message'.

This chapter is not the place to discuss these developments in depth (see Chapter 7). However, we can speculate about the likely effects of Labour's changing media strategy. Definitive conclusions on the electoral consequences of national campaigning are extremely difficult, since there is only one national campaign at each election (though see Miller *et al.*, 1990; Holbrook, 1996; Forrest and Marks, 1999). In any case, parties increasingly see the campaign as semi-permanent. Labour began its 1997 campaign some years before the election, which thereby becomes entangled with other events. To what extent did Labour's strong opinion poll position on the eve of the 1997 election reflect its pre-election campaign as opposed to other political and economic events? We cannot be sure. Strong campaigns in 1987 and 1992 were insufficient to counteract the party's other electoral weaknesses. Even so, it seems extremely likely that New Labour's increased campaigning proficiency at least boosted its developing image as professional, competent and moderate. Certainly it contrasted strongy with the Conservative often directionless and confusing campaigning, which merely served to re-focus attention on Conservative weaknesses (Finkelstein, 1998; Whiteley, 1997). At the very least, the Conservative 1997 campaign does not seem to have helped it; while Labour's campaign produced no unexpected shocks to damage its position.

The national campaign was only one part of New Labour's strategy. In 1995, Labour targeted 90 key marginals the party had to win to gain office (Denver *et al.*, 1998). Much of the party's campaign effort, apart from the national media campaign, was concentrated in these seats. Seats where Labour had no real chance of winning were largely ignored, while in safe Labour seats, campaigning was limited. Within the key seats, the two years before the election were spent in local campaigning and building a picture of Labour supporters and floating voters. Much effort was focused on potential switchers, to encourage them into the Labour camp. By 1997, much of the groundwork in the key seats was done.

The key seats strategy continued into the election. We can examine money spent by local parties on 'official' constituency campaigns, which are subject to legal spending limits and recorded, and which correlate well with other measures of local campaign intensity (Pattie *et al.*, 1994). So by comparing the amount spent in 1997 with the marginality of seats in 1992, we see where campaigning was concentrated. In hopeless seats Labour spent only token amounts in 1997. It spent more in its safe seats, but well below the legal maximum. But in marginals, Labour spent at or very close to the maximum: it concentrated its efforts where they mattered most. The Conservatives spent little in hopeless seats, but close to the maximum in safe seats as well as marginals.

Did Labour's local strategy work? Conventional political science wisdom has argued that in the television age, constituency campaigning is an ineffective anachronism. But the evidence suggests that local campaigning can have an effect (Pattie *et al.*, 1995b; Whiteley, Seyd and Richardson, 1994; Denver and Hands, 1997). In 1997 the more a party spent on its local campaign in a constituency, the better it did there, and the worse its rivals did, especially when the party was the challenger

TABLE 2.6 *The impact of 1997 constituency campaigning on constituency vote change, 1992–97*

	% change in vote 1992–97		
	Conservative	Labour	Lib Dem
% vote 1992	−0.20**	−0.14**	−0.20**
Margin 1992	0.06**	−0.06**	0.04
% Conservative spend 1997	0.05**	−0.01	−0.01
% Labour spend 1997	−0.02**	0.08**	−0.05**
% Lib Dem spend 1997	−0.00	−0.07**	0.10**
Constant	−6.09	13.90	1.55
R^2	0.42	0.31	0.25

Key: ** coefficient significant at $p = 0.01$.

(Table 2.6; also Johnston *et al.*, 1998). Labour won virtually all of its target seats: its strategy did work.

Labour's 1997 gains, of course, went far beyond target seats. It also won seats regarded as hopeless (most memorably Michael Portillo's). Some of these witnessed quite spectacular swings, almost certainly the result of anti-government feeling and tactical voting (Johnston *et al.*, 1998; Evans *et al.*, 1998). This has led some to argue that the targeting did not work (Curtice and Steed, 1997, 312). If Labour could score spectacular victories in hopeless seats, had it really needed to target key marginal seats? But this is in part hindsight. Although some commentators suggested a Labour landslide in 1997, most were more sceptical. The 1992 polls had, after all, wrongly exaggerated Labour's prospects. They might be wrong again, so Labour's caution was sensible. Second, as we have seen, local campaign activism did help Labour. Seat targeting and long-term campaigning are here to stay. Within months of the 1997 victory, Labour was encouraging its MPs to prepare for the next election.

The Electoral System

Finally, Labour was helped in 1997 by the electoral system itself. The tendency of Britain's first-past-the-post system to exaggerate the winning party's margin of victory is well known, though when the result is close, as in 1951 and February 1974, it can produce the 'wrong' winner. In 1997, Labour's 'winner's bonus' was spectacular. With only 43 per cent of the vote, Labour won 418 seats. In 1992, a 43 per cent vote share gave the

Conservatives only 336 seats. In 1997 the system seemed biased in Labour's favour.

One measure of bias is to calculate the difference in seats Labour and the Conservatives would have won on a nationally uniform swing between them sufficient to give them the same vote share. In the example discussed here (taken from Rossiter *et al.*, 1999b), a positive bias indicates an advantage for Labour, and a negative bias means a bias towards the Conservatives. Given the geography of party support after the 1997 election, a uniform national swing producing the same vote share would still have given Labour 82 more MPs than the Conservatives (Norris, 1997b; Rossiter *et al.*, 1999b)! This is especially ironic, as the 1997 election was the first since the 4th Periodic Review of Britain's parliamentary constituencies (Rossiter, Johnston and Pattie, 1999a). In general, boundary reviews have benefited the Conservatives by cutting seats in areas of declining population (mainly Labour-voting inner cities), and adding seats in growth areas (mainly Conservative suburbs in the south). But despite this, the system worked against the Conservatives. Furthermore, the overall bias in the electoral system has changed from pro-Conservative in the 1950s and early 1960s, to large pro-Labour biases in 1992 and 1997 (Table 2.7). The 1997 pro-Labour bias was the largest since 1950. How did this happen?

One way of finding out is to break the electoral bias into its component parts (see Brookes, 1959, 1960). The main sources of bias concern the effective size of constituencies. Parties doing well in constituencies with small populations need to win fewer votes than parties doing well in large constituencies. But 'effective size' variations arise from several different factors. The most obvious is varying constituency size across constituent parts of the UK. Scotland, Wales and Northern Ireland are guaranteed minimum levels of Westminster representation, and as a result can have more MPs than their electorates warrant. Since Labour tends to do better in Scotland and Wales than in England, this 'national electoral quotas' bias favours them, and its value has grown from three extra Labour seats in 1950 to 11 in 1997 (Table 2.7).

Secondly, constituencies vary in size within the nations of the UK, absolute electoral equality being difficult to achieve. Furthermore, population movement means that differences between constituencies change over time. The main post-war population movement has been away from the inner cities and from the north (mainly Labour voting areas) to the suburbs and the south (predominantly Conservative). As a result, it takes fewer votes to elect Labour than Conservative MPs. Since 1955, Labour has gained from this. But periodic boundary reviews, which in part seek to create more equal constituency electorates, have partially reversed the

TABLE 2.7   *Components of electoral bias, 1950–97, assuming Conservative and Labour have equal vote shares (positive bias is pro-Labour, negative is pro-Conservative)*

	NEQ	CSV	A	MPW	NI	MPV	E	I	T
1950	3	−6	−2	−4	−10	−7	−23	−2	−51
1951	4	−5	−4	−4	−10	0	−39	−1	−59
(boundary review)									
1955	4	−8	1	−4	−10	−3	−13	−1	−34
1959	6	1	1	−3	−12	−11	−29	−4	−51
1964	6	13	10	4	−12	−25	−13	−7	−24
1966	6	21	17	4	−11	−22	−13	−5	−3
1970	7	39	17	4	−8	−14	−39	−4	2
(boundary review)									
Feb 1974	5	19	16	5		−32	11	−6	18
Oct 1974	6	19	17	2		−17	−28	−2	−3
1979	8	31	12	1		−20	−1	−5	26
(boundary review)									
1983	10	13	12	12		−19	−28	−5	−5
1987	14	23	10	13		−24	−34	−8	−6
1992	12	29	19	20		−30	−7	−5	38
(boundary review)									
1997	11	13	24	33		−36	48	−9	82

Key: NEQ – national electoral quotas; CSV – constituency size variations; A – abstentions; MPW – minor party wins; NI – Northern Ireland; MPV – Minor party votes; E – efficiency; I – interactions; T – total.

Source: Rossiter *et al.*, 1999b.

advantage Labour has gained from constituency size variations. By 1997, this was worth 13 seats to Labour, down from 29 in 1992.

Abstention, by reducing the effective number of votes a party needs to win a seat, ironically helps parties in seats where relatively few vote. Since the early 1960s, Labour has again been the main beneficiary from this, since turnout tends to be lowest in the seats where Labour is strongest. By 1997 it was worth 24 seats for the party.

The growth of third-party voting since 1970 has affected how far the system is biased towards the two main parties. Most third-party MPs have been returned in seats which would otherwise probably have been Conservative. The more third-party MPs that are returned at an election, therefore, the greater Labour's advantage, an advantage that has grown over time, probably in part through the growth of tactical voting. By 1997, had Labour and Conservatives had the same vote share, third-party wins would have given Labour an advantage of 33 seats. But where the third party does not win, the Conservatives generally gain, since third parties generally come second in Conservative seats. Over time, this pro-Conservative bias has grown too, largely negating, and often eclipsing, Labour's advantage from third-party wins.

But perhaps the most dramatic change in the sources of electoral bias has been in the 'efficiency', the spread of votes. Under first-past-the-post, some votes in seats which a party is bound to lose are wasted, and in seats a party wins some are surplus. Ideally a party will want to minimize its wasted and surplus votes, making most votes as effective as possible. Postwar, the Conservatives have had a more efficient spread of voters than Labour, which has tended to accumulate large majorities in its safe seats. But in 1997, almost for the first time, Labour gained a major advantage from its efficient vote distribution. In part, this was another consequence of Labour's key seat strategy. By not campaigning heavily in seats where Labour was very unlikely to win, it effectively encouraged Labour supporters to vote tactically against the government, rather than 'waste' them on Labour. The Conservatives, by contrast, as the main targets of tactical voters and the main losers of seats in 1997, substantially increased their 'wasted' vote.

Conclusions

Labour remade itself as an electoral force in the late 1990s, not just in terms of winning votes, but also in the ways that it campaigns, its appeal to the electorate, and the groups it wins votes from. It has moved from a 'mass' party based in a declining, and decreasingly loyal social group, to something closer to a 'catch-all' party, drawing support broadly. That change was forced by demographic and political change, and the unprecedented defeats between 1979 and 1992. No change was not an option. In 1983, the party faced the abyss. Even in 1992, although it had seen off the Liberal-SDP challenge, Labour seemed far from power. Undoubtedly, the Conservatives' implosion presented Labour with an opportunity in 1997, but Labour still had to allay voters' fears – it could not assume it would win by default. But after the gloom of the 1980s and early 1990s, the party's situation had been transformed, producing the crushing victory of 1997.

By mid-1999, however, there were some clouds on the horizon, as Labour took a series of knocks in mid-term elections to local authorities, the Scottish and Welsh Parliaments. While Labour emerged as the largest party, its winning margins were narrower than national polls suggested, especially in the English local elections where its 36 per cent of the vote was just three points ahead of the Conservatives, and it lost control of some Labour strongholds such as Sheffield. A month later witnessed a much greater shock when Labour attracted just 28 per cent of votes in the European elections, in second place, eight points behind the Conservatives. The results seriously dented New Labour's hard-won image of a highly professional, effective electoral machine. The European campaign in particular was criticized as lacklustre. These were Labour's first major setbacks since 1992. New Labour looked vulnerable, and there was worrying evidence that support was falling most in its former industrial heartlands. Critics argued that New Labour was alienating its working-class base.

There were still grounds for cautious optimism in Millbank. First, the party had suffered only one major defeat, not the series of defeats inflicted on the Conservatives after 1992. Second, turnouts in most of the 1999 elections were remarkably low, down to 23 per cent in the European elections. It is possible that differential turnout worked against Labour. Experience suggests that voters use mid-term elections to send a warning to unpopular governments. The corollary is that those most disgruntled are most likely to vote, those least unhappy most likely to abstain. If this was true in 1999, then we should expect low turnout to hit Labour. Furthermore, although the European result was quickly seized on by Conservatives as a sign of their recovery, national opinion polls told a very different story: Labour support remained around 50 per cent, while the Conservatives languished close to their 1997 share of the vote.

New Labour faces an increasingly sophisticated electorate, partly of its own making. For instance, several opinion polls prior to the Scottish elections showed voters differentiating between their preferences for Westminster and Edinburgh (where Labour was challenged strongly by the SNP). It is possible that a similar process might operate at the local and European levels too. Labour's loss of local support in its former heartlands can be interpreted as a rejection of local Old Labour, rather than national New, as was the case, to an extent, in Sheffield. In the European elections, Labour's working-class voters were known to be considerably more anti-single currency than its Middle England supporters in what became almost a single-issue campaign. It is consistent with the available evidence that voters prefer different parties for different levels of government.

On this interpretation, despite the setbacks in 1999, New Labour's long-term Westminster prospects remained promising. In part, Labour is aided by the Conservatives' deeply weakened state. That party remains divided, many of its leading figures lost in 1997, or sidelined thereafter. The Conservatives' loss of reputation for competent economic management was a critical blow to their chances in 1997, when around half of all voters said Labour was the best economic manager. Although this dropped to more realistic levels by early 1999 (down to 33 per cent), the Conservatives had not benefited. Whereas 26 per cent rated the Conservatives as best for the economy in 1997, only 19 per cent did so in early 1999 (*The Guardian*, 9 March 1999). Furthermore, the 1997 landslide means that even a spectacular Conservative recovery (of which there is little sign) may not defeat Labour. As noted above, a uniform swing giving Labour and Conservative equal vote shares would still deliver 82 more seats to Labour. Labour has a sufficiently large electoral cushion to make another overall majority at the next election a strong probability. This Labour government might well be the first ever to win two successive periods of safe majority government.

In 1979 Callaghan realized the election contest was slipping away, and commented, in a philosophical moment (Morgan, 1997, 697):

> There are times, perhaps once every thirty years, when there is a sea-change in politics. It then does not matter what you say or what you do. There is a shift in what the public wants and what it approves of. I suspect there is now such a sea-change – and it is for Mrs Thatcher.

As the new millennium dawns, the electoral tide seems to have turned again.

Note

The assistance of the Economic and Social Research Council Data Archive, University of Essex, is acknowledged.

3

New Labour's Third Way and European Social Democracy

BEN CLIFT

Before exploring its relationship to New Labour, we must briefly outline what is understood by European social democracy. Padgett and Paterson identify the principle characteristics of social democracy as:

> a hybrid political tradition composed of socialism and liberalism ... inspired by socialist ideals but heavily conditioned by its political environment and incorporating liberal values. The social democratic project may be defined as the attempt to reconcile socialism with liberal politics and capitalist society. (Padgett and Paterson, 1991, 1)

Crosland (1956) identified the key elements of post-war social democracy as political liberalism, the mixed economy, the welfare state, Keynesian economics securing full employment, and a belief in equality. Each socialist or social democratic party developed within a specific capitalist society, the national setting providing a set of laboratory conditions in which social democracy sought to deliver egalitarian commitments through full employment and extensive welfare states.

Between the wars, socialist or social democratic parties gained political legitimacy and electoral success, either forming governments, as in Britain and Denmark, or participating in coalitions, as in Germany, France and Spain, amongst others. In Sweden, the social democrats were in power in an uninterrupted period from 1932 until the 1980s, and were architects of the Swedish welfare state. After the destruction of socialist parties by fascist regimes in the 1930s and 1940s, social democrats entered the post-war national governments between 1945 and 1947 in Italy, France, Belgium, Holland, Finland and Austria – and thus helped forge the post-war settlements across Europe. Although in power in the Nordic countries throughout the post-war era, elsewhere in Europe social democracy's governmental record is more patchy. In Germany, for example, social democrats did not re-enter government until the grand coalition between 1966 and 1969, and then governed on their own, uninterrupted, until 1982. The 1980s saw governmental successes for 'southern' social democrats in France, Spain and Greece.

Although recent historical research has questioned how distanced the British Labour Party was from European social democracy (Tanner, 1990), the orthodox interpretation sees the party set apart throughout the century from its continental 'sister parties', most of which were founded by Marxists. Part of the explanation can be traced to the particular origins of the party (Minkin, 1991). Unlike most of its European party counterparts, which helped create trade union movements, Labour emerged 'from the bowels of the trade union movement'. This peculiarity created a 'labourist' ethos: a non-Marxist incremental reformism, which, Drucker says, 'set the tone of [Labour's] thought'(1979, 40).

Another source of distance was the legacy of Empire. Imbued with the belief in Britain as a world power, Labour was reluctant to confine its inter-nationalism to a European stage. 'World power' pretensions and Atlanticist commitments hindered European *rapprochement*, delaying membership of the European Union – then almost universally referred to in Britain as the 'common market' and later the European Community (EC) – until 1973. This leads some to argue that until Britain joined, 'the Labour Party, despite its membership of the Socialist International, had very little con-tact with continental socialist parties, and Labour's thinking owed little to continental socialist thought' (George and Haythorne, 1996, 112).

The tide began to turn in the 1960s, with Wilson's first application to join the EC. In the 1960s and 1970s, ambivalence over Europe split Labour. In the 1980s, under Kinnock, the shift was more significant, though there was no damascene conversion. The shift was slow, pushed by harsh elec-toral realities. After the 1987 election defeat, the perception that its European stance had cost votes pushed Labour's leadership towards a more thorough-going Europeanization of the Party. Furthermore, the changing attitude to the EC has been seen as accompanying an alignment with the continental tradition in the party as, from the mid-1980s, Labour began to 'draw heavily from the experience of European social democratic par-ties'(Wickham-Jones, 1996, 220–1). George and Haythorne go further, speculating that 'after a long and difficult evolution, Labour had appar-ently come into line with the positions of other European socialist parties' (1996, 119).

Kinnock's chief economic advisor saw a 'replacement of hostility towards the EC ... with an enthusiasm for the EC as an arena within which Labour's objectives can best be attained'. The industrial potential for Britain of monetary union was recognized, as was the need to pursue 'policies at an EC level which would sustain expansion and employment throughout the Community' (Eatwell, 1992, 335–6). This coincided with the unions seeing Delors's vision of 'social Europe' as 'the only show in town' offering protection against the excesses of Thatcherism (Strange, 1997). Eatwell saw the evolution as a 'wider and more important change in Labour Party thinking ... a turn toward the core ideas of European social democracy, and away from a peculiarly British version of "socialism" – a turn away from the Anglo-American model of the market economy, towards a more efficient European model' (1992, 337).

This reading of the ideological modernization of the Labour Party, as having conformed to the norms of European social democracy, is problematic. First, the path of development taken by the party under Kinnock and then Smith involved explicit self-classification within the continental social democratic tradition. After several years of 'New Labour,' the party is arguably now more influenced by Atlanticist links with Clinton. It is no longer so apparent that the trajectories of Labour and continental social democracy run parallel. Secondly, European social democracy is a heterogeneous tradition, which is changing, as are the socio-economic conditions which once underpinned it. This necessitates careful clarification of what Labour is conforming to.

Although it is a convenient organizing concept, 'continental social democracy' encompasses a complex reality. Factors such as the nature of party competition within the national party system, the financial relationship with the unions, the socio-economic structure of society, and the relative openness and competitiveness of the economy, heavily influence the nature of each national social democratic 'project.' A clear example of this is how the strategic demands of different electoral systems affect ideological positioning. In a recent survey, Bergounioux observed that of all the West European parties of the left, only the Portuguese socialist party, PASOK (the Greek socialists), and New Labour can hope to govern without coalition partners (Bergounioux and Lazar, 1997, 7–8).

New Labour's self-classification as 'centre or centre-left' shows similarities with the Dutch experience, where Wim Kok presides over a coalition government incorporating centrists and (neo-)liberals. However, such centrist self-definition would be unthinkable in the strategic context of France or Sweden, where the nature of party competition and the imperatives of coalition government demand a distinctly left self-characterization. Inevitably, parties are affected by the nature of competition with their coalition partners, be they Greens (as in Germany and France), former Communists (as in Italy and Sweden), or Communists (as in France).

For all this diversity, 'the unifying force of globalization' (Sassoon, 1998) has affected most parties of the West European left in similar ways, leading some to speculate about convergence within European social democracy. Yet whilst we concur with Sassoon that, 'the Labour Party is now far closer to mainstream European social democracy than at any previous time in its history,' significant differences endure (1998, 93). The degree of similarity across the West European left may be unprecedented, but responses to globalization have varied. This chapter will first explore globalization, and then the responses of the left to it. Given their centrality to social democracy, employment policy, welfare policy, and labour market policy will be considered in an attempt to establish the similarities and differences between New Labour's 'Third Way' and its European counterparts.

Globalization and Europeanization

In the 25 years since the collapse of the Bretton Woods system, floating exchange rates and financial deregulation have fundamentally altered the context of economic policy-making. Whereas previously, according to Anderson, national governments had 'the means of steering the capitalist economy to deliver [welfare and full employment]... through monetary policy and fiscal policy', under the new conditions, these policy instruments could not be manipulated with an eye solely, or even primarily, on domestic concerns (Anderson, 1994, 14).

The oil price hikes of 1973–9, and the recycling of the OPEC surpluses 'offshore' through the 'Euro-Dollar' markets, undermined central bank control of international finance. As capital controls were lifted, increasing financial integration facilitated capital mobility beyond national borders. This mobility structurally empowered investors *vis-à-vis* governments, holders of currency and securities having many more 'exit' options and lower 'exit' costs than before. Hence:

> the 1980s may have indeed seen a secular shift in response to increased capital mobility, in which governments all over the world were forced to provide more attractive conditions for capitalists... lower wealth and capital gains taxes... relaxed regulation of financial activities and labour relations.' (Frieden, 1991, 434)

These structural developments interacted with ideological developments. The economic crisis which these developments precipitated coincided with the New Right's ascendancy. Significantly, Thatcher and Reagan were the first to abolish capital controls and deregulate financial services. Their 'sado-monetarism' (Keegan, 1984) of the 1980s led them to tackle inflation by imposing steep interest rate rises. Given internationalized capital markets, others were constrained to follow suit (Scharpf, 1991, 245). Neo-liberals strongly favoured floating rather than fixed exchange rates (Ruggie, 1982). The markets, as Keynes's 'beauty contest' analogy demonstrates, are governed by the average opinion of what the average opinion might be. They are thus dominated by slogans like public expenditure bad, private expenditure good, popularized in the monetarist backlash against Keynesianism. Tagged onto these platitudes is a shift in government's policy agenda: 'Sound money, balanced budgets, low taxation and free markets are the order of the day. Governments no longer have autonomy in constructing their ... social settlement' (Hutton, 1994, 207).

Neo-liberal economic strategies thus facilitated structural changes in the international economy which precluded Keynesianism, formerly the backbone of European social democracy. In partial response to this changing international context, left parties warmed to the process of European construction, seeing the possibility of transferring to the supra-national level the control decreasingly available at the national level. Yet European construction, though led by the likes of Mitterrand and Delors, and influenced by Christian Democracy, was also shaped by the neo-liberal orthodoxy. The consensus over anti-inflationary policies, combined with centrality of reduction of national debt and deficit, are codified in the Maastricht convergence criteria. The acceptance of the new parameters of national economic management thus came at a price for social democracy.

The Third Way

> The middle ground turned out to be like the will-o'-the-wisp, the light which flickers over marshlands by night, beguiling the weary traveller; as he moves towards it, the currents of air he sets up by his movement send it dancing away from him, and he goes on following, stumbling deeper into the mire. (Sir Keith Joseph, 1976)

Students of New Labour may find Joseph's evocative words eerily pertinent to the analysis of the Third Way. One reading puts the Third Way between neo-liberalism and the modernized, circumspect European social democracy of say, Will Hutton. In more abstract terms, the 'Third Way' claims to offer a model of capitalist development distinct both from the 'European' and 'Anglo-Saxon' models, reconciling 'a neo-liberal emphasis on economic efficiency and dynamism with a traditional left concern for equity and social cohesion'(White, 1998a, 17). Here the concern is primarily with the economic policy aspects of the Third Way.

According to Blair (1998a):

> Governments can best improve economic performance by addressing supply-side weakness ... subject to basic minimum standards of fairness in place, the best way for governments to provide job security is through education and an employment service that helps people to new jobs and re-training throughout their working lives.

Influenced by Robert Reich, and 'New Growth' theorist Paul Romer, emphasis is placed on tackling short-termism and market failures, and encouraging investment in 'human capital', innovation and skills. The result is, 'a more sophisticated role for governments: in tax policy, competition policy, corporate governance, support for small business, regional development agencies and education and training' (Balls, 1998, 116). This outlook informs a core concept to the Third Way, 'asset-based egalitarianism' (White, 1998a,b). On this view, more egalitarian market outcomes can only be secured if citizens' endowments of assets are more equal. Education and training are seen as most important, a government's role being to distribute such assets more equally (White, 1998b). Widening access to education and training, it is argued, also helps reduce income inequalities.

New Labour's economic objectives of growth, fairness and jobs are pursued by ensuring minimum standards affecting conditions of work, terms of employment and minimum wages. These standards are justified in efficiency terms, 'efficiency became a word that Labour tried to grab back from the Tories, while the language of social cohesion was now framed in the words of fairness rather than equality' (Corry, 1997, 188–9). Since the beggar-thy-neighbour, low wage path is ruled out by the regulatory framework, firms are pressured into adopting quality-based strategies in order to remain internationally competitive (White, 1998a,b). Within this 'skill-centred growth path', however, a 'ceiling' on pay and conditions is accepted, beyond which profitability would be damaged, harming employment levels.

In establishing how thorough-going the egalitarian commitment is, some have distinguished between a 'radical centre' and a 'new centre-left' within the Third Way's broad church (White, 1998a,b). The fault lines are drawn over the nature of the (shared) commitment to 'opportunity'. Whereas the 'radical centre' frames this commitment to combat social exclusion in purely meritocratic terms, the 'new centre-left' see the goal in terms of the need for greater economic equality. Whilst 'radical centrists' may be content with such indirect egalitarian measures, the 'new centre-left' continue to insist that, 'while asset-based egalitarianism may reduce the need for "old-fashioned" redistribution, it will by no means eliminate it. Redistribution of earnings must remain a central component of social democratic strategy' (White, 1998b, 3; Hutton, 1998a). Reich recently called upon Blair and Clinton to demonstrate the courage to make the better-off underwrite a robust Third Way programme (Reich, 1998). However, as Vandenbroucke points out, the New Labour government, 'lacks an explicit conception of distributive fairness' (1998, 63).

The Third Way and European Social Democracy

Blair's speeches suggest efforts to create a Europe in his own image, based on an emerging 'new European consensus'. He hopes the Third Way will provide, 'the foundation of a reformed European social model of which Britain can not only be part, but take a lead in helping to create' (Blair, 1998a). He argues that:

> Europe has to find its own way – a new Third Way – of combining economic dynamism with social justice in the modern world...active government working with the grain of the market to ensure a highly adaptable workforce, good education, high levels of technology, decent infrastructure and the right conditions for high investment and sustainable non-inflationary growth. (Blair, 1998a)

Although the concept remains ill-defined, tensions between the 'Third Way' and European social democracy are identifiable. Blair asserts, 'the Third Way stands for a modernised social democracy'(Blair, 1998c, 1) insisting that core values remain unchanged:

> My conviction is that we have to be absolute in our adherence to our basic values...These values [are]: solidarity, justice, freedom, tolerance and equal opportunity for all, the belief in a strong community and society as the necessary means of individual advancement. (Blair, 1998b)

However, some would argue that this list underlines a significant change at the level of core values from European social democratic traditions, pointing to the absence of any explicit reference to equality. At the fundamental level of *ends*, New Labour eschews any egalitarian commitment to redistribute wealth. One academic at the heart of the Third Way debate argues that the Third Way is a departure from social democracy. 'Unlike social democracy, it is not egalitarian. There is undoubtedly a commitment to social justice; but it is the kind of social justice that relies on ensuring minimum standards and equality of opportunity rather than on redistribution and equality of outcome' (Le Grand, 1998, 27). Whilst Dutch PvdA and the Finnish social democrats broadly share this outlook (Sassoon, 1996, 741–2), the distinction between such a stance and that of social democrats in Germany, Sweden and France, is significant. An explicit commitment to equality is clearer within the French PS (Parti Socialiste) and Swedish SAP, and the commitment to redistribution is still affirmed in the German SPD.

We may conceptualize the ideological tension between New Labour and European social democracy turning on the implications of globalization, first, for social democratic egalitarianism (and in turn redistribution), and, secondly, for the role of state in the economy. We will examine the policy implications of differing ideological conceptions in terms of macro-economic policy, welfare policy, employment policy, and labour market policy and appropriate minimum standards.

Blair's 'New Economics', Globalization and the Third Way

New Labour's principles of macro-economic policymaking, according to Gordon Brown's chief economic advisor, Ed Balls, 'flow logically from the changes in the world economy and the world of economic ideas over the past twenty to thirty years' (Balls, 1998, 117). 'In today's deregulated, liberalized financial markets,' argues Gordon Brown, 'the Keynesian fine tuning of the past which worked in relatively sheltered, closed national economies and which tried to exploit a supposed long-term trade-off between inflation and unemployment, will simply not work'(Brown, 1998a). As recently as 1987, Labour's macro-economic stance remained Keynesian. However, the backlash against Keynesianism, with New Classical Macro-economics in the vanguard, undermined both the Keynesian paradigm, and Labour's commitment to it. 'By 1992, the policy had shifted markedly, and a new philosophy took over.' The importance of the 'rational expectations' of the private sector, on which the New Classical school so insisted, suggested 'trying to solve everything with demand policies was a mistake' (Corry, 1997, 188).

Third Way economic policy is framed in terms of globalization. 'The global economy' is shorthand for a particular reading of changes in the international economic context in the last 25 years, implying that:

> We must be the enablers of enterprise, equipping our people and business to make the most of their talent and ability...the role of government has

changed: today it is to give people the education, skills, and technical know-how they need to let their own enterprise and talent flourish in the new market-place. (Blair, 1997a)

However, critics point to the disingenuous, rhetorical use of 'globalization'. It is employed, some argue, as justification for what New Labour says and does, without establishing the causal connections within the argument, and as such often 'renders the contingent necessary' (Hay, 1998; Held, 1998). Whilst no one disputes that radical changes in economic context have occurred, a debate rages over the strategic options open to social democratic governments in their wake (Hirst and Thompson, 1996; Vandenbroucke, 1998). Arguably, New Labour find themselves on the opposite side of this debate from the French PS, the Swedish SAP, as well as sections of the German SPD.

The French PS rejects the assumption that 'there is no alternative' to neo-liberal orthodoxy. 'Globalization should not be seen as ineluctable ... often, it serves as a fallacious pretext for harmful, disastrous policies ... [so] fatalism must give way to will.' (Parti Socialiste, 1996) A significant degree of voluntarism, it is argued, remains possible, despite constraining global forces. Lafontaine criticizes Kohl's discursive use of 'globalization' as an excuse for inaction on unemployment, 'Kohl passes the buck. He speaks of globalization, instead of accepting responsibility' (Lafontaine, 1998, 79, 82). How do these different responses to globalization feed through into different policy prescriptions?

Macro-economic Policy

The relationship between Third Way and New Right political economy is important and often misconceived. Balls frames Labour's principle of 'stability through constrained discretion' within, 'the pro-stability but post-monetarist intellectual consensus upon which modern macroeconomic policy-making is based'. This view accepts Friedman's denial of a long-run trade-off between inflation and unemployment, but rejects the idea of a 'natural' unemployment rate unaffected by macro-economic policy (Balls, 1998, 117–8) Hence, tying the government's hands to the sole aim of low inflation is not the answer. As Balls insists, 'achieving stability requires the discretionary ability for macroeconomic policy to respond flexibly to different economic shocks – constrained of course, by the need to meet the inflation target over time' (1998, 120).

New Labour's macro-economic framework thus aims to secure 'price stability through a pre-announced inflation target and sustainable public finances through applying the golden rule, that over the economic cycle current spending should at least cover consumption … combined with a prudent approach to public debt' (Brown, 1998a). Traditional fiscal activism is stigmatized as 'old-style tax and spend', and replaced by 'rules-based decision making' and 'long term fiscal stability that delivers sustainable public finances'. Resulting surpluses will fund the five-year, deficit reduction plan. Public sector net borrowing is also being reduced, the overall aim being to 'lock in the fiscal tightening' (Brown, 1998a).

The objective of securing credibility through sound long-term policies underpins this approach. Credibility boils down to market actors recognizing the soundness and sustainability of government policy, believing that inflation will be held down and assets will not depreciate in real value. Credibility is increasingly important because of the increasing number and speed of economic decisions, taken in deregulated bond and currency markets, which hinge on perceptions of government intentions. Thus, 'the rapid globalization of the world economy has made achieving credibility more rather than less important, particularly for an incoming left-of-centre government' (Balls, 1998, 122). This explains Labour's commitment to increased transparency in economic policymaking, and to 'soundness' through measures such as the independence of the Bank of England.

In this pursuit of credibility, Labour resembles other European left parties. In Spain, former finance minister Solchaga personified the PSOE's anti-inflationary economic orthodoxy, insisting that, 'the problem of macro-economic policy … was not unemployment, since this did not depend on the direction and content of economic policy, but inflation' (quoted in Recio and Roca, 1998, 140). The Maastricht convergence criteria, a yardstick of credibility, were 'defended enthusiastically' by the Spanish socialists (Recio and Roca, 1998, 143).

Balls argues that centre-left macro-economic policymakers face a conflict between the need for government policies to be perceived as sound and sustainable and the desire to retain discretion to pursue social democratic objectives. Yet social democrats differ over how far to constrain discretion to maintain credibility. The French PS, for example, seek to explore any 'room to manoeuvre' despite the convergence criteria, arguing for flexible interpretation to allow spending in a down-turn to increase (Moscovici, 1997). The PS also advocate using macro-policy to counter insufficient demand and create jobs (Parti Socialiste, 1997). The precise location of the limits of the possible is contested, as is Labour's strict, orthodox reading of sound public finance.

Macro-economic Policy and Welfare

New Labour's fiscal tightening, coupled with the waning commitment to redistribution, informs moves towards a 'liberal' (Esping-Andersen, 1990), partially means-tested, welfare state, and away from the inclusive universalism characteristic of social democratic conceptions of welfare. Accessible and generous benefit systems, New Labour argue, hinder employment creation from both supply and demand sides: offering disincentives to work and placing excessive strain on firms in terms of employer contributions, payroll taxes, resulting in slow employment growth and poverty/joblessness traps – what Blair calls, 'welfare systems that lock people in idleness and dependency' (1998a). Dovetailing with this analysis are assumptions about the kind of welfare state compatible with globalization. Such thinking informs the particular conception of appropriate minimum welfare standards – evidenced by less generous benefit levels, and relatively low minimum wage and replacement rates in Britain.

The French PS and Nordic social democrats such as the Swedish SAP remain explicitly committed to equality, and the German SPD to redistribution. This informs the more generous welfare policies they pursue. 'The Swedish social democrats' attitude to the new European tenets of monetary rectitude', Vartiainen observes, 'has been hesitant and uneasy' (1998, 37). The measures enforced by the Social Democratic government elected in 1994, involving tax rises and spending cuts, brought public finances into line with the Maastricht criteria with surprising speed. Even through recent austerity, Swedish social democrats have not embarked on a fiscal downsizing exercise, undermining welfare. The 1998 SAP manifesto pledges to 'develop health care, education and welfare services – without undermining public finances' (SAP, 1998). This difference highlights the unambiguous Swedish egalitarian commitment to redistribution, institutionalized within the welfare state and taxation system (SAP, 1998; Vartiainen, 1998).

Enduring fiscal activism can be explained by the hierarchy of priorities of Swedish social democracy. 'We have high levels of taxation in Sweden because we have high ambitions in our welfare policy. Adjustments in the taxes must therefore take place in a way which does not weaken our welfare system.' (SAP, 1998) In Sweden, most commentators concur that the welfare state's expansion is over, but without implying 'an ideological realignment and a comprehensive retreat of the welfare state' (Vartiainen, 1998, 22). Enduring commitments to universal welfare and redistribution entail a rejection of New Labour's assumptions of the implications of the new economic context for the welfare state.

Macro-economic Policy and Employment

The tendential growth in 'structural' European unemployment levels over the last two decades has weakened the resolve of many left parties, among whom, 'no plausible programme for the restoration of full employment has yet been framed, from any quarter, in the nineties' (Anderson, 1994, 19). Yet so central is full employment to a coherent concept of social democracy that parties such as the Swedish SAP still cling to commitments. The PS and SPD, whilst no longer promising full employment, emphasize the active, interventionist role the social democratic state can play in reducing unemployment. This highlights significant differences between New Labour and some of its continental counterparts about the role of macroeconomic policy in promoting employment.

Balls identifies three pillars of Labour economic policy, 'delivering macroeconomic stability, tackling supply side barriers to growth, and delivering employment and economic opportunities to all' (1998, 113). Underlying this metaphor is a compartmentalization of economic policy. Macro-economic policy provides a stable framework within which the fruits of 'new growth theory' may flourish, whilst job creation is primarily a supply-side issue (White, 1998b). Many European social democrats, including the French PS, are unwilling to renounce demand activism.

Former German Finance Minister Lafontaine insists:

> supply-side economics promised a lower level of unemployment. The result has been the highest level of unemployment since the war ... supply-side economics has failed ... supply-side policies in schools, in education, in research, in development, in universities and so on – fine! But without sufficient demand an economy cannot work either. (1998, 79)

The difference in approach may be traced to the changing philosophical foundations of New Labour's economic thought, outlined above, which led the development of the concept of the 'enabling' state, coupled with an acceptance of the role of market forces, the need to accommodate the interests of the private sector. The corollary was greater emphasis on the supply-side of the economy (Corry, 1997, 188–9).

Whilst realizing that demand management in one country cannot work, European social democrats feel the same need not necessarily be true of the EU level. The 1993 Delors white paper proposed internationally coordinated demand management policies, and a trans-European investment in Public Works to create 15 million new jobs by the year 2000, financed by the introduction of European 'Union bonds' (K. Coates, 1998). Delors's Euro-Keynesianism remains part of the French PS economic strategy, and continues to be a reference point for the Party of European Socialists grouping in the European Parliament. New Labour, however, appear sceptical. As Gamble and Kelly have argued, regarding New Labour's lack of enthusiasm for exploring the 'room to manoeuvre' in terms of progressive taxation and higher public spending which EMU may offer, 'there is little prospect of Labour pursuing any such social democratic agenda' (1998, 28).

The fate of the Employment Chapter (including a commitment to full employment), which the Swedish social democratic government proposed to add to the Treaty of European Union, illustrates New Labour's scepticism. The Employment Chapter proposed annual employment policy guidelines for member states, and a permanent employment committee on a par with the monetary committee, to create institutional pressures to move the EU 'towards more radical goals on employment creation' (Lightfoot, 1997, 111). Fighting unemployment, Persson insisted in 1996, 'is a matter of deep ideological commitment'(cited Lightfoot, 1997, 109). The 1998 SAP manifesto pledges, 'our goal is full employment... The most important goal for Social Democracy is jobs for all' (SAP, 1998).

The battle-lines were drawn up at the PES meeting in Malmö, where Blair urged the likes of Jospin to, 'modernise or die!' (Blair, 1997a). European social democratic coordination could not overcome differences over European job creation policies. At the Amsterdam summit in June 1997, Jospin's wishes to endorse the Employment Chapter and advance towards a 'social Europe' sharpened the division. However, shocked by the intransigence of Blair, and faced with a Blair–Kohl axis, Jospin was forced to back down, settling for a renaming of the stability pact (now the 'Growth and Stability pact'), and a somewhat cosmetic jobs summit, which fell far short of the original Swedish proposals, let alone the Delors white paper.

However, when EU leaders met at Portschach, Austria, in October 1998, Jospin revived plans for, 'a multibillion-pound programme to kick-start continental economies' in the wake of the single currency launch. Of Franco-German origin – Schroeder himself called for a 'European jobs pact' – the plans advocate interest rate cuts to foster growth, large-scale public investment in infrastructural programmes to boost demand and reduce unemployment, as well as an agenda combatting unfair tax competition, setting minimum social standards across the EU and coordinating economic policies – the bulk of Jospin's Amsterdam agenda. What initially changed in the wake of the SPD's election victory in September 1998 was the replacement of the Blair–Kohl axis with an emergent Franco-German axis on state intervention and macro-economic activism to promote employment.

French and German finance ministries agreed to, 'campaign for stronger coordination in economic policy, particularly in the framework of the 11 euro countries, for rapid progress in the harmonization of taxes and for the formation of a real European social model' (cited Lloyd, 1998). The fact that the left currently governs in 11 of the 15 member states can only facilitate this process. The pivotal role of France and Germany within 'Euroland,' and the enthusiastic response of the Swedish, Portuguese, and new Italian governments, made Labour's reticence and scepticism seem out of kilter with the rest of Europe. The subsequent shift, from hostility to a cautious welcoming of the Portschach plans, flies in the face of the 'Third Way', and Labour's refusal to countenance fiscal harmonization leaves Britain isolated (Lloyd, 1998).

Employment Policy and Public Sector Job Creation

As well as different demand-side approaches, there are also significant differences over the supply-side measures advocated by European social democratic parties. In a recent speech, Peter Mandelson claimed, 'economic, industrial and social policy in Europe is increasingly based on common principles that Britain's New Labour Government shares' (1998a, 9). Outlining his putative consensus, Mandelson observed that 'the best long-term policy for job creation is to get the conditions right to enable small and medium-sized enterprises to flourish' (1998a).

However, whilst all accept the importance of small businesses for job creation (see below), many social democrats continue to insist upon the role of public sector job creation in tackling unemployment. State-led employment creation schemes of the kind which have long characterized the Swedish model, and have recently been embarked upon in France, are stigmatized within New Labour's rhetoric as, 'unfocused expansion of the public sector which has led to high taxes and high deficits' (Blair, 1998a). The contrast between Brown's New Deal, which pledged £800 million to help the young unemployed to become self-employed to create 350 000 jobs in the private sector (Brown, 1998b), and the French Socialist's *Plan Aubry*, which pledged 350 000 private sector and 350 000 public sector jobs, encapsulates the differing approaches.

Thirty-five Hour Week

The Jospin government has also implemented a 35-hour working week, aiming to reduce unemployment and to have a redistributive effect between labour and capital. The French law emphasizes job creation, with state aid in the form of reductions in social security contributions offered to firms creating new jobs as a result of the policy. The policy is also seen as an ideological rejection of neo-liberal interpretation of globalization. The inexorable road to flexibility is not the path chosen. The 35-hour week is seen as integral to a French 'model' of capitalism PS seeks to export (PS, 1996).

This alternative path of development has aroused considerable interest among other left parties. As Peterson observes, 'the 35 hour week has now been launched as a realistic option in Sweden, for the same reasons as in Germany and France' (Peterson, 1998, 182). The 1998 Manifesto of the German SPD advocates 'more flexible and shorter working hours... to reduce unemployment considerably', urging, 'parties involved in pay negotiations to create new jobs through shorter working hours' (SPD, 1998). D'Alema's new Italian government is also committed to the implementation of a 35-hour working week. Meanwhile, in Britain, even regulating a maximum 48-hour working week has proved problematic.

Labour Market Policy and Employment-centred Social Policy

Central to Third Way ideas about labour market reform are the imperatives of globalization. A highly flexible and skilled labour market is seen as a condition of international competitiveness. The aim is 'to get social policy and labour markets working in tandem', the poorest are protected, incentives to work are not undermined, and jobs are created. New Labour's 'employment-centred social policy', aims to overcome the problems of both the economies of UK, North America, and Australia which have been creating jobs, but suffering from growing inequality, and Western European economies have witnessed higher wages and narrower income divisions, but also high unemployment (Haveman, 1997, 30).

There has been a significant and relatively recent shift in centre-left attitudes towards the labour market. Many Labour 'modernizers' of the 1980s and early 1990s were attracted to precisely those 'Rhenish' labour market institutions which the Third Way explicitly rejects (Marquand, 1988, 1997; Hutton, 1995). As recently as 1996, in the wake of his Singapore 'stakeholding' speech, many commentators believed that Blair wished to import elements of the Rhenish model (Kelly, Kelly and Gamble, 1997). At the risk of over-simplification, in the ensuing two years there has been a turnaround. Then, Labour contemplated importing elements of the Rhenish model, principally long-termism and cooperative employer/employee relationships. Today, New Labour advocates exporting elements of the

Anglo-Saxon model, principally deregulated labour markets, to continental Europe. The problem, as Soskice noted, is that 'models' of capitalism are an *ensemble*, 'institutionally interlocked' in local contexts from which their extraction and transfer is seldom successful (Soskice, 1997, 220).

Particular policies do overlap, however. Employment-centred social policy can enhance employment through 'in-work benefits' and subsidies, offering financial incentives to employers who hire extra low-skill workers, and subsidies for low-wage workers (Haveman, 1997, 35–9). This mechanism is the inspiration behind the Working Family Tax Credit. Here, New Labour is in step with its European sister parties. The SPD is proposing state subsidies for workers earning between 10 and 18 DM per hour, and employer hiring incentives form part of the French 35-hour week programme. New Labour insists that active labour market opportunities are matched by obligations on the young and long-term unemployed (Blair, 1998a). This explains the element of compulsion in the welfare-to-work programme. The German SPD are working along similar lines, advocating reductions in benefits if the unemployed fail to take work, and exploring the possibility of obliging the unemployed to return to work. Such developments are interpreted by New Labour as a tentative EU realignment along Third Way lines, as Blair has noted (1998a):

> Even in the sensitive area of labour market reform, Europe has made some limited progress. Spain, Italy and Sweden have eased their employment protection legislation … France, Italy and Spain have introduced tax incentives for part time work and together with Austria and Greece have eased legal restrictions on it. Finland, France, Greece, Italy and Spain have relaxed restrictions on working hours.

Most European social democratic parties accept the need for some increased flexibility in labour markets. The view that small and medium-sized businesses are the best job creators, warranting tax breaks and hiring incentives, is common to much of the European left, as is evidenced by close cooperation between the two parties considered at either end of the centre–left spectrum, the French PS and New Labour. The Franco-British Task Force, created by Jospin and Blair, aims to explore how national and European public policy can help small businesses (Blair, 1998b).

However, this brief survey may overstate the similarities in labour market policies. Whilst identifying a common direction (towards a more flexible labour market), it fails to specify the widely divergent starting points (from much more regulated labour markets than the British). Each move to greater flexibility must be placed in national context. Often, the result is dissimilar policies couched in deceptively similar terms. 'Employability,' Swedish Prime Minister Ingvar Persson recently observed, 'is fast becoming a mantra.' He advocates, 'a social contract based on employability ... as a vital part of a strategy to increase employment and bring down unemployment' (Persson, 1998). This extract suggests considerable similarity of outlook between Swedish and British approaches. However, considering Sweden's 90 per cent unionization levels, and the Persson government's 1997 reform of unemployment benefit, raising the earnings-related rate from 75 to 80 per cent of previous income (Vartiainen, 1998, 23), the deceptiveness of apparent similarities can be appreciated.

The degree of flexibility advocated by New Labour's Third Way is difficult to reconcile with regulated continental labour markets, securing higher minimum standards. Nor is it clear that all parties accept that further deregulation is desirable. The assumptions about higher unemployment associated with more regulated labour markets are confounded by recent research, which offers little evidence of continental labour market institutions increasing aggregate unemployment levels (Nickell and Layard, 1998; OECD, 1999).

Thus deeply embedded national characteristics, preventing the import of foreign labour market models, may not be the only explanation for the tepid response to the Third Way. At the intellectual level, there may also be a rejection of some New Labour assumptions, leading to a less thoroughgoing commitment to deregulation. For example, whilst Schroeder may be in favour of increased flexibility, he is conscious of the limits of such an exercise. As Lightfoot notes:

> It is wrong to over exaggerate the similarities between Blair and Schroeder. The latter raised child benefit on taking office and is more convinced by the need for some kind of neo-Keynesian demand management than Blair. Schroeder also sees the reorganisation of work time as an important tool in the fight to reduce unemployment. (1999, 13)

Conclusion

The European social democratic parties are more similar now than at any time this century. However, the importance of the national context to each formation engenders enduring and significant differences between these 'sister' parties. Underlying these differences are a range of conceptions of the implications of globalization for social democratic commitments to egalitarianism and full employment. There appear to be emergent differences at the level of ends between New Labour and other European social democratic parties, notably the absence of firm egalitarian and redistributive commitments within New Labour. Furthermore, the downsizing of the role of the state in securing employment informs a different approach to job creation.

At the policy level, the picture is a complex and variegated one. In some areas, the degree of similarity is remarkable, such as the echoing of calls for greater labour market flexibility. This is not to say there is uniformity – significant differences in national context remain, and there is little to suggest convergence towards similar labour market institutions, even if the rhetoric might hint otherwise. The Third Way's exportability may be limited by the embedded nature of labour market institutions, and the different minimum standards they secure.

Other areas suggest a more arms-length relationship between New Labour's Third Way and the outlook of European social democracy. Whilst all social democratic parties accept the discipline of the new orthodoxy enshrined in the Maastricht criteria as a constraint, New Labour assumes less 'room to manoeuvre' than most. In welfare policy, New Labour's retreat from universalism is not replicated throughout Europe, and, in terms of job creation policies, New Labour's self-imposed prudence and financial orthodoxy continues to engender scepticism towards 'Euro-Keynesianism'. Such scepticism concerning European-level coordination, tax harmoniza-tion, and demand activism is at odds with French and German conceptions of a European jobs pact to promote growth and employment. Furthermore, New Labour eschews public sector job creation or state-orchestrated reduc-tions in the working week as employment strategies.

The Third Way needs more rigorous definition before firm conclusions can be drawn about its compatibility with contemporary European social democracy. Similarly, recent electoral success of many European social democrats has sharpened the need for programmatic clarification on the continent. That said, even at this early stage, it would appear that there are significant obstacles to the exportation of New Labour's Third Way, in terms both of national institutional settings and intellectual aspirations of other social democratic parties. This all gives the lie to the view of the Third Way as the beacon to which the whole of the European left is drawn.

Note

The author would like to thank Simon Lightfoot, Steve Ludlam and Petr Kopecky for their insightful and helpful comments on an earlier draft of this chapter.

4

New Labour and the Party: Members and Organization

PATRICK SEYD AND PAUL WHITELEY

Over the past two decades the Labour Party has changed in a very fundamental manner. Today it has a constitution, programme, policies, personnel, procedures and ethos very different from those of the early 1980s. Other authors in this book examine the alterations to the party's programme and policies. Here we consider some of the extensive and far-reaching changes that have occurred in the party's internal structures and the impact that such changes have had on the party members. Our objective is to consider whether, in the words of a renowned advertisement, New Labour reaches parts that others have failed to reach.

There is no doubt that the Labour Party is a new party in terms of its structures. If one compares the party of today with the party when Labour last formed a government:

- party members elected Tony Blair as their party leader and thus, ultimately, as Prime Minister whereas the previous Labour Prime Minister, James Callaghan, had been elected solely by Labour MPs;
- all Labour MPs elected on 1 May 1997 were selected as candidates by individual party members whereas MPs elected in 1974 had been selected by local party activists;
- constituency party representatives on the NEC are now elected by ballot of all individual party members, whereas they had been elected by delegates to the annual party conference; furthermore, these local party representatives now cannot be MPs, whereas since 1945, with two exceptions, they had always been MPs;
- debates at the party's annual conference are structured around the reports coming from the national policy forum, to which local party resolutions are directed, whereas previously debates were based to a

very large extent upon the resolutions submitted by local parties and affiliated organizations;

- trade unions now cast 50 per cent of the vote at the annual conference, whereas they cast 90 per cent in the 1970s;
- no Labour MP elected on 1 May 1997 has direct financial support from a trade union, whereas 40 per cent of Labour MPs elected in October 1974 had been sponsored by trade unions;
- in 1998 the number of individual party members was officially recorded as 395 000 whereas 348 000 were recorded in 1980 when, for the first time, membership figures were more accurate than in previous years (until 1979 constituency parties had to affiliate, and send subscriptions for, a minimum membership of 1000 to the party; in 1980 the minimum was reduced to 256).

Many of these changes are the result of reforms initiated by Blair's predecessors, Neil Kinnock and John Smith. Nevertheless, the New Labour project in its entirety, involving both party programme and structural reforms, came to fruition after Blair became leader in 1994.

The purpose of this chapter is threefold: first, to examine the major changes which have taken place in party structure; second, to assess what the grassroots party members think of these reforms, and how their opinions about the nature of the party and who it represents have changed over time; third, and finally, to examine the question as to whether New Labour any longer requires its grassroots.

Structural Reforms

For 80 years both the organizational structure of the Labour Party, comprising a large, direct and indirect membership and a strong extra-parliamentary organization, and the organizational principle of delegatory democracy remained constant. However, few efforts had been made to recruit new party members as the traditional, working-class communities and culture began to fragment from the late 1950s onwards and Ware correctly asserts that 'of all the mass membership parties, the British Labour Party is perhaps the one where membership recruitment has been taken least seriously' (Ware, 1987, 146). The party leadership throughout the 1960s and 1970s displayed a relative indifference to membership recruitment based upon its belief that modern forms of communication, such as television and advertising, were more important than door-step campaigners. This belief was reinforced by academic assertions that members were of limited importance as electoral campaigners (Butler and King, 1966; Epstein, 1966). This inertia regarding membership recruitment was not solely confined to the leadership. Many constituency party activists also displayed a hostility towards recruiting new members, primarily because new members might upset local power arrangements (Fielding, 1999). Periodic membership-recruitment campaigns were, therefore, more symbolic than real until Kinnock's leadership in the 1980s when he placed an emphasis upon recruiting new members, culminating in his commitment in 1989 to a party with one million members. Why his enthusiasm for new members?

There are several reasons for this. First, it was a consequence of the party's severe electoral defeat at the 1983 general election and the belief that it was due to the party having been hijacked by extremist activists. The policies on which the party fought that election reflected the activists' priorities and these were unrepresentative of potential Labour voters.

Second, the party was suffering from a shortage of funds. Its dependence upon the trade unions for money was considerable, yet unions had less funds available as their membership was declining. In addition, the party's reliance upon trade union money was increasingly regarded as an electoral liability. For these reasons the leadership felt that the party needed to widen its sources of revenue. Members could play an increasingly important financial role as donors and sponsors, and by the early 1990s the party had succeeded in attracting enough of them to make a significant impact upon the party's income.

A third factor was that, contrary to the conventional wisdom of the 'Nuffield' election studies, the leadership increasingly took the view that members were significant election campaigners. New 'revisionist' research suggested that active members could play a small, but highly significant, role in influencing electoral outcomes (Seyd and Whiteley, 1992b; Pattie *et al.*, 1994; Denver and Hands, 1997) and this was confirmed for the leadership by the party's successful targeting strategy in the 1992 general election, as Clare Short reported to the party conference (Labour Party, 1992a, 74–5).

After Kinnock's resignation, both Smith in 1992 and then Blair in 1994 emphasized, in their leadership election manifestoes, the importance of party members maintaining a very strong commitment to recruit new members (J. Smith, 1992; Blair, 1994). Blair's commitment, in particular, reflected his own experiences in Sedgefield where the local party had become a thriving part of the community.

By recruiting new members and then by giving them a more direct role in party affairs, the party steadily abandoned its key organizing principle of delegatory democracy. The Labour party was established as an offspring of the trade unions and throughout the twentieth century it shared with its trade union allies common customs and traditions (Minkin, 1991). One of the most distinctive of these was the principle of delegatory democracy. The structures of the party enabled individual members, through their branch meetings, to elect and, where necessary, mandate delegates to constituency general committees and from there to annual conferences. Party policy, whatever its source, needed to be confirmed at the annual conference by delegates, often mandated by their constituency parties or trade unions prior to the conference discussions. The only exception to this delegatory principle was in meetings to select parliamentary candidates, where party rules forbade the mandating of delegates, although mandating often occurred among trade union delegations.

In practice, there had been tensions between the norms of parliamentary democracy, stressing the deliberative wisdom of the individual, elected representative, and the collective traditions of the working-class, labour movement (McKenzie, 1955; Minkin, 1978b). Nevertheless, the norm of delegatory democracy prevailed in the party's decision-making structures until the 1990s when the leadership became increasingly intent on communicating directly with the individual member and by-passing the delegates of both the direct and indirect (i.e. union-affiliated) sections of the party as a way of diminishing the powers of both activists and trade unionists.

Labour's abandonment of delegatory democracy and introduction of conventional representative democracy came about in stages following the party's electoral defeats in 1983, 1987 and 1992. In the opinion of Neil Kinnock and then, after 1992, John Smith, much of the party's electoral unpopularity had its origins in the fact that the grassroots had been captured by unrepresentative activists. Activists were the assiduous attenders of branch and constituency meetings with wide-ranging powers, including those of selecting and reselecting parliamentary candidates, voting for the leader and deputy leader in 1983 and 1988, and for the constituency and women representatives to the NEC in annual elections. In addition they were responsible for drawing up the resolutions and amendments to be submitted to the annual conference and, finally, they determined delegates' voting behaviour at the annual conferences. Both Kinnock and Smith believed that the inactive members who did not generally attend meetings needed to be more involved in these decisions, since in their view the inactive members were more in tune with potential Labour voters.

Initially, the reforms concentrated upon the selection of the party's parliamentary candidates, its leader and deputy leader and then, finally, the members of the NEC constituency parties' and womens' sections. The strategy was to open up these recruitment decisions to the wider membership.

The selection of parliamentary candidates was partially opened up to all local members in 1987, and then completely in 1993. Since then decisions have been taken by ballots of individual members rather than by local delegates. No longer are the members who fail to attend party meetings disenfranchised; all paid-up members in a constituency are balloted. Since 1993 the participation of the collective, affiliated trade union membership in the choice of candidates has been terminated (they may still nominate candidates); only individual party members now participate.

Labour party leaders were elected solely by their parliamentary colleagues until an electoral college, consisting of parliamentarians, constituency and trade union delegates, was introduced in 1983 and chose both the leader and deputy leader. When Kinnock and Roy Hattersley resigned in 1992 and were replaced by Smith and Margaret Beckett, constituency parties were required to ballot their individual members but their delegates still met in the electoral college to cast their votes. But in 1993 new party rules abolished this electoral college and obliged trade unions to ballot their political levy payers, and constituency parties their members, in leadership elections and then divide their votes accordingly. This new procedure was used to elect Blair and John Prescott in July 1994. Finally, in 1994 the power to elect the constituency and women representatives on the NEC was removed from constituency party delegates attending the annual conference and given to all individual members.

None of these reforms were adopted without considerable intra-party opposition. Kinnock had first attempted to introduce new parliamentary candidate-selection procedures in 1984 but had been forced to back down; eventually, he succeeded in passing a compromise proposal in 1987. Smith's success in establishing the complete one-member-one-vote (OMOV) procedure in 1993 was only secured after a long and bitter campaign, by making the reform an issue of personal confidence, and by a slender conference majority. Opposition to these one-member-one-vote reforms came, first, from many of the trade unions opposed to the elimination of their collective role within the party and, second, from those on the left of the party who feared that members, who they perceived to be less knowledgeable than delegates, would be swayed by a rightwing media.

After Blair's election as party leader, balloting of members was extended beyond the selection of personnel to the choice of policies also, as part of his commitment to the creation of a very different type of Labour party. First, members voted on whether or not to approve the rewriting of Clause IV of the party's constitutional objectives which committed it to 'the common ownership of the means of production, distribution and exchange'. Only a conference had the constitutional power to amend the constitution, but the ballot was used by the leadership as a means of pressurizing delegates to a special conference called to consider this reform to support the proposed change. Members duly obliged, by 73 288 votes to 12 588. However, on the Director of Organization's membership figures, this meant that only 27 per cent of members voted (*Tribune*, 31 March 1995).

A second membership ballot on policy matters was used in 1996 to approve a short summary of the election manifesto. The simple nature of the document, the question asked, and the pressure placed upon members to vote (some were telephone-canvassed several times by party headquarters), reveal that this was more a public relations exercise as part of the election campaign than a serious attempt to involve members in policymaking.

The use of ballots to give all members the powers to elect their leaders, parliamentary candidates and NEC members, and to endorse leadership-initiated policies, was supplemented by reforms to the party's policymaking procedures immediately after Labour had been elected to office in 1997. The impetus for these reforms came, first, from Kinnock's wish to improve annual conference procedures and, then, as an election victory appeared increasingly likely from 1994 onwards, the new leadership's desire to avoid the strained relationships between the party of government and the party outside government which had occurred when Labour had last been in office.

The party's general secretary, Larry Whitty, had written a broad-ranging document, *Democracy and Policy Making for the 1990s* (Labour Party, 1990a), arguing the need for a thorough change to the party's whole policymaking procedures. However, the proximity of a general election campaign and then Kinnock's replacement as party leader in 1992, resulted in a loss of momentum for these particular proposals. Nevertheless, Whitty's initiative led to the creation of a national policy forum in 1993, with nominated representatives from all sections of the party, as part of the NEC, Shadow Cabinet, and annual conference policymaking process. Between then and the 1997 general election the forum met on eight occasions to discuss a wide range of policy documents. However, ambiguities over its formal constitutional status and financial constraints meant that the forum was limited in both its size and impact.

Whitty's successor, Tom Sawyer, established the 'party into power' project in 1995 'to consider what steps should be taken to help the Party and a future Labour government work together' (Labour Party, 1997a, 2). This wide-ranging NEC examination of 'the predominant ethos, atmosphere and attitudes in the Party, its major symbols and defining characteristics' (Labour Party, 1997a, 2) concentrated upon four specific topics: the role and structure of the NEC, the relationships between a Labour Cabinet, the parliamentary Party and the NEC, the democratic structures and processes of the party and, finally, the individual membership. The reports of the four working parties, incorporated into *Labour into Power: A Framework for Partnership*, were published in January 1997 as a basis for consultation in the party. After six months' consultation, during which 380 constituency parties, 362 branches and 25 affiliated organizations submitted responses, the final document, *Partnership in Power*, was approved at the 1997 conference.

Within twelve months of being elected to office the party introduced new policymaking procedures based upon *Partnership in Power* which significantly modified the structural arrangements that had prevailed over the previous 80 years. A joint policy committee, a national policy forum and eight policy commissions are part of the new framework. The joint policy committee is chaired by the Prime Minister and composed of eight ministers, eight NEC members, and three elected members from the national policy forum. It is charged with the 'strategic oversight of policy development' (Labour Party, 1997b, 8). The national policy forum's 175 members are elected for two years from constituency parties (54), regional parties (18), trade unions (30), MPs (9), MEPs (6), ministers (8), local government (9), and socialist societies, the cooperative party and black socialist societies (9); all 32 members of the NEC are automatically members. The national policy forum is charged 'with overseeing the development of a comprehensive policy programme from which will be drawn the manifesto for the next election' (Labour Party, 1997b, 14). Eight policy commissions were established initially, composed of three representatives each from government and the NEC and four from the national policy forum. The commissions covered economic and social affairs, trade and industry, environment, transport and the regions, health and welfare, education and employment, crime and justice, democracy and citizenship and, finally, Britain in the world. The commissions report directly to the national policy forum. Local policy forums, of which 45 met during the summer of 1998, feed views into these policy commissions.

A two-year cycle of policymaking has been established in which in the first year the policy commissions consult both within the party and outside the party with community groups, voluntary organizations and businesses on the priorities for policy development. Their reports are discussed, first, by the national policy forum and then by the joint policy committee, before being submitted by the NEC to the annual conference for further discussion. The second year of the cycle is more formal and internal, culminating in a draft policy document to the national policy forum. After a policy document has been agreed by the national policy forum it will be widely distributed through the party for formal consultation. Submissions and proposed amendments will be invited and the policy commission will then draw together a final report to the national policy forum. The national policy forum report, which might include alternative proposals representing different points of view, will be debated by the annual conference. In contrast with the past where policy statements 'have been presented to Conference on an all-or-nothing basis', it is proposed that with this new rolling programme 'Conference would for the first time be able to have separate votes on key sections and proposals in the policy statement' (Labour Party, 1997b, 15).

Partnership in Power reaffirmed that '(a)nnual conference remains the sovereign policy- and decision-making body of the Labour Party' and therefore 'no statement would become party policy without being approved by Conference' (Labour Party, 1997b, 7). But the hope is that the annual conference will become a very different type of institution than that which had previously operated. *Labour into Power* stated that '[p]arty conference is a showpiece' (Labour Party, 1997a, 13) and went on:

> Because of its overall importance in the Labour Party and of its particular significance when Labour is in government, any problems or limitations in the working of conference loom particularly large and deserve attention. The more controversial or significant the debates and other events at Party Conference, the more they attract sensational press attention. Gladiatorial contests and deeply divisive conflicts particularly capture attention, irrespective of their true significance; and the alleged power and influence of key individuals, unions or groups are emphasised. As far as possible, and without detracting from the democratic decision making powers of the Conference, we need to beware of providing opportunities for external opponents and critics of the Party to pinpoint Conference as an example of difficulties for the Party in power. (Labour Party, 1997a, 14)

What is being asserted here is that, in this media-dominated age, intra-party democracy has to be tempered by party management in which the sometimes rumbustious and unpredictable, public annual conference is replaced by the private, more discursive and reflective, policy forum.

A key role of the annual conference in the past has always been as a 'bellwether' of party opinion. The conference agenda has reflected the immediate concerns of all sections of the party and has therefore been a simple, if crude, means of assessing activists' opinions. This is no longer the case. Resolutions on subjects being considered by policy commissions go to them and are therefore excluded from the conference agenda. The existence of policy commissions means that 'all year round there are bodies to which branches, CLPs, affiliated organizations can express views and concerns in all areas of policy and through which the party is able to have a continuous dialogue with government' (Labour Party, 1997b, 17). But constituency parties and affiliated organizations are able to submit one resolution to the conference on a topic not covered in the ongoing work of the national policy forum and therefore not addressed on the conference agenda and delegates vote to decide the priority of topics for debate at the conference. At the party's 1998 conference debates were held on four topics determined by delegates' votes.

The new structures are in the first stages of implementation and it is therefore difficult to make conclusive statements about the distribution of power within the party. Only when the two-year, policymaking rolling programme has been completed in all nine subject areas and when the party's manifesto for the next general election is finalized will it be possible to draw some firm conclusions. The extent to which there is a continuous dialogue between the membership and the party leadership in which the latter respond to the former's opinions will take time to assess. However, some immediate observations are possible, based on attendance at national policy forum meetings.

First, in the preliminary discussions of policy documents at the national policy forum, the imbalance of power between the well-resourced ministerial team and others is very apparent. Initial drafts, in which the parameters of policies are being determined, come from ministers. It has to be seen whether later submissions to the policy commissions from inside and outside the party have the authority to challenge ministerial assumptions. Second, the workshop discussions at the national policy forum are guided by facilitators who then produce summary reports of the proceedings, which are the basis for the final statement. This gives considerable interpretative powers to facilitators who are senior personnel in the party organization. Third, the election rather than the nomination of the constituency representatives to the national policy forum has introduced an element of accountability into the process. But the lack of communication between these elected representatives and their electorate minimizes any sense of accountability. Fourth, the national policy forum meets in private, which has the advantage that it allows criticisms of the leadership to be voiced without accusations of undermining party unity; nevertheless, it makes it difficult to mobilize any organized campaigning. Furthermore, the combination of privacy and the relative informality of proceedings eliminates transparency and allows the party leadership greater control over the flow of information. One shrewd commentary on this aspect of the new structures and procedures noted:

Votes are not taken at the forums and minutes are not circulated. Decisions taken (or reports of the discussions held) are passed to the centre but are not distributed to the wider membership. The old system of passing resolutions and having open debates at conferences may have been flawed but at least it was a transparent system. Now, members know only what Labour leaders want them to know. (*Tribune*, 22 January 1999)

Finally, the format of the national policy forum, with its emphasis upon small-group discussions and dialogue, is one in which middle-class professionals feel at ease and are likely to predominate.

One further significant party structural reform, which has occurred since 1997, has been the procedural changes to the selection of candidates to the new Welsh and Scottish assemblies, to the European Parliament and to the House of Commons. The new procedures are, in part, a consequence of the creation of new institutions, the Scottish and Welsh devolved assemblies, and new voting systems, the additional member system for Scotland and Wales, and the proportional, regional list system for the European Parliament. In addition, the leadership is intent on influencing the quality and behaviour of candidates chosen to represent the party in the House of Commons. The NEC has played a prominent role in selecting, rank ordering and then placing personnel in particular constituencies, giving the leadership a greater capability to decide who shall represent the party. Accusations abound that the politically unsound have been excluded and it is argued that the number of leftwing candidates would have been larger if local parties had enjoyed greater autonomy in their choice of candidates (Shaw, 1999).

Impact of the Reforms

What has been the impact of these organizational features of the New Labour project among party members and activists? There have been numerous claims made concerning members and their attitudes, but little hard evidence exists.

One item of evidence is the number of members in the party. Claims and counterclaims are made regarding these numbers because they are of considerable inter- and intra-party significance. There is no doubt that, since the establishment of the national membership scheme in the late 1980s, total figures for the number of members are more accurate. Nevertheless, because party headquarters produce the figures and they are not subject to independent audit they must be interpreted with considerable caution. Furthermore, the party rules enable an individual not to renew his or her subscription for fifteen months and yet still be recorded as a member. At any one time, therefore, the total figure will contain the names of people who, for whatever reason, have decided not to renew their membership.

Between Blair's election as party leader and the general election in 1997 the number of members rose. As we pointed out earlier, a proactive membership-recruitment policy was a key feature of the New Labour project. New members helped confirm Blair's support within the party and deflected those Conservative critics who argued that old Labour was still lurking in the background. Furthermore, in contrast to the Conservative party's ageing and declining membership (Whiteley, Seyd and Richardson, 1994), Labour's growing membership was an electoral asset strengthening both the party's legitimacy and its promise to introduce a new Britain. After 1 May 1997 it became important for the leadership to hold on to its members, whilst some of the government's critics were keen to suggest a loss of members as evidence of political disillusion.

The trend line over a period of time is more important than the figure for one particular year. As can be seen in Figure 4.1, between 1994 and 1997 the trend in recruitment was upwards. Since the election of the Labour government that growth has not been maintained, but the decline has not been precipitous.

Another item of evidence is the votes cast for the constituency representatives on the NEC. These suggest an independence of attitude among members which does not accord with the leadership's wishes. Analysis of the vote is complicated by the party rule that has required one place among the seven in 1994, and three since, to be reserved for women. But Dennis Skinner, associated with the 'hard left', was elected from 1994 to 1997, and Ken Livingstone, a long-standing critic of the leadership, who was elected in 1997, would also have been elected in the earlier years but for the female quota rule. From 1998, MPs could no longer stand for the constituency section. Then in 1998 a very powerful campaign by the leadership to ensure

FIGURE 4.1   *Labour party membership*

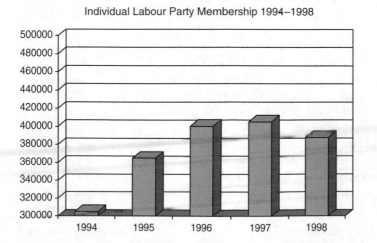

Individual Labour Party Membership 1994–1998

that a slate of 'loyal' nominees was elected as the constituency representatives on the reorganized NEC was foiled by a leftwing, 'grassroots alliance' campaign. Four of the six constituency representatives elected on to the NEC were from this leftwing grouping. The number of members participating in these NEC elections has ranged from 25 to 30 per cent, revealing only limited interest, but clearly members are still willing to support candidates who hold distinct opinions independent of the leadership. Apathy rather than docility seems to be a characteristic of many current party members, making it less easy for the leadership to control the party by using direct democratic methods.

We do, however, have more specific evidence on the membership and its political attitudes (see endnote). Here we are just concerned with members' attitudes on party structures and organization. In the light of the reforms which have transformed the Labour party into a new kind of party, it is interesting to examine what the members think of these developments, and how their opinions have changed over the period during which the reforms took place. This can be done by comparing members' attitudes to the party and the party organization in 1989, at the time of our first survey (see Seyd and Whiteley, 1992b) with attitudes in 1997, the date of our most recent survey (Whiteley and Seyd, 1998).

Comparisons can be made in relation to members' perceptions of the party's image; their perceptions of which groups and organizations the party best represents in the electorate; their attitudes to the leader and their perceptions of his responsiveness to their concerns; and finally, their sense of political efficacy, or the extent to which they feel they can influence the party and policymaking. In addition, it is also possible to examine attitudes to the party in 1997 in relation to whether members perceive it to have moved away from traditional values and beliefs.

As the earlier discussion indicates, the strategy of successive leaders since the time of the first survey in 1989 has several components. First, one aim has been to try to empower members at the expense of activists in order to deal with the problem of extremism; second, and relatedly, to centralize control over decision-making, as exemplified by the changes to the annual conference, as a way of curbing disunity and improving efficiency; third, to weaken the links between the party and the trade union movement, in order to deal with public perceptions that the trade unions control the party; and fourth, to embrace middle-class voters, who play a key role in winning marginal seats, by abandoning traditional leftwing policies.

Accordingly, these changes should have influenced members' perceptions in a number of ways. First, ordinary members, as distinct from the activists, should feel a greater sense of political efficacy if the reforms have been successful. However, this point needs to be qualified to the extent that the centre is perceived to have become more powerful over time. These two tendencies may offset each other. Second, members should perceive that the party is more unified and that the organization is more efficient in the later survey compared with the earlier one. Similarly, there should be changes in perceptions of who the party represents among the voters. We might expect to see a growing perception that the party represents middle-class voters and business interests rather than working-class people and trade unions. Finally, there may be the perception that the party has moved away from its traditional principles and that it is more concerned with media presentation. We address these hypotheses in Tables 4.1–4.5.

Table 4.1 contains data on members' perceptions of the party image in 1989 and 1997. It can be seen from this table that significant changes have occurred in their perceptions over this period. Perceptions that the party is moderate, efficient, united, middle-class and rightwing have grown. In contrast, perceptions that it is badly-run, divided, good for all classes, working-class and leftwing have declined. The most striking change is in relation to perceptions of the party being efficient and united, both of which increased dramatically. However, at the same time perceptions that the party is working-class have halved and perceptions that it is middle-class more than doubled. Thus the evidence shows that the party image has been transformed in the minds of the members in this relatively short period of time.

Table 4.2 examines changes in members' perceptions of the groups that the party is thought to represent in the electorate. In this case there were

TABLE 4.1   *Members' perceptions of the Labour party's image in 1989 and 1997*

Percentage thinking that the party is very or fairly:	1989 (5065)	1997 (5761)
Extreme	6	7
Moderate	54	60
Efficient	62	83
Badly-run	22	10
United	56	77
Divided	27	11
Good for one class	10	12
Good for all classes	70	51
Middle-class	18	38
Working-class	38	19
Leftwing	27	18
Rightwing	27	36

relatively modest reductions in the percentage of members who thought that the party represents working-class people, and modest increases in perceptions that it represents the middle class. The really striking change in this table is in their perceptions of the relationship between the party and the business community. In 1989 only 39 per cent of members thought that the party looked after the interests of big business; by 1997 this had increased to 78 per cent. Thus New Labour is seen by its members as a guardian of business interests in a way that is unprecedented. In contrast, the percentage of members who think that the party represents the interests of the trade unions declined from 90 per cent in 1989 to 62 per cent in 1997. Clearly, the changes which have taken place in the relationship between trade unions and the party have strongly influenced the members' perceptions of these links.

One feature of the whole New Labour transformation is the dominance of the leader over his parliamentary colleagues and over the party in general. However, Table 4.3 reveals that there was only a very modest change in the percentage of members who thought that the leader is too powerful between 1989 and 1997. Thus the leader may be dominant, but members do not perceive this to be a problem. Part of the reason for this is that members are marginally more inclined to believe that the leadership pays attention to them under Blair than they were under Kinnock; in 1989 some 40 per cent thought that the leadership did not pay attention to them, and this had declined to 35 per cent by 1997. Another aspect of the same phenomenon was the marginally greater perception that Blair will stick to his principles in comparison with Kinnock. However, the interesting thing about responses to this statement is the large minority on both occasions who believed that the party leader would not stick to principles.

On the other hand, the thermometer scores of the two leaders show that they were both fairly popular, with Blair being marginally more popular

TABLE 4.2   *Members' perceptions of who the Labour party represents in 1989 and 1997*

Percentage who think the party looks very or fairly closely after the interests of:	1989	1997
Working-class people	89	80
Middle-class people	83	93
Unemployed people	82	69
Big business	39	78
Trade unions	90	62
Black people and Asians	67	67
People on benefits	–	61
The very rich	–	40

than Kinnock. Thus while some members are suspicious of their leader and many think that the leadership does not listen to them, they are nonetheless happy to support the leader overall.

Table 4.4 examines the changes in the members' sense of political efficacy over time. To reiterate the earlier point, there are conflicting signals which emerge from the modernization strategy. On the one hand, reforms

TABLE 4.3   *Members' perceptions of the Labour leader in 1989 and 1997*

		Strongly Agree/ Agree	Neither	Strongly Disagree/ Disagree
A problem with the Labour party today is	1989	15	15	71
that the leader is too powerful	1997	19	21	60
The Party leadership doesn't pay much	1989	40	17	44
attention to ordinary party members	1997	35	24	41
Neil Kinnock/ Tony Blair will stick to his	1989	38	16	46
principles even if this means losing a general election	1997	41	21	38

Mean 'Thermometer' Score, or rating out of 100 for Neil Kinnock in 1989 = 73.5.
Mean 'Thermometer' Score, or rating out of 100 for Tony Blair in 1997 = 78.5.

TABLE 4.4   *Members' perceptions of their influence in the party, 1989 and 1997*

		Strongly Agree/ Agree	Neither	Strongly Disagree/ Disagree
People like me can have real influence	1989	74	12	14
on politics if they are prepared to get involved	1997	72	13	15
Parties in general are only interested in	1989	51	12	38
peoples' votes not in their opinions	1997	44	16	41
By and large, Labour MPs try to represent the views of	1989	74	13	14
ordinary party members	1997	80	13	7
The people who are most active in the Labour party	1989	70	9	20
are the ones who have most say in deciding party policy	1997	64	17	19

have sought to empower ordinary members but, on the other, they have strengthened the power of the leadership. The evidence in Table 4.4 is mixed. On the one hand, perceptions that members can have a real influence on politics if they participate have hardly changed over time; on both occasions close to three-quarters of the samples felt that they could influence politics. On the other hand, there was significant support for the proposition that parties are only interested in votes, and not in peoples' opinions, although this perception had declined somewhat over time.

Again, the belief that the parliamentary Labour Party represents the views of ordinary members was very widespread and it strengthened over time. However, members also recognize that the influence of activists has declined. Generally, Table 4.4 suggests that the reforms have not persuaded members into thinking that they have greater influence on policymaking. But the majority of them believe that they have such influence, and this has not changed very much. The reforms may not have increased political efficacy, but nor have they reduced it either.

Table 4.5 examines responses to questions asked in the later survey only, about recent criticisms which have been made of the party. The basic idea behind these criticisms is that the party is more preoccupied with presentation than with principles and that it has abandoned socialism. It can be seen that members are more likely to agree with the criticism about the preoccupation with a media image than to disagree with it. Moreover, a majority of members believe that the party has moved away from its

TABLE 4.5　*Members' views about party organization and strategy in 1997*

	Strongly Agree/ Agree	Neither	Strongly Disagree/ Disagree
The Labour Party places more emphasis on its media image than it does on its principles	35	21	44
The Labour Party has not moved away from its traditional values and principles	35	13	52
The role of the Party member is to support decisions made by the leadership	42	18	40
The Party conference should be the ultimate source of authority in the Labour Party	39	22	37
The Labour Party is no longer a socialist party because it has dropped its public ownership commitment	33	17	48

traditional values and principles. A near-majority think that it is no longer a socialist party.

However, members are by no means united behind the proposition that they should have a decisive role in policymaking or have a greater influence on party strategy. They are split on the question of the party conference being the ultimate source of authority in the party, and most interesting of all, a plurality of them believe that their basic role is to support the decisions of the leadership. Such evidence challenges the widespread assumption that party members want more power and influence and that they resent any changes to the organization which might serve to limit their power.

Conclusions

Much contemporary academic research on parties suggests that the electoral-professional party (Panebianco, 1988) is now in the ascendancy. Policy and campaign specialists, in particular, speech writers, advertisers, opinion pollsters and media experts, now prevail within parties. So long as parties possess the money to purchase both the specialists and the information and communications technology, there is little need for members. Von Beyme argues that 'electoral campaigns now need capital rather than a work-force of members' (1996, 156; see also Svasand *et al.*, 1996; Jaensch, 1989). Weir and Beetham, in their contemporary democratic audit of Britain, claim that 'high-tech has replaced the 'poor bloody infantry' of local activists delivering leaflets and canvassing door-to-door in the old hit-and-miss way' and that election campaigns 'are now prepared, disciplined and systematic, guided by marketing and media professionals and governed by more and more centralised decision-making' (1999, 66–7). Kavanagh specifically states that the Labour party has become an electoral-professional organization, and believes that 'the targeting of key voters in marginal seats is increasingly conducted from the centre, via direct mail or telephone canvassing, rather than by local activists ... What matters less than ever to each political party is its strong partisans' (1998, 42).

However, the electoral-professional model has been much exaggerated. The regulatory system in Britain limits the extent to which parties can become capital-rather than labour-intensive. There are legal restraints, under the Representation of the People's Act, upon local election campaign expenditures and parties receive only a very limited amount of state funding. Admittedly ambiguities exist regarding local campaign expenditures, such as the extent to which telephone canvassing is declared, and also campaign expenditure is not limited at the national level. But it is nonetheless true that parties in Britain cannot purchase local campaigns in the way that they can in the United States (Brown, Powell and Wilcox, 1995). Local party activists are needed by national parties to run local campaigns.

Both Labour and the Liberal Democrats targeted seats in the 1992 and 1997 general elections. But for these targeting strategies to be effective volunteers are required to conduct the important voter identification exercises on which so much of the subsequent direct mailing at election time is dependent. Moreover, there is evidence to suggest that party activists are not a moveable army and are reluctant to travel to target seats away from their home bases (Whiteley and Seyd, 1998). With the introduction of proportional representation in the Scottish, Welsh and European elections, and the possibility of electoral reform at Westminster, it is clear that parties are going to need an active, grassroots membership in all parts of Britain, if they are to get their message across.

If parties continue to need members both as campaigners and as subscribers and donors they have to provide incentives for individuals to join and become active. The theme of empowering the grassroots membership runs through much of the rhetoric surrounding the reforms we have discussed in this paper. However, the paradox in all of this is the counter tendency for the leadership to try to control the unpredictability of the grassroots membership, by discouraging public criticism and debate, and by interfering in candidate-selection procedures. The restrictions on public debate at the annual conference with the aim of making it a public relations exercise is an example of the former. The interference in the choice of the Welsh Labour leader and the efforts to prevent Ken Livingstone from standing as the Labour candidate for mayor of London are examples of the latter.

As the evidence from the members themselves suggests, there is no widespread discontent with the way that the leadership has conducted the reform process. The reforms have not significantly changed members' perceptions that they can influence policymaking; at the same time they perceive that the activists are much less influential than was true in the past. However, in the long run the leadership will have to balance, on the one hand, the need to empower grassroots members in order to provide incentives to participate with the need, on the other hand, to run a disciplined, united party in order to sustain an electoral appeal. Excessive empowerment runs the risk of returning to the bad old days of the early 1980s, whilst excessive control will severely attenuate the incentives to participate. Only time will tell if this balancing act can be sustained.

Note

Two national surveys of party members were conducted in 1989 and 1997. The 1989 survey was a two-stage, stratified random sample of members. The first stage involved selecting a total of 480 constituencies as sampling points. The second stage involved selecting a systematic random sample of members. A response rate of 62.5 per cent provided a total sample size of 5065. The 1997 survey was a two-stage stratified random sample undertaken shortly after the general election. The first stage consisted of a random sample of 200 constituencies in Great Britain. The second stage involved selecting a random sample of members within those constituencies. A response rate of 62.9 per cent provided a total sample size of 5761. The sampling frame on both occasions was the national membership database held at Labour Party headquarters. For further details of both surveys see Seyd and Whiteley (1992a) and Whiteley and Seyd (forthcoming). Questions regarding members' changing social composition, activism and attitudes on a wide range of policy matters are discussed in Seyd and Whiteley (forthcoming).

5

New Labour's Parliamentarians

PHILIP COWLEY, DARREN DARCY AND COLIN MELLORS

> Jack Cunningham ... told guests at his Christmas party ... that there was no risk
> of contracting CJD from BSE-infected sheep: 'You see, they have their skulls
> and spines removed.' This provoked one wit to reply: 'Just like Labour back-
> benchers.' (*Sunday Times*, 20 December 1998)

The electorate's decisive rejection of the Conservative Party on 1 May
1997 produced the largest change in the composition of the House of
Commons since 1945. Of the 659 MPs elected, 260 (39 per cent) were
entering the Commons for the first time. On Labour's side the proportion
was even greater: 43 per cent (183 of 418 MPs) of the Parliamentary
Labour Party (PLP) were newly elected. The scale of victory was such that
when the Chief Whip first addressed the new PLP he began by saying:
'Normally, I would ask "How are you?" But this time, I should ask, "Who
are you?"' (Draper, 1997, 31). This chapter addresses just that question.
Who are the PLP? And how do New Labour's MPs differ, both from past
PLPs, and from the Conservatives on the opposite benches?

The chapter also addresses a second question: how will they behave?
At the new PLP's first meeting, Tony Blair told his MPs that they were
elected to support the Labour government, 'By all means, speak your mind
but remember what you were sent here to do'. There could be no indisci-
pline. 'Look at the Tory Party,' he warned, 'and then vow never to emulate
them' (Draper, 1997, 31–2). Yet until recently the popular image of the
PLP – if it had an image at all – was of a rebellious, fractious, and troublesome body. The image was born of past behaviour, when the PLP had
'form' and regularly gave Labour's party managers sleepless nights. Why
should this Parliament be any different?

From Workplace to Chalkface

One methodological difficulty in assessing changes in the composition of parliamentary parties is that the nature of occupations changes over time: the notion of a management consultant, for example, would have sounded rather strange in Attlee's time. To make matters worse, different researchers have applied different classifications. Comparisons between extant studies of different time-periods are therefore, at best, approximate and, at worst, misleading. To overcome this problem a new dataset for the 2630 MPs (including 1292 Labour MPs) elected since 1945 has been constructed and assembled in accordance with the Standard Occupational Classification. The resulting data is displayed in Table 5.1.

Since its formation two occupational groupings have dominated the PLP: manual workers and those from the professions. Ross (1955) showed that up to 96 per cent of inter-war Labour MPs came from these groups. Quite apart from an ideological attachment, the preponderant manual representation in the early years reflected social realities. As Norris and Lovenduski (1995) argue, to appreciate social movements at Westminster it is important to recognize demographic trends in the wider population. Thus, the 72 per cent for rank-and-file workers in the inter-war PLP broadly corresponded with the two-thirds of the overall labour force who worked in manual occupations.

However, whilst the proportion of the population defined as working-class fell gradually from a peak of 70 per cent in 1918 to 45 per cent in 1992, Labour's working-class representation in the Commons fell more dramatically. In 1945, 17 per cent of Labour MPs had been manual workers prior to their election; by October 1974 the proportion had fallen to 8 per cent. In the PLP elected in 1997, just 24 of the 418 MPs (6 per cent) were formerly employed as manual workers. This decline – which has been described as the 'single most striking feature of parliamentary recruitment' (Mellors, 1978) – greatly exceeded that of society as a whole.

By contrast, the most significant increase was in associate professional and technical occupations (such as health professionals, social welfare, journalists and authors, and training advisers), a grouping which has increased from one in seven of the PLP in 1945 to one in four in 1997. Almost a third of this grouping is accounted for by social welfare occupations, such as social workers and community organizers; the figure for 1945 was just 8 per cent, with the first social worker elected as late as 1966 (Mellors, 1978).

As in the Conservative Party, the professions have long dominated the Labour benches, both in terms of quantity (since 1945 they have always

TABLE 5.1 *Occupational backgrounds of Labour MPs 1945–97 (%)*

	1945	1950	1951	1955	1959	1964	1966	1970	1974F	1974O	1979	1983	1987	1992	1997
Managers	7	6	6	7	6	6	6	4	3	4	5	5	5	4	6
Administrators	19	15	16	16	17	13	13	12	11	11	12	11	7	9	10
Professionals	33	36	35	34	36	39	42	47	47	48	43	42	43	44	43
Associate professional and technicians	14	14	15	16	15	16	17	16	16	16	16	15	19	19	24
Clerical and secretarial	3	3	2	3	3	4	3	3	3	3	4	5	6	6	7
Craft occupations	6	7	6	6	6	9	8	9	9	8	9	10	8	7	5
Personal and protective occupations	1	1	2	1	1	1	1	1	1	1	*	1	1	1	1
Sales occupations	*	*	*	*	*	1	1	1	2	2	1	2	1	1	0
Semi-skilled manual occupations	11	11	11	10	8	7	5	4	4	4	5	5	5	3	3
Unskilled manual occupations	6	7	7	7	7	6	5	4	4	4	5	6	5	6	3
N	393	315	295	277	258	317	363	287	301	319	268	209	229	271	418

Note: * indicates a figure greater than 0 but less than 0.5.

constituted the largest single occupational grouping) and quality (supplying all but two of the post-war leaders of the party). Irrespective of victory or defeat in general elections, the proportion of Labour MPs with a professional background rose steadily from a third in 1945 to almost a half in October 1974, dropping off slightly since 1979. This category is, however, very broad, embracing law, medicine, business and finance professionals, architects and, significantly, teachers. By looking in finer detail (as in Table 5.2) it becomes clear that the aggregate change conceals significant variations. In particular the proportion who were formerly teachers or lecturers more than doubled over the post-war period.

In 1945, 38 per cent of Labour MPs with a professional background were teachers, by 1966 46 per cent, and in 1997, 61 per cent. Indeed, so well-trodden is the path from classroom and lecture theatre to Parliament that 105 of Labour's current MPs, more than a quarter, are former teachers and lecturers and form the largest occupational group within the PLP. Nine of Blair's first Cabinet – almost half of the Cabinet – were former academics.

While teachers have doubled their representation since 1945, one of the sharpest reductions has been amongst former trade union officials. Although union leaders still do become Labour MPs (for example, the communications workers' leader Alan Johnson was elected in 1997), the days of union bosses, such as Ernest Bevin and Frank Cousins, becoming dominant figures in Labour Cabinets appear to be over. In 1945, one in six Labour MPs entered politics through trade union activities, just one in fifteen in 1997. This change was accompanied by a drop in trade union membership within the Labour Party, from a peak of 6.5 million members in 1979 to 4 million when Blair became leader in 1994 (Pelling and Reid, 1996). New Labour

TABLE 5.2   *Selected occupational backgrounds of Labour MPs, 1945–97 (%)*

	1945	1966	1997	Change 1945–97
Legal professionals	11	15	8	−3
Teaching professionals	13	19	26	+13
Literary and artistic professionals	10	12	7	−3
Social welfare associate professionals	1	1	7	6
Trade union officials	17	11	7	−10
Mining labourers	6	4	2	−4
N	393	363	418	

membership and organizational techniques may have benefited from trade union finance, but their personnel no longer figure large in Labour's parliamentary presence. By contrast, local government remains an effective stepping-stone to Westminster. In 1945, around 45 per cent of Labour MPs had served as local councillors; in 1997 the figure had risen to over 65 per cent.

Significant decline can also be seen in the representation of traditional industries – mining, rail and steel – on Labour's benches, where experience of the chalkface rather than the coalface has apparently become the prerequisite for selection in Labour's strongholds. In part, of course, this reflects the decline of such industries. As pits have closed, 'miners' seats' have fallen to other occupational sectors (Roth and Criddle, 1997). This was exemplified in 1997 in Pontefract and Castleford in West Yorkshire, where three generations of mining Labour MPs dating back to the seat's creation in 1950 were succeeded by a young, female, Blairite journalist.

Long before the Blair, John Smith and Neil Kinnock leaderships, therefore, social change was clearly in evidence inside the PLP (Mellors, 1978; Burch and Moran, 1985; Borthwick *et al.*, 1991). The contemporaneous changes in the Conservative parliamentary party – the gradual shift from 'gentlemen' to 'players', with a decline in the importance of land, law and business – led some to conclude that the two parliamentary parties were 'converging' in composition (Johnson, 1974). Given the changes in the PLP, the convergence thesis is superficially attractive. However, the data presented here clearly lend more support to those who reject it (see, for example, Burch and Moran, 1985; Borthwick *et al.*, 1991; Criddle, 1994; Baker *et al.*, 1995). For whilst broad class differences between the parliamentary parties have weakened, they have been replaced by a new cleavage between public and private sectors (Norris and Lovenduski, 1995). The parties may both have significant numbers of professionals, but they are very different types of professionals. The teachers and social welfare professionals in the PLP are notable for their absence from the Conservative parliamentary party, where the overwhelming majority of professionals are from the fields of law, medicine, business and finance.

In addition, unlike in the Conservative parliamentary party, Labour's 'middle-class' MPs are often the children of working-class parents. As Roth and Criddle point out:

> If you investigate a bit, you find that often [the professional Labour MPs] are the sons of quarrymen, foundry workers, engineers, chemical process workers, Co-op milkmen, drivers, clerks and such, with the children of middle-class professionals in the minority... For every child of a property developer, there are a dozen children of painters and decorators, electricians, carpenters and plumbers. (Roth and Criddle, 1997, v)

A New Comprehensive Generation

One of the most significant changes in the post-war PLP has been in educational backgrounds. The demise of grammar schools, the introduction of comprehensives, and increased participation in higher education are all reflected among New Labour's parliamentarians.

As Table 5.3 shows, there has, since 1945, been a slight change in the percentage who were educated at public (that is, private) schools or Oxbridge (that is, either Oxford or Cambridge). In 1997 just 14 per cent of the PLP had had a public school education; the figure had only ever been as low as that in 1983 and 1987; in the 1950s and 1960s a quarter had been so educated. Almost one in five of the 1997 PLP had had an Oxbridge education, slightly higher than in the 1950s and 1960s, but little had changed since the 1970s. The proportion with both a public school *and* Oxbridge education in 1997 was just 6 per cent; on this, at least, Tony Blair is out of step with 94 per cent of his parliamentary party. The most significant change is in the proportion with a university education, which has risen steadily

TABLE 5.3   *Educational backgrounds of Labour MPs, 1945–97, and compared to Conservative MPs*

	Public school		Universities		Oxbridge	
	PLP (%)	Difference (PLP−CON)	PLP (%)	Difference (PLP−CON)	PLP (%)	Difference (PLP−CON)
1945	19	−61	34	−28	14	−37
1950	22	−59	37	−26	15	−37
1951	23	−44	38	−24	17	−35
1955	23	−54	38	−25	16	−36
1959	24	−51	39	−21	17	−33
1964	24	−53	44	−19	18	−36
1966	23	−56	49	−18	19	−38
1970	20	−54	52	−11	21	−30
1974F	16	−59	53	−14	19	−36
1974O	16	−58	56	−12	21	−34
1979	17	−55	57	−11	21	−29
1983	14	−56	53	−18	15	−33
1987	14	−54	56	−14	15	−30
1992	15	−47	61	−12	16	−29
1997	14	−51	73	−8	19	−35

Note: The difference column shows the % figure for the PLP minus the % figure for the Conservative Parliamentary Party of the same period. In Britain, public school means private school.

since 1945 (when it stood at 34 per cent) to 73 per cent in 1997, mainly through attendance at redbrick or modern civic universities.

As Table 5.4 shows, most Labour MPs went to state schools. But only 50 went to comprehensives, less than those who attended public schools (though among the newly elected cohort of 1997 the figures are closer, 25 and 23 respectively). Whilst, at present, those who attended selective grammar schools comprise the largest single group, by the next election those from comprehensive schools will not be far behind.

Analysis of educational background also confirms the significant occupational differences in the composition of the parliamentary parties noted above. Again, there is superficial evidence of convergence. In terms of university education, the two main parties are now similar. As Table 5.3 shows, the percentage difference between university-educated Labour and Conservative MPs stood at 28 points in 1945. It has been declining ever since, and in 1997 just 8 per cent more Tory than Labour MPs were university-educated. Yet most other indicators of education show little change. The difference figure for public schooling has dropped by just 10 points; for Oxbridge by just 2 points. In 1997, 65 per cent of Conservative MPs had

TABLE 5.4 *Educational backgrounds of PLP in 1997*

	N	%	Difference (LAB – CON)
State schools			
Pre-comprehensive secondary	124	30	+22
Grammar/academy	172	41	+23
Comprehensive	50	12	+10
Public school	59	14	−51
Other	9	2	−4
No information	4	1	
TOTAL	418		
Further and higher education			
FE college	35	8	+5
HE college/poly	35	8	+2
All universities	303	73	−8
TOTAL	373	89	−1
Oxbridge	78	19	−35

Note: The difference column shows the % figure for the PLP minus the % figure for the Conservative Parliamentary Party of the same period.

attended public school compared with 14 per cent of the PLP. Similarly, 66 per cent of Conservative graduates were from Oxbridge, compared to 26 per cent of Labour graduates. And 42 per cent of Labour MPs had been to comprehensive or state secondary schools compared to 10 per cent of their Conservative opponents. Not only do we find significant differences between the parties, therefore, but also that these differences are frequently as large now as in 1945. There has in fact been precious little convergence between the educational backgrounds of Labour and Conservative Members.

Gender Balance

Of all the changes to take place in the social composition of the Commons in 1997, the most dramatic, and the most foreseeable, was in the number of women MPs. By 1992, the UK had fewer than one in ten women MPs. Although broadly in line with parliaments in other developed countries, the figure compared badly with Sweden and Norway where in excess of one-third of MPs were women.

At one level Labour has a long history of leading the cause of women in the Commons. As Table 5.5 shows, in every election since the Second World War (bar one), Labour had a larger share of women MPs than the Conservatives (and in all bar two a larger number as well). The first female Cabinet Minister, Margaret Bondfield, was appointed under Labour Prime Minister, Ramsay MacDonald. But the insufficient number of female candidates has long been clear. The first election where Labour selected 50 women candidates was as recent as October 1974, and it was not until 1987 that women exceeded 6 per cent of the PLP, while 39 per cent of party members were female (Seyd and Whiteley, 1992b).

One explanation is that, despite rhetorical commitments to equal participation, the organizational structures of the Labour party have continued to inhibit the active participation of female members (Perrigo, 1995). In an attempt to address this issue in 1990 the Labour Party Conference supported the introduction of gender quotas, with 40 per cent of party offices and delegations to be filled by women. This was followed, in 1993, by quotas for the selection of parliamentary candidates. All Women Shortlists (AWS) were intended to ensure female candidates in half the seats where MPs were retiring, and half Labour's election target seats (Lovenduski, 1997). In all, 38 women were selected under the system (Criddle, 1997) until, in January 1996, a tribunal outlawed shortlists, ironically under Labour's 1975 Sex Discrimination Act.

TABLE 5.5 *Gender balance within the PLP 1945–97, and compared to the Conservatives*

	N	%	Difference (LAB – CON)
1945	21	5	+4
1950	14	4	+2
1951	11	4	+2
1955	14	5	+2
1959	13	5	+2
1964	18	6	+2
1966	19	5	+2
1970	10	4	−1
1974F	13	4	+1
1974O	18	6	+3
1979	11	4	+2
1983	10	5	+2
1987	21	9	+4
1992	37	14	+8
1997	101	24	+16

Note: The difference column shows the % figure for the PLP minus the % figure for the Conservative Parliamentary Party of the same period.

Labour stood 157 women candidates in 1997. Partly as a result of AWS, many more of these were in winnable seats than would otherwise have been the case. At 64 per cent, the 101 elected represent the Labour's largest success rate ever. Blair's first Cabinet included five women – another record. Positive action had been controversial, but as one commentator suggested, 'a Rubicon had been crossed' (Criddle, 1997).

Representing Ethnic Minorities

Just as female candidates foresaw a breakthrough in 1997, ethnic minority candidates had hoped for one in 1987 when, for the first time since 1924, black and Asian candidates were returned to Westminster, albeit in extremely small numbers. Significantly, Diane Abbott, Paul Boateng, Bernie Grant and Keith Vaz won constituencies where ethnic minorities constituted a quarter of the electorate (Norris and Lovenduski, 1995).

However, 1987 was to be no breakthrough. The number of black and Asian Labour MPs rose to just five in 1992 and nine in 1997.

While positive action became official Labour policy with regard to gender, a much more tentative approach was taken towards ethnic minority representation. Here, the party has remained implacably opposed to quotas, despite evidence of marked under-representation and the strong support of ethnic minorities given to the party (Geddes, 1995). The failure to increase the numbers of ethnic minority MPs has been attributed to several factors. Not least, there is the absence of a single, homogeneous grouping, with divisions in culture, religion and language between minorities, leading to a lack of coherent strategy about how to maximize candidates' opportunities at selection level. There has been no ethnic equivalent of Emily's List, a support system for potential women candidates. And, ironically, the struggle to alter the PLP's gender balance has left little enthusiasm for further positive action (Norris and Lovenduski, 1995; Criddle 1997). Black and Asian MPs currently constitute just 2 per cent of the PLP, with little likelihood of that figure increasingly dramatically in the near future.

That was Then …

There are, therefore, and always have been, significant social differences between the two main parliamentary parties. A second major difference always used to be their behaviour: whatever their background, whilst in government between 1945 and 1979 – as, indeed, before the war – Labour MPs were more likely to rebel against the party line. Note that figures given here for rebels are minima, including only rebel Commons voters, since the reasons for absences and abstentions are, unfortunately, impossible to determine authoritively (see Cowley, 1999a).

Labour MPs were far more likely than Conservatives to rebel in numbers. Under Conservative governments between 1945 and 1970, nine out of every ten Conservative rebellions involved fewer than 10 MPs. By contrast, 58 per cent of Labour rebellions in this period involved 10 or more MPs (Cowley *et al.*, 1996, 5–6). Often the numbers involved were very considerable. Between 1945 and 1951, 6 per cent of Labour rebellions involved 40 or more MPs, with the largest, in April 1947, seeing 72 MPs vote against the National Service Bill (Alderman, 1964–5, 294, 299; Norton, 1975, 21). Between 1964 and 1970 the percentage of Labour rebellions involving 40 or more MPs had risen to 10 per cent, with sizeable revolts over 'virtually all of the major policy positions of the Labour Government'

(Piper, 1974, 385), including the Industrial Relations White Paper, *In Place of Strife*, and the Parliament (No. 2) Bill to reform the House of Lords. During the 1974–9 period, almost a quarter of all Labour rebellions (23 per cent) involved 40 or more MPs; 45 votes saw 50 or more Labour MPs rebel, three times the number in the entire post-war period up to 1974 (Cowley *et al.*, 1996, 7). Moreover, each Labour government saw more rebellions than its predecessor. Between 1945 and 1951 there were 84 rebellions, between 1964 and 1970, 110, and the period between 1974 and 1979 saw a remarkable increase to 317 Labour rebellions, almost a three-fold increase on the preceding period (Norton, 1980, 435).

The effect of the rebellions also increased. Although in previous periods a government might amend or withdraw its policy as a result of backbench opinion (Lynskey, 1970) – as occurred with both *In Place of Strife* and the Parliament (No. 2) Bill, for example – until 1974 a Labour government was never defeated by its own members voting with the opposition. Indeed, although Labour MPs proved willing to vote against their own government on many occasions, they mostly rebelled in large numbers on occasions when the Conservatives were either abstaining from voting or else voting with the Labour government (Norton, 1980, 439). To adapt a canine metaphor once used by Harold Wilson, before 1974 Labour MPs were prepared to bark – sometimes quite loudly – but never to bite.

But between 1974 and 1979, Labour MPs were prepared to bite, and did so frequently. There was a much greater willingness on the part of Labour rebels to vote in a whipped Conservative lobby. The size of the government's majority during this period – a minority in February 1974, a majority of just three after October 1974, slipping back to a minority in April 1976 – meant that one or more Labour MPs voting with the Opposition could risk Labour's majority. As a result, the government suffered 23 defeats caused by its own backbenchers, with a further 36 defeats attributable to its minority status. The figure is remarkable, given that only 34 defeats had occurred in the 67 years from July 1905 to March 1972 (Norton, 1980, 441). It led one observer to talk of a 'new role in policy-making' for the Commons (Schwarz, 1980), and another to note the 'rise of Parliament' (Beer, 1982, 181).

It is important not to overstate the level of rebelliousness. Both in the 1940s (Alderman, 1964–5) and 1960s (Bale, 1997a), even the most rebellious MPs exercised considerable self-discipline. Even in the 1970s, cohesion remained the norm, dissent the exception (Rose, 1983). Yet something did change. Writing in 1970, Ergun Ozbudun (1970, 316) noted 'occasional deviations' from the norm of party cohesion in Britain. Under Labour, such deviations were always more common than under the Conservatives; but by the 1970s they had long ceased to be occasional.

Out of the Wilderness

Previous Labour leaders used to play down their rebellions, arguing either that things were not as bad as people thought, or that some division was a sign of healthy discussion. Blair's strategy was different: he talked about how bad things used to be, in order to talk about how good things now were. The supposed cohesion of New Labour was presented as an important part of its novelty (Bale, 1997a), and a useful contrast with the Conservatives. Not since polls first addressed the question, in the early 1970s, had the Conservatives been so widely regarded as split (Crewe, 1996, 432). By the time Blair became leader, just 13 per cent of people described the Conservatives as united. Labour, however, was perceived to be united by a clear two-to-one majority (Kellner, 1997, 119).

However, empirical analysis of the beliefs and behaviour of Labour MPs revealed a slightly more complicated conclusion. The widespread view in the media before the 1997 election was that Labour rebellions were infrequent; in the words of *The Guardian* (2 July 1996) 'Mr Blair leads a disciplined party where dissent is rare'. In fact, Labour MPs had been rebelling in much greater numbers than Conservative MPs and over more issues (Cowley *et al.*, 1996). The Conservative parliamentary party – widely seen as riven – was no more rebellious than in most previous parliaments; for much of the 1992 parliament it was remarkably cohesive (Cowley and Norton, 1999).

The difference – and it was a crucial one – was that Conservative MPs appeared almost suicidally willing to broadcast their differences (Cowley, 1997, 43). By contrast, even Labour MPs known to have doubts about the Blairite 'project' had for the most part taken what the *New Statesman* described as 'trappist-like vows' (3 July 1996). As Steve Richards wrote:

> Any broadcaster compiling a report of dissent in the Labour Party faces a single overwhelming problem – only a predictable handful of MPs will comment on tape. There are scores of MPs who have private doubts about Tony Blair's leadership, but they won't utter a word in public. Labour MPs are desperate to win. They are more tightly disciplined than they have been for years. (*New Statesman*, 2 August 1996)

It was, though, a discipline of voice rather than vote. If it represented a change, it was, in the terminology of Henry Drucker (1979), one of ethos as much as doctrine. And even some of those who were keeping quiet were prepared to admit that there was little likelihood of their behaviour continuing once Labour were in office.

European integration – the issue which had caused so much difficulty for John Major, as it had for previous Labour governments – was also problematic. Blair accepted that Labour had been split over Europe, and that some divisions remained, but claimed that the 'Labour divisions, unlike the Tory ones, are largely part of the past' (cited in Baker *et al.*, 1996, 353). However, a survey conducted in the middle of the last Parliament discovered a less clear-cut picture. Most Labour MPs were broadly pro-European – for example, only a handful favoured withdrawal, and just 16 per cent thought that EMU was not desirable – and on most issues Labour MPs were more united than the Conservatives. There was also a clear cohort effect, with the newer Labour MPs more pro-European than the older (Baker *et al.*, 1996, 367–9). Blair was clearly right when he claimed in 1995 that 'the centre of gravity in the Labour Party is moving convincingly in my direction' (cited in Baker and Seawright, 1998, 76). But the data also revealed sizeable divisions with the PLP on many key issues, including the role of the European Central Bank, the use of Qualified Majority Voting, and many aspects of economic policy. The potential for the PLP to cause trouble for a Blair-led government was evident before the last election, whatever the official line.

This is Now...

What has happened since May 1997 has been remarkable. The old image of the PLP has been swept away, and replaced by one which would be unrecognizable to Attlee, Wilson or Callaghan: backbench MPs are said to do what they are told, trooping loyally through the government lobbies. The anecdote at the head of this chapter is just one of the many such comments about the high levels of cohesion in Labour's ranks. Whereas the complaint used to be that Labour leaders were not in control of their party, it is now that they are too much in control.

But is it true? Just as with the pre-election image, the reality is slightly more complicated than the picture often presented in the media. There were, in fact, 16 separate Labour rebellions in the first session of the 1997 Parliament. These varied in size, from 5 by a solitary MP, to the 47 MPs who rebelled over lone-parent benefit during the passage of the Social Security Bill in December 1997. There were also sizeable rebellions over military action against Iraq (23 MPs), the Teaching and Higher Education Bill (34 MPs), the Competition Bill (25 MPs), and the Criminal Justice (Terrorism and Conspiracy) Bill (four rebellions of between 16 and 29 MPs). The second session saw 19 rebellions, including sizeable revolts over House of Lords reform (35 MPs), the Access to Justice Bill (20 MPs) and disability benefit (the largest of which consisted of a whopping 67 MPs) (Cowley, 1999b).

There were rebellions by Labour MPs in just 4 per cent of votes in the first session of the parliament. In absolute terms, this was clearly not a high level of dissent: one division out of every twenty-five saw a rebellion – no matter how small – by a Labour MP. The others saw complete cohesion.

Table 5.6 puts these 16 rebellions into historical perspective, comparing the first sessions of post-war parliaments. As the Table shows, in comparison with the most recent parliaments Labour MPs are currently rebelling infrequently, but there is nothing abnormal about their behaviour when seen over a longer time span. Indeed, Labour MPs thus far this Parliament have been more rebellious than government MPs in the first sessions of most post-war parliaments. And when they have rebelled, they have done so in quite respectable numbers: the 47 MPs who rebelled over lone-parent benefits constituted a larger rebellion than any by government MPs in the first session of all but four post-war parliaments. Similarly, only four first sessions have seen larger average rebellions. Expressing the size of the rebellions as a percentage of the PLP produces a similar, if slightly less dramatic, result (Cowley, 1999a).

The 16 separate first session rebellions involved 78 Labour MPs, around 19 per cent of the parliamentary party. This suggests that the tendency to rebel is not restricted to a handful of MPs. Rather, almost one in five in the

TABLE 5.6   *Rebellions by government MPs in first sessions, 1945–97*

Parliament	N	Largest rebellion	Average rebellion
1945	**10**	**32**	**15**
1950	**1**	**7**	**7**
1951	2	22	12
1955	7	22	4
1959	17	13	3
1964	**0**	**0**	**0**
1966	**9**	**59**	**15**
1970	7	39	10
1974F	**8**	**76**	**35**
1974O	**54**	**145**	**29**
1979	32	48	8
1983	76	42	7
1987	61	38	8
1992	93	41	13
1997	**16**	**47**	**14**

Note: Bold indicates a Labour government.

PLP – around one in four of backbenchers – have already shown a willingness to defy their party line.

The scale of Labour's victory brought in many MPs not expected by their party (and often by themselves) to win their seats. These candidates – named the 'unlikely lads' by one of their number – were not as carefully vetted and their election brought fears within the party hierarchy that they might cause trouble (Draper, 1997, 8; *Sunday Times*, 23 November 1997). There is no evidence that these MPs have proved noticeably more likely to rebel, but there are other striking differences between those who have and have not rebelled.

There is, for example, a clear cohort difference. The newly elected MPs were much less likely to rebel than MPs re-elected in 1997. Of the MPs elected before 1997, 23 per cent rebelled at least once in the first session. The figure for the new MPs was just 13 per cent. Of the ten most rebellious MPs, only one – John McDonnell – was a new entrant. The difference between the two groups is statistically significant ($p < 0.01$). A similarly clear effect was found in the British Representation Survey of MPs which showed that the 1997 entrants were significantly more 'Blairite' than their colleagues (Norris, 1998). Blair's belief, expressed before the election, that the new MPs would be supporters of what he termed 'the need to modernize' (*New Statesman*, 5 July 1996) appears to have been confirmed.

The most striking feature of the rebellions, however, has been the absence of women, especially newly elected women. Of all the newly elected women MPs just two (some three per cent) broke ranks in the first session. By contrast, 18 per cent of the newly elected men rebelled, as did 22 per cent of the women and 24 per cent of the men who had been re-elected (with the difference between the newly elected men and women being statistically significant at $p < 0.01$). Of all the behaviour of the PLP since 1 May 1997, it has been the loyalty of the newly elected women which has attracted the most criticism (Purves, 1997; Mitchell, 1998; Watkins, 1998), of which the most hostile was Brian Sedgmore's comparison of the women with the Stepford Wives (*The Times*, 7 February 1998).

Given that two years of the Parliament has yet to come, and given that the number of rebellions is now low, it is probably better not to overplay this gender difference, which may even out after more rebellions. However, two commonly offered explanations can be rejected. First, this is not a pattern seen before. If anything, in the past, women Members have been slightly more rebellious than men. And, as noted above, those Labour women re-elected in 1997 are currently behaving no differently from their male counterparts. This suggests that any explanation for the gender difference needs to look at this particular batch of women MPs and their circumstances.

Second, the difference is unlikely to have been caused by the use of all-women shortlists. Ann Widdecombe, for example, has argued that the process brought into Parliament MPs who, because they had not been subject to the full rigours of an open competition for their candidature, were not up to the job (*Sunday Times,* 4 October 1998). However, only about half of the newly elected women were selected from all-women lists; and there is no evidence of a difference between those so selected and those not. Newly elected Labour women MPs were not rebelling, however they were selected.

Storms to come?

Those MPs who have not rebelled argue keenly that this is not because they are too wet to do so. Rather it is because they do not feel the need, both because they usually agree with government policies and because their concerns are met in private meetings with ministers (see, for example, the comments of Ivan Lewis, House of Commons Debates, 21 July 1998, c.957). As Michael Foster said, 'When new Labour MPs vote with the Government, it may just be that we have already made our point and are happy to be voting for the policies on which we were elected and with which we agree' (*The Observer,* 27 September 1998). Some of the new women MPs have argued that they rebel less frequently because they are better at this behind-the-scenes lobbying than men, and therefore have their concerns met in less dramatic (macho?) ways ('The Week in Westminster', Radio 4, 22 October 1998).

Certainly, before the election the PLP changed its structures to facilitate greater contact between back- and frontbench, in an attempt to channel discontent into more private arenas. Even some rebels argue that the government has been utilizing these channels as much as might be expected, particularly after the scale of the lone-parent revolt made it realize that coercion alone would not prevent rebellions.

It is also true that the ideology of the PLP became more Blairite between 1992 and 1997, also making rebellion less likely. This was clear from surveys conducted both by the British Representation Study (Norris, 1998) and the Members of Parliament Project (Baker *et al.*, 1999). Table 5.7 compares responses to six questions covering economic policy, moral issues and European integration. A sizeable rightward and pro-European shift is evident. Of course, in not all cases did the PLP move so dramatically.

Shifts in response to some other questions were slightly more nuanced. For example, Norris discovered very little change in the percentage who thought that the government should put more money into the NHS between 1992 and 1997, but the percentage who said that they 'definitely should' had fallen from 96 to 65, whilst those who thought they 'probably should' had risen from 4 to 33 per cent (Norris, 1998, 777). The ideological movement in the PLP was not caused solely by the new cohort of MPs entering the Commons; there was also evidence of a (slight) shift in the attitudes of incumbents, as they became converted to Blairite positions (Norris, 1997b, 772–3).

It is, however, best not to overstate the degree to which the PLP has changed in its attitudes. The survey data also reveals considerable division within the parliamentary party on a number of issues. For example, there are still sizeable minorities who would oppose further moves towards European integration, especially over issues of national security (Baker *et al.*,

TABLE 5.7   *Changes in the attitudes of the PLP, 1992–98*

Statement	% agreeing		
	1992 Parliament	*1997 Parliament*	*Change*
Major public services should be in state ownership	70	48	− 22
It's the government's responsibility to provide jobs	65	50	− 15
Young people today don't have enough respect for traditional values	8	23	+ 15
Censorship is necessary to uphold moral standards	17	36	+ 19
The establishment of a single EU currency would signal the end of the UK as a sovereign nation	21	10	− 11
Britain should never permit its monetary policy to be determined by an independent European Central Bank	42	20	− 22

Note: the first four questions are drawn from Norris (1998), and based on surveys done in 1992 and 1997; the last two are drawn from Baker and Seawright (1998) and Baker *et al.* (1999), and are based on surveys conducted in 1995–6 and 1998.

1999). Similarly, whilst the overall shift in attitudes has been to the right, the PLP remains a clearly left-of-centre body. For example, in 1992, just 12 per cent of the PLP did not believe it was the government's responsibility to provide jobs. By 1997, the figure had risen to 22 per cent (Norris, 1998, 776). The Blairite grouping therefore constitutes a minority, albeit a minority which is considerably larger than one would have thought just a few years ago. The PLP is far from becoming a Blairite love-in.

Given this, what should worry the Labour whips is that the first session of a parliament is usually atypical. As Table 5.8 makes clear, in most parliaments the first session sees a lower than average number of rebellions. Only in four parliaments has the first session been the most rebellious. In all the other parliaments – save for February 1974, where there was only one session in the Parliament – the first session has been less rebellious. Importantly, this is true of *all* the first sessions following a change of the party in government (again, excluding February 1974) and it is also true of *every* period of Labour government.

Whilst there is no guarantee that this PLP will behave as PLPs (and Conservative parliamentary parties) have in the past, this strongly suggests that the first session of the 1997 parliament was not typical of what is to come. Not only are the future sessions likely to see more dissent, therefore,

TABLE 5.8   *Relationship between first and other sessions, 1945–92*

Parliament (number of sessions)	Number of rebellions in first session	Mean number of rebellions per session
1945 (4)	**10**	**20**
1950 (2)	**1**	**3**
1951 (4)	2	3
1955 (4)	7	3
1959 (5)	17	24
1964 (2)	**0**	**1**
1966 (4)	**9**	**27**
1970 (4)	7	51
1974F (1)	**8**	**8**
1974O (5)	**54**	**62**
1979 (4)	32	40
1983 (4)	76	51
1987 (5)	61	40
1992 (5)	93	35

Note: The Parliament of February 1974 had only one session. Bold indicates a Labour government.

but they are likely to see disproportionately more dissent. What we have seen so far is probably just a taste of things to come.

Conclusion

The PLP elected in 1997 differed markedly in its composition from that elected in 1945. And for all the talk of convergence, it also differed markedly from the Conservative parliamentary party sitting on the benches opposite. The scale of Labour's 1997 majority – the biggest since 1935, and Labour's biggest ever – does not make defeat impossible. As Mrs Thatcher discovered with the Shops Bill in 1986, even Prime Ministers with 100-plus majorities can be defeated. But it makes defeat unlikely; the odds must be on the 1997 parliament becoming the first not to see the government of the day defeated since the Parliament elected in 1966. This does not mean that Blair can be blasé about the opinions and actions of his parliamentary party. As has already been clear in this Parliament, even failed rebellions have the potential both to influence policy and to be an embarrassment. What we know about the attitudes of Labour MPs makes it clear that the New Labour leadership cannot always rely on enthusiastic support from all its backbenchers. Nor, as the MPs have already shown by their behaviour, and contrary to the popular image, can the leadership rely on timid acquiescence.

Note

Research into the voting behaviour of Labour MPs was supported by grants from the University of Hull and the Leverhulme Trust. Mark Stuart did all the back-breaking work, reading division lists.

6

New Labour and the Unions: the End of the Contentious Alliance?

STEVE LUDLAM

Even before Labour's state wage controls in the 1960s and 1970s, the union-party 'labour alliance' became what an early student of the link called 'the most controversial relationship in British politics' (Harrison, 1960, 12). Thirty long years of indifferent electoral performance later, the phrase was echoed by the alliance's most exhaustive analyst, who portrayed 'a disputatious and controversial relationship – the most contentious in British political life' (Minkin, 1992, 646). Labour governments broke strikes with troops; the Cold War created bitter divisions; conflict over Labour governments' economic, industrial relations and wage policies culminated in the so-called 'winter of discontent' in the 1970s and the internal strife in the 1980s that precipitated the Social Democratic Party (SDP) split. But, confounding its enemies, the union-party link survived, as unions prioritized the electoral defeat of Conservative governments determined to destroy their influence. As Labour celebrated its centenary and re-occupation of Downing Street, though, divorce was again rumoured, the link condemned as the last major obstacle to rebranding Labour as a classless, progressive electoral vehicle. This chapter considers post-war sources of tension in the link, and then concentrates on the position under New Labour, reconsidering the conclusions of Lewis Minkin's *Contentious Alliance* on the future for the labour alliance.

Block Votes, Factions and Wage Norms

Three general sources of post-war tension stand out. First, direct union affiliation (individual unions, not the TUC, affiliate), always unusual, is now unique among Europe's governing parties. Union votes still dominate the party's policymaking conference, and until 1998 determined the composition of the party's Executive (NEC). Depending on political outcomes, consequently, party factions alternatively praised and cursed the union link. Enemies condemned union block voting, funding and patronage, casting Labour MPs as the unions' 'kept men'. Second, organizational unity has meant, historically, that ideological struggles were conducted within Labour and the TUC, that elsewhere in Europe produced bitter competition between mass social democratic and communist organizations. British labour's internal battles between socialist and social democratic groupings have frequently damaged the party's electoral effectiveness and unions' industrial authority. Unwritten, customary rules of union self-restraint within the party have been vulnerable to such conflict over fundamental principles (Minkin, 1978a, 461–2). Such conflict has intensified, thirdly, when Labour governments introduced wage controls to defend sterling and maintain business confidence. Until 1979, post-war governments accepted responsibility for sustaining full employment by Keynesian demand management. Supply-side costs, notably wages, were held responsible for inflation. Tripartite institutions incorporated unions and employers into government economic strategies intended to enable unions to deliver wage restraint. Confronted with the economic problems of an overstretched, declining empire, Labour as much as Conservative governments felt obliged to tackle the 'union problem'.

Each of these factors, constitutional, ideological, and economic, complicated the ambiguous demarcation within the labour movement between industrial and political arenas (Minkin, 1992, 7–9). Unions supposedly concerned themselves primarily with political protection of a voluntary system of industrial relations (Fenley, 1980, 50). Parliamentary politics was the party leaders' territory, though they, in turn, were expected to promote unions' industrial relations policies. This demarcation became most significant as majority Labour governments took office after the war, able at last to legislate without hindrance.

Praetorian Bouncers and Socialism in One Class

Union leaders complained at lack of consultation (Martin, 1980, 296), but Clement Attlee's government delivered unprecedented benefits to unions and workers, as public ownership, full employment, and welfare programmes were implemented after 1945. Conservative anti-union legislation was repealed, and wartime union representation on a vast range of government bodies perpetuated. That most unions cooperated, despite misgivings, in wage policy (V. Allen, 1960, 283–7), and acquiesced in military strikebreaking (Peak, 1984, 83–105), testified to the strength of the link in the cold-war climate of post-war reconstruction.

In the 'thirteen wasted years' between the Attlee and Harold Wilson governments, the principal characteristic of the link was union leaders' 'praetorian guard' role as political bouncers protecting the party against leftwing gatecrashers, sometimes in defiance of their unions' policies (Minkin, 1980, 125–31). Prominent exceptions, in 1960, were the party's support (rapidly reversed) of unilateral nuclear disarmament (Goodman, 1979, 264–309), and rejection of Hugh Gaistkell's attempt to rewrite the party's 'Clause IV' commitment to common ownership (T. Jones, 1996, 46–64).

Notwithstanding such headline dramas, union political activity in this period principally pursued 'the achievement, maintenance or restoration of "free collective bargaining"' (Richter, 1973, 218). It was Labour government challenges to this priority from 1964 that generated the conflict which erupted in the winter of 1978/9 (A. Taylor, 1987, 84–107). Whether viewed approvingly (Dorfman, 1979) or disapprovingly as 'socialism in one class' (Panitch, 1976, 244), analysts highlighted the centrality of union acquiescence in wage controls in Labour's economic strategy. Unions repeatedly collaborated in wage policies on the basis of broader understandings about economic planning and the 'social wage' of public and welfare services. But wage policies were invariably launched as emergency responses to speculation against sterling, and linked with deflationary policies that undermined planning, public services, and employment. Union leaders' political loyalties could only temporarily displace free collective bargaining before workers revolted.

In 1969, when Wilson tried replacing flagging wage controls by making some strikes illegal, the White Paper *In Place of Strife*, 'produced six months of civil war throughout the labour movement ... nearly bringing the government down' (Healey, 1990, 341). The Social Contract reassembled the alliance in Opposition, and formed the basis of the 1974 manifestoes, offering economic and social policy commitments linked to voluntary wage restraint (J. Jones, 1986, 278–88). But, battered by world economic dislocation, the pact degenerated into the worst real wage cuts ever recorded, and the worst public spending cuts of the post-war era, paralysing the alliance when Labour's 1978 wage policy collapsed in the much-mythologized 'winter of discontent' (Ludlam, 2000).

Rebuilding Block Vote by Block Vote

Far from being a simple matter of unions versus party, most such disputes involved both union and party activists in broadly left–right factionalism, complicated by public–private sector union divisions in the 1970s

(Ludlam, 1995). Internal party warfare erupted after 1979, commonly portrayed as unions backing party dissidents to force new constitutional disciplines and leftwing policies on the PLP. In fact, unions were divided, cancelling out each others' votes, leaving constituency activists' votes decisive (Minkin, 1992, 192–5; cf Wickham-Jones, 1996, 176–82). The Thatcher governments, rejecting Keynesianism and tripartism, blamed unemployment not on inadequate government spending, but on monopolistic unions; inflation on government profligacy, not union militancy. The resulting anti-union laws and mass unemployment, combined with the SDP split from Labour and the 1983 election result, quickly brought dissident unions back into line in the party. Thatcher's legislative attempt to loosen the link was defeated by a triumphant campaign to save union political funds (Coates and Topham, 1986, 147–65; Leopold, 1997).

One modernizer described Neil Kinnock's 1984 defeat by union votes over 'one member, one vote' (OMOV) as having 'set back modernization by ten years' (Gould, 1998a, 43). Kinnock recalled, rather, that it taught him to stitch up union votes in advance (Kinnock, 1994, 537–9). Even Peter Mandelson acknowledged at the 1998 TUC Congress, 'how the trades unions helped Neil Kinnock save the Labour Party' (Mandelson, 1998b). Union backing was crucial to Kinnock's expulsion of leftwing activists (Shaw, 1988, 257–90), financing the leadership's independent research capacity (Heffernan and Marqusee, 1992, 148–52), carrying through his Policy Review abandoning commitments to repeal Thatcher's anti-union laws (G. Taylor, 1997, 47–9), and reducing union power in the party constitution (Anderson and Mann, 1997, 312–14). Unions believed modernization was completed with John Smith's 1992/3 review of the link, which abolished monolithic block voting at conference, reducing the total union conference vote to 70 per cent of the total, to be further reduced to 49 per cent as mass membership grew, and established OMOV in both leadership elections (where the union vote was reduced from two-fifths to one third of the total) and in parliamentary candidate selection (Webb, 1995, 1–11). In the latter case, Smith's proposal survived only thanks to a last-gasp abandonment by a large union (MSF) of its mandate (Mortimer, 1998, 448–9). Unions were therefore taken aback by the hostility that surfaced after Blair became leader.

Reassurance, Reassurance, Reassurance

Blair's immediate concern was electoral. His pollsters told him in 1995 that voters needed reassurance on the link, because, 'New Labour is defined for

most voters by Tony Blair's willingness to take on and master the unions …
In focus groups the switchers spoke of little else.' (Gould, 1998a, 257–8)
Blair repeatedly issued such reassurance, insisting:

> We changed the Labour Party, changed the way our members of parliament are
> elected, changed our relationship with the trade unions. We have changed our
> policymaking. We have doubled our membership. We have rewritten our basic
> constitution. Why? To make a New Labour Party that is true to its principles and
> values and is going to resist pressure from them or anyone else. (*The Guardian*,
> 11 April 1997)

At the 1997 election, unions provided unprecedented material support,
demanding little in return. Blair promised little: 'We will not be held to
ransom by the unions … We will stand up to strikes. We will not cave in to
unrealistic pay demands from anyone … Unions have no special role in
our election campaign, just as they will get no special favours in a Labour
Government' (*Financial Times*, 7 April 1997). TUC General Secretary John
Monks pointed out that:

> At previous elections the Trades Union Congress and the Labour Party would
> have agreed proposals on employee-rights questions and then promoted them
> jointly. This time, under the fairness not favours style set out by Tony Blair,
> there have been discussions about new Labour's proposals, but no more than
> there have been between the CBI and the party about the forthcoming business
> manifesto. (*New Statesman*, 4 April 1997)

Union power barely surfaced as a campaign issue, except when the Tories
attacked Labour's imprecise union recognition proposals. Blair's focus
groups reacted with hostility that night, 'because: unions plus Labour
equals danger. Union domination is people's core fear of Labour'. The next
morning Blair reiterated that, 'Anyone who thinks Labour has made
changes in the party to give it all away to the unions or anyone else does
not know me' (Gould, 1998a, 353–4). Blair's intervention ended the campaign crisis, but increased pressure to acknowledge that the recognition
proposals were the final settlement of debt to the unions. In the *Fairness at
Work* White Paper, he again stressed it would 'draw a line under the issue
of industrial relations law' (Department of Trade and Industry, 1998). Polling
evidence suggests Labour's strategists had a point. In 1992, the union link
was the third most important reason given for not voting Labour, behind
tax fears and Kinnock's lack of credibility, but ahead of economic management and defence. Before the 1997 election, Blair's credibility and
Gordon Brown's economic prudence left the fear that the party was 'in the
pockets of the trade unions' the most significant reason for not voting
Labour (King, 1998, 204).

Under New Labour unions hoped to engage in the European model of social partnership they had sought for a decade (McIlroy, 1995, 313–48; Monks, 1998b). But Blair soon insisted 'that we need to reform the European social model, not play around with it', instructing the French National Assembly in the superiority of the Third Way (Blair, 1998a, 1998c). The Third Way contains no positive role for unions. In Blair's *Third Way* pamphlet unions are missing, except in two references to the 'old politics' of the 'Old Left' with its defence of 'producer interests' and its 'armies of unionized male labour' (Blair, 1998c, 1, 8). The same absence characterizes Anthony Giddens' *Third Way*, whose critique of 1980s neo-liberalism does not even mention Thatcher's assault on trade unionism (Giddens, 1998).

Old Wine in New Bottles?

New Labour's novelty can be exaggerated. The contrast with the position in 1974 is, of course, very striking. Then union power was a key issue in Heath's 'who rules Britain?' election, yet Labour stood on its Social Contract with the unions, promising to repeal Heath's Industrial Relations Act, enact pro-union employment legislation, and give unions a leading role in an interventionist industrial and economic strategy. Implementation would be supervised by the new TUC-Labour Party Liaison Committee. It is easy to exaggerate 'union power' in the 1970s (D. Coates, 1983, 70–4) but their access to government was unprecedented (Martin, 1980, 362). Blair repeatedly disowns the 1970s, endorsing Thatcher's legislative reaction:

> There will be no going back. The days of strikes without ballots, mass picketing, closed shops and secondary action are over. Even after the changes we propose, Britain will have the most lightly regulated labour market of any leading economy in the world. (Department of Trade and Industry, 1998)

But, apart from dumping John Smith's pledge to restore employment rights from 'day one' of employment, Blair's industrial relations policy is almost entirely the legacy of the Kinnock-Smith modernization. The decision not to repeal Thatcher's laws was agreed under Kinnock with majority union assent (Hughes and Wintour, 1990, 143–52). Similarly inherited were the National Minimum Wage, statutory worker and union recognition rights (as in *Fairness at Work*), and signing the EU Social Protocol, though none of these could conceivably be branded Thatcherite.

In terms of tripartite macro-economic approaches, however, Blair has followed his Conservative predecessors. He quickly dropped previous

manifesto commitments to a national economic assessment involving tripartite bodies and implying an incomes policy. New Labour also adopted
the Conservative line on flexible labour markets and the charge that the
European social model was economically counter-productive. Blair's
opposition to EU workplace consultation rights infuriated TUC modernizers who see such 'social partnership' as a cornerstone of New Unionism.

So how strong do the incentives to save the union–party marriage
remain? Will the link survive under New Labour? How far, first, does the
party continue to benefit? On Minkin's unrivalled account, the advantages
to the party have been finance, political stability, mutual education, and the
claim to be the 'people's party' (Minkin, 1992, 647–9).

Pipers and Party Tunes

Unions, according to Labour's former media director, 'remain the most
significant obstacle to a new model party ... until New Labour is able to cut
the big outstanding tie that binds: funding' (*New Statesman*, 31 January
1997). Estimates value union backing since 1979 as high as £250 million.
Without union money, insisted one general secretary, there would have
been, 'No Millbank Tower, no Media Centre, no Excalibur, no Instant
Rebuttal Unit, no expensive poster campaigns' (*AEEU Union Review*,
September 1997). Blair has dropped previous Labour policy of state funding for parties, backed by opponents of the union link (Sassoon, 1993),
believing voters would react against subsidizing party politics. Kinnock's
alternative of boosting mass membership income failed (Heffernan and
Marqusee, 1992, 325). Blair has recruited more successfully and by 1998
ordinary individual members contributed 40 per cent of party income,
more than the unions for the first time. Mass membership cannot immediately replace union funds, but Blair has also courted the super-rich, one
such donor confessing, 'My tax bill could have gone up by five or six million ... I didn't want to see the Labour Party in a position where they were
going to be influenced by the trade unions to the extent that the trade unions
would be controlling the government' (*New Statesman*, 27 February 1998).
By 1998, Labour's High Value Donors Unit brought in 20 per cent of
income, helping reduce the union share to 30 per cent, the lowest ever proportion and halved since 1994. New Labour intends to introduce legal limits on general election expenditure, to make it 'far easier for us to cut the
umbilical cord' with the unions, according to one minister (*Financial
Times*, 17 October 1997).

Millionaire donors, though, cannot substitute for a union machine 'mobilizing 10 000 activists to assist Labour in its campaign and coordinating resources, such as telephone banks, campaign headquarters, printing, transport and computer equipment' (National Trade Union and Labour Party Liaison Committee, 1998). Nor can corporate financial loyalty be taken for granted (M. Allen, 1998, 78). Fifty-seven per cent of trade unionists voted Labour in 1997, the highest figure since 1970. New Labour cannot easily replace union organizational support, or risk what the link's supporters insist remains Labour's most dependable core vote. Despite its parliamentary dominance, Labour attracted fewer votes in 1997 than the Conservatives in 1992, and elections in 1999 revealed serious alienation among working-class voters. The unions remain vital to getting the vote out.

New People's Party, Old Bouncers

Minkin's second benefit to the party was the unions' stabilizing role. By 1990 three-quarters of party members, however, believed union block votes brought the party into disrepute (Seyd and Whiteley, 1992b, 51). Union votes have nonetheless protected Blair, blocking awkward conference motions on pensions, rail renationalization, the Private Finance Initiative (PFI), the minimum wage, and electoral reform; and deflected criticism of welfare reform in the National Policy Forum. On the other hand, union votes also carried Blair's *Partnership in Power* reforms, greatly reducing the risk of conference embarrassments. In the 1998 elections to the constituency section of the restructured NEC, union funds controversially (and unsuccessfully) helped fund a loyalist slate against the dissident Grassroots Alliance. When, in the 1999 Welsh leadership election, 'off-message' Rhodri Morgan won party and union membership ballots by three to one, three large unions cast block votes without a ballot, delivering the election to Blair's candidate. Party managers then adopted the same strategy in their desperate battle to defeat Ken Livingstone's campaign to become London mayor. As Monks himself noted during the 1999 TUC, 'most party modernisers now accept that the link is a strength, not least because the unions are vital in their traditional role of counter-balancing the increasingly vocal leftwing within the party' (*The Times*, 10 September 1999).

Minkin's third benefit was educative: giving middle-class parliamentarians insights into working-class concerns. New Labour focus groups and private polling make this function insignificant, and recent changes make it less effective: under Smith the constitutional obligation of party members to join a union was dropped: by 1997 survey research suggested only

34 per cent remained in unions, down from 64 per cent in 1990, a historic shift in party culture (Ludlam, 1998, 39).

Minkin's final benefit was the legitimacy unions brought to Labour's claim to be the 'people's party'. TGWU leader Bill Morris insists that, 'The voice at Labour's table that speaks up for the core of the party's constituency is that of the trade unions' (*New Statesman*, 20 September 1996). But Blair told the party 'We have transformed our Party. Our constitution re-written. Our relations with the Trade Unions changed ... The party, this party, the Labour Party founded by the people, back, truly, as the people's party' (Blair, 1995). New Labour strategists want to hear trade unionists' voices as individual party members, not as affiliated organizations (Mandelson and Liddle, 1996, 226), in a 'new middle class' party (Gould, 1998a, 396–7). In 1999, modernizers began testing new forms of constituency party organization that could end direct local affiliation by union branches. At the 1999 annual conference, the party leadership then launched the 'Twenty-First Century Party' consultation exercise, implying the end of such affiliation.

Built-in Acquiescence

A vital fifth benefit to the party can be added – the tolerance of wage restraint by loyal party-affiliated unions. Now, though, there is no place, in Third Way 'flexible labour markets', for the incomes policies that once politicized Labour's 'union problem' so dramatically. Paradoxically, Blair's neo-liberalism removes the main source of tension in the post-war labour alliance.

For the time being, then, New Labour needs unions funds and election machinery, but none of the other factors benefiting the party remains significant. The unions' voting strength prevents their crude expulsion, so are unions likely to withdraw? Minkin identified four broad factors binding them to the party: 'movement consciousness' – TIGMOO 'This Great Movement of Ours'; conventions of solidarity and unity; access to the policymaking process; and 'shared historical projects' (Minkin, 1992, 653–5).

Forget the Past

Former Prime Minister Callaghan invoked TIGMOO when he warned that the alliance, 'is part of our heritage and it is instinctive in our party and movement that we should keep the link. Anyone who doesn't believe that doesn't understand our history or the natural foundation of our party'

(*New Statesman*, 20 December 1996). Blair had recently told the party, 'There will be fairness not favours for employers and employees alike. The Labour government is not the political arm of anyone today other than the British people ... Forget the past.' (Blair, 1996c). By 1997, only 15 per cent of party membership was manual working class, and of these less than half were in unions (Ludlam, 1998, 68). This mirrors changing union membership: white-collar unions, many unaffiliated to the party, now have the highest membership density rates (Trades Union Congress, 1997a). The historic class basis of labourist sentiment has withered. One loyalist union switched £1 million of its political fund into its own scheme to train working-class MPs, complaining, 'Our fear is that working people will be left behind by New Labour' (*AEEU Union News*, October 1998). After Labour's 1999 election setbacks, even Monks complained that Labour's traditional supporters were being treated like 'embarrassing elderly relatives'.

But union leaders are mostly pragmatists, play a long game, and will not easily be driven out of a party in which only 19 per cent of members (Ludlam, 1998, 72), and only 10 per cent of Labour MPs (*New Statesman*, 3 July 1998), want to end union affiliation. A continuation of traditional union pressure is likely, using party links to campaign on particular issues, like privatizing air traffic control and the Post Office, aspects of welfare reform, the Private Finance Initiative (PFI), implementing EU directives. They continue to back broader factions inside the party, as during the 1998 NEC elections, or on the platform launched in *Tribune* (3 July 1999) and at a conference for 'democratic socialist' commitments to egalitarianism and the labour movement.

Solidarity for Ever?

Minkin's second factor was the convention of solidarity requiring party leaders to help maintain effective trade unionism. New Labour's rapid restoration of union rights at GCHQ was enormously symbolic, but its general attitude has alarmed unions. During a high-profile strike in 1997, a Labour minister announced, with self-evident implications for the public sector, that, 'The presumption must be that in private sector disputes there's no point us taking sides' (*Financial Times*, 11 July 1998). During manoeuvring over *Fairness at Work*, appalled TUC leaders discovered Blair's advisers encouraging employers to toughen their stance, and later pressing German employers to block an EU directive on consultative works councils (*Labour Research*, April 1998). A government officer explained, 'The government does not want to encourage the spread of trade unionism'

(*Financial Times*, 1 December 1998). However, if this factor was crucial, far more serious breaches of solidarity would have ended the link years ago.

Chardonnay and Canapés at Number Ten

Minkin's third factor binding unions to party, access to government policy-making, is far more significant than the first two. A Blair confidante summed up New Labour's view of unions:

> First, that they are in continuing decline; second, that they have nowhere else to go but to Labour; third, that they must not be brought into the central policy-making centres once Labour is in Government. They may take a role in elaborating training schemes and in setting a minimum wage. Beyond that nothing has even been mooted. (*New Statesman*, 9 August 1996)

Early signs were frustrating: only 6 per cent of appointments to Blair's policy taskforces were of trade unionists, compared to 29 per cent of business representatives; most such bodies heard no union voice at all (Platt, 1998b, 10).

Union expectations were correspondingly low. A leaked TUC document on its role under a Labour government set out

> a modest agenda. There are no grand designs, no overarching plans. No return to discredited forms of tripartism. No handing the reins of power to the unions. No likelihood of the reinstatement of a Whitehall department solely for employment issues. Above all, no hint of the unions being offered any role in economic management. (*The Times*, 22 November 1996)

Partners in Progress, the TUC's 1997 election manifesto, did not call for a macro-economic policy based on state planning, let alone demand union involvement (Trades Union Congress, 1997b). No consultation with unions preceded the Royal Mint and air traffic control privatization announcements, and when Post Office privatization was postponed, spindoctors insisted this resulted from electoral and commercial considerations, not union opposition. New Labour did, however, grant unions minor procedural rights, for example in formulating guidance on selling off civil service functions, and vetting companies bidding for PFI contracts.

What is entirely absent is any institutionalized union-government cooperation like the 1970s TUC-Labour Party Liaison Committee, long since disbanded. Blair told the 1995 TGWU conference:

> I want to be quite blunt with you about the modern relationship between today's Labour Party and the trade unions. There was a time when a large trade union

would pass a policy and then it was assumed Labour would follow suit. Demands were made. Labour responded and negotiated. Those days are over. Gone. They are not coming back. (Blair, 1996b, 133)

But access to ministers and departments has improved immeasurably since May 1997, and is a crucial gain repeatedly cited by union leaders as evidence of New Labour's goodwill.

More Partnership, Less Power?

What of union influence through the party? Under Kinnock, party modernization had already markedly reduced their clout (Minkin, 1992, 398–401). Smith's review took the process much further, and revealed Blair's desire to end all union constitutional privileges (Rentoul, 1995, 308–11). In 1995 Blair ended union financial sponsorship of MPs, and triggered the reduction of the unions' conference vote to 49 per cent. In 1996 the most comprehensive internal reform package since 1918 emerged as *Partnership in Power* (Labour Party, 1997b), interpreted as a major reduction in union power (*Labour Research*, October 1997). Before the subsequent changes, agreed in 1997, unions controlled 17 of the 30 NEC seats; *Partnership in Power* left them controlling 12 out of 32. The policymaking roles of the conference and NEC, long since whittled away by Kinnock (Leys and Panitch, 1997, 219–21) were further reduced by the formalizing and expansion of the National Policy Forum, local policy forums, and specialist policy commissions, all subordinated to the national Joint Policy Committee (with no direct union presence) controlled by the party leader (see Chapter 4). On the National Policy Forum, the unions have 30 of 175 seats.

Labour modernizers have argued that unions should use the new structures to shape policy through 'influence and networks' rather than 'resolutions and caucuses' (Taylor and Cruddas, 1998). Unions know that Labour governments ignore unwelcome party policies. Bill Morris argues that, 'Too often in the past, Labour conference has seen us win the vote but lose the policy ... the new structure provides an opportunity to claim both the process and the principle' (*Tribune*, 2 October 1998). There is union representation on all the policy commissions, and unions secured the right to raise urgent issues at the party conference, where their votes still dominate. This last right was very publicly deployed at the Labour's 1999 conference to prevent the government's planned watering down of the Post Office monopoly. Similarly, in return for supporting a national panel of leadership-vetted parliamentary candidates, they negotiated automatic access for candidates 'trained and assessed' by approved union schemes. Unions continue to place great store by the PLP trade union group, whose interventions were crucial over *Fairness at Work*, particularly the last-minute concession of an automatic union recognition route (*Financial Times*, 22 May 1998). The chair of the group made clear that union opinion would be decisive: 'If the TUC accepts it, then I think we will too' (*The Guardian*, 15 May 1998).

Union officers, then, now enjoy access to the government many have only dreamt of, continue to mobilize allies in the parliamentary party, and see some advantages in New Labour's internal party reforms. But what of substantive policies?

Shared Historical Projects

Is there sufficient adhesion left in Minkin's final binding factor – 'shared historical projects' – to keep unions affiliated to New Labour? Beyond a general desire to participate in state policymaking, two further TUC political objectives became central in the context of the post-war consensus: universal welfare provision, and full employment.

Many unions have expressed concern at New Labour's 'targeted' welfare policy, but most accepted the pledge to stick to Conservative spending plans until 1999, welcoming subsequent increases for health and education. When the government invited unions to endorse the assumption that the universal state pension would never again be enough to live on, and to become providers of private 'stakeholder' pensions, the TUC responded enthusiastically (Trades Union Congress, 1998). The AEEU immediately launched its own private pension scheme. PFI funding of public services is unpopular, but opposition by union leaders has been largely symbolic. Related plans to reduce the ratio of public spending to GDP angered important unions, but calls for fiscal stimulation to save jobs were quickly dismissed, government reporting that, 'Union requests to pump money into the economy have received short shrift – this is a new Labour government, not an old Labour one' (*Financial Times*, 20 July 1998). Conveniently, passing control of interest rates to the Bank of England enabled loyalist industrial unions to attack monetary policy without appearing to criticize New Labour. Full employment has been a central TUC objective, though not necessarily at the expense of wage objectives (Taylor, 1993, 20–25). New Labour has never promised full employment, but its 'full employment opportunity' substitute rests on assumptions about the constraints of globalization to which the TUC's New Unionism has also adapted its objectives of social partnership and legal rights for workers. And New Labour 'employability' programmes offer opportunities for New Unionism, notably the 'welfare-to-work' and 'Lifelong Learning' training initiatives. In 1998 the government announced a £6 million 'union learning fund' to subsidize union involvement.

But such opportunities cannot resolve the historic crisis of falling membership. TUC-affiliated membership fell to 6.6 million in 1997, from 12.2 million in 1979, losses unprecedented even in the 1930s. 'Density', the proportion of eligible workers in unions, fell to 30 per cent by 1997, from 53 per cent in 1979; in the private sector to 20 per cent; among workers aged under 20 to 6 per cent (*Labour Research*, August 1998). The membership decline had finally halted by 1999, but how far Blair's 'fairness, not favours' doctrine would help unions rebuild through recognition and recruitment campaigns remained crucial. As Monks repeatedly stressed about *Fairness at Work*, 'Trade union recognition is the key. We will judge the government, in terms of its relationship with the trade unions, over how it responds to this issue ... This is a defining issue for trade unionists. There is simply no room for compromise' (*New Statesman*, 27 February 1998).

Fairness at Work and the Employment Relations Act

Fairness at Work was a legacy of commitments made by Kinnock and Smith. Blair's record as opposition employment spokesperson left unions suspicious (McSmith, 1996, 313–23). But the TUC had recodified its mid-1980s 'new realism' in the 1996 New Unionism project (Monks, 1996), following a series of TUC modernization initiatives (A. Taylor, 1987, 152–99; Bassett, 1987, 44–64; Trades Union Congress, 1991, 1994; Heery, 1998). Unions had accepted Kinnock's insistence on an independent, party industrial relations policy (Anderson and Mann, 1997, 317–19; Hughes and Wintour, 1990, 142–52). Significantly, no organized, left opposition to New Labour emerged within mainstream TUC circles after 1994 (McIlroy, 1998, 554). Indeed New Unionism represents a reorientation as startling as New Labour, notably the shift from voluntaristic industrial relations to a European model of legally enforceable recognition and worker rights (R. Taylor, 1994, 197–216). All three primary union expectations of New Labour – national minimum wage, union recognition rights, and signing the EU Social Protocol – were, significantly, guaranteed by law, not union power.

Blair, it soon became obvious, shared the CBI interpretation of Labour's manifesto commitment that, 'where a majority of the relevant workforce vote in a ballot for the union to represent them, the union should be recognised' (Labour Party, 1997c). On this view, 'majority' meant 50 per cent of the workplace electorate not simply of those voting, an obstacle that even a 70 per cent majority on a 70 per cent turnout could not surmount. Employers wanted to determine the 'relevant workforce', prompting union fears of gerrymandering; exemption of companies with under 50 employees (thus excluding 37 per cent of workers); and 'trigger' ballots demonstrating 30 per cent support before a binding recognition ballot. Some union leaders called for a special TUC Congress, recalling the one that threw out *In Place of Strife* in 1969. Eventually the TUC accepted a 30 per cent voting threshold, and the exclusion of firms with fewer than ten workers. The White Paper announced a 40 per cent threshold, and excluded firms with fewer than 20 workers. The pro-government *New Statesman* complained that, 'Blair's policy of "fairness not favours" towards the unions has been shorn of a third of its words and most of its meaning' (*New Statesman*, 15 May 1998). There was no question of repealing Thatcher's anti-union laws, condemned by the United Nations and the Council of Europe; one prominent QC called *Fairness at Work* 'a statement of defiance of international law' (*Tribune*, 7 August 1998).

Enough had been done to avoid a backbench revolt. Individual worker rights, mostly implementing EU directives, were incorporated, and included the right of any worker to have a union representative at disciplinary hearings, theoretically giving unions access to any workplace. Last-minute concessions included a future review of the 40 per cent threshold; dropping the 'trigger' ballot; unions defining the 'relevant workforce'; and government funding to train union representatives in 'social partnership'. But the crucial concession was automatic union recognition, without a ballot, where unions recruited 50 per cent 'plus one' of the workforce. Blair had earlier rejected this, and employers were furious. The *Financial Times* editorial (22 May 1998) declared 'The scoreline for yesterday's *Fairness at Work* white paper could read: Unions 6, Employers 2. After two decades in which the pendulum has swung against them, there is no doubt that the unions are the winners in yesterday's proposals'.

Unions particularly criticized the exclusion of five million workers in small firms. Peter Mandelson later diluted the White Paper, erecting procedural obstacles to automatic recognition, limiting the right to individual representation, capping and limiting the right of strikers to unfair dismissal compensation. 'We haven't had the fairness, but the employers have certainly had the favours' was the view of Bill Morris (*New Statesman*, 22 January 1999). Nevertheless, the TUC insisted that the balance of power had tilted towards unions, making recruitment easier. And by 1999, in a tone far less critical of unions than his much-resented TUC speech in

1997, Blair offered public support to the TUC's social partnership strategy, providing unions abandoned confrontational 'old ways' and sought to 'add value' and promote business success (Blair, 1997b; 1999).

The national minimum wage package revealed similar compromises. Unions were unhappy that the youth rate applied to 21 year-olds, but employers had wanted it to apply up to age 25. Some unions were angry that the Low Pay Commission's unanimous recommendation on the rate was diluted; Bill Morris called the £3.60 adult rate an 'endorsement of workplace poverty'. But unions welcomed the review function, permitting future argument over the rate. And pressing implementation could help recruit among the 10 per cent of workers who stood to benefit. Monks saw the minimum wage compromise as typical of New Labour's 'quiet revolution' helping the unions (*Financial Times*, 24 June 1998).

So, there is clear evidence that in terms of key union political objectives, a new 'shared historical project' – a New Labourism – could be constructed. The TUC and major unions share enough of New Labour's economic and political assumptions, are sufficiently anxious to act as agencies, in training, pensions, legal representation, for example, and desperate to seize recruitment opportunities, to suggest that a supply-side New Labourism could keep the unions married to the party. If these prospects fail or relations deteriorate, are there viable political alternatives for the unions?

Horses for Courses

Minkin concluded that unions would threaten divorce only if 'sustained frustration and alienation' combined with 'a viable political alternative', suggesting two alternatives: non-partisan pressure-group politics; and other parties (Minkin, 1992, 655–6). The first, that Minkin thought unlikely, has begun to happen, with the 1994 relaunch of the TUC as a more independent pressure group. Monks insists, 'We have done what we can to build relationships with other parties. Our job as trade unionists must be to forge relationships with anyone with a say over the decision we seek to influence' (Monks, 1998a). The TUC's 1997 election intervention, a non-partisan employment rights campaign, with, for the first time ever, no call to vote Labour, was symptomatic, as is New Unionism's mobilization of public opinion through polling and advertising. Such campaigning, and coordinating union financial, legal, welfare and training services, could reposition the TUC as Britain's biggest pressure group, as Monks frequently describes it. Robert Taylor, advising the unions to quit Labour, points to the resources available for such activities if unions stop, 'pouring millions of pounds into the coffers of an ungrateful party' (*Tribune*, 22 May 1998). There have been signs of 'sustained frustration', especially among disappointed public service unionists. In 1998 the RMT (railworkers) conference came within seven votes of disaffiliating from Labour, and in 1999 the FBU (firefighters) conference voted, against its leader's advice, to permit members to specify that their political fund contributions should not go to Labour.

A repositioned TUC is certainly compatible with individual unions affiliating to Labour, and unions need legislative allies, but what of other parties? Minkin dismissed Britain's small, electorally irrelevant, radical socialist and communist parties. Since he wrote, the Socialist Labour Party has split from Labour. Two general secretaries, and one assistant general secretary, of national unions sit on its executive, and a member won election as leader of the train drivers' union in 1998. The SLP has some local union affiliations, but no national ones. Its campaign against anti-union laws has won significant union support, but, crucially, its electoral impact has been negligible.

Perhaps most intriguingly, relocation of UK legislative sovereignty opens new prospects which were over the horizon when Minkin wrote. Recently, one general secretary reminded his members, 'European Works Councils, the working time directive, overtime, shift premiums, and much more, are all being determined by Brussels. Equally, rights at work and health and safety issues are determined by European law and law makers' (*GPMU Journal*, June 1997). For some years larger unions have devoted some of their political funds to EU work (Alderman and Carter, 1994, 337). Social Protocol initiatives such as worker consultation rights, a TUC objective that threatens further rows given the obstructiveness of Blair and his MEPs, might even push unions towards other parties in the European Parliament, and further into EU 'social partner' policy forums. The more worker rights are Europeanized, the less unions need domestic allies to combat hostile Westminster legislation.

The union link has been multilayered, involving national, regional and local affiliation, funding and electoral organization; links between national leaders; and involvement in ginger groups and factions. Historically, such activity assumed the absolute supremacy of Westminster politics. Hence New Labour's constitutional reforms have potentially important consequences. The Human Rights Act will encourage non-parliamentary legal activism on union issues, especially if a European employment rights convention emerges. Other reforms may lead more directly to fragmentation. Partial legislative autonomy in Scotland is the most interesting case, though Wales, the English regions, and directly elected executive mayors in London and elsewhere are others. Proportional representation at

Westminster and sub-national assemblies may well place nationalist, socialist, or red-green parties, or new coalitions, in positions of power. If unions back different party horses for different legislative courses, Labour's monopoly will weaken, though it would continue to receive most of the unions' financial backing whatever their constitutional position in the party. An arms-length union–party relationship might make it easier to secure additional election funding from currently unaffiliated unions, the social profile of whose members makes them unlikely ever to approve affiliation, however many of them are New Labour voters.

Blair is keen to reconstruct the progressive coalition of the late nineteenth century. Then, unions were associated with, but not federally affiliated to, the Liberal Party, though even a close union ally whom Blair knighted, AEEU leader Ken Jackson, is a fierce critic of a Lib–Lab view of modernizing Labour (*Tribune*, 15 January 1999). Certainly, a formal merger with the Liberal Democrats would provoke a crisis. Blair is unequivocally opposed to the unions holding special voting or other powers in the party, as he made clear during Smith's review of the link. If, as seems inevitable, he wins an unprecedented second full term of office, as New Labour, he will feel free to complete the modernizers' unfinished business with the unions. Undertakings to meet regularly with union leaders, and to assist union members to integrate into the party as individuals, might be enough to persuade some friendly union leaders to help lead a voluntary move to change the party constitution, knowing that he might otherwise stake his enhanced authority on another 'Clause IV'-style plebiscite of the mass membership to end the link.

Conclusions

The key factors that once strained the labour alliance have become much less disruptive and damaging. Through centralized control of the party and its dissidents, as well as genuine consensus, ideological tension has greatly subsided. Constitutional conflicts, where they exist, can be processed in the new, and private, policy forums before ratification in the televised annual conference. Principal sources of economic policy tension, tripartite planning and incomes polices, are off the agenda. The party's original 'basic and unifying purpose' (Minkin, 1992, 11) of advancing workers' industrial interests has long been demoted, and frequently contradicted, as class politics became an obstacle to national electoral success. New Labour will not repeal anti-union laws, nor even promise full employment. Unions no longer determine party industrial relations policy; the old demarcation between industrial and political authority is no longer recognized by party leaders. However, a majority of key union leaders support or accept New Labour's economic and social policies, and, partly as a defensive response to Thatcherism, have downgraded industrial voluntarism as a strategy in favour of legal employment rights. The Employment Relations Act provides some such rights, and may help unions rebuild their memberships. And in Blair's 'flexibility-plus' labour market vision, many unions see gains in delivering the 'pluses' of workplace rights and training. The real prospect does therefore exist of a supply-side New Labourism, a new 'shared historical project' engaging New Labour with New Unionism.

But such a New Labourism is a public policy, rather than a party project, and the traditional factors that bound the party to the link are greatly weakened, the more so as New Labour continues to broaden its financial base. The marriage of unions and party may often have been more anguished, but rarely has its fundamental historical rationale been weaker, for either partner. There may be little enthusiasm in the party for acrimonious divorce, but New Labour's 'ultra-modernizers' remain determined to finally to dismantle the federal structures that embodied union control from the party's foundation. From the affiliated unions' point of view, it is an enormous risk to write off a century of investment in the party without a clear alternative. Such alternatives as exist imply only partial fragmentation in the short term. Pressure group activities in Britain and Europe, legislative devolution and electoral reform, and other sympathetic parties in office, may begin to realign unions' political commitments and affiliations. But, whether in a front-page divorce settlement, pressed by modernizers, or a longer process of mutual disengagement, the 100 year-old labour alliance, in its historic, constitutionally united form, is unlikely to last long into its second century.

7

The Hand of History: New Labour, News Management and Governance

BOB FRANKLIN

On Maundy Thursday 1998, Tony Blair flew to Belfast to resolve what seemed to be an impasse in the Northern Ireland peace process. It was a portentous moment for political developments in the province. The international corps of journalists and broadcasters assembled for a press conference at the airport was more than usually attentive to the Prime Minister's briefing. 'This is not a time for soundbites', Blair announced, 'we've left those at home' and then added, with no discernible note of post-modern irony and much less spontaneity, 'I feel the hand of history upon us. Today I hope that the burden of history can at long last be lifted from our shoulders' (*The Guardian*, 11 April 1998). The headlines in the following day's newspapers resonated with the carefully crafted phrase. Politicians' use of such 'soundbites', their need to 'stay on message' and their determination to 'set the news agenda' in their favour, have become crucial components in a modern statecraft which emphasizes the 'packaging' of politicians and policies for media presentation and voters' consumption (Franklin, 1994, 1998).

In the Labour party, such preoccupations are not new. The first Press and Publicity Department was established in 1917 (Hollins, 1981, 46), while intra-party debates about whether election campaigns should be 'image' or 'issue' driven, began in the 1920s (Wring, 1997, 13–14). As part of that continuing debate, Tony Benn criticized Aneurin Bevan for his apparently 'absurd idea that all publicity is unimportant and that all you need is the right policy' (Benn, 1994a, 190). What is undoubtedly new in Labour's political communications strategy, notwithstanding these longer-term trends, is the belief that the presentation of policy is at least as significant as any substantive policy content. 'What they can't seem to grasp', a Labour spin-doctor announced after the 1997 election, 'is that communications is not an after thought to our policy. It's central to the whole mission of New Labour' (Gaber, 1998, 13). Peter Mandelson expressed this commitment unequivo-cally with his suggestion that the government's perception of whether a pol-icy is capable of clear presentation has become central to the government's assessment of that policy's political merit. 'There are some who still deni-grate the presentation of policy as a diversion from its substance, as a super-ficial and unnecessary coating to the main product', Mandelson claimed:

> I take the opposite view ... If a government policy cannot be presented in a sim-
> ple and attractive way, it is more likely than not to contain fundamental flaws
> and prove to be the wrong policy. Once those flaws surface, the unattractive
> alternatives are sticking with it or overturning policy in which significant politi-
> cal capital might have been invested. We do not intend to fall into that trap.
> (Mandelson, 16 September 1997)

This chapter examines Labour's strategy for promoting its policies via news media and argues that such a strategy risks blurring, if not crossing, the important line which separates the commendable and democratic ambition to provide voters with information about government policy, from the unacceptable activity of trying to persuade voters to particular policy choices: in short, the distinction between policy marketing and pro-paganda (O'Shaughnessy, 1996, 62). But since Labour's approach to the media promotion of policy and the news management of policy debates exemplifies a more general trend which I have elsewhere described as the 'packaging of politics', the chapter begins by reviewing the key elements of that development in political communication (Franklin, 1994).

Labour and the Packaging of Policies

Politicians' ever increasing use of media to inform, shape and manage pub-lic discourse about policy, has been variously described as the 'packaging of politics' (Franklin, 1994), the 'modern publicity process' (Blumler, 1990), the activity of the 'public relations state' (Deacon and Golding, 1994), a cen-tral feature of 'designer democracy' (Scammell, 1995), the 'Americanization' (a clumsy word but a more dubious concept) of British political communi-cations (Negrine, 1996; Scammell, 1998), or what Bayley calls the 'poli-tics of Labour camp' where, following Susan Sontag, camp is defined as 'the consistently aesthetic experience of the world ... which incarnates a victory of "style" over "content" ' (Bayley, 1998, 7).

Whatever label is attached to this changing political communications process, the packaging of politics entails three broad propositions. First, politicians in government, political parties and interest groups, have revealed a growing enthusiasm for using the media to market their policies (and their leaders) to the public. In the words of columnist Matthew Parris, 'politicians run on publicity like horses run on oats' (*Sun,* 14 February 1998). Politicians have always been in the communications business, but since the mid-1980s there has been a marked shift in the extent and character of their energy for media-based political marketing. Alastair Campbell alleged that John Major's government was obsessed with 'media manipulation' and 'measured success in the thickness of the press cuttings file and the camera angle on *News at Ten.* We have a Prime Minister' Campbell continued, fashioning an enviably catchy soundbite, 'who will act to stop the *Sunday Times* writing about the recession, but won't act to stop the recession' (Campbell, 1992, 16).

Second, governments are increasingly adept at using media in this way and devote expansive financial and human resources to the enterprise. The Prime Minister's press secretary briefs the Lobby twice daily and gives the government's spin on current policy concerns to the 200 most senior political journalists at Westminster. Governments also enjoy access to the 1000 press and public relations specialists in the Government Information and Communications Service (GICS), the 300 press officers in the Central Office of Information (COI) nationally and regionally, the Strategic Communications Unit (SCU) at Number 10 and the growing band of 'specialist' advisers in departments of state. Governments, moreover, employ private sector marketing consultants and advertising staff to work on particular policy campaigns as well as the more general and perennial task of preening the government's public image. This image grooming is a costly business: the government's expenditure on advertising in 1997–8 was £165 million and approached the peak expenditure of the Thatcher governments of the late 1980s (Franklin, 1999, Ch. 1).

Third, this ambition to package politics poses a number of challenges to democracies. The relationship between government and media can become unduly collusive, with media acting as little more than conduits for government policy messages, drafted by press officers and mistaken by readers and viewers as the work of independent journalists and broadcasters (Franklin, 1997, 19). In these circumstances, the role of media in creating the 'informed citizen' who makes 'rational' policy choices may be substantially diminished as governments try to structure news agendas in ways that exclude certain policy options rather than placing the widest possible policy agenda before audiences and voters.

While the first two propositions have enjoyed broad support from academic observers (Scammell, 1995) this final suggestion is hotly contested (McNair, 1998). McNair acknowledges that 'considerations of image and style are today as important to political success as the detail of policy' but argues that failure to 'participate enthusiastically in "the game" as it is now played' constitutes an 'evil' which 'deprives the electorate of meaningful choice'. Scammell argues more positively that political communication via the media 'heightens the awareness and interest of voters who might otherwise shun dry debates' (Scammell, 1995, 18). This increased voter information and interest may trigger increased electoral participation which, in turn, makes governments more accountable. Consequently, the new media-based politics improves the 'extent, quantity and efficiency of communications between voters and parties' (Harrop, 1990, 283).

But such claims for increased public knowledge are hard to sustain when the crippling banality of some government presentations of policy are considered. On 24 November 1998, for example, the Queen opened the new parliamentary session with the traditional 'gracious speech' – renamed 'The Peoples' Priorities' by Campbell. The highly contentious Welfare Reform Bill, with its proposed reform of welfare's £90 billions budget, was characterised merely as a measure to 'end the something for nothing society'. Little wonder that *The Guardian*'s political correspondent described the policy speech as 'a very New Labour programme: strong on presentation, weaker on detail' (*The Guardian*, 25 November 1998).

New Labour and News Management

Since 1997, the Labour government has imported its election-winning media operation into government: a process described as the 'Millbankization' of government (Gaber, 1998, 10). In his evidence to the Select Committee on Public Administration inquiry into the Government Information and Communication Services, Sir Richard Wilson, the Cabinet Secretary claimed:

> there is a more systematic determined effort to co-ordinate in a strategic way, presentation of government policies and messages in a positive light across the whole of government, than I can remember since the time I have been in the civil service. (Select Committee on Public Administration 1998, xii)

This process has involved the increasing centralization of communications at Number 10, a more assertive relationship with journalists and broadcasters and the politicizing of the GICS.

'Conducting the Communications Orchestra': the Central Control of Communications

Centralizing communications at Number 10 under the control of the Prime Minister's press secretary has been the key priority in Labour's communications strategy. The intention is to establish the government as the 'primary definer' in media discussions of policy, to ensure the consistency of the government line and to minimize the media profile of any dissenting voices. Central control is certainly strict, but effective. The Mountfield report on government communications suggested that 'all major interviews and media appearances, both print and broadcast, should be agreed with the No 10 Press Office before any commitments are entered into. The policy content of all major speeches, press releases and new policy initiatives should be cleared in good time with the No 10 private office' and finally, 'the timing and form of announcements should be cleared with the No 10 Press Office'. Number 10 also coordinates the work of departmental press offices, via a weekly meeting of information officers which is chaired by Campbell, to 'secure a timely and well ordered flow of departmental communications and to see how best departmental communications can play into the broader Government messages and themes' (Mountfield, 1997, 7): what Ingham delighted in describing as 'conducting the communications orchestra' to ensure that everyone 'was following the same score' (Ingham, 1991, 166).

The establishment of the Strategic Communications Unit (SCU) in January 1998, which includes two special advisers (both ex-*Mirror* journalists), is responsible for 'pulling together and sharing with departments the government's key policy themes and messages' (Select Committee on Public Administration 1998, para 19): i.e. keeping spokespeople 'on message'. The unit liaises with media management organizations in individual departments, such as the Strategy and Communications Directorate in the DfEE, to coordinate government policy messages. The SCU also assists with the drafting of ministerial speeches by including common phrases and soundbites to illustrate the consistency of the government's 'message' and 'no doubt they draft some of those "exclusive" articles the prolific Tony Blair writes' (*The Guardian*, 21 May 1998, 20. See also the Select Committee on Public Administration's Second Special report, vi). Since February 1998, the SCU's activities have been supported by 'Agenda', a new computer system which 'helps to co-ordinate government's publicity activities' by listing 'forthcoming newsworthy events, lines to take, key departmental messages and themes and ministerial speeches' (Select Committee, 1998, xiii and Appendix 12).

The government's 'communications day' begins with a 9 am meeting attended by senior communications staffs including Alastair Campbell,

Jonathan Powell the Prime Minster's chief of staff, specialist advisers from the Treasury and the Deputy Prime Minister's Office as well as representatives from the Cabinet Office and the Chief Whip's Office (MacAskill, 1997, 8). The meeting tries to ensure a congruence between strategy and presentation and consigns specific individuals to resolve any particular presentation problems arising that day (Mountfield, 1997, 8). Labour's determination to stay 'on message' requires that nothing is left to chance. The policy 'message' must be carefully scripted, meticulously rehearsed, universally endorsed by party and government, centrally coordinated and favourably presented in the news media (N. Jones, 1999). These communications demands have prompted predictable tensions in the Labour ranks.

In March 1998, for example, Harriet Harman was chastised by Campbell for giving media interviews without his approval: a leaked fax demanded she explain 'why the interviews with *The Guardian, Woman's Hour* and *World At One* were not cleared through this office' (*The Guardian,* 30 March 1998, 5). In July 1998, when Frank Field resigned from government, he was denounced in a Number 10 briefing as an 'impractical, abstract theoretician ... incapable of running a department or translating ideas into workable policy' (*Observer,* 2 August 1998, 1). Field responded by describing the Number 10 press office as 'the 'cancer at the heart of government' (*Jimmy Young Programme*, BBC Radio 2, 3 July 1998). Further 'difficulties' arose in November 1998 when Labour's new general secretary drafted a code of conduct for members of the NEC which demanded that NEC members should 'agree to inform the party press office and to seek their advice before discussing NEC business with the media'. After a brief protest, the 'code' was renamed 'guidance', but the requirement for NEC members to consult Millbank before giving media interviews remains (*The Guardian,* 18 November 1998, 15).

The 'resignation' of Charlie Whelan in January 1999, amid allegations that he leaked information about Mandelson's undeclared loan from a Cabinet colleague, aided this process of centralization. A significant and potentially oppositional centre of spin within government had been closed down: Campbell had been asking for Whelan's resignation since 2 May 1997 (*The Guardian,* 5 January 1999, 2). Hugo Young's description of Labour spindoctors as 'a self justifying, yet also mutually destructive excrescence' proved both precocious and accurate (*The Guardian,* 7 July 1998, 18).

Carrots and Sticks: Labour's Relationships with Journalists

Labour's vigorous and uncompromising news management strategy offers journalists and broadcasters stark choices. If they accept the government line, they will be rewarded with the occasional minor 'exclusive' and be allowed interview access to senior politicians. But journalists who are critical of government will have their bids for interviews denied and will not receive telephone tips about 'breaking stories and exclusives' (Gaber, 1998, 14). In short, the government is playing an old-fashioned game of carrots and sticks (Ingham quoted in Select Committee on Public Administration, 1998, 9–14), although some commentators believe that 'with New Labour ... the game is played with an unprecedented degree of nastiness' (Gaber, 1998, 14).

There is a further reason informing some newspapers' supine coverage of Labour's performance in government; journalists working for the Murdoch press believe their proprietor has agreed a pact with Tony Blair. Murdoch's newspapers' support for Labour since the run up to the 1997 election has been handsomely rewarded by the absence of legislation to outlaw the predatory pricing of *The Times* (despite the opportunity provided by the Competition Bill) and the unwillingness of government to regulate the press's invasion of privacy or Sky's advantageous position in the digital television market. Some journalists argue that Blair is conceding too much policy ground in return for the editorial quiescence of the Murdoch press.

Sticks are more commonplace than carrots. In October 1997, Campbell circulated a memo to all Heads of Information in the GICS arguing that 'media handling' (his preferred term for media relations), must become more assertive. 'Decide your headlines' he insisted 'sell your story and if you disagree with what is being written argue your case. If you need support from here [Downing Street] let me know' (Timmins, 1997, 1). For journalists writing against the government line, 'the 'handling' has become rough! Journalists are privately bullied, publicly harangued and excluded from off-the record briefings.' Andrew Marr, when editor of the *Independent* was told 'you are either with us or against us' (MccGwire, 1997, 11). Complaints from the Number 10 press office seem to influence even the most distinguished journalistic careers. Rosie Boycott's withdrawal of an offer of the political editor's job at Hollick's *Daily Express* to Paul Routledge was attributed by journalists to Routledge publishing a biography of Gordon Brown which was critical of Tony Blair (*The Guardian*, 21 May 1998, 20). Similar rumours surround the departure of *Sun* columnist Matthew Parris after he outed Mandelson on *Newsnight* and the sacking of executive editor Amanda Platell and news editor Ian Walker from the *Sunday Express* following their involvement in the publication of a story about Mandelson's friendship with a Brazilian student (*Financial Times*, 20 January 1999, 10). Given this track record, it is perhaps unsurprising that a biographic article about Campbell observed that 'he performs his onerous tasks with cheerful brutality' (Hattersley, 1998a, 3).

Broadcast journalists, especially those working at the BBC, are subject to similar pressures which were illustrated by the 'Humphreys problem'. In December 1997, David Hill, then the Labour Party's head of communications, wrote to the *Today* programme threatening to isolate broadcasters from government news sources following a particularly robust interview by John Humphreys with Harriet Harman. The letter, which was promptly leaked, is threatening in style, uses military metaphors and subscribes to the belief that it is appropriate for politicians to dictate the style and content of broadcast interviews. 'The John Humphreys problem', Hill began,

> has assumed new proportions after this morning's interview with Harriet Harman. In response we have had a council of war and are seriously considering whether, as a party, we will suspend co-operation when you make bids through us for government ministers ... Frankly none of us feels this can go on. (Quoted in *The Guardian*, 13 December 1997, 12)

Some journalists reflect very thoughtfully about both the efficiency of Labour's news management machinery and the consequences for their effectiveness, journalistic independence and professional integrity. Adam Boulton, Sky's lobby correspondent, acknowledges with admirable honesty:

> the trouble is that the government is operating at a level of news management that is way above the level of British politics. I do not blame Alastair for that. As far as Alastair is concerned, it is all fair in love and war, as long as it's in favour of Tony. On a good day, you can see an intelligent, honest administration at work. On a bad day I feel soiled, when we end up seeing the press conniving in our own manipulation. (Quoted in Toolis, 1998, 31)

But the government's media strategy is subject to constant review. In February 1999, Campbell criticized national newspapers as 'dumbed down' and 'deeply cynical'. He announced the government's determination to address directly the too frequently ignored audiences for live daytime television, as well as the readerships of women's magazines, regional newspapers, the ethnic minority press and European and American news outlets (Campbell, 1999). One such 'cynical' journalist working for *The Guardian* suggested that this shift in strategy reflected little more than the government's belief that its 'message' was much less likely to be contested by generalist and under-resourced journalists working on local newspapers than the specialist If 'troublesome lobby correspondents' (White, 1999, 2). But the establishment of new press lobbies in May 1999, to report the Scottish parliament and Welsh assembly, will undoubtedly challenge the government's ability to present a coordinated policy message via news media.

Red Books and White Lies: Politicizing the Government Information and Communications Service

In government, Labour has access to the resources and services of the GICS, staffed by 1000 civil servants whose press and public relations activities are governed by a code of conduct (The Whitehall Red Book) designed to guarantee their political impartiality. 'Press officers' according to the Red Book, must 'establish a position with the media whereby it is understood that they stand apart from the party political battle, but are there to assist the media to understand the policies of the government of the day' (Cabinet Office, 1997, para 11). One consequence of 'assisting the media' in this way, by presenting 'the government's policies in their best light', is that 'some advantage naturally accrues to the party in power': this is 'entirely proper' (Select Committee, 1998, xv). For the civil service press officer, however, it is never appropriate to 'justify or defend those policies in Party political terms, to use political slogans, expressly to advocate policies as those of a particular political Party or directly attack (although it may be necessary to respond to in specific terms) policies and opinions of opposition Parties and groups' (Select Committee, 1998, xv). By contrast, 'special advisers' such as the Prime Minister's press secretary, 'are not bound by the usual requirements that civil servants should be able to assist governments of "whatever complexion" and that they should be "impartial"' (Select Committee, 1998, xv). The Select Committee on Public Administration, investigating concerns that the Labour government might be politicizing the GICS by ignoring these distinctions, concluded there 'is a very fine line between the promotion and defence of government policy and the promotion and defence of the ruling party's policies'; the Committee further agreed that the policing of that line was a matter for the Prime Minister's press secretary's 'own judgement' (Select Committee, 1998, xv). Since 1997, however, civil servants have expressed growing concerns that this 'line' is too frequently crossed: the 'judgement' of the Prime Minister's press secretary too frequently exercised injudiciously. Senior information officers have warned about the 'creeping politicization of the GICS' (Select Committee, 1998, 80). The government has responded that it concerned only to 'modernize' the GICS to ensure 'it is equipped to meet the demands of a fast changing media world' (Mountfield, 1997, para 2). Four developments have triggered civil service concerns.

First, the government has appointed unprecedented numbers of 'special advisers' to promote government policy: Andrew Rawnsley described it as 'an influx of Labour Apparachiks into posts traditionally occupied by career civil servants' (*The Observer*, 1 June 1997). The Major government's

32 advisers were replaced by 60 within the early days of the Labour government at an additional cost of £600000 (a 44 per cent increase over Conservative expenditure) (Franklin, 1998, 11): the wages bill for the 70 current advisers is £3.5 million (*The Guardian*, 17 November 1998, 5). This is a substantial sum, paid from the public purse, to bankroll partisan propaganda distributed from government departments.

Second, in the first year of the Labour government, 25 heads of information and their deputies, from a total of 44 such senior posts, resigned or have been replaced: the Select Committee on the GICS described this as 'an unusual turnover' (Select Committee, 1998, xviii). The reasons informing these staff changes were varied but included 'the desire of ministers for information officers to be less neutral than they thought was compatible with their regular civil service terms of employment' (Select Committee, 1998, xviii). The retired head of information at the Northern Ireland Office spoke of a 'culling' of Head of Information and their replacement 'by "politically acceptable" temporary bureaucrats'; a process he labels the 'Washingtonization' of the civil service (Select Committee, 1998, 86).

Third, this burgeoning of special advisers has created a 'two tier structure of information' in which the advisers have become the dominant partners over civil servants (Select Committee, 1998, ix). Advisers are chosen by ministers: they are close and trusted friends. By contrast, heads of information are an inheritance of government and judged to be unduly bureaucratic, uncommitted and poorly motivated. Consequently, the significant communications tasks are allocated to the adviser, leaving the civil service press officer with routine day-to-day matters. Jill Rutter, who resigned as head of information at the Treasury, complained that Charlie Whelan had 'taken over three quarters of her job' (*Daily Telegraph*, 6 December 1997, 3). At her leaving party, she claimed she 'felt like Princess Diana had done – that three in a marriage is one too many' (quoted in Lloyd, 1997, 12).

Finally, the most significant change at the GICS has been the need to 'get on message': i.e. to propagandize for government. In October 1997, Campbell sent a memo to heads of information confirming that the central task of GICS publicity was that the 'government's four key messages' must be 'built in to all areas of our activity'. Labour is 'a modernizing government', a government 'for all the people', that is 'delivering on its promises' with 'mainstream policies' that are providing new directions for Britain (*Financial Times*, 9 October 1997, 1). Some information officers have preferred to resign before complying with central dictates which so thoroughly eschew their professional commitments to neutrality.

Many senior press officers have:

> privately expressed their uneasiness at being expected to switch to a more
> aggressive approach where seizing the agenda and occupying the front pages is
> apparently more important than the content, where events and announcements
> are relentlessly pushed rather than being left to find their own level according to
> their news value, and where those media outlets or individuals which did not
> adhere to the 'on-message' approach are penalised by intimidatory tactics and
> the threatened withdrawal of access and facilities. In such a climate presentation
> comes perilously close to propaganda. (Select Committee, 1998, 1–82)

These changes at the GICS prompted an inquiry into the Service in
March 1998. The terms of reference for the inquiry were remarkable by conceding at the outset what the committee was established to decide: namely
whether or not the GICS is impartial. Consequently, the terms of reference
suggested the Committee should try to establish not if the GICS *is* impartial, but 'the extent to which the GICS *should be* politically impartial' and
the 'balance between delivering neutral information and giving a political
spin' (Select Committee on Public Administration, Press Release, 30 March
1998, emphasis added). Given this starting point, the Committee's conclusions were unlikely to be critical of government press operations, but the
eventual outcome of the report's inquiries was unpredictably acrimonious.

An early critical report drafted by the clerk was modified radically by
the Committee's in-built majority of Labour members. The official report,
which was eventually published, contained none of the original criticisms
of Alastair Campbell and the Government Information and Communications
Services nor the many proposals for reform. In the words of one Committee
member, the report 'could have been written by Alastair himself...on
one side of A4 saying everything in the garden is rosy' (*The Guardian*,
5 August 1998, 1). The combined opposition members of the committee
denounced the redrafted report as 'whitewash' and its supporters as 'the
glove puppets of Alastair Campbell' (*The Guardian*, 7 August 1998, 4).
They also published an alternative report reinstating the criticisms and recommendations for changes in the government information machine: four
are significant. First, tapes of Lobby briefings should be 'routinely kept for
12 months' (xxxii) to check if Campbell has been misleading journalists.
Second, advisers who 'undertake significant amounts of party political
activity should be paid from party funds and not the taxpayer'. Third, the
government should 'consider whether the Strategic Communications Unit
gives an undue advantage to the governing party' and, finally, that the
House 'examine the concerns expressed by Madam Speaker on the sharp
growth in "pre-briefing"' [i.e. 'leaking' or 'trailing'] of government policy
statements to the press which undermines the authority of Parliament

(Select Committee Report, 1998, xxxii–iii). The major recommendation in the official report was the suggestion for a new code of conduct to define more clearly government's relationships with the media. The code, to be drawn up and policed by Alastair Campbell, 'would make clear the obligations on special advisors and ministers to work closely with press officers in general and the Prime Minister's official spokesperson in particular' (Select Committee, 1998, xx). It seems nothing less than extraordinary, that the principal recommendation of a Select Committee inquiry into the politicizing of the government information services, should propose the further centralizing of government communications under the control of the Prime Minister's press secretary, especially when that recommendation enjoys the support of only the government members of the committee.

Given this political context to the Select Committee's official and alternative reports, it is perhaps unsurprising that the government, in its official response to the inquiry, 'welcomes the Committee's general endorsement of the key role which the GICS plays in carrying out the important task of effectively communicating and explaining the policies, decisions and actions of the government of the day' (Select Committee on Public Administration, 1999, iv).

Control Freaks or Designers of a New Democracy?

There is an evident irony in Labour's development of such a robust political communications style and practice: Labour's forceful public advocacy of open government and *freedom* of information (albeit delayed), sits ill with the quieter, more private reality of the considerable *management* of information which is conducted by Number 10. Blair's government is controlling the flow of political communications by and about the government to a degree which is unprecedented in the UK in peacetime. The irresistible question which emerges is whether the Labour approach to news management reflects what leader writers are increasingly describing as a 'control freak mentality' or whether there is a more substantive reason; there seems to be more to this than can be explained by individual psychology which invariably concludes in conspiracy theory.

Three reasons for increased 'control freakery' are suggested. First, these developments may reflect the centralizing instincts of British political parties. Second, the loss of clear policy daylight between the major parties, with few substantive policy issues to define differences, has prompted or exacerbated the focus on presentation. Finally, the hierarchical and centralized control of communications may simply articulate the managerial culture of public institutions.

There is a fourth account which warrants further elaboration. The party seems to be developing a new and emergent conception of democracy which, as yet, is far from fully worked through, but which involves recasting the relationship between government, media and citizens in significant ways. Labour's obsession with the media seems to reflect the opportunities which radio, newspapers, but especially television, offer the executive to communicate directly with citizens. This emphasis on taking the debate directly to the citizens has recently been evidenced in the 'Welfare to Work' Roadshows, the 'Town Hall meetings' and the use of focus groups to test budget proposals: this latter is immensely significant since it reveals the extent to which marketing techniques are involved in policy *making*, not merely policy *presentation* as part of a broader process of policy implementation. The developments, moreover, are not confined to Labour. Hague's rather belated 'Listen To Britain' initiative and the reconstruction of Tory Central Office are attempts not merely to keep up with Labour but to create the conditions and processes necessary for the new political communications.

A significant consequence of this direct communication between executive and citizens has been the marginalizing of Parliament. The reduced significance which Labour attributes to the Commons is evidenced in the early changes to Prime Minister's Question Time without consulting the Speaker and the preference for the roving roadshow, described in 'Campbell-speak' as 'The Peoples' Questions and Answers' (what else?) with 'hand picked audiences' designed to 'lend a respectful ear to the Prime Minister' (*The Guardian*, 14 June 1997, 10). But more significant, are Ministers' clear preference for making major policy statements at press conferences rather than informing the House as a first priority. MPs' complaints that they too frequently learn of new policy initiatives from the television are increasingly commonplace. In April 1998, Speaker Boothroyd, in a rare television interview, condemned this practice of 'trailing' policy announcements in news media and warned the Prime Minister and senior ministers to 'rein in their apparatchiks and media spin doctors' (*The Guardian*, 9 April 1998, 5). Whether Tony Blair heard the Speaker's warning is a moot point: he attended only 5 per cent of Common's divisions in his first parliamentary year as Prime Minister. What is certain is that the practice of leaking and trailing stories to the media has continued at an accelerated pace.

The broad assumptions informing what Mandelson described as 'direct' democracy, were first publicly aired in a debate with German Christian Democrat Wolfgang Schauble – although Mandelson's remarks were promptly spun into relative insignificance by the Number 10 Press Office in the now traditional manner; they are worth citing at some length. Mandelson argued that 'the era of pure representative democracy is slowly coming to an end' (cited in Traynor, 1998, 8). Technological innovation (internet and interactive communications technology) has signalled the need for new democratic structures in which citizens occupy a central place which bears more than a passing resemblance to consumers in a marketplace. Democracy involves 'plebiscites, focus groups, lobbies, "citizen's movements" and the internet'. In Gould's more recent statement of this position, 'the new media age' means 'new forms of dialogue must be created. Focus groups and market research are an essential part of this dialogue. So too are the interactive party broadcasts and "Town Hall" meetings at which politicians can be questioned and held to account' (Gould, 1998a, 297–8). This direct democracy must supplant parliamentary democracy to create a new politics that is responsive and closely attuned to public choices and preferences. In Mandelson's early statement:

> Democracy and legitimacy need constant renewal. They need to be redefined with each generation ... Representative government is being complemented by more direct forms of involvement, from the internet to referenda ... that requires a different style of politics ... people have no time for a style of government that talks down to them and takes them for granted ... representative democracy is over. (quoted in Traynor, 1998, 8)

Parliament's Future Looks Bleak

There are at least two reservations to be entered here. First, this changed vision of democracy involves a changed perception of politicians. Governments no longer seem willing to confront political decisions, preferring to return to citizens to 'test' public opinion on issues, to gain a popular verdict on new policies, and implement them accordingly: the result is populist not popular government. Consequently, the status of politicians is substantially reduced. Instead of making political choices, framing political agendas and presenting them to the electorate, politicians seem more willing than ever to become little more then overpaid messenger boys and girls – ever more frantic distributors of questionnaires and frenzied facilitators of focus groups. For their part, the musings and reflections of these small (sometimes tiny), randomly assembled, unelected and unaccountable groups of individuals increasingly seem to weigh more heavily in the decision-making process than the opinions of elected representatives honed in parliamentary debate.

The new politics require politicians to abrogate their moral and political responsibilities, as politics becomes populist. Political decisions are reduced to market decisions and citizens are transformed into consumers. The public sphere becomes a marketplace. But in this marketplace, politicians are no longer seen to be *market driving* (like Thatcher) but *market driven* (like Blair).

There is a second concern. On this account, politicians make naive or perhaps disingenuous assessments concerning the independence and autonomy of citizens' policy choices. Governments' growing enthusiasm for news management and even the publicly funded advertising of new policy initiatives, makes politicians influential in the shaping of those very choices of citizens which are allegedly driving the policy process. Citizens' policy preferences are not constructed in a vacuum. They draw much of their information as well as orientation from news media that are increasingly subject to news management and spin by the GICS, the COI, the SCU and the Number 10 press office. A crucial constitutional function of parliament has been to act as a bulwark of probity against the overheated enthusiasms and ambitions of all governments and thereby to protect the rights and liberties of citizens. It is less clear who will protect citizens' rights in New Labour's, new model, media democracy.

8

New Labour, the Constitution and Reforming the State

DAVID RICHARDS AND MARTIN J. SMITH

The central argument of this chapter is that whilst the new Labour government has acted on a radical agenda for constitutional reform, it has not thought through this programme and how it relates to the operation of the state, nor to the complex inter-relationships that exist within the British constitutional framework. More crucially, the paradoxes of the reform programme are a symptom of Labour's entrapment in a commitment to the long-established British political system and, in particular, the Westminster model. It is interesting that in the first three years in office Blair failed to give a major speech on constitutional reform.

The chapter begins with a brief analysis of Labour's historic relationship with the state and the impact of the Westminister model. It reviews the state New Labour inherited from the Conservatives in 1997. The chapter then examines the present array of constitutional and state reforms that the government is pursuing. It argues that the reform programme has been undertaken in an *ad hoc* manner, based on a set of isolated responses to a series of separate pressures created by the inadequacies within the existing political system. In particular, we will argue that the Labour government has embarked on a segmented programme of state reform, which indicates its failure to understand the organic and interconnected nature of the British constitution. We conclude by contending that the repercussions could finally lead to public exposure of the existing façade of the notion of parliamentary sovereignty which to now has been presented by the political elite as a cornerstone of the British constitution.

Labour, the State and the Constitution in the Twentieth Century

The Labour Party's attitude to the state is perhaps best understood as a product first of its own history and second, its experiences in government. Labour's attitude towards the state has been based on two principles: first, that the state is neutral and second, that it is an effective mechanism for achieving its policy goals. Consequently, Labour governments have accepted the top-down nature of British government and have rarely questioned the key constitutional precepts on which it is based. As Marquand notes (1997, 44):

> Its object has been to win power within the existing political system and to use it to change society in accordance with its ideology and the interests of its constituents. It has shown little sympathy for the proposition that a system permeated with essentially monarchical values might not be compatible with such a project.

The belief was that once in power, Labour governments would retain power for ever, thus allowing for a long-term process of incremental state reform (see Sharpe, 1982, 14). Such a position has meant the Party leadership has consistently failed to question the effectiveness of the long-established and firmly entrenched Westminster/Whitehall system of government.

As a consequence, Labour politicians have been conditioned, as much as Conservatives, by the Westminster model. The Westminster model is an element of the British political tradition which sees governing as a process conducted by a closed elite, constrained by an ethos of integrity with concern for the public good (Richards and Smith, 2000) and contained within the framework of a balanced and self-adjusting constitution (Tant, 1993). Within the model, Parliament is theoretically sovereign, but as a result of parties, and bureaucracy, the reality is executive or cabinet sovereignty. A corollary of this model is the notion of ministerial responsibility, whereby it is ministers who make decisions and are at the head of hierarchical departments and accountable to Parliament. Thus, the primary source of legitimacy in Britain is Parliament (see Judge, 1993). MPs are representatives and not delegates and therefore act in what they see as the public good. Furthermore, the public in general, do not have the necessary information available to make informed decisions. Therefore, secrecy is regarded by the political elite as the best means of ensuring that the right decisions are made in the interests of the people.

Underpinning this position is the fact that any significant shift towards greater openness increases the opportunities available to the media, the opposition parties and interest groups to attack the government. Clearly, this is a reflection of the adversarial nature of the British political system. Yet publicly, secrecy has to be justified and assurances made that a closed system does not lead to corruption. So, the political elite contend that they are imbued with a public service ethos and thus serve the general, not their own, interest (see M. J. Smith, 1999; Richards and Smith, 2000). The relationship between ministers and civil servants is one of interdependence with ministers providing authority and officials expertise (see, for example, Fowler, 1991, 112).

It is therefore significant that in the 1997 election campaign, the Labour Party broke with its tradition and promised a wide array of constitutional reforms. Within days of electoral victory, the Bank of England was made independent and the first parliamentary session produced 12 constitutional acts (see Hazell and Cornes, 1999). One of the defining features of the present Labour government is its far-reaching programme of constitutional reform, marking a significant break from both its Conservative and Labour predecessors. Yet, to understand the implications of this reform programme, it is first necessary to appreciate Labour's relationship with the Westminster system of government and the way that this has affected the reform process. We will argue that Labour sees constitutional reform as being grafted on to the existing system and not changing it. We begin by examining the state which the Conservatives bequeathed Labour in April 1997.

Labour's Inheritance and Its Response

The state which Labour inherited is one that has undergone a fundamental transformation yet has remained, at least rhetorically, wedded to a set of constitutional arrangements which have changed only marginally in the last 50 years. Under the Conservatives, the make-up of the state dramatically changed (see Figure 8.1), as they siphoned-off a whole range of functions upwards to a supra-national level mainly the EU, downwards in the form of agencies, regulatory bodies, quangos and Training and Enterprise Councils (TECs) and outwards, most particularly, in the form of privatization and market-testing.

Paradoxically, eighteen years of Conservatism exposed as a myth the flexible nature of the British constitution: the constitution remained static, while the state had been transformed. Nevertheless, the present Labour government believes that the constitution only requires a degree of adaptation, not wholesale reformation:

> The challenge facing us is that which confronted the Victorian reformers of the last century who, almost uniquely, gave Britain democracy without revolution.

FIGURE 8.1   *The reconstituted state under the Conservatives*

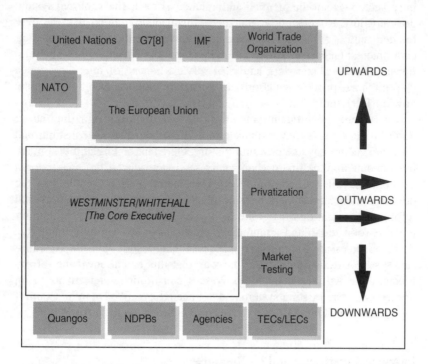

It is to take a *working constitution, respect its strengths*, and adapt it to modern demands for clean and effective government while at the same time providing a greater democratic role for the people at large. [emphasis added] (Tony Blair, in *The Economist*, 14 September 1996)

In the next section, each of Labour's proposals will be examined in order to provide the backdrop from which to demonstrate Labour's failure to understand the organic nature of the constitution. As Riddell (1998, 106) observes:

Many of these proposals tend to be viewed in isolation, with little attempt to relate them to their implications for the position of Parliament – and, in particular, of the Commons – but, in practice, many would have a much wider impact.

Reforming the Core Executive

Labour's reform programme is replete with contradictions. It expects to reform the constitution without undermining its key features; parliamentary sovereignty, traditional notions of responsibility and the neutrality of the civil service. It wishes to decentralize and disaggregate power whilst retaining, or increasing, central control.

Whilst advocating greater devolution of power, Tony Blair has maintained that: 'People have to know that we will run from the centre and govern from the centre'. This statement was made in light of concerns over the tendency of the Party to fragment, the institutional divisions within the central state, and the risk of changing patterns of governance fragmenting further the central state (see Kooiman, 1993; Rhodes, 1997).

These three factors led the Blair leadership team to conclude that the government would have to strengthen the coordinating abilities of the core. The new government was aware of a lack of any institutionalized co-ordinating body *solely* responsible for safeguarding and enforcing broad government strategy and preventing a slide into departmentalism. The Blair government's programme for reforming the machinery of government was based on the notion of moving towards 'joined-up government'. In particular, there was much anxiety over whether the organizational structures and the existing operational style of the core executive were capable of delivering a co-ordinated policy programme.

The most effective antithesis to departmentalism is a strong, coordinating agency located at the centre of the core executive. The problems of the British core executive has always been that it is institutionally strong in departments but institutionally weak at the centre. In particular, conflict arises between three co-ordinating centres: the Cabinet Office, the Prime Minister's Office and the Treasury.

Ironically, the government's first action was to augment the process of fragmentation by making the Bank of England independent and establishing the new Monetary Policy Committee conferred with the power to determine the base lending rate. More generally, Labour accepted the majority of the reforms which the Conservatives had introduced during the previous 18 years. In particular, Labour rejected the option of bringing functions back into the public sector which had been privatized under the Conservatives. As Blair (1998d) contended:

> Big government is dead. The days of tax and spend are gone. Much of the deregulation and privatisation that took place in the 1980s was necessary. But everything cannot be left to the market. We believe there is a role for active government.

Despite Labour's acceptance of the state it had inherited, it soon became clear that the new government would make central control and coordination of both policy and presentation the cornerstone of its programme of reform for central government. If 'departmentalism' was the disease festering at the heart of British central government, then Labour's antidote was 'joined-up government'. In order to affect this, Labour adopted the twin strategy of centralization and the establishment of *ad hoc* policy reviews,

i) Centralization

The first twelve months of the new government saw the centre strengthened through: the creation of the Strategic Communications Unit with a staff of six whose remit was to harmonize public relations initiatives of Cabinet Ministers (see Chapter 7); an expanded Prime Minister's Policy Unit; a new Social Exclusion Unit whose function is to examine deprivation across all tiers of society; and the appointment of a minister without portfolio whose role is to assure coordination in government policy. Indeed, this role was handed to Peter Mandelson, but he soon came into conflict with a number of other high-profile Labour ministers who also saw their formal position as being responsible for cross-departmental coordination. In particular, Lord Irvine the new Lord Chancellor, regarded part of his role as being, formally, to coordinate the machinery of government and, informally, to act as chief adviser to the Prime Minister. There were clearly tensions arising over the creation of these particular power bases at the centre of the Labour government. During the 1998 summer reshuffle, Mandelson was moved to the DTI and his previous role was merged with that of the Chancellor of the Duchy of Lancaster (following the sacking of David Clark) to create the new post of Minister for the Cabinet. Jack Cunningham was given this new portfolio which included: overall responsibility for the work of the Cabinet Office, including the Modernizing Government agenda (see below); providing strategic direction to the Cabinet Office's function for coordination; and Minister for the Civil Service. He was subsequently replaced by Mo Mowlem.

Also in 1998, the Cabinet Office was strengthened by the addition of a number of new units that were primarily a response to the (internally published) 'Wilson Report'. Most important, was the creation of the Performance and Innovation Unit which, crucially, reports directly to Number 10 and hence commands Prime Ministerial support. The aim of the Unit is to improve the effectiveness of government policies, their implementation and service delivery mechanisms by working with departments on cross-cutting and innovative projects. The key functions of the new unit are to evaluate the performance of existing policies, while at the same time providing innovative thinking in policy areas which have traditionally been locked-in by the strength of the departmental view.

There has also been the creation of a new Centre for Management and Policy Studies incorporating the existing Civil Service College with the aim of introducing more outside influence on policy thinking. Finally, the Management Board for the Civil Service has been established in order to emphasize and harmonize the corporate objectives of government as a whole. Whereas, during the Conservative years, reform was targeted almost solely at introducing and improving managerialism and economy in government, the present raft of reforms emphasize the need to improve on policymaking, in particular, policymaking which cuts across the old departmental boundaries (see Bichard, 1999). As the present Cabinet Secretary, Richard Wilson (1998) observed:

> I do worry that the management reforms of the last decade may have focused our energies very much on particular objectives, particular targets, performance indicators in return for resources and delegations. And that we have in some measure taken our eye off what we used to be good at – and still can do – which is working more corporately across the boundaries. And it may be … that personnel reforms that we have introduced have also given people a sense that they work more for Departments rather than for the wider civil service.

Under Tony Blair, the importance of the Prime Minister's Office continues to grow because Blair sees himself as having a continued role in the development of policy (see Kavanagh and Seldon, 1999). This is indicated by Blair's attempt to replace the official appointment of principal private secretary with a political appointment as chief of staff. In the end, the official civil service post was retained with Jonathan Powell being given an explicitly separate political post. For Blair, political appointees and a strengthened policy unit are crucial elements in imposing coordination on government. The number of political appointees has nearly doubled and there are clear lines of communication between political appointees in Number 10 and the departments (*The Guardian*, 3 June 1997).

Finally, in relation to centralization, one of the key tools available to the machinery of government to facilitate communication and coordination is IT. In particular, one of the aims of joined-up government is to introduce an intranet system compatible across all government departments, smart cards and call centres.

ii) Ad Hoc Committees

The second element of Labour's strategy for joined-up-government has been the establishment of *ad hoc* policy reviews. Indeed, during the government's first 12 months, 192 policy reviews, taskforces and a Royal Commission were set up (see Platt, 1998b). The most important element of this strategy has been the creation of 'taskforces' that cut across the traditional policy arenas established by Whitehall to address 'wicked issues' which have no single, departmental home. As Daniel (1997, 27) observes:

> Unlike the Royal Commissions and reviews of previous governments, the task forces are not intended to sweep issues under the carpet. They are emblems of Labour's desire to be seen to be implementing manifesto pledges briskly and in a spirit of trust.

TABLE 8.1   *Task forces set up by Labour government, 1997*

Task force	Chair	Task force	Chair
Youth justice	Norman Warner	Export forum	Torm Harris
Welfare to work	Sir Peter Davis	Special educational needs group	Estelle Morris
School standards	David Blunkett	Advisory group on continuing education	Bob Fryer
Literacy	Michael Barber	Review of the CPS	Iain Glidewell
Numeracy	David Reynolds	Review of film policy	Tom Clarke and Stewart Till
Creative industries	NA	Review of pensions	Tom Ross
Tax and benefits	Martin Taylor	Review of health ineqalities	Donald Acheson
Private finance	Adrian Montague	Review of London health service	Leslie Turnberg
NHS efficiency	Alan Milburn	Review of surrogacy law	Margaret Brazier
Better regulation	Chris Haskins	Civil litigation and legal aid plans review	Peter Middelton
Football	David Mellor	Working group on teacher bureaucracy	Peter Owen
Advisory group on competitiveness	Margaret Beckett		

Source: Daniel, 1997.

The taskforces themselves do not simply consist of ministers and civil servants, but draw on an array of people from the private and public sector, trade unions, as well as opposition MPs. Some of the more high profile taskforces have been on youth justice, school standards, NHS efficiency, welfare-to-work and football (see Table 8.1).

Yet the taskforces themselves are symbolic of Labour's broader problem in their programme for reforming the machinery of government: by attempting to strengthen the centre, Labour has recast the old problem of competing power centres based on strong departments but at a different level and in a different guise. As the new government has attempted to improve coordination at the centre of the core executive, it has established a number of competing centres of power. Indeed, paradoxically, the unforeseen and unintended consequence has been to create confusion over where power at the centre resides. The different central bodies themselves have become locked into a struggle for ascendancy. This has left those in the traditional, government departments, unsure over which power centre to engage with, in order to secure their own departmental goals. It would, at least potentially, appear that Labour may have recreated the problem of ineffectual, central co-ordination, rather than overcome it. Further, the style they have adopted could, at a future point, lead to fundamental splits within the present Cabinet and, more broadly, policy drift in Whitehall, as the traditional networks for securing policy success have become blurred. In 1998, Sir Richard Wilson, the new Cabinet Secretary, examined the processes of coordination in Whitehall and suggested that there needed to be greater cross-department co-ordination and increased strategic capacity. But as Hazell and Morris (1999, 152) highlight: 'there was no mention of the impact of constitutional change; and no awareness that there may need to be more radical reconfiguration at the centre as it adjusts to its new role at the centre of a quasi-federal, more rights-based, more transparent system of government'.

Labour appears to have continued the Thatcherite tradition of by-passing the Cabinet system and Blair does not regard the Cabinet as an: 'effective decision-making forum. Only on a few occasions has Blair allowed sufficient time for Cabinet to be discursive... he tries to focus on strategic issues' (see Kavanagh and Seldon, 1999, 408). His preference is to work through bilateral meetings with Cabinet colleagues. Likewise, despite the existence of Cabinet Committees, they are much under-utilized. This leads Hennessy (1998, 3–4) to suggest that the Blair government has abandoned Cabinet government replacing it with a '"Napoleonic" style of government'. Here, the implication is that strategies are centrally prepared and then imposed on departments, which are regarded as units whose function is one of implementation. Furthermore, instead of Cabinet, Labour seems to be relying on taskforces to deal with interdepartmental issues/problems and this raises a number of constitutional issues. The key difference with Cabinet committees is that these bodies have been set up to deal with specific issues and they include a large number of outsiders (Daniel, 1997). Interestingly, of the 23 taskforces only 4 are chaired by ministers. These bodies indicate a more pluralistic approach to policymaking and less reliance on civil servants for advice. For traditional mandarins, like the former Cabinet Secretary, Sir Robin Butler, the use of so many outsiders is potentially leading to poor advice, policy errors and lack of accountability (*The Guardian*, 5 January 1998). Indeed, the absence of ministers does raise the question of the weight the final reports will carry within government. Unlike Cabinet committees, their decisions will not carry Cabinet authority and may lack the necessary departmental support to be implemented.

Although the Cabinet Office has certainly had its profile raised and power extended under Labour, the role of the Treasury remains crucial. One of Labour's key concerns has been to present itself as the government of financial prudence. In the first two years, the government was committed to remaining within Conservative spending plans. This has given the Treasury considerable influence over policy developments. It also ensured departments conducted spending reviews 'to determine how best their programmes can contribute to the achievement of the government's objectives, The Treasury used the reviews to release finance for priorities in health, welfare and education. As a consequence the Treasury has had a direct impact on policy development.

The Labour government has attempted to address the fundamental problem of coordination which exists within British central government but, in a contradictory style, they have further fragmented the state with the creation of new institutions. However, these changes have been made without any reference to wider constitutional changes. The state and the constitution are perceived as mutually exclusive entities, thus limiting the radicalness of constitutional change. So, change in the constitution is not regarded as directly affecting the way the nation is governed. The Blair government is sustaining the principles of parliamentary sovereignty, secrecy and elitism that underpin the core executive. Yet, the problem for the government is that the programme of constitutional reform is not consistent with these principles. For example, the key tenet underpinning the process of reform is increased pluralism, achieved by devolving power away from the centre. In practice, this is a principle that directly opposes elitism and parliamentary sovereignty.

Finally, it is worth pointing out that the dynamic driving Labour's reform programme is the need to install greater checks and balances on the power of the executive. This has nothing to do with ideology or notions of equality, but is opportunistic, a reaction to the 1980s and 1990s and Labour's drawn-out experience in opposition. Comparisons can be drawn with the Liberal Party in the first quarter of the twentieth century which embraced ideas of constitutional reform, once its electoral fortunes had gone into permanent decline and the existing system no longer worked in its favour. Similarly, in the 1990s, the modernization project of the Labour Party came round to adopting a number of elements of constitutional reform as a reaction to the manner and extent to which the Conservative governments had used the state apparatus during the 1980s. The rest of the chapter will highlight the tensions which may develop between Labour's notion of the state and the aims of the constitutional reform programme. The problem is that the programme of constitutional reform will produce direct challenges to the various elements that collectively make up the Westminster model, which Labour claims will be strengthened, not further damaged.

Devolution

Britain is a unitary, though not necessarily uniform, state (see Bogdanor, 1997, 15). In response to regional demands and concern over democracy, Labour was committed to devolve greater power to Scotland, Wales, Northern Ireland and to England through the establishment of new English regional assemblies. Indeed, their commitment to such a policy is arguably one of the most radical elements in their agenda for reforming the state. However, Labour's approach, in particular to Scotland and Wales, has been based on political pragmatism. Their commitments have been framed in the context of devolving greater power to the territories, in order, paradoxically, to strengthen and reinvigorate the unitary character of the state, not as a transitory stage on the path to complete separation or federalism. The key dynamic underpinning this stance has been Labour's reluctance to risk the strong, electoral position it spent 18 years striving for.

Three principal problems arise in relation to devolution. First, devolution is a threat to parliamentary sovereignty. Second, there is not one but at least four forms of devolution proposed and third, the consequences may be greater fragmentation and conflict within the British State.

Parliamentary Sovereignty

The government's argument is that devolution neither threatens parliamentary sovereignty nor undermines the integrity of the United Kingdom. For 'Sovereignty rests with Westminster because we are proposing devolution – local services to be run here by the people of Scotland. It's not separation' (cited in Riddell, 1998, 105).

However, in the case of Scotland, the central tenets of the reform package have been to establish a Scottish Parliament, based in Edinburgh, with powers to make law, provide limited scope for raising taxes and to represent Scotland in the European Union. The White Paper, *Scotland's Parliament*, proposed that

> The Scottish Parliament will have law-making powers over a wide range of matters which affect Scotland. There will be a Scottish Executive headed by a First Minister which will operate in a way similar to the UK Government and will be held to account by the Scottish Parliament. The Scottish Parliament and Executive will be responsible for: health, education and training, local government, social work and housing, economic development and transport, the law and home affairs, the environment, agriculture, fisheries and forestry, sports and art, research and statistics in relation to devolved matters.

There has also been a conscious attempt to reject the Westminster ways. For example, proportional representation, more sociable working hours and the use of electronic voting methods were embraced.

The Scottish Parliament consists of 129 members, of which 73 were directly elected on a constituency basis, with the remaining 56 members elected by the Additional Member System. The Parliament will have the power to increase or decrease the basic rate of income tax set by the United Kingdom Parliament by up to three pence.

However, in conceding the above range of powers to a Scottish Parliament, the Labour government made clear that the UK Parliament would remain sovereign. In particular, Westminster would retain powers over issues concerning: UK defence and national security; UK foreign policy including relations with Europe; the UK constitution; the stability of the UK's fiscal, economic and monetary system; common markets for UK goods and services; employment legislation; social security; and over most aspects of transport safety and regulation. Despite this reassertion of the sovereignty of the UK Parliament, it is increasingly clear that divergence exists over the interpretation of the nature of sovereignty between the Labour Cabinet and the views emanating from the Scottish Constitutional Convention. The 'Claim of Right' adopted at the inaugural meeting of the Scottish Constitutional Convention on the 30 March 1989 stated:

> We gathered at the Scottish Constitutional Convention do hereby acknowledge the sovereign right of the Scottish people to determine the form of Government best suited to their needs, and do hereby declare and pledge that in all our deliberations their interests shall be paramount. (cited in Riddell, 1998, 105)

It is questionable whether notions of tax-raising powers and representation in the EU are compatible with notions of sovereignty. The fact that MPs are pressurizing the government to prevent Scottish MPs from voting on English matters indicates that the unified sovereignty of Parliament is already being undermined. The *de facto* sovereignty of Parliament could be further threatened if proportional voting increases nationalist representation and breaks the links of dependence that would be maintained through a Labour Scottish Assembly. The rejection of the Westminster model may produce a less executive-centred, more open and responsive assembly unbound by the Westminster traditions and consequently less elitist. Moreover, the assembly may have greater legitimacy than Westminster, thus effectively restraining central government from ever reducing the powers of the Scottish Parliament.

The principles of parliamentary sovereignty are further undermined by the form of devolution in Northern Ireland. The Northern Ireland Assembly is made up of 108 members, elected by a single transfer vote based on the existing Westminster constituencies in Northern Ireland. More importantly, the Assembly operates where appropriate on a cross-community basis and is the prime source of authority in respect of all *devolved* responsibilities. The Assembly has authority to pass primary legislation for Northern Ireland subject to a number of checks including the European Court of Human Rights and the Westminster Parliament which continues to legislate on *non-devolved* issues. Furthermore, a North/South Ministerial Council has been established to bring those with executive responsibilities together in Northern Ireland and the Republic to develop consultation, cooperation and action on matters of mutual interest. Finally, a British–Irish Council has been established under a new British–Irish Agreement in order to promote the 'harmonious and mutually beneficial development of relationships between the North, South and the mainland'. Thus, this agreement brings in non-Westminster elements into the policy process and further questions the notion of territorial sovereignty within the United Kingdom.

Different Models of Devolution

There is no single model of devolution but effectively four types, one for each nation of the United Kingdom. As we have seen, Scotland and Northern Ireland will have considerable autonomy, whilst in Wales and the English regions policy competence will be much less. While Scotland will experience a real and discernible transfer of power from Westminster to Edinburgh, the same cannot be said for Wales. Labour's proposals, set out in the July 1997 White Paper, *A Voice for Wales*, aimed to revitalize Welsh participation in the political process and reinvigorate faith in the UK political system. However, it offered only executive, not legislative, devolution of power to the Principality. Unlike Scotland, the Welsh Assembly is not to be conferred with either power to raise taxes or primary legislative powers. Instead, the Assembly constitutes 'executive devolution'. It consists of 60 members also elected by the Additional Member System and its responsibilities will include: health; education; industry and training; agriculture; environment; roads; planning; arts and heritage. More particularly, the Secretary of State continues to represent Wales in the Cabinet, providing a formal link between the Assembly and Westminster.

Unlike Scotland, the establishment of a Welsh Assembly should not create the same degree of tension surrounding issues of sovereignty, nor is it as likely to provide a staging post on the path towards full separation. However, the danger Hazell and O'Leary (1999) identify is leap-frogging, whereby a Welsh Assembly sees a successful Scottish system and consequently demands more powers. This may increase tensions with Westminster and lead to greater autonomy for Wales.

Labour is contemplating some form of regional governance for England. The 1997 Labour Manifesto embraced many of the proposals stemming from the 1995 Labour consultation paper, *A Choice for England*. In particular, it advocated the creation of regional chambers based on ten Integrated Regional Offices with co-ordinating functions over a range of policy areas. Furthermore, the manifesto proposed that, depending on the outcome of regionally held referenda, directly elected regional assemblies could be created. Again, as in the case of Wales, these assemblies would lack tax-raising or legislative powers, but apart from providing a strong coordinating role, would perform a vital function in making sub-central government more accountable. However, the momentum behind regional devolution seems to be declining, with little progress in this area. Only in London with the creation of an authority and executive mayor has there been any devolution within England, although there is some suggestion that executive mayors will be extended to other cities.

Constitutionally and practically, it may not seem a problem that the constituent parts of the UK have different forms of devolution, but two issues arise. First, these developments undermine the notion that Britain is a unitary state because not all people are being governed in the same way. Second, if devolution is popular in Scotland and Northern Ireland pressures may develop for similar forms of government in Wales and the English regions. Such developments, and the pressures they may cause for greater independence, will further undermine the Westminster model as a value system for legitimizing government. We have already seen the issue of student loans being affected by developments in Scotland.

Fragmentation and Conflict

The notion of a unitary state is difficult to maintain when a range of forms of governance are operating within various parts of the UK. This problem will prove even greater if conflicts develop between the core executive and the regions. A crucial point made by Hazell and O'Leary (1999) is that devolution is not an end point, but a process of continual negotiation and development: 'Devolution may never reach a stable equilibrium'. Relationships will vary according to circumstance, political control and the tactics of the various parties.

The government also maintains that devolution is not a threat to a unified civil service (Hazell and Morris, 1999, 138). However, it is likely that over time varied traditions and cultures will develop in each of the regions which, in effect, may produce a range of types of official. The desire for the newly devolved bodies not to operate within the confines of the Westminster model implies that civil servants are likely to work within different rules of the game and therefore political/official relationships will vary from the Whitehall model norm. Hazell and Morris suggest (1999, 138) that: 'There will be pressure from the Scottish Parliament and Welsh assembly to have their own civil service, like the Northern Ireland Civil Service'.

Devolution may result in new structures of dependency within the British system of government. Whilst, currently, the most important relationships within the core executive are between the Prime Minister and departments, the Treasury and departments, and ministers and officials (M. J. Smith, 1999), devolution will establish important new relationships between the centre and the regions. For certain policies, the Prime Minister and departments will be dependent on devolved bodies for delivering policies and important process of exchange will occur over issues such as finance and legitimacy. This may create an important constraint on the activities of the centre, especially if regional governments are controlled by nationalists or coalitions. These new structures of dependency are likely to make greater coordination and joined-up government difficult to achieve because the government will not have direct control over the devolved bodies. The impact of these new dependency networks have already been made apparent in the area of agriculture. The Welsh and Scottish bodies have levered extra assistance to all farmers and in return the UK agricultural secretary has had to put pressure on his Welsh and Scottish counterparts to lift the ban on beef on the bone.

However, it is important not to overstate the impact of devolution. Mitchell (1999, 608) points out that it is possible to classify Britain as a union, rather than unitary state where 'integration is less than perfect and that pre-union rights and institutional infrastructure preserving some degree of autonomy and serving as agencies of indigenous elite recruitment are preserved'. In other words, a strong degree of autonomy has always existed, especially in Scotland, and devolution is about changing the form of legitimation rather than governance. In addition, the choices that the Scottish parliament makes will be greatly constrained, particularly by financial imperatives. Finally, the fact that all EU negotiations have to be conducted through UK representatives reinforces the position of national sovereignty.

Electoral Reform

The Labour government has also embarked on a process of electoral reform which it hopes will modernize and revitalize Britain's democratic tradition. For example, in the case of Scotland and Wales, the alternative member system has been introduced. At least half of the members are elected locally by first-past-the-post (FPP) procedures, while the remainder are allocated proportionally at regional level with electors having two votes. In the European elections in June 1999, the Regional List System was used, whereby electors voted for a particular party and seats were then allocated proportionally from a closed list of party candidates. In the case of the direct election for a mayor of London, a variant on the alternative vote system will be used. Here, voters will be able to rank their preference between first and second choice and votes are then redistributed until one candidate has 50 per cent or more of the votes cast. In the case of the London Assembly, electors will vote for a first-past-the-post candidate based on the 14 area members, while the remaining 11 London-wide members will be allocated proportionately on a party basis.

The other main initiative Labour has instigated in relation to electoral reform has been based on Westminster itself. In December 1997, a cross-party electoral reform committee was established, chaired by the Liberal Democratic peer Lord Jenkins, to recommend an alternative, broadly proportional system to the existing first-past-the-post system based on four criteria: stable government, an extension of voter choice, the maintenance of the constituency link and broad proportionality. The *Report of the Independent Commission on the Voting System* recommended the 'Alternative Vote Plus' system. This is a mixed system containing two features; a constituency element and a list top-up. Electors will have two votes – one for an MP based in 500 constituencies and the other from the party of their choice (open list) creating between 98 and 132 MPs drawn from 80 top-up areas across the country. Following the Report's publication, the government did not formally commit itself either way to its findings. However, there were an immediate number of dissenting voices – most notably Jack Straw and John Prescott. It has been suggested that a UK referendum will be held after the next General Election.

There are a number of problems for Labour in relation to electoral reform. In one sense, it has conceded the principle that first-past-the-post is not a legitimate electoral system by abandoning it for all but central and local elections. At the same time, the national party is still ambiguous on the issue. It is torn between the desire to have a majority, in order to implement the New Labour project, and at the same time seeing PR as a way of realigning the party system to ensure that Labour remains in office for a long period. Furthermore, it faces the problem that PR in devolved assemblies and possibly the House of Lords will give these institutions greater legitimacy than the Commons elected on FPP. This, potentially, may reduce the power of the executive or force a shift to PR.

Such a sequence of events has the potential to impact seriously on the Westminster model. If there is electoral reform for the Commons and coalition government becomes the norm, key elements of the Westminster system will change. First, collective responsibility may be harder to maintain with multi-party government. Conflicts within the government could become party-based, as well as departmentally. This would alter the nature of dependency within the core executive. A by-product may be greater openness as parties leak, in order to achieve their own goals. The power of the executive may be more difficult to maintain. Policy could depend on compromise between coalition partners, rather than direction and this may produce a role for backbenchers and parties in negotiating agreements in order to pass legislation. It will increase the opportunity for Parliament to win concessions from government. Third, when parties are offered ministerial portfolios as part of a coalition deal, it will increase the autonomy of the minister. If the Liberal leader is made foreign secretary in return for supporting Labour, the Prime Minister cannot sack him or her without the possibility of bringing down the government. Consequently, PR will change the relationship between ministers and the Prime Minister. Finally, different party and department agendas within government will again fragment the policy process and create new problems of coordination.

House of Lords

Labour's commitment to reform the House of Lords has been a two-stage process. There was considerable controversy surrounding the first stage which saw the dismissal of both the Conservative and Labour leaders in the Lords and the House itself adopting a discernibly entrenched position in relation to the lower chamber. However, Labour has pushed on with the first stage of its strategy and removed all but 92 hereditary peers. At the same time, a Royal Commission was appointed under the guidance of the Conservative Peer, Lord Wakeham, to look at suitable alternatives to the present arrangements. The 12-member Commission report supported three options with a mostly appointed second chamber with a modest, indirectly elected element being preferred. This would not be problematic for Labour, who, though committed to removing what they perceive as the antiquated, unjust hereditary element to the Lords, do not wish to see a newly constituted Upper Chamber with real power and democratic legitimacy capable of challenging the Lower House.

Human Rights

Human rights is also having an impact on the constitutional settlement Labour inherited. In October 1998, the Labour government received Royal

Assent for its Human Rights Bill, which incorporates a version of the European Convention on Human Rights into United Kingdom Law (although this will not come into effect until October 2 2000). This will enable UK citizens to appeal to any level of UK courts on the grounds of a breach of the convention. However, the Bill has been specifically designed by the Labour government, in order that, it does not breach the principle of absolute parliamentary sovereignty, while at the same time strengthening the European Convention's guarantee of effective redress to citizens whose freedoms and rights have been infringed. However, it is clear that, despite the bowdlerized version of the Bill which Labour has introduced, it will still have a substantial impact on the rights and freedoms of UK citizens.

Throughout the passage of the Bill, the Home Office Minister, Lord Williams, strongly defended it, arguing that it would in no way impinge upon the concept of parliamentary sovereignty by devolving power and responsibility to the judiciary. However, despite the guarantees of protecting the freedoms and rights for the individual citizen, Lord Williams's pledge to the sanctity of parliamentary sovereignty appears less than certain. For example, on 27 January 1999, Jack Straw signed the 6th Protocol of the European Convention of Human Rights, part of which abolishes the death penalty in the United Kingdom. The implications for Parliament will be that future governments will not be in a position to reopen the debate on the death penalty without first overturning the entire European Convention on Human Rights. Therefore, although there has been much rhetoric from the Labour Cabinet that parliamentary sovereignty has in no way being impacted upon by signing up to the Convention, the reality is that clear and discernible structural constraints have now been placed upon Parliament.

Freedom of Information

As with Human Rights, the Labour government's proposals to introduce Freedom of Information legislation will also have serious constitutional implications. The first stage in introducing a Freedom of Information Act occurred in December 1997, when the government published the White Paper, *Your Right to Know*. Constitutionally, the key area of any legislation concerning freedom of information centres on reconciling ministerial accountability with a statutory right of information. Following the publication of *Your Right to Know* it was clear that the government's priorities lay in protecting the convention of ministerial responsibility. The key elements of the White Paper are: individuals would have a legal right to see almost *all* information; an Independent Commissioner would be appointed to police the Act and handle appeals; the law would be applied right across the public sector; and it would be user-friendly to protect sensitive information. The seven categories which come under protection are; national security, defence etc., *the internal discussion of government policy*, law enforcement, personal privacy, business activities which could unfairly damage a company's commercial standing, the safety of individuals, the public and the environment; and references, testimonials etc. However, following the White Paper, the Minister responsible, David Clarke, was sacked and the development of the Bill was passed to the more constitutionally conservative Home Office.

The Bill drawn up by Jack Straw and the Home Office was the subject of widespread criticism and was seen as a retreat from the radical proposals of the White Paper. The principal and crucial change is that under the White Paper the 'guiding principle was that disclosure should be the norm' unless the authority in question could prove 'substantial harm' to the public interest. In the Bill, the government interest just has to be prejudiced which as Hugo Young points out is 'virtually impossible to challenge' (Young, 1999). In addition, the commissioner who can decide on 'substantial harm' is no longer independent. The government can use a parliamentary order to exempt any information. According to Young (1999):

> This bill is a triumph for the forces of reaction in Whitehall, a reward for the patience of mandarins. They opposed it from the start. They knew it would take time for ministers to lose their idealism, and arranged with Straw's connivance, for time to pass.

Crucially, the Bill excludes any documents relating to policy advice from the act. This raises two problems. First, policy advice can be used to cover much of the information that is passed through Whitehall. Second, it is only through revealing the advice of ministers that the processes of policymaking can be really opened up. Without this change the policy process will continue as closed and elitist and officials will not be held to account for poor or misguided advice. Indeed, it is only by opening up this procedure that citizens could really become involved in policymaking and that the nature of advice given to ministers could be improved.

Effective open government would ultimately destroy the Westminster model. It would end the closed, elitist value system that had underpinned the British system of government. Openness would create external supervision but more importantly expose the myth of ministerial and collective responsibility. It would reveal, as the Scott Report did, that officials make a whole range of decisions often without ministerial support. In addition, it would open up official advice to scrutiny and accountability and allow outside groups to challenge the assumptions of official advice, thus allowing for more pluralistic and inclusive policymaking. For these reasons the government does not intend to have open government. Freedom of Information will not include advice to ministers even though such a change is necessary to make the core executive democratic and open. Much of what will be revealed under the FOI Act is already available under the Conservative government's changes. As Hazell and Morris (1999, 147) confirm:

> At the policy level little will change. Departments will be required to publish all their internal manuals and staff instructions; but this requirement has already existed for five years under the Open Government Code of Practice ... Few if any policy papers will be released until after decisions have been made. Overseas experience suggests that will not be related to increased public participation in policy making ... To sum up, most FOI requests will be relatively low level; and FOI will not be the great reforming panacea which its proponents sometimes propose.

Conclusion: Labour and the Unravelling of the Constitution

During 18 years of Conservative government, the British State underwent a programme of almost continuous transformation (see Figure 8.1). Where some commentators would have expected a period of consolidation under Labour, instead, the government has pursued a programme of reform which will again fundamentally redraw the contours of the state (see Figure 8.2).

Labour's policies on the constitution and the state fully reveal the dilemmas of New Labour. On the one hand, it is extremely radical and is new in the sense that it owes very little either to old Labour or Thatcherism. On the other, it is bound by tradition and pragmatism. Labour has grappled with many features of the constitution – devolution, electoral reform and the House of Lords, but without recognizing the ways in which the core executive and the Westminster model are fundamentally linked to the reform process. Thus, many features of the constitution are being changed without any real consideration being given to its foundations. This is a fundamental problem because the changes that Labour are introducing have profound implications for the Westminster model which the government has failed properly to consider. It is difficult to have devolution, a Human Rights Bill, and an independent Bank of England and maintain notions of sovereignty. The fragmentation of the policy process and proportional voting will threaten executive sovereignty and further reveal the tenuous nature of

FIGURE 8.2 *The reconstituted state under Labour*

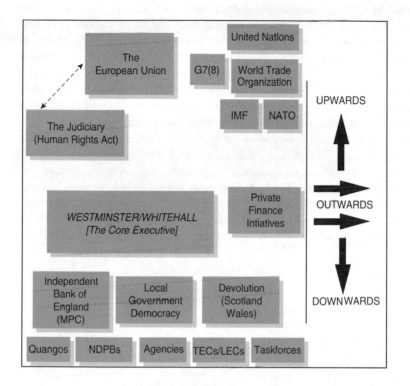

ministerial responsibility. The greater use of referendums, will lead to questions concerning the centrality of parliament. This reveals the contradictions of the reform programme. Finally, while notions of ministerial and collective responsibility are continually used to mystify how decisions are really made, the system will remain difficult to democratize. So, under Labour, the framework of the Whitehall model remains, whilst key elements of the model are undermined. For example, the disaggregation of the decision-making process could make greater co-ordination and joined-up government much harder to attain. This leads us to suggest that, despite the malleable nature of the British constitution, under Labour, its point of elasticity may be surpassed and the façade of the Westminster model left openly exposed.

Finally, if one adopts a holistic view of Labour's programme of reform, the degree to which, since 1997, political power has conditioned their actions soon becomes apparent. As we have seen, Labour does have a state-led project to modernize British society and the polity. It is a project conditioned by pluralistic sentiments aimed at devolving power away from the centre, in particular, as a safeguard against any future Conservative government using the state in the same way as occurred in the 1980s. However, the reality of implementing this project has not necessarily proved compatible with the dispersal of power. Since Labour was elected, it has not displayed wholesale willingness to relinquish power in the way it promised prior to April 1997. Changes such as devolution, freedom of information and electoral reform have evolved within the context of maintaining the executive power which was so useful to the Thatcherite project. This creates an almost impossible task: New Labour is trying to reform the constitution and the state without surrendering the powers of the state. Consequently, reform will be deformed or limited or it will produce outcomes unintended and, possibly, more far-reaching than the government expected. Moreover, in office, Labour have appeared willing to trust the nations (through the devolution of power to the periphery) while still not trusting its own Party.

9

Labour's New Economics

ANDREW GAMBLE AND GAVIN KELLY

New Labour is widely perceived as having broken with traditional Labour party policy on the economy. Some critics have complained that the break is so complete that Labour's economic policy is now little different from the policies pursued by the Conservatives between 1979 and 1997, and that Labour has accepted and consolidated the neo-liberal economic policy regime on the economy that was established at that time. It has been claimed that Labour's policies in its first year in office represent 'the final triumph of monetarism and the defeat of Keynesian economic policies' (Arestis and Sawyer, 1998, 41). On this reading New Labour has become the agent of a neo-liberal consensus which gives priority to price stability over full employment, and promotes the free movement of goods and capital. In sharp contrast to old Labour its rhetoric is said to be pro-business and anti-union; it advocates reducing taxation, regulation and other forms of direct government involvement in the economy whenever possible as the best means of stimulating growth and enterprise, and recommends concentrating government effort on the supply-side of the economy to make markets more flexible by removing obstacles to competition and improving the skills and employability of the workforce.

New Labour is certainly different from old Labour but the judgement that it is just neo-liberalism under another name is too simple, and also premature. The last years of the first term may turn out very differently from the first, and a second term of office may be different again. It is not easy to decipher the precise character of Labour's economic programme; the evidence is contradictory, and it is often difficult distinguishing between rhetoric and reality. It is after all hardly surprising that the economy still bears a neo-liberal imprint so soon after the downfall of a committed neo-liberal government. All governments have to work with what they inherit, occasionally making major changes, more often negotiating incremental

167

adaptations. It is the type of shifts that have been made and the nature of the compromises that have been struck that need examining.

This chapter argues that New Labour's record in government shows elements of both continuity and discontinuity, both in relation to past Labour theory and practice, as well as in relation to the Conservative economic policy regime. It seeks to identify which aspects have changed and which have remained the same. To do this it will briefly survey the development of Labour party policy since 1945 and earlier modernization episodes under Hugh Gaitskell and Neil Kinnock, before turning to the modernization attempted by New Labour, and the impact which this has had on the course of policy since 1997. In reviewing Labour's economic policy care has to be taken to disentangle economic rhetoric from economic substance, to understand the very different dynamics of policymaking in government and in opposition, and to recognize how the wider context of economic policy has changed.

Labour Party Economic Policy Since 1945

There have been two central tensions in Labour's economic policy. First, as the political arm of the trade unions, the party sought to defend and advance the labour interest within a capitalist economy, but as an electoral machine it also needed a social democratic programme for governing in the wider public interest. Over time the latter has come to overshadow the former; under New Labour it has eclipsed it altogether. Governing the economy in the labour interest meant above all sustaining voluntarism in industrial relations; protecting the independence of unions both from employers and from the state by preserving and strengthening their ability to bargain collectively and freely. Governing the economy in the public interest meant in practice trying to make capitalism work better. There was a potential conflict between any such national social democratic programme and the defence of the labour interest. When this conflict has flared up, Labour governments have been destroyed or gravely weakened by it, most notably in 1931 and 1979.

A second tension in Labour's economic policy has been between socialist ideological rhetoric, which proclaimed the replacement of capitalism by socialism as the ultimate goal of the movement, and the pragmatism of Labour governments which gave priority to making capitalism run smoothly. The gap between rhetoric and reality has often been considerable. In practice Labour governments have been obliged to secure the cooperation of those who owned and controlled productive assets, but the ideological hostility in the party towards capitalism and markets has remained strong, repeatedly creating uncertainty and mistrust in financial markets about Labour's ability to run the economy competently. New Labour is new in terms of the Labour tradition because of the degree of its detachment from the labour interest and its effort to secure business confidence.

The Attlee Government

The programme of the Attlee Government (1945–51) has come to exercise a powerful hold over the Labour imagination, setting a standard against which later Labour policies have been judged. It sought to deliver full employment, economic growth, significant redistribution of income and wealth, and comprehensive social security. The means it chose were public ownership, industrial planning, high progressive taxation on income and capital, and universal welfare programmes. Intervention as a mode of governance was treated as intrinsically superior to markets, and enlargement of the public sector as good in itself. Economic intervention was justified on the ground that, in the public interest, countervailing power had to be exercised by the state to restrain private capital.

National economic management, if it was to work, however, had to serve the interests of capital as well as labour. Labour governments presented themselves as governing in the national interest, as even-handed between labour and capital. The understanding between the political and industrial arms of the Labour movement was that, in return for welfare and full employment policies, unions would accept restrictions on their freedom to press for higher wages. They resisted, however, the kind of incorporation, into economic decision-making at the level either of the firm or of national government, common elsewhere in Europe (King and Wickham-Jones, 1998).

The Attlee government was the main architect in Britain of what became known as the Keynesian welfare state. Keynesian economic doctrines provided justification for an active macro-economic policy aimed at promoting full employment and economic growth, bolstered by universalist welfare programmes, funded from general taxation. As a proportion of GDP, public expenditure (including transfer payments) and taxation had risen to over 60 per cent during the war. It now fell back but remained at over 40 per cent, substantially higher than before 1940 (Peacock and Wiseman, 1961). At this level public spending programmes provided the kind of automatic stabilizers required by Keynesian policy.

Modernization Round 1: Gaitskellism

The Attlee government established an economic policy regime and a set of institutions which the Labour party tried to defend for the next forty years. But changing domestic and international circumstances meant that the party periodically sought to modernize its programme. This process began almost as soon as Labour lost office in 1951. Rising living standards combined with low inflation and full employment during the 1950s and 1960s encouraged Hugh Gaitskell, Tony Crosland and others to argue that the primary goal of social democracy was not wider public ownership but greater economic and social equality. Public ownership was only one means to achieve it and was no longer appropriate. Much more relevant were policies to increase equality of opportunity and redistributing income and wealth. The public sector and the private sector should not be rivals but essential partners for economic success and achieving the social democratic programme (Crosland, 1956).

The Gaitskellites failed to persuade the party to drop its constitutional commitment to public ownership, but the party became less interested in extending state control and more concerned with how the public sector could help 'modernize' the economy in partnership with the private sector. A proactive state would encourage faster growth through indicative planning, stimulating and coordinating public and private sector investment. Prices and incomes policies together with reform of industrial relations became key counter-inflationary instruments.

Failure to achieve modernization targets in the 1960s and 1970s, or to install workable corporatist arrangements, combined with the unravelling of the Bretton Woods system of fixed exchange rates, produced a crisis of the Keynesian policy regime in the 1970s, producing major political alternatives on right and left (Holland, 1975). In the Labour party the discrediting of modernization created space for many variants of the 'alternative economic strategy' (Wickham-Jones, 1996). After 1979 this perspective gained ascendancy. By 1983 the party was committed to withdrawal from the European Community, extending public ownership, boosting public investment, and restoring controls on foreign exchange and trade to promote full employment and redistribution within Britain.

Modernization Round 2: the Policy Review

The election defeats in 1983 and particularly 1987 forced a fundamental rethinking, set out in the 1989 Policy Review (Labour Party, 1989;

Shaw, 1996; Smith and Spear, 1992). The most important changes for party economic policy were the turn away from protectionism, and acceptance that national economic policy had to be conducted within the constraints imposed by the global economy and membership of the European Community. The extent of the shift was apparent when the Conservative government finally put sterling into the Exchange Rate Mechanism (ERM) in 1990: preconditions for entry which Labour had previously insisted on were quietly dropped, and the party supported the decision.

The most significant policy thinking under Kinnock sought a distinctive supply-side policy – a medium-term industrial strategy – aimed at improving long-run economic performance. The party remained pledged to take back into public ownership some, though no longer all, of the industries privatized by the Conservatives, but there were no new nationalization proposals. Similarly, although the Labour leadership still had major disagreements with monetarism and Conservative macro-economic policy, the party no longer supported the high spending, public sector investment programmes aimed at generating full employment which had characterized the alternative economic strategy. The party also gave positive endorsement to markets, and returned to advocating partnership with the private sector, as well as signalling that it would not seek to overturn many elements of the new industrial relations framework (Shaw, 1996).

The Policy Review returned Labour to the pragmatic economic policy which Labour governments had always pursued, substantially narrowing the gap between ideology and policy. But it remained a social democratic strategy of the type Labour had embraced since the 1940s, with substantial commitments to the public sector and progressive taxation, and a continuing belief in the importance of state regulation of markets. Underlying this programme was an analysis of the systemic failures of the British model of capitalism and the identification of specific government remedies, for example proposals for a compulsory training levy (King and Wickham-Jones, 1998). As in the 1960s the social democratic economic model which Labour sought to emulate was drawn from European experience. It became an article of faith that the European social model was superior to the Thatcherite model of capitalism both in terms of economic efficiency and social justice (Eatwell, 1992).

Modernization Round 3: New Labour

After 1994 a new phase of modernization opened under Tony Blair's leadership. Blair and his allies wanted to overcome the gulf between rhetoric and substance in Labour policy, and to affirm the party's identity as a social democratic party rather than a trade union party. 'New Labour' was a rhetorical device to help promote these changes. An important symbolic moment was the decision to change Clause IV of the party constitution, which committed the party to common ownership of the means of production, distribution and exchange – the single most glaring example of the mismatch between the party's ideology and the policy it was prepared to pursue in government.

This success was reinforced by the New Labour concern finally to dispel the idea that Labour in government would promote the labour interest above the business interest. The structural weakness of unions in the 1990s allowed the party leadership to position Labour openly, for the first time, as a pro-market and pro-business party, endorsing most of the industrial relations reforms of the 1980s, whilst simultaneously (and also for the first time) committing itself to a distinctively social democratic agenda on industrial relations developed under Neil Kinnock and John Smith, involving individual employment rights and a minimum wage (Crouch, 1998, 1999).

Other important New Labour messages concerned taxation and spending. Although research has cast doubt upon the relationship between taxation and votes, Labour was widely perceived, not least by leading modernizers, to have lost the 1992 election because the Shadow Chancellor, John Smith, announced plans to raise taxes to pay for improved services (Shaw, 1996). The leadership sought to overcome Labour's 'tax and spend' reputation by making specific pledges on rates of taxation and levels of spending.

Labour's aim was to emphasize that it was now moderate, cautious, and safe to vote for. Labour won the election in 1997 helped by a strong mood for change, but committed to few actual changes in policy. The Conservatives were criticized less for their objectives than for their methods. Labour argued that inflexible Conservative attempts to achieve macroeconomic stability, by adhering to fixed targets first for the money supply and later for the exchange rate, had precipitated two major recessions (in 1980–81 and 1990–92) as well as the ERM debacle in 1992 (CPPBB, 1997). Similarly, Conservative supply-side reforms were judged inadequate to remedy the gaps in investment in human capital (training and skills) and in physical capital (new technologies and infrastructure) and raise levels of productivity towards those in Germany and the United States (Kelly, 1997). Conservative welfare reforms were criticized for failing to make work pay for those at the lower end of the labour market. Labour now promised a far-reaching programme of welfare reform and labour market initiatives, including the New Deal, to increase employment and reward relatively low-skilled work. Employment policy and welfare reform were flagged as central components of economic and social policy under a Labour government, alongside macro-economic stability.

New Labour in Government

Since May 1997 New Labour economic policy has had two main strands: macro-economic stability; and giving employment and economic opportunities to all by tackling supply-side barriers to growth (Balls, 1998). These were developed in the context of two key external commitments – on the global economy and on the European Union. The new government affirmed more clearly than any Labour predecessor its support for an open world economy, renewing the strong Atlanticism of Labour governments and Labour leaders since the 1940s. This commitment was demonstrated when Gordon Brown played a leading role in designing a more robust system of international financial regulation and supervision, aimed at increasing the effectiveness of the existing Bretton Woods institutions in responding to the kind of financial turmoil experienced in East Asia and Latin America.

On Europe the new government quickly demonstrated its positive engagement by signing the social chapter of the Maastricht Treaty. It faced a bigger challenge over economic and monetary union because of its major implications for national economic strategy (Gamble and Kelly, 2000). After some hesitation the government decided not to join the euro at its launch in 1999, but gave unmistakable signals (urged on by much of the business community) that it intended to hold a referendum as soon as practicable after the next election, and in February 1999 it launched a National Changeover Plan to prepare Britain for the euro if there was a yes vote.

Macro-economic Stability

Within the context set by its commitments to an open world order and cooperation in Europe, Labour set out to demonstrate that it could deliver its election commitments, and pursue a sound money policy as the bedrock for other policies. By macro-economic stability the new government meant both stable outcomes (principally low inflation and sound public finances) as well as a stable policy framework (stability in economic instruments, such as interest rates). The principal means of achieving stability was to be an inflation target. The chosen target of 2.5 per cent was symmetrical: the monetary authorities were not to allow inflation either to overshoot or undershoot the target by more than one per cent. Their actions were constrained by the need to pursue the target, but they had to exercise considerable discretion and judgement to meet it (Balls, 1998). As such it has permitted policy activism, very different from a fixed policy rule as prescribed by monetarists such as Milton Friedman.

Central to this approach was credibility, which the government believed it could obtain by long-term policies which the financial markets considered sound, by transparency in decision-making, and by making pre-commitments ruling out certain policy options. It adopted a code for fiscal stability containing two key rules: the 'golden' rule stipulating that, over the economic cycle, government borrowing is only legitimate for capital investment and not to fund current spending; and a rule requiring public debt to be held at a stable and prudent proportion of national income over the economic cycle.

The most striking example, however, of the bid for credibility was Brown's unexpected decision to give the Bank of England operational independence. The party which had nationalized the Bank in 1946 handed interest rate control to the Bank's Monetary Policy Committee (MPC) of eight members, five appointed by the government. The MPC was charged with conducting monetary policy to achieve the government's inflation target. Responsibility for supervising the banking system was removed from the Bank to another agency.

This change built on the greater openness on the setting of interest rates introduced by the publication of discussions held between Conservative Chancellor, Kenneth Clarke, and the Bank's Governor, Eddie George, but went further. The Bank had always given advice on setting interest rates, but the final decision had been the Chancellor's. The symbolism of the change was all-important. Labour wished to demonstrate that low inflation would remain its primary objective. It wanted to reassure the financial markets that this Labour government would not be blown off course by the kind of financial pressures which had shipwrecked its predecessors.

Another target of the government's bid for credibility was political credibility in the eyes of the voters. It had pledged not to increase the standard or higher rates of income tax, and to keep spending within Conservative planning totals for 1997–9, including planned cuts. Some of these backfired politically, like the reduction in single parent benefit in November 1997, but the general message was maintained – Labour would not allow any dramatic rise in public spending to meet pent-up demands implying substantial new borrowing or increased taxation. The government even tried to underline the point by cutting some taxes with a high political profile, even though other increases meant that the overall tax burden was projected to rise. In the budget in March 1998 it announced a reduction in corporation tax from 31 to 30 per cent. The March 1999 budget introduced substantial increases in support for pensioners and children, a new 10 per cent income tax band, and a reduction in the standard rate of income tax from 23 to 22 per cent.

The early insistence on fiscal prudence and monetary credibility made the government appear far more orthodox than it was. As with previous Labour governments there remained a gap between the rhetoric of the government and the substance of its policy. For once, however, the substance was more radical than the rhetoric. In its rhetoric, for example, the government never mentioned redistribution, dissociated itself from 'tax and spend' policies, and stuck rigidly to inherited spending limits. But this did not prevent Brown from raising substantial additional revenue from other taxes, such as the £5.2 billion windfall tax on the privatized utilities announced in his first budget in July 1997. Pension Funds Tax credits for Advance Corporation Tax were also abolished, intended to raise £5.4 billion. The impact of this was largely hidden, penalizing those with personal pensions. In the 1999 budget various tax reliefs such as the married couple allowance and mortgage tax relief were abolished, national insurance on higher income earners was raised, and an energy tax introduced. Such measures raised revenue on a scale that was politically difficult to contemplate through straightforward changes in income tax.

From the outset Brown sought to increase spending on health and education, and to finance the welfare-to-work and other key initiatives. Existing expenditure was re-prioritized to have a more redistributive impact, and the Comprehensive Spending Review in July 1998 announced significant spending increases for the final three years of the parliament, as well as cuts in certain programmes such as defence. These medium-term plans broke with the annual planning model which had dominated spending reviews since the mid-1970s, and committed Labour to increased spending totalling £57 billion over three years, on health (£20 billion), education and science (£19 billion), housing (£4.4 billion), poor pensioners (£2.5 billion) and transport (£1.7 billion).

The plans were attacked because they assumed a rate of economic growth and unemployment which many thought unrealistic, particularly as the turmoil on world financial markets was expected to translate into lower growth and possibly recession. In response, the 1998 Autumn pre-budget statement reduced the growth forecast to 1–1.5 per cent in 1999, rising to 2.75–3.25 per cent by 2001. The Treasury claimed it had built in sufficient flexibility to cope with any variation in economic performance; the CBI agreed, although other independent forecasters suggested that the projections might prove optimistic. The dominant view, however, was that the plans were prudent, carefully costed, and still allowed for a significant recasting of public spending priorities and a modest redistribution of resources over the planning period. Indeed, the Treasury pre-budget statement in 1999 confirmed earlier forecasts.

The new fiscal rules meant no return to fine tuning, but observers noted that the increase in spending was planned to be broadly counter-cyclical, and that Labour still talked about stabilizing public sector investment at a high level. Underlying its Comprehensive Spending Review was an approach retaining some links to Keynesianism, even though it was condemned as monetarist by the left. Perhaps the stance is best characterized as an eclectic blend between macro-economic pragmatism (the rejection of doctrinaire approaches to economic management); monetarist ideas (particularly setting targets for inflation and accepting the existence of a 'natural' or non-accelerating inflation rate of unemployment – NAIRU); and New Keynesian ideas, particularly that policy activism can improve economic performance. It was a highly prudent approach aimed at permitting relatively progressive policies, including some counter-cyclical fiscal policy and an activist monetary policy.

Supply-side Reforms

Labour's long-term policies for raising economic performance and personal prosperity, and for better public services, centred on reforming the welfare state, particularly through welfare-to-work. Welfare-to-work was part of a wider strategy aimed at making work pay, improving employability, and getting those able to work off benefit and into jobs (Oppenheim, 1998). The strategy relied heavily on incentives to workers and employers. The centrepiece was the New Deal, funded by the 1997 windfall tax: £3 billion was allocated for getting the young unemployed into jobs or training. The 1998 budget then introduced a working families tax credit, raising tax thresholds for the poor, and guaranteed a minimum income of £180 a week to a family with one full-time worker. Child benefit was also increased. These welfare reforms were complemented by efforts to raise standards in education, increase access to further and higher education, and establish Independent Learning Accounts as part of a lifelong learning strategy.

The supply-side strategy stressed the need to raise the economy's long-term growth potential. Alongside welfare-to-work, the government looked for ways to stimulate investment in machines, technology and innovation, skills and infrastructure, particularly through new forms of partnership between the public and private sector, and new institutions such as Regional Development Agencies (RDAs). This built on policies developed under

Kinnock and Smith, although a greater emphasis was now placed on private sector-led schemes such as the Private Finance Initiative (PFI).

In its industrial relations policy Labour reassured the business community that it would not reinstate the legal immunities which unions once enjoyed. Nevertheless the *Fairness at Work* proposals did confer some important rights on trade unions as collective bodies, and perhaps more significantly it extended employment rights for individuals. It marked a decisive shift away from voluntarism in industrial relations, and the articulation (for the first time) of a recognizable social democratic approach to industrial relations which accepted legal structuring of employment relations and an emphasis upon individual rights (R. Taylor, 1998; see Chapter 6). It also pressed ahead with the introduction of a minimum wage, the first time Labour had ever introduced one. The rate was set at £3.60, and for workers under 21 the rates were still lower. But in winning the intellectual argument an important principle had been established that there was a floor below which wages should not be pushed.

On mergers and competition policy government rhetoric was again highly reassuring to business, floating proposals for removing decisions on mergers and monopolies from the remit of politicians altogether. On industrial policy the government signalled that it wished to ditch any remnants of an interventionist industrial strategy and ruled out any return to a pro-manufacturing stance. It was revealing that one of the five tests as to whether the UK should join the euro concerned the financial sector; no mention was made of manufacturing. The substance of its view was set out in the Competitiveness White Paper, which gave priority to sectors in the new knowledge-based economy and stressed the limited, if important, role which could be played by government.

At the same time, however, elements of more familiar centre-left industrial policy have crept into policy debate. Under Margaret Beckett the Department for Trade and Industry (DTI) set up a Company Law Review to examine the legal framework under which companies operate in the UK; and the Treasury began to look in detail at productivity. Both signalled an interest in investigating the links between structures of corporate governance and the supply of capital. The DTI also lobbied hard and successfully for a substantial increase in the science budget to protect the science base and encourage research partnerships between universities and industry. The Review of Banking Competition was set up to look at ways in which finance for investment for small and medium enterprises could be improved, and there were signs that the new RDAs might prove to be more interventionist than government rhetoric suggested. There are some major continuities here with the kind of industrial policy developed by Kinnock and Smith, not least the concern over the impact of the operation of banking and the City on corporate investment and productivity. The major difference is the much clearer pro-business rhetoric adopted by New Labour, particularly under Margaret Beckett's successors at the DTI, Peter Mandelson and Stephen Byers, and the apparent downgrading of the importance of trade unions. But whether the substance of the policies is much different is not yet clear.

Can New Labour Deliver?

No previous Labour government has stayed in office for two full terms, one of the principal reasons being the failure of Labour's economic policies, in particular an inability to reconcile ambitions for greater public spending with the fiscal and monetary discipline needed to satisfy financial markets. They failed, as a result, to achieve many of their other policy objectives. Will New Labour be any different? The New Labour government has tried to avoid past pitfalls by establishing a credible set of institutions to govern fiscal and monetary policy. It faces a number of dilemmas.

Critics of New Labour's regime worried that the government would have less control over how the economy is steered, and that the MPC might have a deflationary bias and keep unemployment too high. Others argued that the policy continued to rely too heavily on interest rates, and urged greater use of fiscal policy. The CBI in March 1998 appeared to endorse this, calling for a £2 billion increase in taxation on consumers to moderate demand and allow the MPC to reduce interest rates. But Goldman Sachs calculated that the increase in taxation would have to be at least £9 billion to reduce interest rates by 1 per cent. Subsequently interest rates fell sharply as the Bank took into account the rapid fall in consumer and business confidence. These events do not suggest there is *no* role for fiscal policy in stabilization, but monetary policy is more easily adjusted to changes in aggregate demand.

The judgement of monetary conditions remains highly complex, and the scope for misreading unfolding trends and making policy mistakes is as great as ever. The level of unemployment, for example, below which inflationary pressure starts to build (NAIRU) is a crucial assumption in macroeconomic models, but there is a range of calculations as to where it lies. During the later years of the Conservative government the consensus for the UK was that it lay between 1.5 and 1.75 million unemployed, or 6–7 per cent of the workforce (Philpott, 1998). Other estimates put it higher, and some lower. Indeed, during this period there was a tendency for estimates of falling unemployment to reflect the latest rate of unemployment.

The problem for policymakers has been to stabilize aggregate demand at a level which keeps unemployment close to NAIRU, at the same time as supply-side policies are introduced which seek to reduce the theoretical level of unemployment at which NAIRU operates.

Macro-economic stability appears a simple enough goal, but it can be defined in different ways and there is much confusion about whether the object is stability in the policy instruments, or stability in the policy outcomes. Most statements on the subject promise both, but there is often a tension between them. New Labour's inflation target certainly gives priority to stable outcomes, and pursuing it has so far meant no stability at all in the main instrument, interest rates. Focusing on inflation rather than several other objectives simultaneously at least simplifies the task for policymakers, but there will still be considerable fluctuations in levels of unemployment and output, which may exact a high political cost. However, it is far from clear that adopting a formal employment target instead would reduce these swings; moreover within a dynamic economy policymakers cannot and should not seek to iron out all fluctuations and uncertainty in key economic variables. In the government's favour is the fact that interest rates peaked at a far lower level during the upturn which ended in 1998 than they did in the 1980s, although how much of this is due to prudent economic management as opposed to international factors is unclear.

Like previous governments, Labour's programme depends on achieving macro-economic stability and at the same time increasing the long-run growth potential of the economy. It needs the economy to keep growing at its long-term potential rate to fund the spending plans necessary to deliver Labour's wider policy commitments before the next election. Macro-economic stability is seen as a condition for increasing the underlying growth rate, if only by 0.25 per cent. In historical terms this would still be a large shift and would make possible the aim of reducing the number of workless households. Labour is determined not to commit macro-economic mistakes which undermine its wider reform programme. It is keen to avoid the macro-adventurism and large-scale policy regime switches which characterized the Conservative era. This programme is often said to be highly cautious, but it is still high risk because it depends on assumptions about economic growth and unemployment which are not within the power of the government to deliver.

The new regime is also threatened by the turmoil in world financial markets which may yet plunge the global economy into a major depression, sweeping away New Labour assumptions that the international policy regime will remain broadly what it has been for the last twenty years, and introducing quite new considerations into national economic policy. Even a smaller recession would pose a severe test, probing the soundness of Brown's fiscal framework and undermining its flagship policy, the New Deal.

A second dilemma is posed by economic and monetary union. Joining the euro, and locking Britain into a regime which many believe would deliver macro-economic stability, would be a natural development of New Labour policy since 1997. Many British businesses feel that if Britain stays out of the euro they will face significantly higher costs as well as interest rates higher than the rates prevailing in the rest of the EU. In these circumstances the pressures to enter are likely to intensify. Nonetheless the government faces a number of problems.

The first is the political task of winning the referendum against the opposition of the Eurosceptics. A second problem is that transferring responsibility for macro-economic stability to the European Central Bank (ECB) intensifies the disadvantages of transferring that responsibility to the MPC. The ECB operates a monetary policy with an implicit inflation target of 0–2 per cent in contrast to the symmetrical target in the UK, creating a serious risk of monetary policy being too deflationary, threatening very high unemployment in some European regions. If the ECB is not properly accountable for its policy stance its legitimacy will also be undermined. With national governments constrained by ECB independence the political consequences could become explosive. One important remedy for supporters of European integration is to ensure that there is not just monetary union but economic union as well. According to this view Europe has to acquire an economic government which can ensure a monetary and fiscal policy mix which avoids a deflationary bias, and takes into account the very different context of the global economy of the late 1990s.

A third potential dilemma lies in the supply-side strategy, which is so heavily focused on work and effecting structural changes to get the unemployed back into jobs. The government has toned down its claim that welfare reform, by taking many of the unemployed off benefit, will release sizeable resources to switch into programmes such as education and health. It is committed, like previous governments, to the long haul. An alternative approach to welfare developed by Frank Field was briefly floated within the government, but with Field's resignation in July 1998, the Treasury appeared to resume full control of the welfare reform agenda, favouring more directly redistributive means-tested strategies which also contain financial costs. The government is committed to tackling social exclusion, and sees getting those on benefit back into jobs as the key (Robinson, 1998a). But the pool of unemployed remains large, the welfare bill continues to grow, and the scale of the problem which Labour has inherited (as revealed for instance in the 1998 Acheson Report) means that progress will be slow.

The issue for the government is whether a bolder supply-side strategy would have more impact. Labour's diagnosis of Britain's industrial failings was that it was locked into low-productivity, low-wage, low-skill jobs in too many sectors. Remedying the lack of investment in human capital through better training and education and the lack of investment in physical capital through better research and development, and improved infrastructure, are Labour's solutions. Many on the centre-left question whether Labour can deliver the long-term improvement in economic performance it seeks without broader institutional reform aimed at changing the vocational training system, the accessibility of lifelong learning opportunities, and structures of corporate governance, to develop more companies keen to train and retain skilled workforces and to establish long-term stakeholder relationships with their employees (Hutton, 1995).

Conclusion

As indicated at the beginning, in analysing the economic policy of a new government, it is tempting to tell a simple story – emphasizing either continuity or discontinuity with the past. But such stories are rarely adequate, because they cannot capture the complexities of the policy process. This is especially true of New Labour. Extreme interpretations that the government is pursuing either a wholly 'new' economic policy which marks a sharp break from the past, or exactly the same policies as its predecessor under a different label, should be rejected.

Some suggest that at least as far as its economic policy is concerned Labour is now a neo-liberal rather than a social democratic party, because it appears to have fully accepted most of the consensus on economic policy, its assumptions and constraints, established during the 18 years of government under Thatcher and Major. But neither neo-liberalism nor social democracy are fixed and unchanging. The context in which they are applied changes and evolves, and ideologies and political parties have to adapt (see Chapter 15). Many of the changes credited to Thatcherism were changes which would have happened whatever government was in power. If Labour had not adjusted to these new realities it would have faced political extinction or at best marginalization.

Those who believe that New Labour represents a fundamental break with social democracy (rather than with Labourism) have to demonstrate that there is no continuity between New Labour's programme and that fashioned by Kinnock and Smith. This is quite difficult since although there are some important differences, particularly as regards macro-economic policy, there are also many common emphases, particularly on the importance of the supply-side, on 'skills and education', on the limits of intervention, on the commitment to open trade and open regionalism, and on the industrial relations reforms which for the first time have introduced individual employment rights and minimum wage legislation. These reforms make Labour more like a European social democratic party than ever before.

One major apparent difference between New Labour and the party of Kinnock and Smith is in their attitude to tax. Labour's high tax reputation had been exploited ruthlessly by the Conservatives in the 1992 election, and it became one of New Labour's main aims to dispel that perception. Kinnock and Smith were prepared to use the tax system to underpin redistribution. New Labour's decision to rule out raising direct taxes was taken as meaning that it had abandoned redistribution. Certainly the word 'redistribution', at least officially, rarely figures in New Labour rhetoric, mainly because of its taxation implications. But, as argued above, redistribution remains an important objective for New Labour, reflected in Brown's budgets (see Chapter 11). Taxation was raised in other ways, and expenditure re-prioritized to achieve a positive redistribution of resources. Far from turning its back on redistribution it could be argued that New Labour has sought to redistribute incrementally by every means possible except direct taxation. It is redistributing through tax credits, changing expenditure priorities, and shifts in the National Insurance system. It is, however, a very particular type of redistribution, because it has targeted specific groups: those with children, low-income pensioners, and the working poor. It has done little, at least directly, to help the workless poor.

There is obviously much greater discontinuity if New Labour's programme is compared with Labour programmes between 1979 and 1987. But one of the main reasons for the contrast is that the international context in which policy is now made has been transformed. National economic protectionism is no longer politically or economically viable. A second important change compared to the 1970s and 1980s is the general lessening of inflationary pressure, with many economists now predicting a deflationary era (Bootle, 1997).

A third change is the revaluation of the market and the state as different modes of governing the economy. Under New Labour the market, and with it the private sector, has assumed a central place, and the commitment to the public sector as both morally superior and economically more efficient has disappeared. In its place there is (at least at the rhetorical level) a much more pragmatic evaluation of whether public or private agencies are best placed to deliver services, in a world in which the dividing lines between public and private have become increasingly blurred. Some on the centre-left fear that Labour now accepts the innate superiority of the market.

This does not mean, however, that Labour has simply succumbed to neo-liberalism. There remains a sharp contrast between Labour and the Conservative governments of the 1980s and 1990s in their attitudes towards the state. Labour retains a much stronger belief in the role of an active state in promoting a fairer and more prosperous society than did the Conservatives. One consequence is a much more positive attitude towards the public sector. What is new about New Labour in relation to the Labour tradition is the linking of a commitment to macro-economic stability with an active policy to incease employment opportunity, redistribute resources and find new ways to combat social exclusion. This does not put New Labour outside the Labour tradition as some have suggested. It places it squarely in the long tradition of economic revisionism which has been such a distinctive feature in the evolution of the party in the last fifty years.

Since the advent of New Labour the gap between rhetoric and reality has been significantly narrowed, but there still remains a gap, as there does for all parties, between aspiration in opposition and delivery in government. The transition is often painful, and many politicians do not survive it. The problem is designing effective policies. Much centre-left economic analysis, however eloquent, offers little guide to translating aspirations into reality. Governments need strategic vision but they also need detailed, rigorous, painstaking and unglamorous analysis.

The other historical tension in Labour's economic policy – between defending trade union interests and pursuing a social democratic programme – has also been eased through the modernization of the party and its programme conducted first by Kinnock and Smith, and then by Blair (see Chapter 4). This modernization weakened Labour's ties to the unions, at the same time redefining the content of its social democratic programme. Labour may no longer articulate many of the themes which used to identify social democracy, but it is still a party of social reform and active government, with an increasingly unified economic and social policy. Its hopes of holding its electoral coalition together and implementing its wider programme of reforms depend more than ever on its economic policy being a success.

10

New Labour and Education, Education, Education

COLIN McCAIG

This chapter will examine the nature of education policy under New Labour. It will begin by setting the context for immediate post-war developments in education policy. It will then discuss the dynamics of what has been termed the 'Old' Labour period, and contrast this with 'New Labour'. It is the contention of the chapter that New Labour's educational philosophy is one which is designed to appeal to the aspirant parent, voter or consumer, whilst at the same time remaining within the broad church of the Labour Party's ideology. There has clearly been some movement by Labour in terms of the programme offered to the electorate, but rather than talk of this movement in left–right terms, this chapter asserts that New Labour is more easily explained as moving from egalitarian to libertarian positions on a values distribution in a search for the vote-maximizing position. Changes in education policy are often legitimized by reference to the needs of a competitive market and improving individual choice. However, policy change cannot be traced entirely to developments since the advent of Blair and New Labour in 1994. Indeed it has involved changes to the policymaking structure of the Labour Party from the mid-1980s.

Context: the Post-war Settlement in Education

The educational context for the first half of the post-war period was set by the Butler Education Act of 1944 which the Labour government of 1945 enacted. This provided free secondary education for all, and to that extent satisfied some inter-war Labour Party policy aims (Barker, 1972, 54). However, the Butler settlement entrenched selective education, with a grammar school system which provided certification for the top performing

20 per cent of pupils in competitive exams at the age of 11. The remaining 80 per cent of pupils were redirected into secondary modern or technical schools in a division of abilities to suit the assumed correct division of labour (S. Tomlinson, 1997a, 4). Throughout the 1950s this situation increasingly came to be seen as anachronistic, neither satisfying the growing middle-class demand for grammar-style education, nor the requirements of equity and the provision of opportunity for all. A radical solution, multilateral (or comprehensive) schools which would take all abilities within a given age range, had been Labour Party policy since before the second world war (Parkinson, 1970, 27–32). Labour clearly stood against the inequities of the system and supported its own earlier policy:

> Labour will get rid of the segregation of children into separate schools caused by 11-plus selection: secondary education will be reorganised on comprehensive lines. (Labour Party, 1964, 31)

Perhaps as importantly, after the 1964 General Election, Labour-controlled LEAs became attracted to progressive pedagogic techniques which focused on the individual child. Although Labour in Government could not claim to have legislated progressive education, it presided over the publication of the Plowden Report (HMSO, 1967) which gave an intellectual lead to an education system in which all children were given the opportunity to develop at their own pace (Pinder, 1979, 134).

Beyond the concerns of party politics, comprehensive education conceptually represented a balance between the interests of egalitarians, through its collective ethos, and the interests of libertarians through the emphasis on meritocratic aims based on the needs of the individual pupil (Tasker, 1997, 4–5). Egalitarian and libertarian left positions set the parameters in compulsory education, creating an uneasy balance between ensuring all children received a rewarding education and embracing the concerns of the aspirational middle classes that the Labour Party wished to attract about state education. It was in this sense that successive party leaders Gaitskell and Wilson chose to portray comprehensive reorganization as levelling up towards 'grammar schools for all' (Gaitskell, 1958; Labour Party, 1964). The essentially compromised nature of this internal party balance (Panebianco, 1988, 8) made it politically difficult for Labour to respond to changes introduced by an ideological Conservative government after 1979.

However, from the late 1960s criticisms of comprehensive education began to grow. In 1976 Labour Prime Minister, James Callaghan, enunciated widespread concern about the efficacy of the comprehensive education. The speech and the *Black Paper* questioning of comprehensive, child-centred learning had implications beyond compulsory schooling. The attendant

'Great Debate' also led in the 1980s to calls from employer organizations for the vocationalization of secondary education to address the shortfall of skilled workers (Ainley, 1988, 105). Subsequently much Conservative legislation has been concerned to make education more valid to employers, for example the introduction of Technical and Vocational Education Initiative (TVEI) and City Technology Colleges (CTCs) (Ainley, 1988, 133). In higher education, the post-war era has encompassed a contrast with the expansion of the 1960s which was only curtailed after the oil-price crisis of the mid-1970s and the attendant pressure on public spending. Thereafter, despite periods of rapid growth in the sector (particularly the doubling of intake among the 18 year-old cohort between 1988 and 1992) the declining unit value of students in an era of increasing public accountability created the context for the university system of the mid-1990s.

'New' Versus 'Old' Labour

Traditionally, Labour was not intrinsically interested in education and was prepared to leave the details of pedagogy and curricula to professors of education so long as schooling was free, a condition largely satisfied by Butler's 1944 Education Act. Such caution was emphasized by the eschewing of party policy on comprehensive reorganization throughout the 1945–51 governments. However, following Crosland's *Future of Socialism* (A. Crosland, 1956), the Robbins expansion of higher education (Robbins, 1963, 69) and the introduction of the Industrial Training Boards in 1963, even old Labour began to view education as crucial to economic policy, enjoining a consensus around the idea of human capital which survives into the New Labour period. It is difficult, then, to sustain the old Labour/New Labour divide in terms of either detailed policy or philosophy in education and training matters. Where we can trace differences is in the development of policy and in the presentation of a coordinated appeal to aspirant middle-class voters during the 1980s and 1990s.

Although Labour after the 1960s benefited from association with the introduction of comprehensive education, training levies and the expansion of the higher education sector, these were largely in response to a consensus about the changing needs of the economy and social demand from middle-class activists. Middle-class demand was particularly well served by the Open University, which many Labour educationalists believed was a waste of time and money in terms of industrial demand (Reisman, 1997; D. Robertson, 1997, 117–30). The fragile nature of the comprehensive consensus was also based on the individual assumptions of millions of parents that it was the most effective system to deliver opportunities to their off-spring. This was well encompassed by the ambiguity of leading Labour Party figures throughout the 1950s and 1960s. When the system came under attack from the series of *Black Papers* after 1969, and especially during the 1980s, the party became naturally defensive about the comprehensive settlement and its attendant philosophy of equity, pluralism and optimism. Such defensiveness is understandable given that Labour Party policy at this time was largely written to satisfy a party audience and the educationalists close to the front bench.

Party institutional interests were also evident in training policy, which for the first time after 1964 was based on compulsory funding by employers (B. Evans, 1992, 7–8), and the new Industry Training Boards (ITBs) provided the trade unions with a permanent seat in government policy circles. ITBs were part of a bipartisan attempt to plan the economy in response to changes in the bases of demand, an essential and consensual component of Keynesian demand management (Gunter, 1963). Following the oil price crises of 1974 and 1979 and the election of the Conservatives in 1979, central planning became discredited as employers argued for labour flexibility in response to open markets.

This made Labour and trade union attachment to the corporatism of the ITBs anachronistic during the 1980s, when many on the left sought to introduce more general education into post-16 programmes for workers and the growing young unemployed. However, the trade unions' representation on bodies such as the Manpower Service Commission (until 1988) and the Health and Safety Commission (into the 1990s) preserved the illusion of influence and acted as a blockage to new policy ideas, causing continual difficulties within the party (Minkin, 1991, 444). A further important element of old Labour's attachment to the 1960s settlement was a belief in the local democratic control of education and training through LEAs and Further Education colleges. In further and higher education, expansion and widening access were traditionally accepted as intrinsically good things, although such plans often had to be sidelined in response to crises in the economy, especially during the 1974–9 government.

In contrast to this, New Labour, following the lead set by the internal Policy Review of 1987–9, embraced open markets and the need for supply-side reform in response to globalization (Smith and Spear, 1992, 31). Even as New Labour chose to be less interventionist with regard to markets, the logic of supply-side reform has meant becoming more interventionist in the education system. While this can still be conceptualized as human capital planning, the centralizing of powers in the DfEE reduced professional autonomy and the influence of LEAs in determining policy and spending priorities. This New Labour anathema towards local democratic control has extended to insisting on private and voluntary sector input into nursery education, following the removal of the Nursery Voucher Scheme, declining to take Further Education colleges (incorporated after the 1992 Act) back into local authority control and threatening to remove LEAs' responsibilities for the school system. Partly this can be seen as accommodating to the New Right thesis that local authorities represent an unnecessary layer of bureaucracy between producer and consumer, but it can also be portrayed as a pragmatic and modern attempt to face up to continually pressurized public spending and the need to address poor school performance.

Politically, New Labour is also more interventionist than old Labour, with a sharper idea of what kind of society it wants to create (see Chapter 11). In education, this social authoritarianism is enunciated by home–school contracts, homework time guidelines, and the provision of homework centres after school time, although all these have had to remain voluntary. Conceptually, New Labour treat education problems as if there is no debate about what constitutes 'best practice' (R. Alexander, 1997, 224), while it is suggested that education professionals need to adopt a 'what works, works' approach to pedagogy (Labour Party, 1996a, 8). 'What works' is to be decided centrally at the DfEE, and made to 'work' by LEAs across the board, under the threat of abolition and replacement by Education Action Zones (EAZs). This clearly denigrates the role of educational theory (Tooley and Darby, 1998; OFSTED, 1998) and reinforces the centralization of powers with the Secretary of State. In this purely managerialist way, some New Labour advisers hope to eradicate failure in state schools (Reynolds, 1998a; 1998b). This prescribing of the professional role of teachers is augmented by a continuation of attacks on poor teachers, and investigations into ways of making schooling more responsive to modern lifestyles (changes to the school day and year to suit parental demands) also presage changes to teacher's employment contracts (DfEE, 1998d).

To tackle the recruitment shortages in some subject areas New Labour aims to attract new teachers into the profession with the promise of fast-track career development for high-flying entrants and Advanced Teacher Status for excellent existing classroom teachers. The proposed introduction of performance-related pay and incentives for teachers in some subjects is also designed to increase the social value attached to teaching as a career. In return, the DfEE offers support and reduces the pressure on teachers by prescribing exactly what to teach and for how long. Teaching will henceforth involve less professional discretion and more emphasis on delivery skills. The National Curriculum has also been reshaped by New Labour, reflecting the need to raise standards and incorporate social responsibility through compulsory citizenship classes (DfEE, 208/99, 1999b). This type of interventionism in the name of the Secretary of State also places real pressure on the government to meet its formal targets (HM Treasury, 1998). While planning was an intrinsic element of the human capital environment of the 1960s, the measurement of school performance outcomes now makes target setting and accountability a question of management rather than politics.

If old Labour were traditionally non-interventionist in terms of education, but interventionist in economic matters, this was largely in response to the requirements of the economy. However, the accepted need for flexible workforces in the knowledge economy of the future obliges New Labour to be socially and educationally interventionist. This means, in compulsory education, offering the kinds of specialism which will produce a differentiated and flexible workforce, although clearly there are also political dividends from offering consumer choice. As in the 1960s, the Labour Party has taken elements of social demand and the unpalatable imperatives of the economy, and presented them in such a way as to appeal to elements of the broad coalition that the party still represents. However, the political imperative and the centrality of economic concerns to education policy has meant that both Old and New Labour have been non-radical in matters of higher education. With little sense of crisis in the quality of outcomes from higher education, New Labour are able to continue to balance the egalitarian and libertarian left elements within the coalition, acting decisively only on tuition fees, and then without leaving the boundaries of the consensus among higher education pressure groups.

Policy and Process: from Modernization to New Labour

During the immediate post-war decades, as we have seen, social demand was translated into government policy indirectly through the efforts of empowered and vocal middle-class groups and their supporters in academia. From the mid-1970s, social scientists began to measure satisfaction with the education system through a series of opinion polls and surveys which asked respondents to cite the 'most important issue facing Britain today' on a regular basis. Thereafter public satisfaction or dissatisfaction with the education system could be traced across time-series, providing politicians and reformers with a directly tangible measure of consumer demand. In becoming more public, the performance of the education service would become more political and this was realized as respondent concern with the education service grew steadily after 1986 (MORI, 1998). To Labour modernizers and electoral strategists, such as Peter Mandelson and Philip Gould, these concerned respondents could be conceptualized as either 'worried middle class' or 'aspirational working class' and targeted by a new emphasis on policy presentation (Gould, 1998a, 218–20).

Changes in the nature of Labour Party policymaking during the Kinnock and Smith leadership periods made it easier for the political targeting of aspirant middle-class voters, in harness with the new emphasis on central control in the hands of the leadership (see Chapter 4). The impact of centralization was seen in the case of training policy, and it was after a long period of stalemate within the Manpower Liaison Committee that the front-bench team set the precedent of developing policy and then putting it before the NEC for discussion (Minkin, 1991, 444). The Policy Review changes accelerated the trend with the introduction of broad, Shadow Cabinet-led Policy Commissions, although they were considered unwieldy and soon fell into disuse (Blunkett, 1996a). The outcome was the piece-meal development of frontbench-led 'mini-commissions', made up of advisers and colleagues chosen by the shadow minister.

Labour's policy development throughout the long period of Conservative control has seen the party adapt to ever-changing consensus positions, with an increasing emphasis on individualist concerns. In tertiary education, widening access and attacking the cuts in higher education after 1981 became the main themes that both the egalitarian and meritocratic left could agree on during the 1980s. However, thanks in part to the critical journalism of commentators such as Melanie Philips in *The Guardian*, the liberal press began regularly to highlight poor standards in education during the early 1990s (R. Alexander, 1997, 228), thus disconnecting the Labour-voting middle classes from automatic support for the state comprehensive system. The 'failure' of metropolitan schools became dinner-table conversation material and the phenomenon of middle-class flight to more salubrious catchment areas grew throughout the period. The first acceptance that tuition fees should be repaid by students also came in confidential party memoranda during John Smith's leadership, although this was not yet seen as electorally palatable (Labour Party, 1994b).

Process and Outcomes: Labour in Opposition, 1994–7

In 1994 the Labour Party produced *Opening doors to a learning society*, written by shadow education secretary, Ann Taylor. The paper expressed hostility towards the publication of league tables of school performance, and pledged that grant maintained schools would be returned to LEA control (Labour Party, 1994a, 17, 29). Tony Blair, however, contradicted this policy document even as it was being prepared for the 1994 Annual Conference (Young, 1997a), and David Blunkett replaced Taylor as shadow education secretary soon afterwards. Blair and Blunkett then set out to alter the public perception of Labour and education by emphasizing the modernization of the comprehensive principle through higher standards and more parental choice (Labour Party, 1995, 1996a, 1997a).

With the Conservatives promising to extend selection in grant maintained schools and place a grammar school in every town (Conservative Party, 1997, 54), both major parties highlighted education during the long pre-election period, with New Labour using the more reformist and modernizing rhetoric. Beyond the compulsory sector the concept of lifelong learning, utilized across the political divide since the 1980s, was reflected in the Employment Department's absorption by the Department for Education and Employment (DfEE). New Labour adopted the lifelong learning slogan as its own during the early 1990s as the party sought to offer opportunities for the individual to improve his or her occupational prospects periodically, in response to the new demands of the knowledge-based economy (Labour Party, 1996b; Barber, 1996a; Ainley, 1997, 14–15; D. Robertson, 1997, 117–30). Some saw this as natural Labour territory (S. Tomlinson, 1997b), because lifelong retraining implied open access and the opportunity for the first time to create transferable credit structures which could incorporate academic, vocational and work-based learning (Richardson, Spours, Woolhouse and Young, 1995; D. Robertson, 1996).

During the 1994–7 period New Labour tapped into real working-class concerns about the failings of education policy and focused on the issue of raising standards (Blunkett, 1996b; Blair, 1996b; Barber, 1996b). This message also addressed the concerns of aspirational middle-class parents. The politicization of 'standards' was clearly intended to be beneficial in terms of extra votes for the party. However, a far more difficult task was to persuade the Labour Party that the structure of the education service was separate from concerns about standards. The egalitarian left argument, and the basis of the comprehensive settlement, was that only by ensuring all abilities within a catchment area shared the same school experience would real equality of either opportunity or outcome be realized. Even Wilson, who, echoing Gaitskell, saw comprehensivization as levelling up (and thus an egalitarian policy which would improve standards), made no serious attempt to close the grammar and independent school sectors. Nevertheless, comprehensive education served as an important symbol within the party and the electorate at large. It allowed parents to assume that no one else was getting any better education than their own offspring, unless they paid for it. Conservative changes made this myth difficult to sustain by the 1990s, but an evolving comprehensive system also reflected social change. In metropolitan areas, many aspirational parents were willing to move house to come under more desirable state school catchment areas, thereby denuding urban state schools of supportive and motivated middle-class parental role models. Grant maintained schools, whose heads and boards of governors had chosen to opt out and which received transitional funding, were most often found in wealthier suburbs, and drew part of their intake from a widely selected pool. The problem for New Labour was to address this new reality of a steady erosion of the comprehensive principle, without abandoning comprehensive education as a symbol for the left or alienating the aspirant parents who had benefited from GM and City Technology College (CTC) schooling.

This problem was addressed in *Diversity and Excellence* (Labour Party, 1995) which tried to square the political circle by retaining the freedom of grant maintained schools (renamed as Foundation Schools) to control more of their education budget, while at the same time bringing them back into the LEA fold for the purpose of inspection and accountability. The remaining schools were also to be awarded control of 90 per cent of their own funds in what was, in effect, a levelling up towards the GM principle of Local Management of Schools (LMS) for all. However, foundation schools were to retain the right to select up to 10 per cent of pupils by 'aptitude' in a particular skill or curriculum area. This apparent acquiescence to selection, and the choice of selective schools for their own children by senior New Labour figures such as Tony Blair and Harriet Harman, led to problems at the 1995 party conference. At the heart of the argument were New Labour's attachment to providing some individuals with opportunity through subject specialization, and competing definitions of ability and aptitude (Hattersley, 1998b). In response to the ongoing debate within the party, Blunkett had to amend his 1995 Conference pledge of 'watch my lips; no selection' to 'no further selection' in 1996 (Blunkett, 1996b), acknowledging the reality of foundation status.

New Labour attempted to subsume the row over selection by concentrating on standards as the election neared. The 1996 policy document *Excellence for Everyone* promised more focus on the core skills of the National Curriculum, and a much harder line on poorly performing teachers. This can be seen as the culmination of the long battle over education standards first seriously joined by left-inclined journals such as *The Guardian* during the winter of 1991–2 (R. Alexander, 1997a, 228).

For the first time since coming into government in 1964, the Labour Party overtly linked improved school performance with diversity and competition among schools, even promising to extend the range of specialist schools. By concentrating on improving the standards of poorly performing schools in particular, and promising to target such schools with extra funding as 'action zones', by 1997 New Labour were able to point to progressive policies aimed at improving the education of 'the many, not the few' (DfEE, 1997b).

New Labour were also more adept at tailoring choice to aspirant parents, compared to the Conservative promise to allow all schools to select and create 'a grammar school in every town' (Conservative Party, 1997, 24, 54). Despite the presentational emphasis on egalitarian comprehensive education, New Labour now promised to preside over an education system which offered a meritocratic hierarchy of institutions: independent schools; grammar schools; CTCs; foundation (GM) schools; other specialist state schools; voluntary aided (usually church) schools; comprehensive schools; and secondary modern schools in areas where grammar schools persisted. Of these eight categories, seven would be state funded, while all but comprehensives and secondary moderns would select a proportion of their intake by ability, aptitude or religious persuasion. Alongside these categories were education action zones (EAZs) as a signal of failure and a new category of Beacon Schools, which would be designated local centres of excellence as an example to others; again, a clear signal to parents of where good (and bad) state education could be found.

The idea of raising standards was also used symbolically by New Labour, along with the abolition of the Nursery Voucher Scheme (which had yet to go nationwide after selective piloting), and on the abolition of the Assisted Places Scheme (a subsidy for the independent sector to recruit poorer children), the savings from which would fund a maximum class size limit of 30 for all five, six and seven year-olds. These policies can be interpreted as symbolic because they represented totems of egalitarian left positionality which could be embraced without serious economic or political cost to New Labour.

Beyond the compulsory sector, symbolism was also evident in the rhetoric of lifelong learning which infused such documents as *Lifelong Learning*, and *Aiming Higher* (Labour Party, 1996b,c). The first of these was concerned mostly with higher education, while the latter was concerned with producing an appropriate structure of post-compulsory qualifications and courses which would help make further and higher education more relevant. In both documents, New Labour were accommodating the policy development of the government (DfEE, 1997a) and shared much of the language. While New Labour joined the consensus around the need to rationalize tertiary (third level) education, the party failed to take on the autonomy of the university sector by backing the reform of A levels as the main route for university entry. Here the desire to maintain standards won out over calls to democratize or redistribute opportunity within higher education as the research-dominant, liberal élite universities fought for autonomy and against any ideas of financial redistribution (Thompson, 1998a). Much of the developing policy here took place outside public debate; Sir Ron Dearing's Commission on Higher Education was not scheduled to report until after the 1997 election, after which the party that won would have to tackle the critical issue of student finance.

The Development of Policy since May 1997

Following the General Election, New Labour stayed true to its promise to change the education landscape rapidly, with two major Bills scheduled for the first year as well as the single-clause Bill to abolish the Assisted Places Scheme (HMSO, 1997). The government's first political concern, however, was the Dearing Report, due for publication in July 1997, and how to present its own plans alongside the report's recommendations. The government intended to introduce charges to students' families of around a quarter of tuition fees (£1000 per year of study), whilst replacing maintenance grants with a new, fairer loans system. Dearing himself had recommended keeping grants, while New Labour had pledged to remove them in the manifesto (Labour Party, 1997c). The manifesto had failed to signal clearly the introduction of tuition fees, however, even though the *Lifelong Learning* document had praised the Higher Education Contribution Scheme (HECS) from Australia as an example of an international trend towards students paying part of their own fees (Labour Party, 1996b, 21).

Despite the fierce backlash from many on the left over the sacrifice of 'free higher education', the New Labour government persevered with the student finance provisions in the Bill which also contained regulations preventing older universities from charging top-up fees to reflect the extra demand for places. The government was determined to avoid top-up fees because of its commitment to widening access and to avoid the appearance that introducing flat-rate fees would end the possibility of bright working-class students getting into élite institutions on merit (Carvel, 1997; DfEE, 1998a). The ensuing controversy led to the Teaching and Higher Education Bill suffering several defeats in the House of Lords, and the introduction of 197 amendments during its passage (Rafferty, 1998a; H. Richards, 1998).

One of the major problems was the 'Scottish anomaly' which arose because English, Welsh or Northern Irish students on a course of HE in Scotland would have to contribute £4000 in fees because of the traditional fourth year of study, while this final year charge could not be made to Scottish or European Union-domiciled students attending Scottish universities. Devolution has complicated the situation and created an alternative system of funding in Scotland. It also became clear during the passage of the Bill that New Labour plans were partially redistributive, as tuition fee income from the traditionally middle-class intake of universities would be targeted at institutions that could promise wider access for under-represented groups, with most of the expansion envisaged in further, not higher, education. New Labour, however, were themselves reluctant to portray fees as redistributive (*THES*, 1997), preferring to stress the necessity of maintaining excellence in higher education.

Other aspects of the Bill were controversial, but proved less problematic for the government. Here, New Labour were on the safer political ground of raising standards in schools. The Bill established a General Teaching Council largely free from teacher union influence (DfEE, 1997c), inspections of teacher training colleges and the establishment of a mandatory headship qualification. Again this heralded criticisms of over-centralization of the education system, but, unlike the universities, the school sector did not have a record of excellence through autonomy to point to in their defence. Nor did the teacher unions have the same influence on New Labour policymaking as they had in the past. The distancing of Labour from the teaching unions had begun under the Kinnock leadership. By contrast, in higher education, the Committee for Vice Chancellors and Principals (CVCP) were at the forefront of developing New Labour policy in an area which attracted less public scrutiny. Revealingly, the government was not afraid to take on teachers and headteachers who were apparently failing children through inadequate performance, and indeed the nation through the failure to develop sufficient human capital; in this case, because of the politicization of the standards message, New Labour could override professional groups and sound tough to the electorate. The overall effect of the Bill was to send the message that New Labour were not afraid to tackle a tough decision (tuition fees) which would inevitably hurt the middle classes.

Following the *Excellence in Schools* White Paper (DfEE, 1997d), the second major piece of legislation, the School Standards and Frameworks Bill, concentrated on standards and the legislative changes required to launch New Labour's preferred school structure. The Bill was launched in November 1997 and received Royal Assent in the summer of 1998.

The major change designed to improve standards was the introduction of Education Action Zones where LEAs had failed. The intention was to vocationalize secondary education in areas with persistently poor examination results and a correlation with such factors as a high ratio of pupils with English as a second language, free school meals and high unemployment. If necessary the management boards of Zones could introduce radical changes in the implementation of the National Curriculum, to the structure of the school day, employment contracts and in relationships with both private and voluntary sectors (HMSO, 1998). The threat to close failing schools, to be reopened with a new head and a 'Fresh Start', also showed that New Labour meant business on standards, and there were proposals to make it easier for the DfEE (with the assistance of the General Teaching Council) to sack poor teachers. In terms of centralization, the 1998 Act was believed to rival the Education Reform Act, 1988, with up to 100 new powers in the hands of the Secretary of State (Rafferty, 1998b).

The new school structure, with Foundation schools to replace Grant Maintained status and Community to replace council and county state categories, further endorsed specialization. Selection by aptitude in new specialist schools was to be set at 10 per cent, but remain higher at 15 per cent for former GM schools. In an example of the new powers of centralized intervention, the DfEE's numeracy and literacy taskforces prescribed what had to be taught and in what way. New Labour ministers and advisers such as Michael Barber and David Reynolds sought to bring pedagogy under political control, prescribing whole-class teaching and subject-setting and streaming as the norm even in primary schools (Robinson, 1998b, 142–9).

Funding issues in education were covered by the pre-election announcement that New Labour would stay within Conservative spending limits for the first two years of the administration. Thereafter, a comprehensive spending review (CSR) would establish New Labour priorities for the remainder of the parliament (Hackett and Thornton, 1998). Despite the headline figure which suggested that the government were planning to increase expenditure by over £19 billion, the CSR settlement in education was set to amount, after inflation, to an extra £1.9 billion in 1999–2000, £2.3 billion 2000–1, and £1.8 billion 2001–2 according to the Institute for Fiscal Studies (Hackett and Thornton, 1998). Education as a share of GDP across the UK was projected to increase to 4.9 per cent in 2000–1 and 5.0 per cent in 2001–2, compared with 4.8 per cent in 1996–7 (DfEE, 1998b). However, to set this increase in context, education spending was 5.2 per cent of GDP in 1994 after the effect of the Conservatives' pre-1992 election spending had been taken into account (Rafferty, 1998c). Under New Labour, education spending would not reach such a level again until well into the new century. However, given the low starting point, after the CSR settlement, local authority Standard Spending Assessments were to increase by an average 3.4 per year in real terms, capital spending on schools was set to double, and funding was released for another extra 500 000 students for further and higher education (Major, 1998). However, funding growth only looked generous in the context of the Conservative legacy covering the first two years of the Labour administration.

In other public pronouncements during the first two years of the administration there was no let up on the rhetoric of improving school standards, against the expectations of many educational professionals (Kane, 1997; Tooley, 1997). This was underlined when Secretary of State David Blunkett let it be known that Chris Woodhead, Her Majesty's Chief Inspector of Schools, was to have his contract as head of the Office for Standards in Education (OFSTED) extended, rather than shortened as some had hoped (Leadbetter, 1997, 12). To the consternation of many on the left, New Labour began its term of office by naming and shaming 18 apparently failing schools (Judd, 1997). Education Action Zones, mentioned for the first time in the manifesto, were also developed specifically to encourage private input into state education, raising the possibility that the private sector could eventually replace local democratic control of schools in problem areas, if that was what it would take to raise standards (DfEE, 1998c). New Labour seemed to circumvent the development of EAZs however, in 1999 with the introduction of a new (and apparently *ad hoc*) redistributive package which offered help to all inner-city schools and slowly developing pupils through the use of school mentors. Although this package, amounting to a further £350 m for secondary education, was designed at least as much to appeal to middle-class users of the comprehensive system, the targeted redistributive element suggested a much broader scope and faster timetable than existing EAZ plans (DfEE, 1999a). This perhaps reflected concerns about the lack of private finance (and thus rapid improvement) promised by EAZ bidders.

In vocational training, voluntarism and exhortation has been the government's preferred method, in keeping with the Conservative tradition. However, the CSR money which has gone into further education and the promise of funding from university tuition fees represented a redistribution of opportunities. Out of the announced expansion of higher education by 500 000 places, 420 000 students were expected to be taking sub-degree qualifications (for example Higher National Diplomas and Certificates) in further education colleges, many of them part-time. However, after the rhetoric of lifelong learning there was general disappointment in the tertiary sector when it was realized that Labour's plans involved no changes to the law, with the long awaited White Paper downgraded to Green Paper consultative status (Hillman, 1998, 63–72).

In New Labour discourse, lifelong learning is best seen as a unifying slogan rather than a unifying policy aimed to absorb the varied and hierarchical qualification structure. Adopting consensus positions in further and continuing education necessarily meant retention of the A level at the pinnacle for entry to universities and as a signal clearly valued by employers (E. Williams, 1997). While the overarching plans of more radical reformers (Richardson *et al.*, 1995) have been sidelined, other initiatives such as the university for Industry and Individual Learning Accounts, outside the DfEE's purview as Treasury policy areas, have been only slowly established. New Labour's reluctance to take more radical positions on tertiary education and training highlights the power of the higher education lobby with its message of defending autonomy and excellence.

Adapting to Consensus: Continuities with the Conservatives, 1979–97

How much of what has ensued can be traced back to the legacy of Thatcherism? There is a clear danger of attributing any new policy direction to the effects of the immediate past administration; given the usual levels of policy continuity and cross-party consensus, such an argument can be tautological. Even as Labour in power in the 1960s and 1970s was able to satisfy internal ideological pressure for expansion and wider access at tertiary and higher levels, the government was responding to changes in the nature of employment which would have confronted any government of the period. During the very different conditions of the 1980s, Labour responded slowly to the Conservative reforms about choice and standards, constrained by association with the teacher unions and elements of egalitarian left ideology. In government the Conservatives drove the educational agenda; consensus politics, which would make Labour electable again, required responding to that agenda. This meant the individualization of training and tertiary education programmes, the emphasis on employer imperatives in the development of vocational qualifications (Jessup, 1991, 10), and in compulsory education, it implied the sacrifice of the all-encompassing comprehensive school district and the political power of local education authorities.

Consumer concerns were first raised by the Conservatives on assuming office in 1970, and more effectively after 1979 as the fragile consensus among middle-class parents around the efficacy of comprehensive education deteriorated in the wake of the so-called 'Great Debate' sparked off by Callaghan's 1976 speech. Discontent about the appropriateness of comprehensive education for either the pupils or their future employers (the main concern of Callaghan) was translated by the Thatcher government into a series of Education Acts. The 1980 Act obliged Local Education Authorities (LEAs) to make examination results available to parents and gave them the right to challenge the authorities' decision on which school their children should attend. This threatened the basis of the comprehensive settlement, reliant as it was on catchment areas designed to incorporate all classes of children (P. Smith, 1992, 141).

The Education Reform Act of 1988 legislated for a National Curriculum and delivered as many as 500 new powers into the hands of the Secretary of State (Rafferty, 1998a). In 1992, a further act made it possible for schools to opt out of LEA control, and manage as much as 90 per cent of their own budgets. Funding would henceforth follow the child, rather than the needs of the school's socio-economic characteristics, further weakening the progressive comprehensive principle. The Act also created Grant Maintained schools which could opt out of LEA control and benefit from the receipt of transitional funding. Such schools were also allowed to select a proportion of pupils by their aptitude in one or more specialism the school offered (DFE, 1992).

While egalitarian and libertarian left ideas were encompassed within the comprehensive consensus, the fragile nature of middle-class support for comprehensives resulted in the Labour Opposition of the 1980s having to come to terms with an individualized, fragmented state school system as a Conservative legacy. In this sense, New Labour's construction of education policy between 1994 and 1999 can be seen as continuing general post-war developments, always responding to social demand with the hope of reaching beyond the working-class base of traditional Labour Party support. The reality of declining school populations throughout the 1980s also has to be understood as the context for the Conservative's introduction of competition between schools for the declining numbers of school age children. Changes to the pupil funding regime placed the emphasis on schools to attract more units of a resource which was becoming scarcer. The change from needs-related to pupil number funding challenged one of the main redistributive aims of progressive education.

One major thematic continuity has been the centralization of powers in the DfEE, involving changes to the National Curriculum and prescribing pedagogy. Clearly, New Labour have also adopted much of the popular rhetoric of the Thatcher and Major years; parental choice of schools facilitated by information released by LEAs; the presence of selection as a market signal to the aspirational middle class; the accountability for public expenditure typified by league tables of performance; local management of schools' funding (LMS), which New Labour have extended to all schools; and the centrality of standards to the education debate. However, this chapter has sought to argue that most of these changes are related to the changing basis of demand for labour and social demand for educational opportunity, rather than from any deliberate ideological departure from the left. The exceptions would seem to be the emphasis the Conservatives placed on returning to selection of pupils by schools, and a desire to see more private money invested in the running of schools. Although selection may benefit the education of a few, even where presented as specialization, it is not designed to respond to national economic needs nor to deliver the best education to 'the many, not the few' (Beckett, 1998a). Politically, moves towards private finance and selection by New Labour are best understood as the offering of a set of market signals designed to appeal mainly to non-traditional Labour supporters, holding out the prospect of better funded schools offering real consumer choice. This can be seen as the direct consequence of constructing policy aimed at vote maximization, rather than as a reflection of the wishes of the party membership or institutions.

As for private sector involvement, the responses to the bidding for EAZ status show once again the difficulties most private companies envisage in making a profit from running state schools, an echo of the Conservatives' original plans for City Technology Colleges in the 1980s (Beckett, 1998b, 8–10, 1999, 8–9). Philosophically, the erosion of the principle of state funded compulsory education implies a no-nonsense and un-ideological attitude to an essentially managerial problem; how to increase the amount of money in education without adding to the public burden. This can be interpreted as meritocratic, technocratic planning or indeed as egalitarian if the policy's best effects are on the educational performance of children from deprived areas. State-only funding and local democratic control are not intrinsic elements of improving opportunities and outcomes among the poorest in society.

Conclusion

So what is new about New Labour's education policies? Educationally there are clearly large areas of continuity with the Conservative era, and some aspects, such as the centralization of pedagogy and the application of private finance to failing state schools are new at least in degree, if not intent. Politically New Labour can more readily be seen as radical, having advanced policy with regard to selection, choice and local authority control. The party remains, however, New Labour rather than the 'New Party' because it has successfully presented policy change as emanating from within the corpus of party ideology, which had always encompassed egalitarian and libertarian, meritocratic values. Under the (perhaps convenient) cover of modernization in response to globalization, New Labour have reconceptualized a comprehensive education system designed to meet the needs of its new individualistic and aspirational voter base. New Labour can thus be seen as a synthesis of three elements. First, it has inherited a vague, plural ideology from the several guises of its 'old' Labour history, balancing egalitarians and meritocrats, authoritarians and libertarians in the famous 'broad church'; this allows the party leadership some manoeuvrability within the confines of the ideology, without provoking exit (Panebianco, 1988, 8). Second, the Labour Party developed a centralized policymaking structure around the time of the Policy Review which has steepened the party hierarchy. Now there are fewer intermediate institutions between leaders and membership such as trade unions and party caucuses such as the NEC; almost all power is concentrated in the hands of senior parliamentarians who can direct policy in an embodiment of Michelsian party domination by oligarchy (Michels, 1962, 35), with a plebiscitary relationship between leader and led. The third element in the synthesis is electoral popularity which the party began to court systematically again during the mid-1980s. In education this has been reduced to a partially symbolic emphasis on standards and choice, with simple clear messages for the electorate provided by the Conservatives in office. Labour are 'new' because of the emphasis now given to the electoral impact on key aspirational middle-class groups. In the 'old' Labour period, middle-class groups were attracted to a collective form of school organization which the party benefited from association with (as long as it was thought to be successful). After the Conservative interregnum, the aspirational middle class is now attracted to individualist forms of organization and signals of opportunity and excellence. New Labour's electoral success has been built on creating an association with such individualist responses to aspirational demand. Without the option of voter 'exit' in Britain's two-party, first-past-the-post electoral system, New Labour has adopted some elements attractive to the libertarian and meritocratic left and has still benefited from the grudging support of the party's egalitarian wing. This balancing process has undoubtedly restricted the political manoeuvrability of New Labour, but the party's attachment to public opinion does not preclude adapting to more egalitarian solutions to social and educational problems if they are shown to appeal to the middle class in the future.

11

New Labour and Welfare

CLAIRE ANNESLEY

The reform of the welfare state is, together with constitutional reform, a key pillar of New Labour's project to modernize Britain. The direction and content of these reforms have been widely debated since the election of 1997. There is much disagreement about how to characterize these reforms within the conventional understanding of the British welfare state, and in relation to Labour's traditional welfare policy. New Labour's welfare reform has been criticized on the one hand for being a continuation of the neo-liberal Thatcherite agenda, and on the other as typical of Labour's 'nanny state' instincts. To dismiss New Labour's welfare plans in this way is easy. What is harder, but more useful, is to attempt to assess whether there is something new about New Labour's approach to welfare. Most important, though, is assessing to what extent welfare reform under New Labour is likely to create either an equal or a divided society, particularly given Tony Blair's statement that, 'I believe in greater equality. If the next Labour Government has not raised the living standards of the poorest by the end of its time of office it will have failed' (Blair, 1996a).

This chapter will first examine the extent to which the shift in welfare policy represents a substantive break from the post-war welfare consensus and traditional Labour welfare ideology. It will then outline the factors motivating the reforms, and question whether these are driven by electoral considerations, demographic imperatives, a new moral philosophy, or a changing socio-economic environment. The concept of social exclusion will be used to illustrate how the combination of changing economic, social and political conditions challenge the ability of the welfare state to promote social citizenship. Then the policies which have been proposed to manage those social exclusions will be outlined. Finally the chapter will summarize some of the academic and political debates, in ideological terms and within the discourse of social justice and social fairness.

Welfare Modernization: a Labour Tradition?

To what extent does New Labour's welfare modernization represent a break from the post-war model constructed by Beveridge? Labour's welfare ideology has been dominated by a statist view which maintained that social equality could be achieved through increased welfare spending, which in turn was to be financed through sustained economic expansion achieved through Keynesian demand management. A successful government was defined as one which presided over high welfare expenditure. Furthermore, the post-war welfare state was intended to extend existing civil and political citizenship rights to the social sphere. Social citizenship was understood as an economic status within a welfare state, independent of a citizen's contribution to society. This approach was 'linked with ideas about the universality of welfare, the need to avoid stigma, the growth of a concern with rights and the belief that benefits could contribute to a more egalitarian society' (Plant, 1998, 30). However, this ideal model of welfare has been constantly challenged since the 1960s, when the necessary levels of economic growth became harder to achieve and poverty was 'rediscovered' (Lowe, 1993, 135–41). Although on the whole the party remained ideologically committed to the universal welfare model and high levels of redistribution, Labour governments with budget constraints were required to limit welfare expenditure, mostly by resorting to means-testing. Indeed from 1974 onwards, even prior to the visit of the International Monetary Fund (IMF) in 1976, Labour governments were advocating cuts in public spending (Ludlam, 1992, 716).

During the early 1980s, Labour in opposition reacted to welfare retrenchment of the Thatcher government by adopting a more traditional stance, characterized by commitments to restore the principle of universalism and high levels of benefits, especially pensions and child benefits. However, following two electoral defeats in 1983 and 1987, Neil Kinnock initiated a Policy Review which sought to rethink welfare policies taking account of changed economic and social circumstances, and to re-examine the relationship between welfare policy and economic planning (Alcock, 1992, 137). In social policy terms the 1989 Policy Review is significant in that it opened a debate about alternative models of welfare and social security provision. It acknowledged the limits of the role of the state and accepted individual liberty over social equality as a primary goal of social policy (Ellison, 1997, 51). The Review was widely criticized by party traditionalists for representing accommodation to the Thatcherite market-led agenda. However, many have argued that it was more a response to socio-economic change, for example changes in size and composition of the working class, and to electoral failures since 1979. Supporters claimed that it sought a long-term modernization strategy which can be understood as a continuation of the process of modernization started by Gaitskell in 1959. As such, this process of social policy modernization can be seen as a Labour tradition which pre-dates Thatcher (M. J. Smith, 1992, 18).

Following a fourth electoral defeat in 1992 and Kinnock's resignation, Labour commissioned an independent policy review. The Commission on Social Justice (CSJ) was established in December 1992 at the instigation of the new leader, John Smith. The Commission's aim was to promote social justice by developing a long-term strategy for reversing Britain's failure to respond to the three 'revolutions' – economic, social and political – which had altered the shape of Britain over the past 30 years (CSJ, 1994, 61–90). Social justice was defined as a hierarchy of four ideas: equal worth of all citizens; the right of all citizens to meet their basic needs; primary distribution and redistribution of opportunity to promote life chances; the reduction and, where possible, eradication of unjust inequalities (CSJ, 1994, 17–18). The CSJ asserted that social justice could best be achieved by an Investors' future, defined as a long-term strategy not simply tailoring existing policies but rather setting a new direction (CSJ, 1994, 398). Most importantly it recognized that social justice should not be tackled though the welfare state alone, but that co-ordinated and complementary policy approaches in all sectors of social policy were needed. The Investors' future saw economic prosperity as the basis for social justice. It 'combines the ethics of community with the dynamics of the market economy … demands strong institutions, strong families and strong communities'. This was contrasted with the Levellers' future (old Labour) and the Deregulators' future (Thatcherism). The former was rejected because, although it shares many Investor objectives, its strategies for achieving social justice are different. Most importantly, the Levellers are perceived as not recognizing the importance of economic renewal in achieving social justice. The Deregulators' future is rejected for being a short-termist and risk-fraught option which, rather than promoting social justice, would result in a 'future of extremes' (CSJ, 1994, 4–5).

The CSJ policy review called for an 'intelligent welfare state' which would respond rapidly to the changing circumstances and needs of welfare recipients. The four propositions which run through the CSJ policy proposals assert that the welfare state should be transformed 'from a safety net in times of trouble to a springboard for economic opportunity'; that access to training and education must be improved and that investment in the talent of all citizens is required; that the 'real choices across the life cycle for men and women in the balance of employment, family, education, leisure and retirement' need to be promoted and finally that the 'social wealth of our country' must be reconstructed (CSJ, 1994, 1–2). Throughout, the CSJ remained committed to welfare universalism and a model of citizenship which stressed a balance between rights and responsibilities.

The CSJ provides us with the key to understanding New Labour's welfare ethos. There is a common recognition by the CSJ and the New Labour government that economic renewal and overcoming structural deficiencies require approaches which depart from the existing strategies of the post-war welfare state. Moreover, this adoption of new strategies is necessary if the social justice aspirations of the post-war welfare state are to be upheld. However, there is evidence that New Labour's position on social justice shifted between the publication of the CSJ and the election of 1 May 1997. During the Stakeholder debate in 1996–7 the balance between rights and responsibilities became weighted in favour of responsibilities, although this debate appeared to remain firmly committed to universalism over means-testing (Hutton, 1995; Kelly *et al.*, 1997). However, the defining value of New Labour in government appears to be social fairness not social justice, and some have suggested that this shift amounts to more than rhetorical detail (Hall, 1998, 12). Whereas the goal of policies informed by the concept of social justice is to extend inalienable social citizenship rights to the maximum number of people, placing a strong emphasis on universal benefits, social fairness is concerned with reducing the gap between those most deprived of social citizenship rights and mainstream society. This can be seen in New Labour's move towards a culture of targeting and means-testing. Frank Field, who was Minister for Welfare Reform 1997–8, claimed that New Labour in government has moved away from a disengagement with means-tests before the election and has instead set sail in the opposite direction into a 'means-test morass'. Field attributes this shift to the Treasury-domination of welfare reform which is more concerned with the state of public finances than social justice (Field, 1998).

In this review of the development of the Labour Party's welfare policy it is also important to place the New Labour approach to welfare in the context of 18 years of Conservative welfare policies. Social policy between 1979 and 1997 was generally centred around attempts to cut the cost of public expenditure by limiting the scope of social welfare provision. Conservative governments moved social policy away from universal provision and placed a greater emphasis on means-testing, self-provisioning and individual responsibility. This was coupled with a shift from rights-centred social policy towards attaching obligations to the receipt of welfare and coercion into work, best illustrated by the introduction of the Job Seekers' Allowance (JSA) in 1996. However, attempts to cut welfare expenditure largely failed due to the increased demand for welfare services caused by mass-unemployment and demographic change and the rising aspirations of citizens (Hills, 1998, 7). Instead of redistribution through the mechanisms of the welfare state, Conservative governments relied on market forces to trigger a 'trickle-down' effect whereby increased national wealth would benefit all income groups. The market-led approaches of the New Right culminated in the widening of income and social inequalities, between the lowest and highest income groups.

Under the Tories, the scope of government responsibility for welfare was reduced and the role of the private sector in providing aspects of welfare was encouraged (Lister, 1997a). The New Right saw the welfare state as a barrier to independent citizenship 'crowding out' otherwise active civil society organizations, voluntary associations and individual self-provisioning (Green, 1993, 147). It can be argued that New Right policies have reinvigorated a spirit of individual responsibility which was absent from the statist period of welfare that prescribed welfare roles to citizens. The welfare approaches of the New Right and New Labour have in common a recognition of the failure of the statist approach to welfare to meet the diverse needs of welfare recipients in increasingly heterogeneous social conditions – a point which has been made forcefully by new social movements and pressure groups since the 1960s.

Challenges to the Welfare State

New Labour's reform of the welfare state is being motivated by the belief that 'welfare needs of today are not being met by the welfare state of yesterday' (Blair, 1996a, 142). This is a situation which has arisen because the 'welfare system has failed to keep pace with profound economic, social and political changes' of late twentieth-century Britain (DSS, 1998a). These profound changes affecting advanced industrial economies are outlined in government consultation papers on welfare reform in four broad categories. The first is the change in the nature of work over the last 30 years with a shift from manufacturing to services, towards flexible employment and an increased importance of skills and training. The full-time, lifelong model of employment, upon which the welfare state relied for the funding of social security both through the insurance principle and tax-based welfare, exists only for a minority. The phenomena of mass- and long-term unemployment have placed strain on the principle of social insurance and meant a shift towards means-tested, tax-based benefits. Second, the increased involvement of women in the workplace has altered the nature of the labour market and welfare state, undermining the male-breadwinner assumptions of the post-war Beveridge welfare state. Third, families have changed in size and form because of, among other factors, high divorce rates and a growth in the number of lone-parent families over recent years. Finally, demographic trends point towards an ageing population which places a burden on the welfare state by no longer being adequately provided for by either state or private pensions schemes. It is estimated that one in three people retiring in 50 years' time will be poor enough to be dependent on means-tested support (DSS, 1998a).

Two exogenous processes – globalization and Europeanization – are perceived as creating constraints on the ability and scope of nation-states to determine their levels of public expenditure. It has been argued for a while that high levels of public expenditure have a negative impact on the ability of nation-states to compete in a global environment, although this is now also widely contested (Hirst and Thompson, 1996; Held *et al.*, 1999). For some, the process of European integration is understood as an economic project which renders social goals a second priority. In addition, the convergence criteria for qualification to the European Monetary Union (EMU) placed constraints on public borrowing which led to welfare 'belt-tightening' in many European states. Others see the European Union's social agenda as a positive influence on New Labour's welfare policy understood in its widest sense.

Social Inclusion: the Motivation for New Labour's Welfare Reform

It can be argued that the cumulative impact on societies of the endogenous and exogenous influences outlined above reduced the ability of welfare systems to meet the needs of large groups of citizens who fall out side the post-war welfare framework. These citizens thus become socially excluded – they enter into a 'process of being detached from the organizations and communities of which the society is composed and from the rights and obligations that they embody' (Room, 1995, 243). The inability of existing welfare structures to guarantee social inclusion for all citizens is New Labour's justification for prioritizing welfare reform in its modernization agenda. Unlike the New Right, New Labour recognizes the role and duty of government to intervene in issues of social inequality and believes that welfare states are still a mechanism for tackling social disadvantage: 'Helping those who are not in a position to help themselves is a mark of a civilised society' (DSS, 1998a). Unlike old Labour, New Labour employs a wide range of strategies to achieve this aim.

In many ways social exclusion discourse is an extension of the CSJ and Stakeholder debates. They are all broadly concerned with the same themes: how to break the cycle of multiple disadvantage and how to reconcile social and economic change with social and economic equality. Social inclusion, it is argued, can be promoted in part with the traditional tax and benefits framework of the post-war welfare state. However, it also requires 'joined-up' strategies which involve policies and actors in different spheres (public, private and third-sector partnerships) and at all levels of governance (nationally, regionally and locally). In 1998 the government established the Social Exclusion Unit (SEU) which operates from within the Cabinet Office but co-ordinates work and policy development across a range of departments to better understand and tackle the phenomenon and cycle of social exclusion. The SEU covers England; the Scottish Office also established a Social Exclusion Team with similar goals but with a particular emphasis on rural communities. In Wales and Northern Ireland, community renewal and regeneration strategies are also being developed.

During its first year to July 1998, the SEU's remit was to concentrate on the four problem areas of school truancy, drugs, street living, and the worst estates. The second phase of the work plan will continue on the truancy and homelessness issues, as well as teenage parents, and 16–18 year-olds. This new social inclusion approach to welfare has been interpreted in various ways and has been both warmly welcomed and widely criticized (Levitas, 1998). Critics see it as a strategy which focuses more on the cosmetic and moral dimensions of social disadvantage, rather than tackling deep-rooted and multiple deprivation or material poverty. It has also been criticized for concentrating on the redistribution of opportunity – helping people help themselves – rather than redistribution of income.

Policy Reform to Promote Social Inclusion

This section concentrates on the dominant themes which run through the Labour's welfare reform aimed at social exclusion. These link up with the four categories of social and economic change outlined above, which have contributed to the inability of the existing welfare regime to meet the needs and demands of its citizens. These categories are for analytical purposes only. The stated intention is that 'joined-up' policies reinforce each other across the categories, so that those most affected by social exclusion will benefit from the widest range of measures, if they fulfil their responsibility to society. For each category the policy proposals and the debates surrounding them will be outlined.

Work

New Labour's welfare reform is dominated by work-centred policies aiming at rejuvenating the work ethic (Hills, 1998; Kelly and Oppenheim, 1998). Mirroring Beveridge, New Labour's reconstruction of welfare is founded on the conviction that work represents the best means of reconnecting citizens with the organizations and communities which promote social inclusion and prevent material poverty. Research indicates that workless households are over-represented in the bottom fifth of income distribution and that the best chances of moving to a higher income group accompany a shift to employment (DSS, 1998g).

Policies aimed at reinserting key groups into the labour market take a variety of forms. First, there are activation policies. The New Deal welfare-to-work schemes have been set up for those groups who experience the greatest difficulty moving into employment: 18–24 year-olds and the long-term unemployed participate on a compulsory basis, lone parents and the disabled on a voluntary basis. However, all new claimants are required to pass through a Single Gateway for benefit assessment, in which able-bodied claimants will be required to attend a series of interviews to discuss plans. Disabled claimants will be required to take a reformed All Works Test to assess their ability to work (the original test assessed the degree of their disability). After the period of assessment, New Dealers are offered either subsidized employment; a training option; work on an environmental taskforce; voluntary work; or assistance with self-employment. Those who do not comply are subjected to benefit sanctions.

Second, the work-centred social policy recognizes the existence of so-called benefit and poverty traps, which act as a disincentive to low income groups entering the labour market. Policies have been developed to 'make work pay' by increasing the incomes of the lowest paid, and improving general employment conditions. To this end the government introduced a national minimum wage which, it is anticipated, will increase the incomes of between 12 and 15 per cent of 18–21 year-olds (*Labour Market Trends*, 1998, 629). In addition the government has introduced a lower, ten pence tax band to give low earners higher disposable incomes, and has reformed National Insurance contributions. Other labour market policies were outlined in the *Fairness at Work* White Paper. Some are national policies (for example, trade union recognition) while others result from EU Social Protocol directives on part-time work and parental leave.

The third strand of getting people back to work involves improving employability through permanent up-skilling and retraining, known as Lifelong Learning. This aims to ensure that 'all those capable of work are encouraged to develop the skills, knowledge, technology and adaptability to enable them to enter and remain in employment throughout their working lives' (HM Treasury, 1997, 2). This recognises that those most harshly affected by unemployment are the low-skilled, and is also a response to evidence from countries such as Germany that investment in human capital boosts macro-economic performance.

New Labour's social policy is based on the principle of 'work for those who can; security for those who cannot' (DSS, 1998a, iii). This rejuvenation of the work ethic has raised many concerns among those to the left of New Labour. As noted above, social citizenship under the post-war welfare consensus was guaranteed by unconditional, mostly universal, rights to welfare. There are concerns that work-centred policies represent a regression from these aims of post-war welfare regimes, which sought to detach social welfare from economic activity. The New Labour approach suggests an overt shift towards a second model of citizenship that places equal emphasis on responsibilities and on rights; on contribution and on receipt. Plant characterizes this form of social citizenship not as a 'pre-existing status, but rather something that is achieved by contributing to the life of society' (Plant, 1998, 30). Lister and others argue that New Labour's harsh enforcement of the work ethic could highly stigmatize the economically inactive, who do not or cannot contribute to society through work, and create an underclass of citizens who rely on benefits. Such critics believe that unpaid work and a care ethic should be equally valued and rewarded (Lister, 1998; Levitas, 1998). Economic arguments against the welfare-to-work programmes question the sustainability of activation programmes at different points of the economic cycle, while others criticize the focus on the supply-side of the labour market which promotes training or retraining rather than supporting demand-side policies creating jobs.

Equal Opportunities and Family Friendly Policies

The success of the post-war welfare state relied on the breadwinner model which assumed full employment for men, and domestic and informal roles for women. Now women comprise roughly 50 per cent of the labour force, but are over-represented among the lowest paid and the lowest income group, and remain responsible for the majority of childcare. Research has also revealed that children are over-represented in low income groups, with one fifth of children living in poverty. These issues are addressed in the Home Office publication *Supporting Families I*, which lays out a range of policies aiming at: providing better services and support for parents; providing better financial support for families; helping families balance work and home; strengthening marriage and offering better support for serious family problems (Home Office, 1998).

The most noteworthy policy in this document is the Working Families Tax Credit (WFTC) which replaced Family Credit in October 1998. This policy provides working families with a guaranteed minimum income paid through the wage packet. This policy is reinforced by the Childcare Tax Credit (CCTC) to help with childcare costs for working parents, and the National Childcare Strategy which seeks to improve the availability of quality childcare for working parents. Policies for families have been criticized by the Conservatives as state intrusion into citizens' private lives, and as such a continuation of Labour's 'nanny state' instincts. The policies have been cautiously welcomed by women, who expressed concerns about the shift in payment of benefits from women as prime carers (Family Credit) to men as main breadwinners (WFTC). In addition, women have highlighted paradoxes such as training lone mothers to become childminders through the New Deal: paid to look after other people's children but not supported to care for their own at home.

Ageing Society

New Labour's reform of the pensions system addresses two issues: 'The current pensions system does not provide adequate security for people who cannot save and does not have the trust of people who can afford to do more to help themselves' (DSS, 1998f, 23). The radical solution to the pensions problem proposed by Frank Field would be to introduce compulsory, private sector, stakeholder pensions linked to individual saving accounts, while providing basic pensions for the poorest. The Green Paper *Partnership in Pensions* rejects privatization of the entire pensions system and only goes as far as replacing the Serps scheme with a pay-as-you-go Second State Pension whilst introducing a parallel system of strictly regulated, mutual-run, stakeholder pensions plus a range of incentives to make them appear attractive. The Green Paper avoided compelling people to pay into private pensions, relying instead on various incentives to encourage saving, even among lower income groups.

The level of poverty amongst pensioners has steadily increased since the early 1980s, when pensions increases became linked to prices rather than average incomes. This has made record numbers of pensioners eligible for means-tested income support, whose take-up has been very low. New Labour has been addressing the problem by encouraging the take-up of income support, with a minimum income guarantee of between £72 and £83 per week for single pensioners.

Health

New Labour's manifesto pledged to reduce waiting lists in the National Health Service (NHS), by redirecting money saved through cutting the administrative costs of the internal market. In government it has redirected large amounts of extra funding to the NHS in its first budgets and the Comprehensive Spending Review. It has set up Health Action Zones (HAZs) to improve health through local partnerships in areas marked by pronounced deprivation and poor health.

Public expenditure on the NHS still commands popular support – arguably because of the universality of its provision – and any indications of privatization in the form of the private finance initiative (PFI) meet with criticism. PFI was introduced by the Conservatives in November 1992 to transfer the financing of public investment from the state to the public sector, in an attempt to lower the Public Sector Borrowing Requirement. New Labour has relaxed the PFI rules – it is no longer compulsory to consider this option – but it remains a popular means of raising funds. Critics of PFI argue that the NHS could raise capital more cheaply itself, that this *de facto* privatization of the NHS has damaged services, resulted in higher overall costs, and destroyed cohesion in the NHS (Hutton, 1998b).

The Debate Surrounding New Labour's Welfare Reform

Since the election of 1997, New Labour's welfare proposals have been widely debated and criticized. The critiques, from a wide range of political and academic viewpoints, constitute attempts at positioning New Labour on the political and ideological spectrum. They are summarized in this section.

Many to the left of New Labour see its welfare reform programme as an obvious continuation of the Thatcherite agenda. Martin Jacques argued in *Marxism Today* that, 'it is the continuities rather than the ruptures that characterize the Blair era' (Jacques, 1998, 3). He cites as continuities the refusal to raise income tax, and the adherence to the Tories' spending plans for the first two years in office. The latter decision has been criticized by many on the left as unnecessary self-constraints, imposed in pursuit of electoral popularity (Hills, 1998; Jacques, 1998). New Labour was especially heavily criticized in autumn 1997 for implementing the cut to lone parents' benefit which was part of these Tory spending plans. This move was read as a blatant attack on the most vulnerable and excluded, which exposed the neo-liberal instincts of New Labour. This critique continued over the cutting of incapacity benefits in February 1999 when the Welfare Bill came before Parliament. Both incidences provoked major backbench revolts.

This New Thatcherite view sees New Labour working within the constraints of the New Right agenda, resigned to the rule of the markets, rather than attempting a radical project for social improvement. It is seen as a continuation of the neo-liberal agenda, in the absence of an alternative left response to structural change (Lister, 1997a). In terms of social policy, the Blair project, according to this argument, seeks not to eradicate poverty and promote equality by changing the socio-economic framework, but to 'mollify' growing inequality (Jacques, 1998, 3). This is viewed as a complete break from the Labour tradition of seeking social justice through the tools of the welfare state. However, the choice to limit public spending can also be interpreted as a realistic electoral strategy to ditch Labour's tax-and-spend image, in order to win the support of Middle England, and reconstruct the welfare consensus which eroded during the Thatcher and Major administrations, while reducing the public debt which mounted under the Conservatives.

A further *Marxism Today* critique of New Labour focuses on the unapologetic acceptance of globalization as a law of nature, marking a failure to break with neo-liberalism (Hall, 1998, 11). Bill Jordan, too, sees Labour's welfare reform as a 'positive and proactive response ... to the phenomenon of globalization', and influenced by Clinton's welfare reforms. The so-called Blair–Clinton orthodoxy for a global world relies on a strong emphasis on the work ethic, stricter conditions regarding benefits entitlement, the rejection of class analysis and exploitation in the analysis of social justice, which have been superseded by the notion of equality through opportunity (Jordan, 1998). There is a certain amount of evidence which suggests that New Labour is adopting an understanding of welfare that is a 'narrower American term – means-tested cash support for those outside paid work – rather than the more helpful definition which includes universal services and draws wider political support' (McCormick, 1997, 110). Certainly, the Working Families Tax Credit (WFTC) was a policy which New Labour borrowed and adapted – by inserting more aspects of voluntarism – from the American Earned Income Tax Credit (EITC). Tax credits look set to become an increasingly important tool in Labour's reformed welfare state, providing basic incomes to certain groups. The idea of an integrated tax and benefits system had been rejected by the Commission on Social Justice, due to technical and administrative complexities: it would be like 'using a sledge-hammer to crack a nut' (CSJ, 1994, 258–60).

Whilst New Labour's welfare approach is often interpreted as a shift to a more residual, American regime of welfare, it is also worth noting parallels with European welfare states. Most other social democratic welfare states have introduced workfare policies with strong(er) elements of obligation, and even the states with the most developed traditions of universalism (for example Sweden, Denmark, Finland), resort to means-testing in order to target limited welfare resources (Heikkila *et al.*, 1999). New Labour's approach to welfare mirrors efforts in European welfare states to tackle social exclusion using a combination of tools, actors and levels of governance. The influence of the social policy of the European Union (EU) is also worth noting, since New Labour signed up to the Social Chapter and is more and more influenced by EU social policy strategies.

New Labour is increasingly working according to the principle of subsidiarity – a concept from Christian Democracy introduced to EU politics with the Maastricht Treaty in 1992 – which implies that problems should be solved at the level closest to the citizens. The New Deal for Communities, outlined in the SEU report on neighbourhood renewal, stresses the importance of 'involving communities, not parachuting in solutions' (Social Exclusion Unit, 1998, 10). The concepts of partnership and civil society that encourage participation by non-state actors in the provision of welfare was first used in the post-war period by the Conservatives. They were used by the New Right as part of a strategy of aiding the state's retreat from the provision of welfare. New Labour's mantra of 'helping people to help themselves' is understood by the left as the state's retreat from the responsibility for the welfare of its citizens, and there are many on the left who still see the state as the most appropriate provider of welfare. However, these concepts can also be seen as ways of re-empowering citizens, involving them in forming innovative and appropriate solutions to social exclusion.

The government's social inclusion approach, which prioritizes redistribution of opportunity over income redistribution through the tax system, has been widely criticized. In a letter to the *Financial Times*, Ruth Lister along with 53 other social policy professors (*FT*54) accused New Labour of creating a 'false dichotomy' between redistributing opportunity and incomes. They called for redistribution of incomes, and benefit levels, to be replaced on the political agenda (Lister, 1998, 14). Many recent reports on social exclusion have shown that low incomes are a fundamental obstacle to exiting social exclusion. The Child Poverty Action Group (CPAG) has shown that poverty can create barriers to learning through poor levels of nutrition, health and clothing, access to books and participation in school activities (cited in Lister, 1998, 15). The *FT*54 argued that inadequate benefit levels 'could weaken the Government's own anti-exclusion strategy' as '[r]esearch suggests that the effectiveness of education reforms could be undermined by unacceptably high levels of child poverty and that impoverished benefits claimants are not the best recruits for "welfare-to-work" programmes' (Lister, 1998, 15). Furthermore, low incomes remain an obstacle to entering the labour market, since loss of benefits, most notably housing benefit, tends to offset the financial advantages of moving into a job. The *FT*54 suggested that increased benefit levels would, rather than reduce the incentive to work, ease the transition from employment to unemployment and, given the flexible and insecure nature of the British labour market, the transition between jobs (Lister, 1998).

The absence of redistribution from New Labour's rhetoric conceals the fact that the first two budgets were the most redistributive budgets for years, albeit achieved with tools other than income tax (for example, the windfall tax on the privatized utilities to fund the New Deal). Three areas of welfare still enjoy widespread public and electoral support – health, education and children – and in these areas the principle of universality has been strengthened by supplementary funds and increases in benefit levels in Gordon Brown's first two budgets, and in the Comprehensive Spending Review. At the same time, however, universal benefits are being increasingly replaced by means-tested social security, and these in turn are being increasingly targeted at poorest households and children (Timmins, 1999). Labour's welfare policy appears to be a balancing act between universal welfare funding of consensually sound areas (health, education and children), and generous means-tested benefits targeted at the poorest groups.

Research has revealed four major problems with means-tested benefits. First, they are expensive to administer. Second, they penalize saving. Third, the most needy often do not benefit from means-tested benefits to which they are entitled, as take-up rates are affected by ignorance about availability or the stigma attached to claiming. Finally, research suggests that claimants' behaviour alters according to their entitlement for benefit, and that this encourages dishonesty and fraud which the government is eager to eradicate. Tackling fraud is a priority issue of the New Labour reform of welfare. This is viewed by many on the left as an insult to the most deprived in society. Both critics and supporters of New Labour have pointed out that control of the incomes of the poor is misplaced. It should, they claim, be more concerned with tax-evaders and the 'voluntarily excluded' in the high income brackets who opt out of the welfare state through private pensions, schools and health provision. The inclusion of these groups is seen as essential for rebuilding the welfare consensus. Giddens recognizes that strategies need to be developed to stem voluntary social exclusion at the top, the so-called 'revolt of the élites' (Giddens, 1998). The rich can only be included, he argues, through 'a benefit system that benefits most of the population [and] will generate a common morality of citizenship', most likely to be achieved through universal benefits (Giddens, 1998, 108).

Left, Right or Third Way?

How easy is it to characterize New Labour's welfare approach in political terms? Is it still part of the social democratic tradition? During 1998 New Labour tried to reconnect its project to the left through the Third Way debate. This debate was concerned with whether New Labour had transcended the conventional boundaries of the old left, which believed in an active role for the state in welfare provision funded through tax and benefits, and the neo-liberal Right, which advocated a rolling-back of the state in welfare provision. In his Fabian pamphlet, *The Third Way*, Blair stated that New Labour was working according to the principle of 'permanent revisionism'. This is defined as a 'a continual search for a better means to meet our goals, based on a clear view of the changes taking place in advanced industrialized societies' (Blair, 1998c, 4). This position maintains that only by permanently reassessing the underlying socio-economic foundation of the welfare state can a government legislate effective social policy that address serious problems such as social exclusion. In many ways, Blair's Third Way mirrors the Investors' future outlined in the CSJ. Giddens uses the term 'positive welfare' to describe the Third Way approach to welfare provision, promoting autonomy, active health, and education, as a continuing part of life, well-being and initiative (Giddens, 1998, 128). Citizens are expected to be more active in determining their own welfare. Again, parallels can be drawn here with the 'intelligent welfare state' proposed by the CJS. The Third Way approach has been most criticized for being an unprincipled response to current welfare problems, and for offering no long-term strategy. This view maintains that the New Labour's welfare policy is *ad hoc*, reactive and driven by cost-cutting motivations.

The Third Way debate also left New Labour open to the criticism that it was ditching old social democrat ('old Labour') traditions. According to Blair, the Third Way is concerned with pursuing a model of politics designed for the new socio-economic conditions of the late twentieth century, which departs from post-war assumptions, and reconnects with earlier traditions: the Third Way 'draws its vitality from uniting the two great schemes of left-of-centre thought – democratic socialism and liberalism – whose divorce this century did so much to weaken progressive politics across the West'

(Blair, 1998c, 1). The Third Way therefore represents a break from the statist preferences of the post-war welfare consensus, but its ambitions remain clearly connected with the left by the commitments to emancipation and social inclusion (Giddens, 1998).

Conclusions

This chapter concludes, first, that New Labour's welfare ethos can be clearly distinguished from the market-led, neo-liberal policies of preceding Conservative governments, which expressed no interest in social justice or social inclusion. Second, rather than being a compilation of unprincipled and value-free measures, there is a coherence and a clearly defined aim to New Labour's welfare strategy. The programme of welfare reform seeks to identify and overcome the complex phenomenon of social exclusion. This is being achieved through targeted but generous welfare benefits, which are being used to redistribute resources from the top half of income distribution to the bottom half, and to those with children from those without. Given the wide disparities which, at the time of writing, still exist between the highest and lowest income groups, generous, targeted means-tested benefits are best suited to overcome inequality. At this stage, universal benefits would fail to promote social equality, in fact, the most excluded would benefit least. Put another way, policies which aspire to the more universal values of social justice cannot be attempted until social exclusion has been eradicated.

Third, with regard to the issue of New Labour's long-term vision for the welfare state, I shall propose an optimist's and a pessimist's conclusion. The pessimistic conclusion asserts that the Third Way ethos of 'permanent revisionism' restricts New Labour to short-termist responses to the most pressing welfare issues. Its strategy is motivated by the desire to remain popular with Middle England for electoral reasons. In order to keep these key voters content, welfare expenditure is maintained at a level sufficient to alleviate the situation of the most socially excluded, through the flexible mechanism of tax credits in order to ensure a minimum of social fairness.

The optimistic conclusion in contrast maintains that New Labour's commitment to achieving social justice in the long term remains strong. This view sees a radical approach in New Labour's welfare reform which, in the short term, seeks to manage in parallel the eradication of social exclusion and the reconstruction of the welfare consensus. In the long term, once social exclusion becomes a subject for historical analysis, we may be witnessing the emergence of a new model of welfare which expands the minimum incomes, already guaranteed for certain groups, to all citizens who fulfil certain responsibilities. The aim could conceivably be a universalistic citizens' income model as proposed in the CSJ, informed by the concept of social justice.

Note

The author would like to thank Michael Kenny, Steve Ludlam and Joanne Cook for their comments on earlier versions of this chapter.

12

New Labour's Foreign and Defence Policy: External Support Structures and Domestic Politics

JIM BULLER

Two initial points are worth noting in the context of this survey of New Labour's foreign and defence policy. First, in a world of increasing economic and political interdependence, it is now accepted that the separate study of 'domestic' and 'foreign' policy is no longer feasible or accurate (to the extent that it ever was) (S. Smith, 1991). One implication of this observation is that students of this subject are faced with an enormous 'analytical site'; especially if we accept that a historical perspective is vital to understanding New Labour (Bale, 1999). Second, it is misleading to talk of a specific Labour Party approach to external affairs since 1945. As a number of commentators have noted, foreign and defence policy is an example of the post-war consensus par excellence, although the scope of this agreement applies only to the front benches at Westminster and officials in Whitehall (P. M. Jones, 1987). One obvious implication is that socialist principles and ideas have played less of a role than in domestic policy.

What follows is not a general description of Labour's foreign and defence policy. Instead this chapter explores the more specific question of how Labour Party leaders have managed the link between domestic and external policy in historical perspective. More particularly, it highlights the willingness of the leadership to embrace and enmesh itself in external commitments and constraints, as a means of achieving governing competence and electoral success. Indeed, on rare occasions, these politicians have been capable of creating external institutions in pursuit of these domestic objectives. Despite New Labour's explicit attempts to distance itself from much of the party's governing performance in the post-war period, this chapter argues that policy in this area shows important continuities with this earlier period.

External Opportunities and the Cold War: Labour's Foreign and Defence Policy, 1945–67

Perhaps the most important structural backdrop facing all British foreign policymakers after 1945 was the need to reverse Britain's decline, or at least to manage it in a way which caused as little disruption to domestic politics as possible (Kennedy, 1981; Bulpitt, 1988; Gamble, 1994). The main features of this decline are well documented. While Britain's deteriorating economic performance was not confined to the post-war period, the precarious financial state of the economy came into sharper focus after the Second World War. During this conflict, Britain had lost approximately one quarter of its wealth. By the end, £1.2 m of exports were required just to maintain the wartime level of consumption. Unfortunately, the war had reduced the volume of exports to £400 m, a mere 46 per cent of its pre-1939 total. More significantly perhaps, Britain had acquired $13 m of overseas liabilities (the so-called 'sterling balances'), which increased the pound's vulnerability. This weakness was compounded by the resurrection of the pound's reserve currency status, as part of the new Bretton Woods fixed exchange rate regime negotiated in 1944. In this context, the Attlee government procured a £3.75 m US loan to strengthen Britain's economic position. Unfortunately, such assistance did not stop sterling from being devalued in 1949 and 1967: both times when Labour was in office (Gardner, 1969; Morgan, 1984, 144–8; Ryan, 1987, 13).

A second aspect of this decline was Britain's political descent from its hegemonic position within the international system; its dwindling military prowess became increasingly apparent as the post-war period developed. The granting of independence to India in 1947 was a symbolic blow, although perceived by ministers to be inevitable (Porter, 1984, 315–18). Perhaps the defining moment came with the aborted invasion of Suez in 1956, largely because of a withdrawal of US financial support. Cancellation of the Blue Streak nuclear missile in 1960 (Bayliss, 1981, 67) compounded this image of impotence, and Britain's final entry into the EU in 1973 (after two failed attempts) confirmed its status as just another European regional power.

After 1945, the response of the Attlee government was to appropriate and reform its external environment in a way which helped to disguise this gradual decline. At the centre of these efforts was the so-called 'special' relationship with the US. In recent years, a number of revisionist historians (Deighton, 1987; Ryan, 1987; P. J. Taylor, 1990) have argued that it was Britain, as much as any other country, which intensified the momentum towards the Cold War, thus creating the external conditions for this Anglo-American alliance. It is not necessary to agree with the full thrust of this contentious interpretation to appreciate that this bi-polar world provided opportunities as well as constraints. Britain could portray itself as Washington's close and loyal lieutenant; a role strengthened after the formation of the North Atlantic Treaty Organization (NATO) in 1949.

From the Labour leadership's point of view, this 'external support structure' conferred a number of governing benefits. First, the American connection allowed Britain to acquire a defence capability unrivaled in western Europe. The possibilities for such collaboration were not always evident, especially when the Truman Administration's 1946 McMahon Act prohibited the exchange of atomic information between the US and any other nation. Attlee and Bevin responded by agreeing secretly to the development of Britain's own atom bomb, a decision which some analysts argue played an important part in keeping alive future chances of cooperation (Bayliss, 1981, 26, 62). Indeed, in 1958, the McMahon Act was repealed, allowing Whitehall sole access to American information on the design and production of warheads. More generally, by tying the US into the defence of Europe in this way, Britain enjoyed considerably more protection than it could have ever afforded unilaterally.

Second, this policy supported the Labour leadership's attempt to create and maintain an image of credibility and competence in the area of economic management through preserving the pound's reserve currency status and avoiding a repeat of the devaluation in 1949. US financial support remained important in the post-war era. For instance in the 1960s Wilson, along with Callaghan, then Chancellor of the Exchequer, negotiated secret US financial support to stabilize the pound. Of course there were strings attached. Washington insisted that the Labour government maintain its defence role east of Suez, despite the increasingly obvious gap between resources and responsibilities in this area. That said, this 'understanding' helped protect the level of sterling and was perceived to be an important contributory factor in securing Labour's re-election in 1966. Devaluation in the following year marked an end to this compact (Ponting, 1989, Ch. 3; Pimlott, 1992, 365).

Third, this new bi-polar, geo-political environment helped Labour's leadership discipline expectations within the party concerning the possibilities of injecting socialist ideals in the conduct of British statecraft. The leadership cautioned against the usefulness of 'ideology' in the conduct of foreign affairs. The international system was an environment fraught with fluidity and uncertainty, as states in pursuit of their own national interests continually manoeuvred for position and power. In such a context, Labour was right to pursue a flexible, 'practical' approach (B. Jones, 1977, Ch. 8; P. J. Taylor, 1990, 57–67). As the Cold War became a reality, a socialist foreign policy was a luxury that Britain could not afford.

One final observation concerning this period is worth making, if only because it is pertinent to the argument pursued below. The management of foreign policy, as interpreted in this way, implies a picture of rational and coherent elite behaviour. In fact, as a number of authors have noted, British statecraft during this period was fraught with contradictions. The 'American connection' may have provided short-term economic (and governing) palliatives, but financial assistance from Washington came at a price: a continued presence east of Suez and the stationing of troops in Germany necessitated a higher level of defence spending than elsewhere in Europe, thus diverting precious resources from domestic expenditure. It was almost as if Labour leaders took solace from immersing themselves in these external constraints. With such external vulnerability came a perverse sense of domestic freedom. Maintaining Britain's Great Power status could be presented as given: all domestic policy options and, indeed, all domestic groups would have to submit themselves to this 'template' or 'discipline'.

Détente and Domestic Divisions: Labour's Foreign and Defence Policy, 1967–87

If the period after 1945 had witnessed an attempt by the Labour leadership to 'arrange' external policy in a way which complimented its domestic interests, changes in the international field from the late 1960s challenged this strategy and a new era of *détente* in the 1970s increased fears in Whitehall concerning Washington's commitment to the future defence of Europe. The Strategic Arms Limitation Talks (SALT II) demonstrated the real possibilities of a US–Soviet 'condominium', operating independently of Britain. This was particularly worrying in the light of Soviet superiority in short-range nuclear weapons in Europe (Camps, 1972; Owen, 1991, 379–80; Byrd, 1991, 19–22). At the same time, changes in the international economy compounded political uncertainty. The creation and growth of the Euro-dollar market and the collapse of the Bretton Woods fixed exchange rate system in the early 1970s complicated the implementation of foreign economic policy. In 1976, Labour politicians once again found themselves 'on the end' of these adverse external developments, as sterling plummeted from $2.00 to $1.50. Whilst it is now accepted that this 'Sterling Crisis' had little to do with economic fundamentals at the time, it went down as another legendary episode in the 'ungovernable' 1970s: something which Labour leaders found difficult to forget (Browning, 1986, 71–98; Donoughue, 1987, Ch. 4; Healey, 1990, 426–36).

The response of the Labour leadership during this period was twofold. It reflected an uneasy mix of continuity and change in British foreign and defence policy at this time. On the one hand, these politicians instinctively attempted to shore up as much of the old external support system as possible. Wilson and Callaghan made a number of unpublicized decisions aimed at maintaining the 'special' relationship and preventing US disengagement from Europe. These included: the purchase of additional F111 aircraft, capable of launching a nuclear strike; a decision to proceed with the Chevaline programme; and the initiation of discussions concerning a possible replacement for Polaris (Owen, 1991, 380–2 and 404; Keohane, 1993, 27–9; Morgan, 1997, Ch. 25).

At the same time, some Labour leaders began to accept that membership of the EU provided the best alternative means to maintaining a seat at the international top table. The domestic impact of this policy shift was always likely to be unpredictable. Rather than publicly embracing the pro-EU rhetoric of the EU's founding fathers, Wilson concentrated on trying to manipulate the domestic agenda in a way that presented membership as inevitable. Analysis in Whitehall focused primarily on the economic arguments rather than constitutional issues, which were likely to be more controversial. Even then, the discussion was compartmentalized. The effect of the 'common market' on each area of the British economy was studied separately because the overall picture was always likely to be adverse in the short term (Castle, 1980, 236; see also Jay, 1985, 354–62 and 382–6). Other arguments stressed Britain's growing isolation and lack of influence in a world fast dividing into regional blocs. Faced with this management style, it was perhaps unsurprising that the Labour Party's conversion to Europe proved to be a slow and painful process. Delegates at the 1980 conference actually voted to withdraw, although this policy was gradually reversed under Kinnock's leadership.

However, if external policy had helped to support the leadership's autonomy from the demands of the rank and file, these tensions within the international system helped expose increasing divisions within the party. After the 1979 election defeat, evidence of elite manoeuvring provided fertile ground for those who sought to argue that the leadership had 'betrayed' Labour's socialist principles. In the 1970s, both the Wilson and Callaghan governments had patently ignored manifesto promises to remove Polaris and reduce UK defence expenditure to a level commensurate with other western European countries. This slavish worship of the 'special' relationship, it was argued, had not only left the country vulnerable to a nuclear strike, it had diverted precious resources needed for genuine socialist planning (Kaldor *et al.*, 1979; Williams and Williams, 1989, Ch. 4; Owen, 1991, 422–4). As a result, the party moved towards unilateralism in the 1980s, thus signifying the first breakdown of the frontbench consensus on external relations since Suez. The precise electoral effect of this move is contested by psephologists (see Crewe, 1983; P. M. Jones, 1987, 119–20; Keohane, 1993, 71). Of more importance is the fact that the Labour leadership increasingly perceived the consequences of unilateralism to be deleterious (see quote by Hattersely in Conservative Research Department/European Democratic Group Secretariat, 1984, 6; Keohane, 1993, 67–8).

European Support Structures and Domestic Politics: the Changes and Continuities of New Labour's Defence Policy

Whilst the 'second' Cold War halted a number of geo-political trends evident in the 1970s, by 1990 Whitehall was faced with an international environment markedly different from anything it had witnessed since 1945. Progress on nuclear disarmament was overtaken by events, as communism collapsed in 1989 (Sanders, 1993). The reunification of Germany in the following year further complicated the security vacuum in eastern Europe (Baun, 1995/6). Both events compounded pressure towards further European integration, which had already begun as a result of the destabilizing effect of the dollar on the workings of the ERM (Thompson, 1996, 73–4; Grahl, 1997, 71–2). These changes represented an uncomfortable and uncertain future for British foreign policymaking (Coker, 1988, 33–45). The old external support system had finally crumbled. This was most graphically symbolized by the (already widely accepted) fact that Washington now gave primacy to its dealings with Germany in the broader context of US–Europe relations (Treverton, 1990).

In the defence field, these geo-political movements represented an opportunity: they provided convenient 'structural cover' for a leadership hoping to return the party to a policy of multilateralism. Put simply, international treaties establishing cuts in intermediate nuclear weapons rendered null and void arguments concerning the urgency of unilateralism. A more sensible option was to retain Britain's deterrent and then place it in appropriate disarmament talks. By 1989, the document, Meet the Challenge,

Make the Change, asserted that the Trident submarine would not now need to be abolished under a future Labour government, although plans for a fourth submarine would be cancelled (Keohane, 1993, 112–28). By the 1997 election, a bi-partisan consensus had been re-established, allowing the defence issue to be successfully depoliticized. Indeed, the emphasis on rapid and flexible force deployment in Labour's Strategic Defence Review could be presented as evidence that the party had done some creative thinking on the subject of British security in the twenty-first century (McInnes, 1998; *Financial Times*, 9 July 1998).

The Europeanization of the Labour Party

In other areas of foreign policy, the Labour Party responded to these external challenges by accepting the need for change. Between 1983 and 1987, Kinnock had gradually coaxed the party into reluctant acceptance of EU membership. After 1987, party publications began to assert positively that the only way for Britain to retain influence and power in this fast changing international world was to play a leading role in influencing the EU agenda (Robertson, 1990; Labour Party, 1990b, 45, 1991, 52). While this message was helpful in outflanking the Tories under Thatcher, it differed little from Major's 'heart of Europe' strategy. Indeed, despite a willingness to sign the Social Chapter and the acceptance of an increased use of majority voting in 'limited areas', there was little to choose between the party's EU policies at the 1997 general election. Labour leaders seemed, though, to have devoted little attention to analysing why this co-operative strategy had actually failed under Major's leadership. Instead, the impression given was that a united party and sufficient political will was all that was needed for a New Labour government to forge a new left-of-centre consensus across Europe (see Young, 1997a; see also George and Rosamond, 1992; Tindale, 1992; Daniels, 1998; Hughes and Smith, 1998).

In fact, initial optimism that a change of government might herald a new chapter in Britain's relations with the EU seemed well-founded. Within a matter of months, negotiators discovered that employment policy provided an area whereby New Labour could be seen to be making the running on the future development of the EU. Ministers stressed that a 'middle way' existed between an Anglo-Saxon emphasis on labour-market flexibility and the well-trained, but often highly protected workforce that existed on the continent. By reducing the burden of 'red tape' on small businesses, encouraging the growth of venture capital and reforming the dependency culture of welfare, Britain could show the way to the 'Holy Grail' of job creation (Brown, 1997; *Financial Times*, 5 June 1997). At the same time, these ideas proved attractive to European delegations during the complex machinations of EU summitry. For example, it has been argued that during the negotiation of the Amsterdam Treaty, British policy suggestions helped ameliorate splits between France and Germany over the inclusion of a commitment to job creation within the EMU-inspired Stability Pact (*Financial Times*, 16 June 1997, 17 June 1997). More generally, this success seems to have been partly responsible for the creation of a joint task-force with Germany to explore further the question of labour-market reform (*Financial Times*, 3 November 1998).

However, question marks remain over the possibilities for alliance-building in this area. Many social democratic leaders in Europe are said to dislike Blair's habit of lecturing them about the imperatives of modernization (Anderson and Mann, 1997, 114; see Chapter 3). More importantly, in many cases, these politicians face formidable obstacles in the implementation of UK-style reforms as Schroeder has discovered in Germany. On the one hand, many northern European countries still possess centralized union movements, used to a system of corporate bargaining which has developed over decades. Alternatively, economies in many central and southern European countries contain an industrial relations culture which has traditionally been resistant to labour-market deregulation and flexibility. By the Portschach Summit in October 1998, newspaper commentators were noting Blair's relative isolation, as he could only manage a 'cautious welcome' to proposals agreeing to set up an employment pact with Maastricht-style job creation targets (*Financial Times*, 26 October 1998). Indeed, three months earlier, Blair had called for a fundamental review of New Labour's policy towards the EU. This was not just a sign of disillusionment with the present state of this 'charm offensive': it represented an admission that it would take Britain ten years to establish itself at the 'heart of Europe' (*Financial Times*, 1 July 1998).

The review concluded that foreign and defence policy might provide an alternative opportunity for the pursuit of a leadership role within the EU. In a significant departure from Whitehall's previous thinking on the subject, ministers have suggested scrapping the Western European Union (WEU) as a way of augmenting the Union's defence capability. The WEU's military role would be transferred to NATO, thus strengthening the European pillar of this organization. Conversely, the WEU's political role would be folded into the EU, thus enhancing the authority of the new position of 'high representative' created at Amsterdam (*The Times*, 21 October 1998). George Robertson, whilst Labour's Defence Secretary, followed up this initiative with a speech calling for EU access to NATO military assets in circumstances where the Union alone might want to conduct operations

(*Financial Times*, 10 March 1999, 13 May 1999). These efforts seemed to pay off in December 1998, when British negotiators signed an agreement with their French counterparts to develop Europe's out-of-area defence potential. Moreover, this process may receive a significant boost as a result of the EU's perceived over-reliance on US hardware during the Kosovo crisis.

However, whilst publicly promoting moves to imbue Europe's foreign and defence policy with greater coherence, ministers have presided over a number of decisions which have arguably militated against its desire to play a leadership role in this area. Labour's unilateral support for the Clinton Administration's invasion of Iraq in the winter of 1997/8 was initially made without consulting her European partners. Dutch Foreign Minister Merlo went as far as to criticize publicly Britain for neglecting its duties as current holder of the Presidency of the European Council (*The Guardian*, 25 February 1998). Moreover, on the issue of EU defence restructuring, the Blair government's rhetoric sits awkwardly with the Ministry of Defence's decision to pull out of the three-nation military satellite programme and the Horizon frigate project. Just as embarrassing was British Aerospace's decision to purchase the defence arm of General Electric at the start of 1999. This move makes the British company significantly larger than its European competitors. At the same time, analysts agree that the possibilities for the creation of a pan-Union venture in this area are more problematic (Nicoll, 1999).

Perhaps the biggest contradiction within this strategy has been Labour's policy on the single currency (see Chapter 9). The decision in October 1997 not to join the first wave was understandable, in light of the fact that Britain's economic cycle was still significantly out of sync with that of its European partners. Nevertheless, the Labour leadership's hesitation in putting its full weight behind a public campaign to educate the electorate about the benefits of this policy was something that politicians on the continent found increasingly incomprehensible. For them, participation within the Single Currency was the benchmark against which commitment to the EU project was to be tested. They began to warn British diplomats of the dangers of becoming increasingly marginalized unless New Labour signalled its intention to abolish sterling soon. These predictions seemed to be borne out as early as December 1997, when Gordon Brown found himself excluded from membership of the newly formed Euro-11 committee. This body was set up as a counterweight to the European Central Bank (ECB), which allowed Europe's political leaders to debate issues and problems arising from the operation of the single currency. Ministers in London began to worry that these decisions would harden into a shared perspective, allowing representatives from the Euro-area to 'pre-cook' decisions made at the Council of Finance Ministers (Barber, 1997; Hutton, 1997; Young, 1997b; Stephens, 1997).

A survey of domestic opinion makes it easy to understand Labour's apprehension in launching a public campaign in support of the euro. In general, the electorate remains sceptical concerning the wisdom of such a project. Since Labour's victory, opinion polls have indicated that, on average, approximately 60 per cent of the British public are opposed to joining the single currency (*The Guardian*, 8 April 1998; *Financial Times*, 6 October 1998). This scepticism has been reinforced by much of the press, particularly those papers owned by the Murdoch empire. One chink of light for the pro-Europeans lie in findings from a Demos report, which indicate that 75 per cent of the public considered themselves to be ill-informed about the EU (*Financial Times*, 4 August 1997). This indicates that a battle of political ideas still needs to be fought in this area and could possibly be won. One unknown factor is the state of opinion in the party. As already noted, Europe is an issue which can complicate the task of party management. A survey of Labour MPs just before the election showed that a substantial minority agreed with the view that domestic monetary policy should never be determined by an independent ECB (Baker *et al.*, 1996, 358). It remains to be seen what effect the new influx of MPs after 1997 has had on the state of party opinion on this question.

Yet, there seems no reason to doubt that New Labour will join the single currency, providing it wins the next election with a working majority and that the euro is perceived as strong and successful. Officially, the party accepts this policy in principle and has argued in the House of Commons that there is no 'constitutional bar' to entry. Moreover, this policy exhibits strong historical parallels with the practice of previous Labour governments. By again immersing itself in external constraints, the leadership may once and for all dispel the myth that Labour is a party which is soft on inflation and prone to devaluation. By tying the conduct of economic management to another currency area in this way, membership of the euro provides the 'final solution' to an old governing problem: how to discipline the expectations and profligacy of the party rank and file, thus maintaining a semblance of leadership autonomy and governing competence (for similar arguments concerning ERM membership, see, George and Rosamond, 1992, 181–2; Anderson and Mann, 1997, 70). Indeed, the decision to grant the Bank of England operational independence to set interest rates provides an interesting preview of such benefits. When, in the spring of 1998, the Treasury came under fire for neglecting the high value of the pound in British exporters, it rejected charges that it had not raised taxes high enough to take pressure out of the economy. Instead, it made clear that primary responsibility lay with the Bank's Monetary Policy Committee, which had failed to raise interest rates quickly enough when faced with evidence of a sustained up-turn (Chote, 1998; Stephens, 1998; Woolf, 1998).

If New Labour's enthusiasm for the single currency can be partly explained as a new version of an old governing strategy, its management of the domestic agenda also shows distinct similarities with the past. The absence of a public campaign is not necessarily an indication of political inactivity on this subject. As with the Wilson government of the 1960s and the 1970s, much of the current debate has focused on the economic arguments, thus allowing the democratic consequences of such a decision to be side-stepped. At the same time, a slow, yet inexorable process of preparation has begun under the auspices of the government's new Standing Committee on this subject. Initiatives have ranged from the production of information guides, television advertisements, business-led road-shows, through to legislation designed to help business accommodate the process of monetary union. In September 1998, the Treasury introduced measures allowing companies to redenominate share capital in euros (*Financial Times*, 28 September 1998), whereas in February 1999, a full-scale National Changeover Plan was finally published. In this sense, there may be something to Conservative claims that New Labour is conducting a campaign of 'Europeanization by stealth' (*Financial Times*, 24 February 1999). Again, this strategy also probably reflects the view that the inevitability of the single currency process is perhaps the best argument the pro-euro camp has (see, for example, Young, 1998).

'The Ethical Dimension'

If the Europeanization of the Labour Party reflected broad themes of continuity as well as change, one area which appeared to herald something of a departure is the new commitment to an 'ethical' foreign policy. In the 1990s, the emergence of a number of dubious practices in the defence field under the Conservatives made this sort of gesture attractive from a party political point of view. The Pergau Dam affair revealed that the Thatcher government had agreed to finance a dam project in Malaysia in return for the purchase of British arms, despite civil service objections about poor value for money. Alternatively, there was the Scott Report into the Arms to Iraq affair, which saw the then Thatcher government secretly relaxing its policy on the sale of weapons to this dictatorship. In this context, New Labour could appear to offer a break with these 'sleazy' activities by offering to 'clean up' foreign policy; a theme which chimed well with its message on domestic politics. Indeed, two weeks after the election, Cook signalled his intentions in a blaze of media publicity. Labour would inject a new 'ethical dimension' into British statecraft. No longer would Whitehall accept: 'that political values can be left behind when we check in our passports to travel on diplomatic business' (quoted in Wheeler and Dunne, 1998, 847).

When it came to unpacking these claims concerning a new ethical dimension, two particular features of the policy merit attention. The first is New Labour's intention to put the worldwide pursuit of human rights at the centre of its diplomatic actions (speech by Robin Cook, 12 May 1997). Nation-states now inhabit a new global international community and it is the obligation of all countries to abide by the rules of membership. Central to this conduct was a respect for and, the observance of, the UN Charter of Human Rights. In stressing such rights, Labour was only demanding that all countries be able to enjoy the same conditions that Britain took for granted (speech by Robin Cook, 17 July 1997). Second, at the domestic level, an ethical foreign policy meant 'opening up' the process and making it more transparent to the outside world. By the time of writing, New Labour could point to a number of notable achievements. These included: the negotiation of the Ottawa Agreement banning the production, import and export of landmines; playing a key role in setting up a new International Criminal Court to deal with war crimes; the publication of an annual report detailing the government's record on human rights; and the exchange of personnel between the Foreign Office and non-governmental organizations (NGOs) such as Amnesty International and Save The Children.

These achievements aside, Labour's ethical foreign policy has not been without its critics. Take, for example, the government's policy towards the recent conflict between the Serbs and the ethnic Albanians in Kosovo. Blair's absolute determination not to countenance the atrocities and evidence of ethnic cleansing during this war should not be doubted. However, the means through which New Labour sought to implement these objectives have sometimes played into the hands of those quick to levy the charge that this agenda smacks somewhat of 'cultural imperialism'. In this sense, Britain's support for Washington's argument that NATO intervention in Kosovo could take place without further UN authorization has given the contradictory impression that ministers are willing to sideline an organization whose universal values they are so quick to endorse in principle (Nicoll, 1998a; Benn, 1998; Carlson and Ramphal, 1999). Indeed, such action has had the effect of actually increasing tension within the UN Security Council. Both Russia and China have expressed continual opposition to what they perceived as US hegemony; a fact not helped by NATO's accidental bombing of the Chinese embassy in Belgrade (*Financial Times*, 11 May 1999). Moreover, Western insistence that NATO, rather than the UN, form the core of a future International Protection Force in the province has helped to sharpen these perceptions.

Similar observations can be made concerning New Labour's support for the US bombing campaign against Iraq mentioned briefly above. Once again, Blair's sincerity about defending the 'international community' from the perceived threat of the Iraqi regime is not in question. Indeed, the bombing campaign against Saddam, after the latter rejected UN access to Presidential sites suspected of containing biological and chemical weapons, was defended on these grounds. The problem with this argument is that, what is 'good' for the 'international community' is always likely to be essentially contested at any particular time. In operational terms, Blair and Clinton found themselves isolated, with the British premier being the only leader to lend substantial military support to the United States.

In other areas, Labour's record shows a rather depressing continuity with the activities of previous governments. The policy on arms exports is an obvious example. One could point to the decision to proceed with the sale of Hawk aircraft to Indonesia. Alternatively, as Wintour (1998) has argued, Whitehall's plans for new rules on the disclosure of exports were watered down after interdepartmental lobbying. In response to criticisms outlined in the Scott Report, this White Paper on Strategic Export Controls recommended the replacement of existing rules under which the 'government has an unfettered power to impose whatever export controls it wishes and to use those controls for any purpose which it thinks fit'. Instead, these powers should be subject to parliamentary approval. Disappointingly, the Blair government rejected as impractical the idea that every application for an export licence could be examined by MPs, despite the existence of this practice in other countries (Nicoll, 1998b, 10). For example, Sweden operates a system whereby a parliamentary select committee vets sensitive licence applications, whereas in the US prior and public disclosure of arms exports valued in excess of $14 million is a legal requirement.

In this context, New Labour's willingness to consider fundamental institutional reform is perhaps the single biggest obstacle to change in the area of arms exports. As the Scott Report argued in 1996, more effective control of activity by British firms is inhibited by the fact that the DTI is responsible for both the promotion and licensing of exports: a dual role which serves to structure outcomes in favour of the former function (Scott, 1996, 111). Moreover, recent export issues demonstrate that the Foreign Office continues to be defeated by the institutional interests of the DTI and the Ministry of Defence over arms exports. If we keep in mind the importance that ministers attach to the link between the defence industry and the protection of jobs in the domestic economy (see, for example, Cmnd. 3861, 1998), it is hardly surprising that Whitehall should continue to demonstrate an institutional bias in favour of granting licences whenever possible. Indeed, ministers seemed rather complacent about this issue of structural change. In evidence to the Foreign Affairs Committee at the start of 1998, Cook saw no reason to alter the fact that no written rules existed concerning cases where human rights clashed with the interests of other departments (see HC 100 II, 1998, 49–50, 54–9, 150–51 and 159–60). It remains to be seen whether Amnesty International's proposal for a single independent authority with responsibility for export licence applications will make any headway (Amnesty International, 1998, 30).

Finally, the Arms-to-Africa affair in 1998/9 has made rather a mockery of Labour's commitment to open up the foreign policy process. This incident refers to allegations that the Foreign Office approved a shipment of arms by Sandline International (a British firm) to Sierra Leone despite a British-sponsored UN embargo on such activities. Although ministers and officials were subsequently cleared of complicity, they hardly conducted themselves in a transparent way throughout the investigation. It was admitted that 'restricted' telegrams informing Whitehall of Sandline's activities, had 'gone missing' (*Financial Times*, 14 May 1998). Ministers were confused and unclear in their answers to Parliament, when detailing exactly when they were made aware of the customs investigation of this impropriety. Cook initially rejected the release of the remaining telegrams to the Foreign Affairs Committee, which was conducting its own inquiry into the subject. When summaries were finally provided, they were reported to be so brief as to be 'almost meaningless' (*Financial Times*, 17 July 1998). Finally, Ernie Ross, a Labour member of the Committee, was caught leaking a copy of the resulting report to the Foreign Office before it was published (25 February 1999). No wonder Cook was reported to have given up using the phrase 'ethical' foreign policy, complaining that it had been continually misrepresented (*Financial Times*, 12 November 1998). The ethical policy became increasingly problematic in early 2000 when Blair appeared to sanction the sale of fighter aircraft parts to Zimbabwe.

Conclusions

It has been argued that broad continuities exist between the Blair government and the conduct of foreign and defence policy under previous

Conservative and Labour administrations. However, if this chapter has demonstrated anything, it is the importance of history to understanding claims about contemporary policy change. History is not just something which provides the 'context' to our appreciation of the present. It is a property that can be endlessly appropriated, re-interpreted and employed to justify existing behaviour and future plans. New Labour leaders may be right to bemoan the performance of their predecessors during the 1960s and 1970s, but part of the reason for increased discontent during this period was rank and file agitation at a foreign policy seen as subverting Labour's domestic programme. In conducting this statecraft, the leadership had become too divorced from the wishes of its followers. Any future attempt to join the single currency represents a similar dilemma for Blair and Co. In light of the electorate's (and party's) present scepticism towards this policy, the challenge for these leaders is to ensure that this mistake does not happen again.

13

Interpreting New Labour: Constraints, Dilemmas and Political Agency

MICHAEL KENNY AND MARTIN J. SMITH

Three years into the life of the current Labour administration, observers remain as divided and uncertain about its nature as they were before the election. In this chapter we consider some of the prevalent views of the government's political trajectory, noting particularly the popularity of interpretations which juxtapose Blair's policies with Thatcherite Conservatism and those that regard the government as the culmination of a tradition of 'modernization' of the party according to the changing realities of post-war society. Both of these perspectives have something to offer to our understanding of Labour's current political direction, yet each throws only partial light on it. As an alternative, we propose a general framework for comprehending this complex political phenomenon and offer a rather different account of the ideological and political 'meanings' of so-called 'New Labour'. Though the emphasis in our argument is on treating Labour's development in the 1990s as a complex political problem which requires a multidimemnsional and disaggretated interpretation, some broader 'generic' conclusions about the political trajectory of the government are also offered. In particular, we hope to show that a better balance needs to be struck between attention to the constraints under which Labour has been operating, a sense of the dilemmas that flow from these pressures and obstacles, and a more nuanced consideration of what sorts of response have been offered to them.

What's in a Name – 'New' Labour?

Why has the Labour Party in the last few years invested so heavily – in symbolic, electoral and political terms – in presenting itself as new?

Most obviously, such a claim is based on an attempt to differentiate the party from the 'old', and, in particular, the experiences of both the Labour administrations of the 1970s and the recent past when Labour was in opposition. But 'New' also signals an ambiguous relationship to some of the ideals and values embodied in the party's history, and its policy programmes (Kenny and Smith, 1997a; Hay, 1999; Gamble and Kenny, 1999). Two stances can be discerned within the party's public discourse – a revealing tension at the heart of its public philosophy. On the one hand, nearly all the leading figures in the party and Cabinet have at some point, and with varying degrees of enthusiasm and sentiment, asserted that there is nothing wrong with the core values of the Labour tradition. It is the means needed to realize these ends that require 'updating' (Bevir, 1999a; Kenny and Smith, 1997b). Yet something more ambitious has also been hinted at. At times, members of the inner circle present the political programme that they are carrying out as representing the transcendence of 'labourism' and indeed of political traditions in Britain altogether, a claim that is often yoked together with the belief that Labour has been repositioned as the natural custodian of the centre-ground of British politics. Thus, the modernizing impulse is at times deployed to signal both a break from some of the party's most cherished traditions and indeed some of the nation's political past – for instance the moves towards constitutional reform and some rather tentative steps towards closer economic involvement in Europe. There consequently exist both conservative and radical 'faces' to the Blair 'project', hence the vibrancy of the continuing disagreement about its political character. The radical element of Labour's thinking might encourage a thorough transformation of Britain's social and political institutions, a shift away from the Westminster model of British governance, and far-reaching reforms in the fields of education and welfare. The conservative impulses make even piecemeal reform hard to envisage, and have shaped a macro-economic strategy built upon a promise of no increase in direct taxation and numerous concessions to business interests. Blair and his team shift between both claims, with individual figures positioned uneasily on a spectrum between these different poles.

This ambiguity is reflected in academic analysis of the Labour government. A number of historians see little that is really new in current Labour politics (see Bale, 1999). Important elements of Blair's own political agenda can be understood only as continuities with programmatic change overseen by the previous leaders, Neil Kinnock and John Smith. Some historians have also identified similarities between Blair's rhetoric and the language adopted by, for instance, Harold Wilson in the period 1963–4 (Pimlott, 1992). One might go further and suggest that Wilsonite modernization has exerted some influence upon the rhetoric and aspirations embodied in

'New Labour's modernizing programme, especially in the months preceding the 1997 election. The twin catchphrases of party programmes under Blair – social justice and economic efficiency – predominated in earlier periods, informing the mind-set of Labour as a governing party. Writing before the 1997 election, David Coates went even further in arguing that many of the pressures facing an incoming Labour administration remained broadly similar to those encountered previously and the likely response of the current Labour leadership was comprehensible in terms of prior behaviour:

> What previous Labour governments actually did was work with the grain of market forces, in a collaborative relationship with senior managers in major companies, to trigger privately-generated economic growth; and that, of course, is precisely what New Labour is saying that it intends to do as well. (Coates, 1996, 67)

Such continuities are important in both political and interpretative senses. Even in its own terms, Blairite discourse about Labour's past is rather ambivalent. Golden 'moments' in the party's progress throughout the twentieth century are contrasted with the dark years of opposition and government mismanagement. Indeed, one of the most intriguing elements of its public discourse about Labour's past is the narrative of genesis which some of its leading figures employ: Labour needs to be returned to its point of origin, at the head of a 'progressive coalition' with other social and political forces, most notably the Liberal party (Mandelson and Liddle, 1996). Its mission remains unfulfilled – to turn Labour into a hegemonic party of government, and thereby exclude the Conservatives from the political mainstream for the foreseeable future. The rhetorical claims to embody all that is modern and new, and to be the force that will deliver the reversal of a perceived pattern of decline and failure, are actually rather old. They involve borrowing from a rich stock of rhetorical resources deployed by the political elite at different points throughout the century (Eccleshall, 2000). The claim to have transcended past squabbles and divisions, and the zealous imagination of a 'new Britain' about to be born, can be detected as far back as Ramsay MacDonald and indeed have stemmed from the moralistic rhetoric of the ethical socialist tradition of the late nineteenth century (Bevir, 1999a).

The claim to have transcended the past, to have moved beyond the constraints of 'the British tradition' and to be developing non-ideological solutions to contemporary problems is thus a rather old feature of British politics. Given the significance that the language of modernity achieved during the Thatcherite period, it is no surprise that Blair has highlighted this theme, and the likelihood is that any Labour leader would have done much the same; though Blair is unique for the lengths to which he has gone to separate the contemporary party from its past. One interesting dimension of this rhetoric concerns the political space it may generate for party leaders. By declaring Labour's history to be packaged up and boxed off from the past, Blair has created a degree of freedom of manoeuvre in terms of policy development and innovation, the capacity to respond with 'flexibility' to particular crises and problems and indeed the opportunity to outflank political enemies on key issues (Bale, 1999). Consequently, Labour's policy-makers define contemporary policy primarily with the notion of Labour's past as the 'other'; in a number of fields, policy, it seems, has to be seen to have moved on or away from long-standing commitments associated with earlier eras in the party's history.

Interpreting New Labour – Thatcherism Mark II?

But this sense of the historical roots of current political themes has been somewhat obscured by the recurrent assertion that Thatcherite policies and neo-liberal political economy are the key contexts for understanding Labour. Critics have rightly pointed to some important elements of continuity between the policy agendas developed during the Conservative administrations and Labour's record in government.

Several different accounts of this connection have emerged. Theorists like Przeworski (1985) point to the inhospitable conditions facing social democratic parties in liberal democracies, and regard the compromises that left-of-centre politicians have to make to the principal vested interests represented by national and international capital as inexorable and inevitable (see Wickham-Jones, 1995b). A less structural and more agency-centred account of the link between Thatcherism and Labour in the 1990s has been offered by some of the 'New Left' intellectuals (the New Left itself has adopted a range of positions in response to Labour's political development over the last four decades) who were associated with the controversial magazine, *Marxism Today*. A number of *Marxism Today*'s writers deployed the notion of 'hegemony' utilized in the writings of the early twentieth-century Italian Marxist, Antonio Gramsci, to interpret the significance and character of Conservative politics in the 1980s. They interpreted Thatcherism as a hegemonic 'project' that sought to

> construct a new consensus, a new definition of our social situation; one that would reverse 'common sense' and undermine any automatic assumption that a welfare state and mixed economy, managed by a state that would represent a genuine social interest, were inviolable features of the British form of capitalism. (Finlayson, 1999, 272)

The implications of this understanding of the phenomenon of Thatcherism are various; most significant for our purposes is the stress upon the importance of a broadly based strategy of counter-hegemony as a necessary precondition for a successful alternative political strategy.

Measured against the backdrop of this reading of hegemony, and the derived notion of a 'counter-hegemony', Blairite politics is something of a disappointment – a judgement publicly aired by the former editor of *Marxism Today*, Martin Jacques, and the well-known New Left theorist, Stuart Hall, prior to the 1997 election. From 1994 to 1997, they argued, Labour's political agenda narrowed rather than broadened as issues of contention, where differences might have been staked out from the Tories, were kept to a minimum; and frequent assurances were offered that Labour policy remained proximate to the neo-liberal 'common sense' forged by the Conservatives. In office too, it has been suggested, Labour has tapped into a deep vein of popular authoritarianism on a range of social issues in a manner set down by Conservative predecessors. Colin Hay similarly suggests that from the time of the major Policy Review undertaken during Neil Kinnock's leadership of the party, Labour's attitude towards the electorate shifted from what some political scientists call 'preference shaping' to 'preference accommodation' (Hay, 1999, 135). Slowly but surely, the Labour leadership, first under Neil Kinnock, then under John Smith, and finally under Tony Blair, gave up on the possibility of imagining either 'the need for' or 'the possibility of, such an alternative to the ascendant neo-liberalism of the times' (Hay, 1999, 135). For these critics Labour has accepted 'the considerable extent of the Thatcherite legacy' (Hay, 1999, 35; Heffernan, 1999).

The Modernizer's Dilemmas?

Such arguments possess an empirical and political force, and have to be incorporated within analytical understanding of Labour in the 1990s. But they do not adequately capture the totality of this political phenomenon, as we shall suggest more fully below. Some critics who stress the failure to break from the perceived hegemony of neo-liberal assumptions are hostile to the idea that Labour's development can be explained and justified through the notion of 'modernization'. But here too, we would suggest, there is something to be learned.

In many usages the term 'modernization' has become infused with a sense of ineluctable progress, and is strongly teleological. In the political realm, modernization is frequently used to signal the need to bring the political world into line with changes conceived to have occurred in other domains, principally society, economics and culture. As Hood (1999, 195) argues, '"modernization" is a rhetorically successful idea because when the powerful but implicit metaphor of technological development that underlies it is carried over into human organization it is inherently ambiguous' and so lends itself to very different political worldviews. The claim that New Labour represents the completed modernization of Labour merits careful examination. Hay detects a generic 'modernization thesis' to which supporters of the government tend to subscribe; in this, Thatcherism is seen as facilitating the 'necessary accommodation' of Labour to 'a qualitatively global economic environment characterised by the heightened ... mobility of goods, labour and especially capital' (Hay, 1999, 60). For proponents of this 'story', the major review of its policy undertaken from 1987 to 1991 was an important moment in a larger process of ideological renovation – a necessary response to the experience of wilderness in opposition. Both the review and the associated shifts in policy, notably in the economic domain, were less concessions to Thatcherism but 'rather an overdue modernization which had, for too long, been thwarted by the cloying influence of the trade unions and the inertial impulses of left extremists' (Hay, 1999, 61). Hay and others are quite right to suggest that, in this form at least, this thesis is in danger of conflating the dictates of electoral expediency with a tendentious account of current economic imperatives.

But a closer inspection of the literature suggests that it is quite hard to locate a single modernization narrative or thesis (see, for instance, Smith and Spear, 1992; G. Taylor, 1997; Shaw, 1994; Anderson and Mann, 1997). More accurately, there are competing analytical assessments and normative responses to the processes and meanings associated with 'modernization' – and consideration of the ideas and writings of Labour's inner circle yields important differences. It is certainly the case that a teleological, and quasi-determinist, account of 'modernization' constitutes one strand of the party elite's current self-understanding; hence arguments claiming that modernization is about reshaping Labour's political programme in accordance with socio-economic realities that are endogenous and unalterable by political forces. The notion of the arrival of a global economy is frequently invoked in this way. Other accounts of the contemporary economy – framed through the notion of the information economy or the weightless economy – are sometimes advanced in rather determinist fashion, as if politics is a process of endless adaptation to an already altered terrain, not a site of creative interaction with and shaping of economic as well as other forces (Leadbeater, 1999; Finlayson, 1999).

But this is not all that 'modernization' means or has to mean. First, commentators who emphasize the importance of a tradition of 'modernization' are not merely seeking to justify every twist and turn of Labour's programmatic development; they are also pointing in a less normative fashion to the causal impact of some of the re-thinking and re-evaluation of Labour's ends and means that has been a continuous feature of its internal intellectual life since at least the 1950s (M. J. Smith, 1994; Kenny and Smith, 1997b). We should regard this rich and plural tradition as a key resource which has been borrowed and modified by recent political actors. And, second, it is clear that concepts like 'modernization' have to be understood as essentially contested – and hence open to very different interpretations in different settings. In historical terms, 'modernization' has been invoked and appropriated at different points in the history of the left not only by the trimmers and political 'realists'. The New Left, for example, hoped that Wilson's modernization programme would undermine Britain's *Ancien Régime*, at least before his term of office (Anderson and Blackburn, 1999; Kenny, 1995). Later, the idea of a modern democratic constitution, to bring Britain into line with other European states, was central to the arguments of the radical grouping Charter 88 and can be traced back into the nineteenth century. Equally, the idea of modernizing the economy has been a useful rhetorical device for those calling for greater state intervention and direction of economic life. Certainly a figure like Blair thrives upon the ambiguities of concepts like 'modernization' but we have to recognize and understand how such terms provide invaluable resources (of a symbolic and rhetorical kind) for political actors, in all periods, rather than expel this term from our own interpretative lexicon. Its ambiguous character in the current period is neatly illustrated by its invocation to justify rather populist policies in relation to crime and disorder, as well as steps toward the devolution of power within the UK (a 'modern Constitution' for Britain).

It is certainly logically possible to include 'external' social and economic developments in an account of political change without succumbing to determinism. This kind of question touches on some of the foundational keys underpinning social science research, eliciting questions such as how to evaluate the relationship between political perception, action and other environmental factors. 'Modernization' may still be a useful motif to deploy in relation to Labour's development, less in terms of justifying all that Blair and his team have done, but certainly as a route into the self-understanding of parts of the party leadership and indeed of the membership more broadly. The point, in analytical terms, is to decode usages of modernization rhetoric and to probe their meanings in combination with other concepts. Equally attention to modernization discourse leads to a recognition of the importance of aspects of Labour's internal intellectual history since at least the 1950s, an important source of contemporary ideas and policies. We look at the deployment of some of Labour's traditions in this regard later in the chapter. The notion of 'modernization' was not invented in the 1980s, nor has it merely been deployed to justify the wholesale abandonment of party principle. It has, however, become integral to the construction of a new conceptual-political terrain upon which questions of principle and policy have been recast and reconsidered within the party.

Constraints, Dilemmas and Political Responses

If Blair's Labour government cannot be understood solely in relation to Thatcherism and its own internal history of 'modernization' how might we develop a better understanding of it? We agree with those authors who have pointed to the need to transcend interpretations lodged within the 'modernization' and 'accommodation' narratives described above (Wickham-Jones, 1995a; Driver and Martell, 1998). The remainder of this chapter therefore offers a multidimensional framework within which Labour's development can be more fruitfully grasped. The key premise of this framework is that we can detect at least three analytically separable dimensions of the political behaviour of this government. These need to be balanced more completely by Labour's interpreters. The first dimension concerns the *constraints* facing Labour in the British context; we use this term to signal entrenched obstacles and biases arising from certain social and political factors as well as the recurrence of certain challenges over the medium and long terms. Several of these constraints and their significance for understanding Labour's development are outlined indicatively here. Against one recent trend in the analysis of British politics, we believe that there are 'real-world' constraints, structural pressures and causal factors. Yet it is also important to observe that actors' perceptions of what constitutes an obstacle can themselves become a constraint upon what political actors feel able or willing to do. In the study of Labour politics, historians have pointed to the impact of such ideologically generated constraints throughout the party's history. Constraints come in different forms: there are objective ones, the existence and character of which are open to profoundly different interpretation, and also subjectively determined ones that flow from the belief-systems of actors at particular points in time. Both are pertinent in considering the politics of Labour. Our suggestion is that these constraints only enter the realm of everyday politics when they become constructed as 'dilemmas' by political actors.

The second dimension to which we need to attend therefore in understanding contemporary political phenomena is the political *dilemmas* facing the current government (for an extended conceptual discussion of dilemmas see Bevir, 1999b). We use this term to signal the emergence of a host of more immediate and often contingent problems and challenges. Many of these stem from the constraints that we can observe, which have been converted into immediate problems and challenges by political actors. Dilemmas assume an immediate and often contingent form. Many dilemmas emerge from the mismatch between actors' perceptions and traditions of belief and the confusing and complex realities that surround them (Bevir, 1999b), resulting in a fairly ongoing process of ideological adaptation and adjustment. Interpreted in this way, dilemmas can be regarded as 'constructed' within the webs of belief that actors hold (though again a wider philosophical debate raises the question of whether these exist solely in these perceptual fields). Finally, we separate from both of these dimensions the *responses* that actors adopt to pressures and constraints arising from the social, economic and political contexts in which they operate. These responses take many different forms – from legislative action to internal party debate. They are never predetermined by either the constraints or dilemmas, but they are heavily influenced and their infinity circumscribed by the ways in which 'dilemmas' are actually constructed. Hence the Blair government conceives itself as facing a number of contingent dilemmas – concerning macro-economic policy decisions – arising from the constraints attendant upon its perception of the realities of the global economy. Its responses, in policy and political terms, to these dilemmas are to a large degree shaped by how the constraints and particular dilemmas are perceived. Yet these responses are not foreclosed by the latter: as we shall see, a variety of response-pathways are always available to actors and interpretation needs to be sensitive to these. In the remainder of the chapter we provide a brief indication of how this framework might be operationalized.

Constraints

The Economic Environment

As some of the 'classic' studies of Labour politics in the twentieth century have rightly observed, the party's policies have often been thwarted through the structural and lobbying power of capital either through capital flight (a key backdrop to the sterling crises Labour experienced in, for instance, the 1960s), direct veto or non-co-operation from business élites. Proposals for greater industrial democracy contained in the Bullock report, for instance, were blocked by a combination of pressure from the CBI and some Cabinet opposition (see Stones, 1990; Coates, 1980; Grant and Marsh, 1977 for consideration of this and other examples). One major constraint facing Labour, and other social democratic parties in (capitalist) liberal democracies concerns the influence (or structural power) which can be wielded by entrenched economic interests (see Lindblom, 1977; Poulantzas, 1976; Przeworski, 1985, for a theoretical discussion).

In government, Labour has on occasions abandoned or ignored its own policy commitments; delivery has rarely matched promise. As early as 1968 Labour was attempting to reduce the levels of public expenditure and lessen its commitment to universalism in the provision of welfare benefit levels (see Bale, 1997b). Public expenditure cuts have been forced on Labour in order to reassure the markets (see Bale, 1997b; Wilson, 1974). In this sense Blair and his Chancellor, Gordon Brown, have internalized a form of argument popular in some academic circles: that there is no option for social democratic political actors except to reassure the principal components of finance capital. This submission to the pressure of capital and the market is a continuous problem for social democratic parties. Consequently, the pressures of a competitive party system have tended to inflect social democratic politics in a generally 'accomodationist' direction with regard to socio-economic arrangements. On certain occasions Labour leaders have translated parts of the social democratic traditions that they have inherited into relatively 'radical' policy-frames, for instance, by developing a 'national plan', calling for the introduction of high marginal rates of taxation, instituting planning agreements with industry, increasing public expenditure in the 1960s, developing proposals for industrial democracy and, at various points, promoting the nationalization of key industries. But the increasingly apparent convergence in policy terms between social democratic parties across central and western Europe (which is rather masked by rhetorical differences over a putative 'third way') suggests that these constraints are both common across different political systems and have been 'framed' in a similar way as a set of powerful dilemmas which appear to necessitate certain programmatic responses (Sassoon, 1997).

Constraints have existed too, since the late 1960s, in the shape of the changing character of the international economic environment, as well as through the perception of these developments by those who have shaped Labour's economic policymaking. For a while now, some of the key decision-makers and opinion-shapers around the government have adhered to a 'strong' version of globalization theory to make sense of economic change, though again one can detect alternative ideas in high places until the early 1990s (Gould, 1998a; Giddens, 1998). This constraint is most apparent in two areas. Public expenditure policy is developed around the imperative of not upsetting the global financial markets. Within this perceived structural constraint, Labour's strategy is not to be forced to abandon policy because of the pressure of capital. Blair has chosen to adapt social democratic principle to capitalism in a way that hollows out much of the former. The almost unbridled acceptance of capitalist economic organization combined with a commitment to social justice hints at the influence deriving from US Democrats rather than social democratic thinking here. This particular example illustrates the analytical complexity involved in delineating constraints. Some are undoubtedly external and 'objective' in kind, yet these are extremely hard to separate from the 'baggage' of actors' perceptions of circumstances, the latter representing constraints of a different kind.

The British Political System

The party has also been historically constrained by the nature of the political system in which it operates. Though Labour established itself as a presence within the mainstream of political life in the early years of the twentieth century, its value-system and policy priorities have been ambiguously positioned in respect of the prevailing traditions of the British polity. The relationship between Labour and these different ideological and cultural traditions is a complex and nuanced one, being as much about osmosis and adaptation as clear-cut ideological separation. Despite the recent emphasis upon constitutional reform, Labour has not managed to break the embrace of parliamentarianism and the continued potency of key actors' reverence for the Westminster model (see Chapter 8). Indeed it is torn between the degree of control the Westminster system provides for the executive and commitments to considering proportional representation.

Electoral Factors

Labour has been constrained by the changing nature of its electoral coalition and particularly the changing social composition and experiences of its 'core' constituency, the working classes. It is impossible to understand Labour's evolution in the 1990s without attending to the impact that repeated electoral failure had on the party. Labour's vote declined overall from 1951 to 1983 (though it rose in the short-term in the elections of 1964, 1966 and October 1974), a trend that seemed to require explanation through social as well as political factors. Moreover, the scale of the defeat in 1983 was such that it devastated the party, the leadership and the left opposition. It particularly highlighted the extent of the electorate's disillusionment with the party and undermined the party left's claim that the erosion of support was caused by its drift to the right. Increasing divergence between the policies of Labour and the views of the electorate (Crewe, 1983; Whiteley, 1983) reinforced these electoral problems. The divergence was a reflection of significant social change during the post-war period. The size of the skilled manual workforce has declined whilst there has been a growth in clerical occupations (see Castells, 1996, 307). Moreover, the character of work has changed greatly, with many more people working part-time and substantially more women being employed throughout the economy. In addition, the standard and quality of life have altered, both qualitatively and quantitatively, over the last few decades (Hobsbawm, 1998). In order to win, Labour came to believe that it had to attract a more diverse and volatile electorate whose preferences and concerns were harder to detect and more 'post-material' in kind. And there was evidence to suggest that popular concern had shifted towards issues which come under the heading of 'quality of life' and that the limiting of tax liability had become a major economic priority for the middle classes and skilled working classes.

DILEMMAS

These are closely linked to and often arise from the recurrent constraints such as those suggested here, though they take an inevitably contingent form in different political eras. Several illustrations can be provided:

Economic Competence

Particularly challenging for Labour's leadership after 1994 was the question of establishing a relationship of trust with parts of the electorate beyond its core constituency, and regaining the electorate's confidence in the realm of economic policy. There is considerable evidence that voters did not trust Labour on the economy until the Tory economic debacle of black Wednesday in September 1992 (see Sanders, 1996; Wickham-Jones, 1996; Gould, 1998a). As late as 1996 there was still a perception amongst voters that economic improvement would be jeopardized under a Labour government (Gould, 1998a, 276). Fundamental to Labour's strategy under Blair both in opposition and in government, therefore, has been the need to prove that Labour is economically competent and will not repeat the errors that led to the crises of the 1970s. The dilemma that arises from this perception is how to generate the image of competence and make headway in delivering on the goals of social justice. Labour has chosen to 'resolve' this dilemma by reproducing the self-imposed constraints in public expenditure established by the Tories (and indeed by surpassing them in reducing public spending), expressed as a proportion of national income in comparison with the Tories (*The Guardian*, 25 August 1999), reducing the burden of public debt, and maintaining a balanced budget in the medium term. Much of Labour's economic policy has been concerned with retaining the confidence of voters, especially in the imagined community of 'Middle England' and the financial markets. More broadly we might label this the strategy of presenting Labour as the country's 'natural' economic manager. This particular stance is connected in Labour's current rhetoric with the challenges associated with participation in the open and fast-moving international economic environment.

Building an Electoral Coalition

Despite the overwhelming nature of its victory in 1997, Labour's electoral position has presented a number of dilemmas (see Chapter 2). A convincing electoral victory requires the votes of its core working-class supporters as well as significant middle-class voting. The coalition that Labour needs to marshal through the ballot box has only been successfully stitched together on three occasions – 1945, 1966 and 1997. A recurrent dilemma for the party's leadership has therefore arisen around the delivery of some of its core values in what it perceives as a hostile electoral environment. The invention of 'New' Labour can thus be seen as a slightly different response to this dilemma, an adjustment to the party's ethos and arguably its very mission in order to secure the Holy Grail of stable electoral support from divergent social constituencies. Not surprisingly, in ideological terms this has encouraged a shifting of the party's political centre-of-gravity, towards the middle of the political and ideological system. Blair is particularly conscious that

> With the possible exception of 1964, Labour has hitherto been unable to recreate the strong consensus of 1945. The truth that we must take seriously is that 1945 was the exception not the rule. (Blair, 1996b, 5)

Though different commentators have pointed to the significance of the electoral dimension to Labour's current development, less attention has been focused upon the precise degree and ways in which the parameters of policy have been affected by this 'external' (and now hugely internalized) pressure. Sceptics are right to observe that such factors provide a powerful rationalization for party leaders who want to reorientate the ideological trajectory of the party. But less attention has been devoted to what meaningful alternatives were available to a party operating in a competitive two-party system, facing the kind of challenges that Labour did in the early-mid 1980s. A number of questions need more serious attention here. Would any of the alternative figures displaced, marginalized or replaced by Blair (John Smith, Bryan Gould, Ken Livingstone come to mind) have been able to lead the party to electoral victory without succumbing to the pressures facing the Labour leadership? What degree of space for alternative policy pathways was actually available? Would the more authentically postulated social democracy hinted at as the missed normative alternative by critics (Hay, 1999) really have fared any better in these electoral and political circumstances? These are much harder questions to answer than the rather certain tone of much of the academic writing on Labour in the 1990s implies, and actually requires a greater methodological self-consciousness than has hitherto been displayed. Certainly it is wrong to consider the response to these dilemmas pursued by Labour under Blair as the only one available; this would be to make the error of determinism. But it is equally wrong to posit a pristine political-normative alternative path as the lost or abandoned trajectory which might have magically maintained Labour's true traditions without all the painful compromises and disappointments that the period in office have produced.

The Thatcherite Inheritance

A particular dilemma worthy of emphasis concerns the challenge awaiting a party that has to take over the reins of power following more than a decade of government by the opposition party, and the different policy context that the latter has undoubtedly brought into being. This issue is most usefully disaggregated to examine the differential impact of Tory governance in different policy areas, but it is important to consider the most fundamental and generic set of changes which have bequeathed some traps for Labour. The machinery of the British state that Labour has inherited in 1997 looks very different from that which it gave up in 1979. In the first place, through the public sector it could exert indirect control over roughly 20 per cent of the economy at this earlier date. By 1997 the only major industry still in the public sector was the post office. In 1979 there were 505 815 civil servants; and by 1997 there were 431 400, three-quarters of whom work in Next Steps Agencies. In 1979 the state had a range of mechanisms enabling it to intervene within the production process, for instance through the 1972 and 1974 Industry Acts and the creation of the National Enterprise Boards and Sector Working Parties. These mechanisms were reinforced by a range of corporatist institutions such as the National Economic Development Council, the Price Commission and the Manpower Services Commission, all of which were designed to ensure that capital and labour had institutionalized contact with government and the potential to influence policy outcomes. The Thatcher government effectively dismantled this machinery, and even abolished the sponsorship bodies within the DTI (later to be reintroduced) which gave departments contact with key industrial sectors. The DTI itself was emasculated in the Thatcher years; its expenditure was cut dramatically and it shifted from an industrial department to one concerned with trade, the single European market and deregulation.

Consequently, Labour inherited a state that did not have the same capacity for intervention as that which existed in the 1960s and 1970s and that operated according to a very different set of internal 'logics'. To re-establish such a state would have involved tremendous costs, in both resources and political energy. Moreover, the incentives for re-establishing such a state form are low. The collapse of the Labour government in 1979 was linked closely to the failure and collapse of the corporatist, interventionist state model. Certainly a fairly profound adaptation of rhetoric and imagination to the 'realities' of the Thatcherite state is apparent, with the advocacy of public/private partnership, multiple-service delivers, and intervention through incentives. It is significant that Labour now adopts the language of 'provider-client' rather than 'state-citizen' relationships (Freeden, 1999b, 2). In different respects, there is evidence to suggest that this is not merely a shift of élite opinion. Many within the Labour party now accept that markets should be deployed to deliver a range of goods and services, in both the local and central states. Equally, a distrust of the state is no longer a provenance of the right. Increasingly thinkers on the left are suggesting that social problems need much more complex solutions than the state can provide (see, for example, Hirst, 1997). As Freeden (1999b, 1) notes, in Blair's discourse:

> The state is reduced to the status of one actor among many, both internationally and domestically, appearing as pathetically subservient to global economic forces, unwilling to generate policies through its bureaucracies because it no longer believes in the power of politics as a central force for change. Societies have simply become too complex for wielders of political power and authority to manage.

This particular example of the institutional legacy of the Tory governments is important both in its own right and equally as an illustration of the space for political agency that needs to be made in our conceptualization of political challenges (Bevir and Rhodes, 1999); the latter can be handled in different ways, the range of possible response being in part determined by wider circumstances and pressures. The exercise of agency – the aspects of the political responses of actors that could have been 'otherwise'

(Giddens, 1998) – needs to be central to academic understanding of Labour, contrary as that is to the self-understanding of the key political actors involved.

Political Responses: Ideas as Resources

The third dimension highlighted in our interpretative framework is concerned with how responses are generated from the dilemmas facing political actors. Understanding of this process actually requires a context-dependent analysis as well as a consideration of the traditions of thought mobilized by these actors. In particular, we need to consider whether Labour's many responses can be understood as informed by a coherent ideological package or stem from purely pragmatic considerations, as many commentators attest. It is important to consider Labour's development in relation to established political traditions through the notion of 'path dependency'. Current praxis emerges out of the history of the party's thought and practice, as well as in relation to some of the broader traditions of the polity. Indeed these traditions ought to be seen as some of the principal resources enabling the exercise of political agency (Bevir, 1999b; MacIntyre, 1981). For all the anti-traditional claims made by Labour's apologists, our suggestion is that 'New Labour' can in fact only be understood through attention to the selective mobilization of some important intellectual and ideological lineages within British politics.

For example, Labour's current approach to economic matters is particularly dependent upon the economic decisions taken with great difficulty by the party élite during the 1970s when the Labour government abandoned the commitment to full employment and other mainstays of its macro-economic thinking. The intellectual shift which generated the proto-monetarist policies adopted then – a neglected precursor to current Labour thinking – are signalled in Prime Minister James Callaghan's famous speech to the 1976 Labour Party conference:

> For too long, perhaps ever since the war, we postponed facing up to fundamental choices and fundamental changes in our society and in our economy. That is what I mean when I say we have been living on borrowed time ... We used to think that you could spend your way out of a recession and increase employment by cutting taxes and boosting government expenditure. I tell you in all candour that that option no longer exists. (Callaghan, 1987, 425–6)

But considering the relationship between a particular phase in the history of a political party and its ideological lineages more broadly is a fraught exercise, generating major questions about the relationship between political thought and practice, and collective beliefs and actions. A further complication arises if we consider which agents are deploying and subject to the different ideological influences that we can identify. It is easier to pin down the belief-system of particular individual actors or the upper echelons of the party machine, yet a complete account of Labour's transformation in these years requires attention to the different levels of the party – right down to the level of ordinary members' attitudes. Studying ideological influences in relation to collectivities represents a major analytical challenge, hence the tendency of most commentators to focus on the leadership or key individuals at the head of the party. And, finally, we have to be careful not to fall into the trap of 'reifying' the relationship between particular traditions and current beliefs. Mark Bevir (1999b) illustrates the methodological limitations of interpreting traditions in terms of unchanged 'essences' that can be used as yardsticks to consider ideological developments. Thus we ought to be alert to the role of traditions as resources which undergo active modification by agents in the development of their understanding. Similarly, Freeden (1999a) shows the inadequacy of searching for a single tradition as the sole measurement of changing political perceptions: assessing the rather complex and overlapping set of social democratic discourses that have historically occupied the intellectual high-ground of the centre-left, he develops an analysis that simultaneously illustrates the resources upon which Labour has been able to draw, from the political ideas of Ramsay MacDonald, the Fabians, pluralists like Harold Laski and G. D. H. Cole, through to Crosland, as well as the degree to which the plural repertoire of social-democratic thinking in Britain is a necessary but ultimately insufficient backdrop to understanding the political trajectory of Labour in the twenty first century.

The latter's ambiguous relationship to social democracy is central. Some critics have presented this in rather stark terms. According to David Marquand, Labour 'has abandoned the tradition once exemplified by such paladins of social democracy as Willy Brandt, Helmut Schmidt, Ernest Bevin and Hugh Gaitskell. It has also turned its back on Keynes and Beveridge' (Marquand, 1998). But such a judgement is in danger of leading us too far away from what remains one of the sources of current Labour values. Though the state has clearly been shrunk, in ethical terms, support for the moral purposes enshrined in the welfare state remains strong throughout the party, and the state is still confidently envisaged as the agency for intervention to tackle a range of social and economic problems (see Chapter 12). State mechanisms and subsidies have been given an important role in transport, employment, economic and social policy. As one government white paper asserts:

> There has been a presumption that the private sector is always best, and insufficient attention has been given to reward in success in the public service and to equipping it with the skills required to develop and deliver strategic policies and services in modern and effective ways. (Cm 4310, 1999, 11)

The institutionalization of the minimum wage and the government's much trumpeted 'New Deal' for the unemployed are, for example, underpinned by a philosophy of public intervention which differs markedly from Thatcherite thinking. Citizens are to be helped (trained) to help themselves, and the undergirding ethic is equality of opportunity. As Gordon Brown has put it:

> We argue for equality not just because of our belief in social justice but also because of our view of what is required for economic success. The starting point is a fundamental belief in the worth of every human being. We all have an equal claim to social consideration by virtue of being human. And if every person is regarded as of equal worth, all deserve to be given an equal chance in life to fulfil the potential with which they are born. (Quoted in Routledge, 1998, 320)

The quotation signals the ethical understanding of state and community underpinning these interventions which is clearly demarcated from some of the utilitarian and individualist strains found in Conservative discourse in the 1980s.

But Marquand and others are right to emphasize that we may also need to look beyond the most familiar traditions of the left to understand some of the ideological influences upon Labour. Most obviously, liberalism, or at least aspects of this dense heritage in the British context, has been proposed as a more suitable genesis for the thinking of the current government. Freeden highlights particularly Blair's attempts to lay claim to the political heritage of such figures as David Lloyd George, L. T. Hobhouse, William Beveridge and John Maynard Keynes. John Gray, on the other hand, sees in New Labour the triumph of the politics of liberal individualism – in both the economic and social domains. And Sir Samuel Brittan sees the distinguishing feature of Labour's current practice that it has 'fully accepted competitive markets, private enterprise and the profit motive as the motor of the country's economy', though he is less enamoured by what he perceives as its socially illiberal ethos (Brittan, 1999). Several critics have noted the 'Gladstonian' aspects of the constitutional reform agenda unveiled by the government and the proclamation of an ethical foreign policy.

It is equally valid to consider the impact of aspects of conservative thinking, in part through the immediate influence of Thatcherite conservatism. Clearly there are also one-nation strains in New Labour's attempt to represent Britain as an imaginary political community in which distinctions of class and culture matter less than ever before, and in the appeal to the nation to rally together beyond sectional divisions. Some commentators have been ready to interpret the apparently 'authoritarian' and socially conservative register struck by Labour ministers, and notably the Home Secretary, Jack Straw, on a range of issues as evidence of the continued hegemony of conservative discourse.

In addition, some of these aspects of Labour's public talk, and occasionally its behaviour, may well make sense in relation to aspects of the intellectual pedigree of the left and Labour's governmental history. Thus Labour figures have frequently voiced socially conservative themes, as well as on occasions more liberal, cosmopolitan values. Wilson and Callaghan were often opposed to what they termed the permissive society and presented Labour as the guardian of 'traditional' moral values. Callaghan was a socially conservative Home Secretary and as Prime Minister attempted to shift education back to educational basics away from fashionable 'liberal' thinking (see Chapter 10). Much of Labour's current familial conservatism can be detected further back in the party's history. Moreover, the juxtaposition of a model of community with emphasis upon individual responsibilities as a supplement to rights can be seen as representing a revival of earlier forms of socialist communitarianism, and ethical socialism. New Labour's response to certain contemporary dilemmas can be usefully read in terms of the redeployment of strands of ethical socialist thought. Certainly there are many clues in the public discourse and writing of leading New Labour figures (via the theologian John MacMurray) that the ethical socialist tradition has been mobilized in fairly conscious ways by Labour. Whilst it may be more reassuring for those disappointed by the record of Labour in office to place blame on the capitulation to alien ideologies, a less comfortable reading may actually force us to face those elements of its agenda that have their origins in some aspects of the left's own ideological heritage. Equally, the formation of the Labour party cannot be understood without reference to liberal thought and politics. Socialist and especially social democratic ideology in Britain has enjoyed a symbiotic and mutually sustaining relationship with liberal thought, as evidenced through figures like John Stuart Mill who constituted important bridgeheads between these different traditions but also in terms of the political ambitions of early Labour politicians. To discover liberal motifs, particularly from the collectivist and progressivist 'churches' of the early century, in the words and thought of

Labour figures and factions, even on the left of the spectrum, should no longer be the occasion for surprise. Some Labour figures are now prepared to give a public voice to this common heritage (Freeden, 1999b).

Conclusions

The central argument of this chapter is the need to consider the 'New Labour' phenomenon in a multidimensional and disaggregated form, a recognition which encourages scepticism about essentialist characterizations of its political trajectory and meaning. Yet it remains important to consider whether there are any core or generic themes within the politics of the current Labour administration, and whether interpretation of this macro-political phenomenon can be organized around them.

We considered earlier two particular 'narratives' which have been used to fix the meaning of current Labour politics – the story of Thatcherism's total political and ideological success, on the one hand, and the inexorable unfolding of a modernization agenda designed to bring Labour into line with the 'real' world, on the other. Both of these stories, if used on their own, lead us to underestimate the complexity of Labour politics in the 1990s. This is not to deny that elements of Thatcherite thought and action have cast a long shadow over this government. Labour has been impressed by the willingness of the Thatcher administrations to restructure the economy, control inflation and avoid blame for economic misfortune. Equally Blair's reconstruction of the party's policymaking machinery can be understood as an attempt to enable rapid programmatic shifts, akin to those made under Thatcher's leadership of the Conservative party, in response to electoral signals. In substantive terms, the government has reproduced fiscal conservatism and the privileging of an anti-inflationary strategy within macro-economic policy; indeed it has outdone the Conservatives with its adoption of new fiscal rules and granting of operational independence to the Bank of England.

But Labour's current trajectory cannot be reduced to an echo of Thatcherism, as if the prior histories of the party were wiped clean in 1979. Not only does such an argument underplay the complexity of Labour's transformation but it simultaneously leads to a misreading of the party's political and ideological centre-of-gravity. A roughly coherent political framework, hewn from an eclectic mix of traditions, has been developed under Blair's leadership of the party and it amounts to something other than Thatcherism Mark II. Crucial elements of it are the notion that public expenditure should be increased, though within the framework of 'value-for-money' and as the public sector itself is modernized, as well as a commitment to an active state designed to equip the nation for the 'new economic paradigm' (commonly labelled the information economy) within which it is suggested that we now live. Equally Blair and his allies have sought, in ideological terms, to transcend some of the antinomies of recent political discourse (markets vs the state, or justice vs liberty) though frequently one detects the prevalence of one ideological tradition over others in different domains – conservatism in social policy, liberalism (of a nineteenth-century vintage) in terms of the international economy, as well as a distinctly Whiggish attitude towards the modernization of some of the constitutional and institutional features of the state. For all these different emphases, Blair and his allies feel confident that Britain now offers a 'model' of sorts, outside the social market model favoured by some continental social democrats. Though it is a long way from social democracy as we have known it, and looks a lot like the politics of Christian Democracy practised in other European party systems, this model is clearly not neo-liberal in any straightforward sense.

A discontinuous understanding of contemporary trends in political economy – underwritten by presumptions about the qualitatively new economic paradigm in which we live – offers one interpretative key to Labour's development, and clearly represents a priority within its overall thinking. Another imperative within the New Labour value-set, around which other ideas and policies fall into place, concerns the politics of electoral coalition-building. This has been turned into an imperative of such salience that arguably it has come to underpin the 'governing code' through which the party has developed its policies since 1994. The politics of coalition management also provide the site of a number of debilitating political contradictions and tensions. The attempt to meld a range of traditions with the goals of retaining both party support and a broad electoral coalition creates a number of problems for Labour. How can Labour retain the middle-class support it needs for re-election without alienating its core supporters? Many of Labour's traditional voters hoped for resources to be diverted into welfare and benefits expenditure, but the government prioritizes the imperative of not alienating more prosperous voters with higher public expenditure and increased taxation. And how can the party convince its core support that its programme represents a modernized version of an older social democratic vision when its key opinion-framers are simultaneously convinced that we have moved into a new social and economic era in which the ideological maps of yesteryear no longer work? And, finally, how can Labour service a diversity of social constituencies whilst simultaneously undermining the position of a range of group interests through its 'modernization' of the public sector in the image of the private? These questions may well provide the axes along which key positions will be staked and internal differences will arise in the next few years, especially if a second term is won. To gain a meaningful purchase on them and why they have arisen, students of British politics will need to think beyond the horizons of the political narratives bound up in emphases upon inexorable 'modernization' and the continuing influence of Thatcherism.

Note

The authors are grateful to Mark Bevir, Andrew Gamble and Steve Ludlam for their comments and criticisms.

14

Conclusion: the Complexity of New Labour

MARTIN J. SMITH

However one interprets the government of Tony Blair and New Labour, there can be little dispute that Blair's project has been successful in both electoral and, so far, governmental terms. In the mid-1980s Labour was in danger of becoming the third party and the question of 'Can Labour win?' was a constant refrain of psephologists. In 1997 Labour routed the Conservatives and despite the caveats raised in Chapter 2, could present itself as the only truly national party in Britain. In governmental terms Labour in 1979 had lost claims to governing competence. The party lost power after a period of rising unemployment, high levels of inflation, the breakdown of the social contract with the unions and the loss of Keynesian tools to provide a social-democratic welfare state. In making large public expenditure cuts, Labour had lost its *raison d'être* and consequently was divided between an ideologically bankrupt centre-right and a dogmatic and electorally unpopular left. Consequently, voters lost faith in the ability of the party to govern. One of Blair's greatest achievements is first to create trust in Labour and second to restore Labour's reputation for governing competence. New Labour in government has learnt the lessons of old Labour in government and therefore isolated itself from the trade unions and carefully assessed and reassessed its spending commitments in light of economic circumstances.

In assessing the newness of New Labour and answering the question raised in the introduction of how much Labour owes to 'Old' Labour, how much to Thatcherism and how much to the modernization process of 1983–94, it is important to place Blair and New Labour into context. First, whatever the arguments over modernization (see Chapter 13), Blair's success cannot be divorced from the process of party adaptation that occurred under Kinnock and Smith. Kinnock, coming from the radical wing of the party, was able to persuade the party to accept the perceived realities of the party's electoral position: that it could not get elected unless some key policies were changed. Kinnock laid the groundwork for Blair and it seems unlikely, although unknowable, that Blair could have been elected without Kinnock. Thus, many of the element of Blair's New Labour project are found in Kinnock's policy review; the reconciliation with the market, a new conception of the role of the state, a new relationship with the trade unions and close integration with Europe. Nevertheless, there are significant differences in terms of industrial policy, the view of taxation, the radical reforms to the welfare state and the single currency.

In addition, Labour's apparent dominance owes much to the implosion of the Conservative party. Black Wednesday undermined the Conservative economic policy almost to the same extent as the IMF crises had delegitimized Keynesianism. The consequences of the debacle was a chronically split party that was unable to reconcile either its relationship to Europe or the broad themes of economic policy (see Ludlam and Smith, 1996). The Conservatives lost their reputation for governing competence, a perception which was reinforced by the continual stream of sleaze allegations. More importantly, the Conservatives split from key elements of their natural class. Much of Thatcherite economic policy had been based on liberating the City of London as a mechanism for encouraging the growth of the service economy. It was this sector, which received the full fruits of the 1980s economic boom, that strongly favoured greater European integration in order not to lose markets and to ensure the City remain Europe's financial capital. By adopting a Euro-sceptial position, the Conservatives lost the support of elements of the Capitalist class.

Whilst we would reject the notion that New Labour can simply be defined as a Labour version of Thatcherism, there is little doubt that the Thatcherite inheritance has influenced and constrained the direction of New Labour. Richard Rose has raised the question of whether parties make a difference pointing to the weight of constraints on governments which force them to adopt policies that are similar to those of their predecessor. Even the post-war Labour government and the 1979 Conservative government, which have been seen as agenda-setting governments, were both constrained by their situation and to some degree followed policies of their predecessor. As Addison (1977) demonstrates, many of the roots of Labour's 1945 government welfare state are to be found in the wartime coalition. Likewise monetarism, cuts in public expenditure, reductions in the size of the civil service and the selling of public assets were all undertaken by the Callaghan government. Consequently it is unrealistic to think that the New Labour government will be completely distinct from the Conservatives. The state they inherited did not have the mechanisms to carry policies like those of previous Labour administrations. People appear unwilling to accept increases in income tax and external financial pressures, whether perceived or real, favour the maintenance of a market-based economy with external money markets demanding prudence. Labour could choose to ignore these pressures but the political consequences could be high, as previous Labour governments discovered.

Analysis of New Labour will be superficial unless proper account is taken of the way in which the state both enables and constrains the activity of the government. As a wealth of research demonstrates, governments cannot quickly change the general policy direction of the state (see Rose and Davies, 1994; Marsh and Rhodes, 1992; Richards and Smith, 1997). Thatcher, despite some fairly clear programmatic goals, was unable to make significant impacts on the DTI until after 1985, on education, welfare and health until the late 1980s, and in Home Affairs it was only under Major that the policy direction really changed (see Ludlam and Smith 1996). The state has constrained Labour in three ways. First, in terms of the actual capabilities that exist for achieving goals. Second, as Chapter 8 demonstrates, through the continued adherence to the British tradition and Westminster model which constrains the potential developments in democratizing the British state. Third, as is illustrated in Chapter 12, through the way international factors are impacting on the British state. Greater integration into Europe, shifts towards monetary union, the continuing importance of NATO, and the development of new transnational organizations such as the World Trade Organization affect what government can do and the choices that can be made. In new institutionalist terms, the Labour government is 'path dependent'. Britain's position in the world economy, its history and the consequences of 18 years of Conservative rule shape the nature and dilemmas of New Labour. New Labour can only be understood in relationship to Thatcherism; this does not make it a product of Thatcherism.

Whilst Thatcherism has remained an influence, so too has old Labour. Some of the elements of old Labour are perhaps difficult to discern but nevertheless do exist. There is a commitment to a welfare state which includes the free provision of health and education and a system of welfare benefits to those in need. Whilst the means and focus of this welfare system may have changed, there can be little doubt that the bases of Labour's post-war ideological position remain in place (see Chapter 11). There is a shift from universal benefits to targeted benefits and, as Will Hutton has argued, with the abandonment of social insurance Labour has rejected a 'core social democratic position' (*The Observer*, 23 May 1999). Nevertheless, unlike the Conservative administration Labour has rejected the notion of a natural level of unemployment with a commitment to 'a higher percentage of people in work than ever before' and is committed to abolishing child poverty within 20 years. The commitment to 'lifelong' equality of opportunity and the belief that social justice can be achieved through state action marks Labour as significantly different from the Thatcherite right (see Chapters 10 and 11).

The point that several chapters of this book have emphasized is that there is a complex relationship between New Labour, old Labour and Thatcherism. Any decision by the Blair government is shaped by complex and contradictory pressures. As Kenny and Smith highlight, Labour's traditional commitment to ethical socialism and social democracy cannot be ignored. At the same time, fear of the failures and difficulties of old Labour are not far from the minds of the present leadership. Undoubtedly, the policy successes and failures of the Conservative years have embedded certain policy ideas into British government. Moreover, the Labour Cabinet is undoubtedly keenly aware of the feelings of the electorate (see Chapter 2). Finally, all previous Labour governments were at some point knocked off course by the financial markets. In 1949, 1966, 1969, 1975 and 1977, Labour was forced to change policies and cut spending in order to satisfy the markets. Brown and Blair restate financial rectitude in order to preempt City demands.

Gamble and Kelly demonstrate that economic policy is probably the area where the most complex juxtaposition exists between Thatcherism and Labourism. On one side both Thatcherism and Labour were adjusting to new realities. There is no party in western Europe, or perhaps the world, which is now using Keynesian demand management. The existence of the WTO means that all countries are now committed to liberalization of trade. Labour could potentially buck the trend but such a strategy is likely to result in the sort of humiliating U-turn that the French Socialists suffered in 1983 (see Chapter 3). Whilst fiscally conservative, Labour is committed to interventionist supply-side measures and to incremental redistribution through the tax system.

This complexity is evident in other policy areas again highlighting the limited extent to which Labour is new. For instance, as the chapters by McCaig and Annesley reveal, both education and welfare policy can be seen as condensation of three important influences. First, is the old Labour concern with welfare and education as mechanisms for improving the life chances of individuals. Public provision of welfare goods is not inherently inferior to the market and it is not on the whole a safety net (although there are, for example, clearly safety net elements in the future plans for pension provisions). Labour does retain a strong commitment to publicly funded education. Second, Labour has not ignored or dismantled the policy frameworks developed by 18 years of Conservatism, partly because of the costs of dismantling all that they have found and partly because they addressed some real world concerns which are recognized as such by voters. So, for example, whilst Labour has abolished the assisted places scheme because of the implicit private-sector bias, they have continued the Conservatives' national curriculum, the emphasis on standards, auditing of teachers, the use of private funds (and in Islington private-sector provision) and league tables. However, the end Labour desires is not a market in education or an exit to the private sector but a high-quality education that prepares people for a competitive market and that enhances opportunity. It is the goal that is New Labour; a combination of market concerns with a belief in the social value of education to all; and the belief that inner-city and deprived children have a right to good-quality education. Of course, what it could be argued is missing is the necessary financial largesse to achieve this goal. Infusing all these pressures is the desire to keep on board the aspirational upper working-class and lower middle-class voters.

As Chapter 11 highlights, welfare policy is subject to similar cross-cutting pressure. The principle of universality remains in certain areas of policy; child benefit; heating and TV licences; benefits for pensioners; and health. However, in other areas Labour have continued the Conservative emphasis on increasing sanctions on the long-term unemployed and targeting benefits particularly in relation to single parents and the disabled. And, while the universal basic state pension will continue to fall in value, second pensions will not be compulsory, and the 'minimum income guarantee' to pensioners will be means-tested. Social security policy has also been clearly shaped by the Treasury line that costs should be controlled and there is a strong acknowledgement that the Beveridge welfare state is not suitable to what are seen as increasingly competitive, global markets where the tax burden has to be reduced. Yet, what sets New Labour apart is an ethical socialist belief in the dignity of labour, the belief that the social exclusion produced by Thatcherism must be undone and a commitment to state-led redistribution. Unlike old Labour, the government sees many problems in the Beveridge welfare state but unlike Thatcherism it does not see the welfare state as an inherent corruption of the market mechanism.

Whilst economic, welfare, education and foreign policy have to be seen as a complex amalgam of ideas, policies and institutional structures which have been influenced by old Labour, Thatcherism and new thinking, certain changes can be seen as more distinctly new. Where Blair's Labour party seems to have broken with tradition are in the areas of constitutional reform, news management and party organization. Previous Labour governments had made lukewarm attempts at devolution and freedom of information whilst Conservative governments had rejected completely the need for constitutional reform (see Chapter 8). The extent and rapidity of New Labour's constitutional reform thus seems a significant break with the past. Nevertheless, as Chapter 8 emphasized, the flaw in Labour's constitutional package is its unwillingness to confront the British tradition and reconsider the core elements of the British constitution such as parliamentary sovereignty and ministerial responsibility. Thus the danger is that constitutional reform is corrupted by the existing constitution and will fail to enhance the quality of democracy in Britain.

In terms of party and news management, New Labour seems to have made a qualitative leap ahead of the Conservatives and certainly old Labour (see Chapter 7). Franklin highlights how the media have increasingly become a control mechanism initially for electoral purposes and subsequently for governing purposes. Philip Gould's insight into new Labour strongly emphasizes the extent to which the party leadership is concerned with manipulating the news and sees controlling the party as an important element of this strategy. The leadership's role in the European elections, the selection of the leader of the Welsh Assembly and the problems of the London mayor emphasize the increasing grip that the centre has on the party. However, whilst the New Labour leadership may be more effective in this area than any other party, it is clear that they are to some extent building on pre-existing developments. The professionalizing of campaigning and news management owes much to lessons learnt from the Conservatives and initiated by Kinnock's campaign team (which included Mandelson and Gould) and the imposing of party discipline is also a development of policies under Kinnock. Moreover, Cowley, Darcy and Mellors demonstrate (in Chapter 5) that despite the strong desire to control, there have been significant rebellions amongst Labour backbenchers. Indeed, the government has been forced to make concessions in order to secure the passage of the Freedom of Information Act and changes in disability benefits.

Nevertheless, it is important to see New Labour as a specific Labour response to the crises of the Keynesian Welfare State. Labour's post-war governing strategy was undermined by a combination of the collapse of Bretton Woods, the end of the post-war boom, the power of the trade unions and the consequent inability to trade off unemployment against inflation. As a consequence Labour was forced to adopt a new governing strategy and, if anything, it was the government of Callaghan which adopted

Thatcherism because of its inability to develop a centre-left alternative to Keynesianism. The alternative strategy was the Alternative Economic Strategy with its proposals for a policy of national protectionism (see Gamble, 1992). This policy was made unviable because of its lack of legitimacy in the party, the electorate and the City. Whilst the Conservatives under Thatcher developed a strategy for governing in the post-post-war boom world, Labour was left foundering trying to marry its traditional spending commitments to new economic and electoral demands. Consequently New Labour should be seen as an attempt to fill this vacuum and rebuild Labour's electoral viability and its reputation for governing competence. Blair and the New Labour leadership have been astutely aware of Labour's problems of governing competence, electoral decline and party division. In many ways New Labour can be understood as a response to these problems. It is in many ways less programmatic and more a strategy to try to deal with electoral, party and governing issues. In a sense the essence of new Labour is the need to get and keep the party in power.

BLAIR'S STRATEGY FOR NEW LABOUR

Electoral

As Chapter 1 suggests, it is impossible to understand New Labour without comprehending the severe impact that Labour's electoral failure had on the party. Chapter 2 highlights the degree of that failure. Consequently, in order to rebuild Labour's electoral base, fundamental to Blair's vision of New Labour is a strategy for permanently linking the working class, the lower middle class and a significant element of middle-class support. Such a bloc is the mechanism for ensuring that Labour can be a successful 'catch-all' electoral party (see Chapter 2) and a serious governing party for the foreseeable future. Blair's vision of Labour is very much of a party that can place itself in the centre and consequently build a wide coalition of support.

Blair's concern is to create a permanent coalition and this goal, which is an artefact of electoral necessity, provides a great constraint on Labour's policies. It explains the need to overcome traditional antagonisms, the reclaiming of patriotism and why certain policies such as high marginal rates of taxation and nationalization are no longer an option. This is not an acceptance of a Thatcherite agenda but an awareness of the need to build a wide electoral coalition. Central to the electoral strategy is the party strategy.

Party

One of the main problems both for the electoral strategy and the governing strategy was the role of the party. There was a belief that the divisions in the party, the strength of party activists and conflicts between the party and the leadership were both undermining electoral support and creating perceptions of governmental failure. The belief of leaders as far back as Gaitskell was that activists wanted policies that were not supported by the electorate and that activists through accusations of betrayal were creating expectations of a Labour government that could not be met in the 'real world'. These problems were exacerbated in the 1980s when party activists increased their say over party policy, the selection of candidates and the election of the leader. The fear of the party is emphasized in the famous leaked memo by Patricia Hewitt that stated:

> It is obvious from our own polling, as well as from the doorstep, that the 'London effect' is taking its toll: the gays and lesbians issue is costing us dear among the pensioners, and fear of extremism and higher taxes/rates is particularly prominent in the GLC area.

Thus Blair's party strategy has been concerned with reasserting central control and moderating party policy. As Seyd and Whiteley demonstrate in Chapter 4, there have been significant changes to party organization under Blair, in particular the declining role of conference, which is a significant change from the party organization of old Labour.

Although many of the organizational changes are new, it is important to note that Blair was not the first Labour leader concerned with reforming the party in terms of a notion of modernization. Gaitskell was acutely aware of the need to change Labour's ideology and policy in the light of economic and social change. Wilson wanted to present Labour as a modernizing party and clearly saw the role of nationalization as a means rather than end. Finally, Neil Kinnock initiated the process of modernization that has been carried further by Blair. However, what makes Blair's modernization different is that it is more fundamental than previous attempts, that it tackled the issue of Clause IV, and it is linked with electoral success.

A fundamental and defining component of Blair's modernizing project was the reform of Clause IV. Blair quickly decided that he would drop Labour's commitment to common ownership of the means of production. The impact of the decision was far-reaching. Blair was demonstrating a break with the past and a symbolic ending of the link that Labour had with state ownership. This was a confirmation of a fundamental change in the ideological position of the party. The party was unconditionally disassociated from state socialism and it dispelled the myth that Labour 'would nationalize everything'. It was intended to send a clear message to voters about how Labour had changed. It also indicated in an unambiguous way that key elements of the party ideology would change. By giving the leader a mandate it stamped Blair's authority on the party. In supporting the reform of Clause IV the party was supporting Blair's whole programme of modernization. Yet Blair was concerned with reassuring the party:

> The process of what is called 'modernisation' is in reality, therefore, the application of enduring, lasting principles for a new generation – creating not just a modern party and organisation but a programme for a modern society, economy and constitution. It is not destroying the left's essential ideology: on the contrary it is retrieving it from an intellectual and political muddle.

Once Clause IV was reformed Blair quickly consolidated the reforms to the party machinery that Kinnock had begun. Blair strengthened one member one vote and through the development of the policy forum he effectively undermined the role of conference in policymaking. Likewise, the NEC, which at times had been a troublesome critic of the leadership, became increasingly Blairite whilst its policy role was significantly reduced (see Chapter 4).

The aim of these reforms has been both to reduce the influence of party members and to re-educate them. The party leadership can offer policies that are attractive to voters rather than the party and in pursuing such policies not be accused of betrayal. Central to Blair's strategy is an attempt to eradicate the 'culture of betrayal' by pointing to the political and economic constraints that will prevent Labour achieving many of its policies in the short term. In an article in *The Guardian* of July 1995 he urged members to be realistic about what can be achieved:

> With the ideological and organisational change, there has to come the attitude of mind of a party to govern. Part of this means activists should not rise to every bait held out by the press or revive the old 'betrayal' psychology that has dogged the party before.

Undoubtedly as Chapters 4 and 5 indicate, much of New Labour's strategy is concerned with imposing discipline on party members and MPs. However, these chapters also indicate that the New Labour leadership has not completely recreated the rest of the party in its image. Whilst there are some indicators of acceptance of the New Labour agenda, there is still some resistance among MPs and party members. Cowley, Darcy and Mellors indicate that there is not always enthusiastic support amongst MPs for New Labour legislation. However, as Seyd and Whiteley demonstrate, whilst there is some belief that Labour has abandoned principles, most members are satisfied with the changes that have occurred in party organization and democracy.

Central to the need to reposition the party and to avoid some of the conflicts of the past was a reordering of the relationship with the trade unions. As Ludlam highlights in Chapter 6, many of these changes occurred under Kinnock and Smith and Blair's industrial relations policy derives from the Kinnock–Smith era. However, under Blair there was a qualitative change in the nature of the relationship between party and unions in particular with the rejection of a privileged position for unions. In one of the most significant breaks from the traditions of old Labour, and his immediate predecessors, Blair has aimed at creating a distinct distance from the trade unions. This underplaying of the trade union link is fundamental to the strategy of maintaining electoral support, avoiding party conflicts and ensuring that the union problems of previous Labour administrations do not re-emerge. The union link in its present form will be lucky to survive into the twenty-first century.

The cold-shouldering of the unions emphasizes the importance of the rhetorical device of old/New Labour. If there is an enemy left, and one that is strongly identified by certain elements in Blair's leadership, it is 'Old Labour'. The reality of old Labour is that it is a combination of the right of the party, the left and dissidents but its rhetorical importance is that it is a way of distancing New Labour from its past and indicating to the electorate that the Party has fundamentally changed. Consequently, the negation of old Labour is an important element in shaping what is new. The problem, of course, is that the dichotomy is false and many of the concerns, if not directly the policies, of the present government are similar to previous Labour governments. All past Labour administrations have been concerned to find a middle way between free-market capitalism and state-centred socialism and have effectively attempted to run the British economy successfully in order to produce some fruits for redistribution. Other 'New Labour' themes such as the importance of education, traditional values and law and order have appeared in past administrations, particularly the socially conservative Callaghan administration. Labour is not free from its traditions and the themes of social conservatism and social justice that recur in New Labour have a strong resonance with the past. Moreover, the appeal to realism in the membership is a theme that has reoccurred in Labour administrations. This invocation of realism in the party is central to Labour's governing strategy.

Governing

Labour's statecraft is essential to New Labour. Labour has to govern in a way that does not unravel its electoral coalition (thus enabling a second term) and therefore it is important that party criticism does not undermine its essentially conservative governing strategy. What both Blair and Brown have been mainly concerned with is ensuring that the Labour government is perceived as competent and, therefore, it is important to avoid the sort of economic and union crises that have dogged previous Labour administrations. This governing strategy can be clearly seen in Blair's commitment to 'run from the centre'. There is within the government a need to try to control in order to prevent policy disasters.

The central point is that the electoral, party and governing strategies are interlinked and in that sense part of New Labour has to be seen as non-ideological; it is a mechanism for ensuring the continuation of the party in office. This position, of course, creates a problem. Whilst Blair and Brown have a vision for a long-term modernization of the British polity, economy and society, the short-term goal of electoral victory may contradict its achievement. The electoral impediment may force the government into conservative incrementalism rather than radical measures necessary to achieve their social goals as demonstrated in Chapter 11.

The Importance of the External Environment

Whatever the arguments concerning the nature and impact of globalization, New Labour can only be understood within the context of external changes. As the chapters by Clift and Buller demonstrate, New Labour's ideology and policy goals have to be understood within the perspective of changes to social democratic parties more broadly and to changes in Britain's position with the world order. The ending of the Cold War, the reluctant acceptance of Britain's lesser status in world politics and new perspectives on the European Union, have allowed or encouraged the abandonment of key old Labour policies such as withdrawal from the EU and unilateral disarmament. The end of the Cold War has reduced the salience of these policies.

Moreover, the Conservatives' hostility to the EU and the sense in which Europe provided the only intermediate institution that was able to ameliorate the worst excesses of Thatcherism shifted the perspective on most of the left over the issue of European integration. The collapse of the eastern bloc has also resulted in nearly all, except the old Trotskyist left and new anarcho-communist groupings, accepting that (rightly or wrongly) capitalism is here to stay. Thus without being determined by the international context, Blairism is of its time and many of New Labour's policies have derived from a particular international context.

Conclusion

In developing policies New Labour draws on often contradictory and conflicting traditions of social democracy, social conservatism, Thatcherism and pragmatism. Consequently, New Labour is essentially ambiguous and Janus-faced. Gordon Brown can at the same time express Labour's commitment to equality and social justice whilst proclaiming the need to set business free and to reduce their tax burdens. There are clearly non-Thatcherite elements to New Labour: the minimum wage, the New Deal, extra benefits to pensioners, the relationships to the EU. At the same time some of the welfare reforms and key elements of economic policy would not look out of place in a Conservative government. This ambiguity is extremely useful in terms of the interlocking governing, electoral and party strategies. The leadership can draw on varying traditions according to the principal goal or audience at a particular time. Whilst this may be an efficient means of maintaining Labour in power, it is questionable whether it provides the mechanisms for a radical transformation of Britain. The problem is that the means may undermine the ends.

At the moment New Labour contains within it both radical and conservative potential. If Labour was to accept proportional representation for Westminster elections, restructure the welfare state, create a highly skilled workforce within the context of increasing levels of employment, join the single currency whilst continuing and extending the process of redistribution, it is clear that Britain in ten or fifteen years' time would be very different from the Conservative Britain of 1997. By rejecting the low-skill, low-wage, free market exporting economy of the Conservatives, it would have a dramatic impact on the long-term trajectory of politics and the economy in Britain. If, however, the government remains cautious in it constitutional reform programme, focuses on welfare reform rather than redistribution and makes its central economic policy fiscal conservatism, it is likely that the radical modernization of Britain will be delayed yet again.

Guide to Further Reading

1 The Making of New Labour

The fullest account of Labour since 1945 is Shaw (1996). The most useful studies of the Wilson and Callaghan governments of the 1960s and 1970s remain Ponting (1990) and D. Coates (1980); Whitehead (1986) adds the personal views of many Labour leaders on the 1960s and 1970s. For alternative analyses of the rise and fall of the Labour left from the 1970s see Seyd (1987) and Leys and Panitch (1997). On Labour's long march back to office after 1983, Kinnock has provided his own account (1994). Smith and Spear (1992), Shaw (1994) and G. Taylor (1997) provide analysis of components of the process, and friendly and hostile histories are provided, respectively, by Hughes and Wintour (1990), and Heffernan and Marqusee (1992). P. Gould (1998a) provides a significant inside account by a key modernizer. Mandelson and Liddle (1996) and Blair (1996b) were early New Labour statements of intent. Early studies of New Labour included Brivati and Bale (1997), Anderson and Mann (1997), and Driver and Martell (1998); more recent analyses will be found in Hay (1999) and Kastendiek, Stinshoff and Sturm (1999).

2 New Labour and the Electorate

Denver and Hands (1992) offers a collection of keynote work covering much of the post-war period, and is especially helpful on the volatile period since 1964 and the crucial arguments (for Labour) about class voting. Landmark empirical studies have included Butler and Stokes (1969), Crewe and Särlvik (1983), and, on the 1983, 1987 and 1992 defeats, Heath, Jowell and Curtice (1985, 1991, 1994). Johnston, Pattie and Allsopp (1988) unravel the importance of regional effects. Successive editions of *British Elections and Parties Review* contain much valuable material, not least the volume covering the 1997 election, edited by Denver, Fisher, Cowley and Pattie (1998). Other early studies of the 1997 election have included Butler and Kavanagh (1997), Geddes and Tonge (1997), Norris and Gavin (1997), and A. King (1998).

3 New Labour's Third Way and European Social Democracy

For extensive surveys of the parties of the European left, not least of the dilemmas and transformations of the 1980s and 1990s, see Piven (1991), Padgett and Paterson (1991), Scharpf (1991), and Anderson and Camiller (1994). Sassoon (1996) adds a grand historical sweep. For a view from Europe, see Bergounioux and Lazar (1997). For contrasting views of the implications of globalization, see Held, McGrew, Goldblatt and Perraton (1999), Hirst and Thompson (1996), and, from Labour's think tank, Vandenbroucke (1998). For recent views of key European parties, see Lafontaine (1998) on the SPD, Parti Socialiste (1997), Peterson (1998) on Sweden, and Recio and Roca (1998) on Spain; and for a recent view of social democratic convergence in Europe, see Lightfoot (1999).

4 New Labour and the Party: Members and Organization

The detail and dynamics of Labour's internal democracy and discipline for much of the post-war period are captured in Minkin (1980, 1992) and Shaw (1988). Among other insights, Whiteley (1983) includes results from an attitude survey of Labour members, as does Seyd (1987); their joint work analyses the first mass attitude survey of Labour members nationally (Seyd and Whiteley, 1992a), and their forthcoming work on New Labour will analyse their subsequent survey. Key Labour Party documents (1990a, 1997b) explain and describe many recent changes internal organization. The earlier changes of the 1980s are discussed in Shaw (1994), Seyd (1987; 1993), and Heffernan and Marqusee (1992). Insights into the New Labour leadership's view of the party's function and functioning can be gleaned from Mandelson and Liddle (1996) and P. Gould (1998a), and are discussed in Seyd (1998). Surveys of parties in general, across the period, include McKenzie (1955), Epstein (1966), Ware (1987) and Panebianco (1988).

5 New Labour's Parliamentarians

Important studies of the socio-economic composition of Labour's parliamentary party since 1945 include Mellors (1978) and Burch and Moran (1985). Results of the first British Candidate Study, covering the 1992 election, appeared in Norris and Lovenduski (1995). The origins and composition of the 1997 Parliamentary Labour Party are described in Criddle (1997) and Roth and Criddle (1997). Records of Labour parliamentary dissent since 1945 are set out in detail in Norton's exhaustive studies (1975, 1980), and in Piper (1974). The results of a key survey of Labour MPs' attitudes to Europe are reported in Baker, Gamble, Ludlam and Seawright (1996). An earlier analysis of Blair's backbenchers appeared in Cowley (1999).

6   New Labour and the Unions: the End of the Contentious Alliance?

The union role in Labour politics in the early post-war decades is analysed in Harrison (1960) and Richter (1973), and closely observed in Minkin (1980). The tensions in the years of incomes policy are captured from different perspectives in Panitch (1976) and Dorfman (1979); for the whole period see R. Taylor (1993). For Social Contract years, the memoirs of Denis Healey (1990) and Jack Jones (1986) are instructive, and resulting strains considered in Ludlam (1995). Union–party links in the 1970s and 1980s are analysed by A. Taylor (1987), and by Minkin (1992) whose study of the century-long alliance is most detailed on the 1980s. The union role in Labour's modernization is discussed in Kinnock (1994), Heffernan and Marqusee (1992) and Hughes and Wintour (1990). John Smith's review of the union link is discussed in Alderman and Carter (1994) and Webb (1995). The modernization of trade union politics during the 1980s and 1990s is dealt with in Bassett (1987) and Rosamond (1998), and the TUC's 1990s reorientation in R. Taylor (1994). The significance of New Labour's industrial relations legislation is assessed in R. Taylor (1998), and initial reactions recorded in Ludlam (1998).

7   The Hand of History: New Labour, News Management and Governance

The impact of modern political communication on democracy is analysed in McChesney (1999), and the techniques involved in N. Jones (1995). The role of the Government Information Services is discussed in two key official reports, Mountfield (1997) and Select Committee on Public Administration (1998). New Labour's media strategy in the 1997 election is extensively dealt with in Norris, Curtice, Scammell and Semetko (1999), and in Crewe, Gosschalk and Bartle (1998), in which Philip Gould, director of Labour's Shadow Communications Agency gives an explanation of why Labour won. New Labour's 'spinning' in government is covered in

Franklin (1998) and, by a frontline political journalist, in N. Jones (1999). Many insights can be gained from Philip Gould's memoir (1998a), and from a study of Labour's senior spindoctor, Alastair Campbell, by Oborne (1999).

8 New Labour, the Constitution and Reforming the State

The elements of Labour's constitutional reform programme are well reviewed in Hazell (1999). Labour's historical position on the state is outlined in Alexander (1997) and Marquand (1992). The nature and impact of the core executive and the Westminister model is examined in M. J. Smith (1999), Richards and Smith (2000) and Tant (1993). For an examination of Taskforces see Daniel (1997) and Barker *et al.* (1999). For the governments approach to the reform of central government see the White Paper *Modernising Government* CM 4310 (1999).

9 New Labour's Economics

For the crucial economic and economic policy contexts of most of the post-war period see Cairncross (1992). Wickham-Jones (1996) provides a full account of party economic policy from 1970 to 1983, and Kinnock's economics adviser (Eatwell, 1992) has surveyed policy development between 1979 and 1992. G. Taylor (1997) considers the economic sections of the 1989 Policy Review, and Thompson (1996) puts the turn towards supply-side socialism in its historical perspective. The key modernization debate on stakeholding is presented in Kelly, Kelly and Gamble (1997), and the notion is strongly advocated in Hutton (1995). The debate on globalization is analysed from every angle in Held, McGrew, Goldblatt and Perraton (1999). New Labour's approach to economic management is set out by Gordon Brown's chief adviser in Balls (1998). The early studies of New Labour listed in the further reading for Chapter 1 above all contain material on New Labour's economics, which are extensively attacked in Hay (1999). The Treasury's website is a convenient source of keynote speeches and other documents on New Labour economic policy.

10 New Labour and Education, Education, Education

For an understanding of Labour's past education policy see S. Tomlinson (1997) and Pinder (1979). For a discussion of the great debate see

Ainley (1998). For an outline of the ideological background of old Labour see A. Crosland (1956). For a discussion of policy during the Kinnock period see R. Alexander (1997). An outline of New Labour policy is provided in Blair (1996b) and Blunkett (1996b). For policy in government see DfEE (1997d) and (1999a), and Robinson (1998b).

11   New Labour and Welfare

Labour's post-war record of social policy is surveyed in Lowe (1993), and its modernization in the 1980s in Alcock (1992). The crucial report of John Smith's Commission on Social Justice (1994) argues for many policy changes that New Labour has since taken up; its content is discussed in G. Taylor (1997) and put in historical context by Ellison (1997). Many aspects of New Labour's welfare policy approach can be studied in Field (1996), Giddens (1998), Oppenheim (1998), Kelly, Kelly and Gamble (1997), and in chapters in the early studies of New Labour listed in the further reading for Chapter 1 above. Important recent work on New Labour's welfare reform strategy includes Hills (1998) and Levitas (1998). Social Exclusion Unit (1998) is an early outcome of the attempt to practice joined-up government on poverty. Gordon Brown (1999) defends New Labour's approach to social equality, as does Tony Blair in his Third Way pamphlet (1998c).

12   New Labour's Foreign and Defence Policy: External Support Structures and Domestic Policies

For the historical and political context on Britain's foreign policy see Kennedy (1981), Bulpitt (1988) and Gamble (1994). Sanders (1993) provides a good account of post-war foreign policy. For the importance of nuclear issues see Bayliss (1981). For the importance of economic constraints on foreign policy see Thompson (1996) and Grahl (1997). The changing position of Labour on Europe is covered by George and Haythorne (1996) and Daniels (1998). For discussion of EMU membership see Stephens (1998) and for an examination of ethical foreign policy see Wheeler and Dunne (1998).

13   Interpreting New Labour: Constraints, Dilemmas and Political Agency

The debates concerning New Labour can be found in Hay (1999); Heffernan (1999), Kenny and Smith (1997a) and Anderson and Mann (1997). For an account of the process of modernization see Shaw (1994) and (1996), Smith and Spear (1992) and Wickham-Jones (1995b). For ways of understanding New Labour, Bevir (1999b) and Freeden (1999a and 1999b) are useful. For Blair's position see Blair (1996b and 1999c) and for Brown's see Brown (1999). The key insiders' account of Blair's vision is given in Mandelson and Liddle (1996).

References

Abrams, M., Rose, R. and Hinden, R. (1960) *Must Labour Lose?* (Harmondsworth: Penguin).

Adonis, A. and Hames, T. (eds). (1994) *A Conservative Revolution? The Thatcher–Regan Decade in Perspective* (Manchester: Manchester University Press).

Ainley, P. (1988) *From School to YTS: Education and Training in England and Wales 1944–87* (Milton Keynes: Open University Press).

Ainley, P. (1997) 'The Crises of the Colleges', *Education Today and Tomorrow*, Vol. 49, No. 2, Summer 1997.

Alcock, P. (1992) 'The Labour Party and the Welfare State', in Smith, M. and Spear, J. (eds) (1992).

Alcock, P. (1996) *Social Policy in Britain: Themes and Issues* (Basingstoke: Macmillan).

Alderman, K. and Carter, N. (1994) 'The Labour Party and the Trade Unions: Loosening the Ties', *Parliamentary Affairs*, Vol. 47, No. 3.

Alderman, R. K. (1964–5), 'Discipline in the Parliamentary Labour Party 1945–51', *Parliamentary Affairs*, Vol. 18, No. 3.

Alexander, G. (1997) 'Managing the State' in Brivati, B. and Bale, T. (eds), (1997).

Alexander, R. (1997) *Policy and Practice in Primary Education: Local Initiative, National Agenda*, 2nd edn (London: Routledge).

Allen, Liz (1996) of the Labour Party Policy Directorate, interview with author, Millbank Tower, 29 October.

Allen, M. (1998) 'British Trade Unionism's Quiet Revolution', *Renewal*, Vol. 6, No. 4.

Allen, V. (1960) *Trade Unions and the Government* (London: Longman).

Amnesty International (1998) UK Foreign and Asylum Policy: Human Rights Audit (London: Amnesty International).

Anderson, P. and Blackburn, R. (eds) (1999) *Towards Socialism* (London: Collins).

Anderson, P. and Camiller, P. (eds)(1994) *Mapping The West European Left* (London: Verso).

Anderson, P. and Mann, N. (1997) *Safety First: The Making of New Labour* (London: Verso).

Anderson, P. (1994) 'Introduction', in Anderson, P. and Camiller, P. (eds) (1994).

Arestis and Sawyer, M. (1988) 'New Labour, New Monetarism', *Soundings*, Vol. 9, pp. 24–41.

Artis, M. and Cobham, D. (eds) (1991) *Labour's Economic Policies, 1974–79* (Manchester: Manchester University Press).

Atkinson, M. (1998) 'It Won't Always be Yes Minister', *The Guardian*, 6 June.

Atkinson, T. (1998) 'Targeting Poverty', *New Economy*, Vol. 5, No. 1.

Baker, D. and Seawright, D. (1998) 'A "Rosy" Map of Europe? Labour Parliamentarians and European Integration', in Baker, D. and Seawright, D. (eds), *Britain For and Against Europe: British Politics and the Question of European Integration* (Oxford: Oxford University Press).

Baker, D., Fountain, I., Gamble, A. and Ludlam, S. (1995) 'The Conservative Parliamentary Elite 1964–1994: The End of Social Convergence?', *Sociology*, Vol. 29, No. 4.

Baker, D., Gamble A. and Seawright, D. with Bull, K. (1999), 'MPs and Europe', in Fisher, J., Cowley, P., Denver, D. and Russell, A. (eds) (1999) *British Elections and Parties Review Volume 9* (London: Frank Cass).

Baker, D., Gamble, A., Ludlam, S. and Seawright, D. (1996) 'Labour and Europe: A Survey of MPs and MEPs', *Political Quarterly*, Vol. 67, No. 4.

Bale, T. (1997a) 'Managing the Party and the Trade Unions', in Brivati, B. and Bale, T. (eds) (1997).

Bale, T. (1997b) 'Sacred Cows and Common Sense: the Symbolic Statecraft and Political Welfare of the Labour Government' (unpublished Ph.D. thesis, University of Sheffield).

Bale, T. (1999) 'The Logic of No Alternative? Political Scientists, Historians and the Politics of Labour's Past', *British Journal of Politics and International Relations,* Vol. 1, No. 2.

Balls, E. (1998) 'Open Macroeconomics in an Open Economy', *Scottish Journal of Political Economy,* Vol. 43, No. 2.

Barber, L. (1997) 'Life on the Outside', *Financial Times,* 3 December.

Barber, M. (1996a) *The Learning Game* (London: Victor Golancz).

Barber, M. (1996b) *Everyone Deserves Success, Times Educational Supplement,* 6 September 1996.

Barker, A., Byrne, I and Veall, A. (1999) *Ruling by Task Force* (London: Politico's).

Barker, R. (1972) *Education and Politics, 1900–1951: A Study of the Labour Party* (Oxford: Clarendon Press).

Barr, N. and Hills, J. (eds) (1990) *The State of Welfare: The Welfare State in Britain since* 1974 (Oxford: Clarendon Press).

Barr, N. (1998) 'Towards a "Third Way"? Rebalancing the Role of the State', *New Economy,* Vol. 5, No. 2.

Bassett, P. (1987) *Strike Free: New Industrial Relations in Britain* (London: Macmillan).

Baun, Michael. J. (1995/6) 'The Maastricht Treaty As High Politics: Germany, France and European Integration, *Political Science Quarterly*, Vol. 110, No. 4.

Bayley, S. (1998) *Labour Camp: The Failure of Style Over Substance* (London: BT Batsford Ltd).

Bayliss, J. (1981) *Anglo-American Defence Relations 1939–80* (London: Macmillan).

Beckett, F. (1998a) 'Grammars for the Hammer', *The Guardian,* 3 November.

Beckett, F. (1998b) 'Business Snubs Blunkett's Big Idea', *New Statesman,* 19 June.

Beckett, F. (1999) 'Blunkett Accepts Schools for Profit', *New Statesman,* 15 January.

Beer, S. (1982) *Britain Against Itself* (London: Faber).

Benn, T. (1989) *Against the Tide: Diaries 1973–76* (London: Hutchinson).

Benn, T. (1994a) *Years of Hope: Diaries, Papers and Letters 1940–1962* (London: Hutchinson).

Benn, T. (1994b) *Tony Benn: The End of an Era, Diaries 1980–90* (London: Arrow).

Benn, T. (1998) 'Serbia Will Not Be Bombed Into Submission', *The Observer,* 11 October.

Bergounioux, A. and Lazar, M. (1997) *La Social-démocratie dans l'Union Européenne* (Paris: Fondation Jean Jaurès).

Bernstein, K. (1983) 'The International Monetary Fund and Deficit Countries: The Case of Britain, 1974–77' (unpublished Ph.D. thesis, Stanford University).

Bevan, A. (1952) *In Place of Fear* (London: Heinemann).

Bevir, M. (1999a) 'New Labour and Ethics: A Study in Ideological Change' (unpublished manuscript).

Bevir, M. (1999b) *The Logic of the History of Ideas* (Cambridge: Cambridge University Press).

Bevir, M. and Rhodes, R. A. W. (1999) 'Studying British Government: Reconstructing the Research Agenda', *British Journal of Politics and International Relations*, Vol.1, pp. 215–39.

Bichard, M. (1999) *Modernizing the Policy Process* (London: Public Management and Policy Association).

Birch, A. (1998) 10th edn, *The British System of Government* (London: Routledge).

Blair, T. (1994) *Change and National Renewal* (London: The Labour Party).

Blair, T. (1995) *Speech to the 1995 Annual Conference of the Labour Party* (London: The Labour Party).

Blair, T. (1996a) Interview, *Independent on Sunday*, 28 July.

Blair, T. (1996b) *New Britain: My Vision of a Young Country* (London: Fourth Estate).

Blair, T. (1996c) *Speech to the 1996 Annual Conference of the Labour Party* (London: The Labour Party).

Blair, T. (1997a) *Speech to the Party of European Socialists Congress*, Malmö, 6 June 1997 (London: The Labour Party).

Blair, T. (1997b) *Speech to the 1997 Annual Trades Union Congress* (London: Trades Union Congress).

Blair, T. (1998a) *A Modern Britain in a Modern Europe: Speech at the Annual Friends of Nieuwspoort Dinner, The Hague, 20/01/98* (London: The Labour Party).

Blair, T. (1998b) *The Third Way: Speech to the French National Assembly, Paris, 24 March 1998* (London: The Labour Party).

Blair, T. (1998c) *The Third Way: New Politics for the New Century* (London: Fabian Society).

Blair, T. (1998d) 'Modernising Central Government' Speech to the Senior Civil Service Conference, London, 13 October.

Blair, T. (1999) *Speech to TUC Partners for Progress Conference* (London: The Labour Party).

Blank, S. (1977) 'Britain: The Politics of Foreign Economic Policy, the Domestic Economy, and the Problem of Pluralistic Stagnation', *International Organisation*, Vol. 34, No. 4.

Blumler, J. G. (1990) 'The Modern Publicity Process', in Ferguson, M. (ed.), *Political Communication: The New Imperatives* (London: Sage).

Blunkett, D. (1996a) interview with author, Sheffield, 22 Auguest.

Blunkett, D (1996b) *Speech to Annual Conference of the Labour Party*, 2 October, (London: The Labour Party).

Blunkett, D. (1997) interview with author, Leeds, 13 September.

Bogdanor, V. (1997) *Power and the People* (London: Victor Gollancz).

Bootle, R. (1997) *The Death of Inflation: Surviving and Thriving in the Zero Era* (London: Nicholas Brearley).

Borthwick, G., Ellingworth, D., Bell, C. and Mackenzie, D. (1991) 'Research Note: The Social Background of British MPs', *Sociology*, Vol. 25, No. 4.

Bosanquet, N. and Townsend, P. (eds) (1980) *Labour and Equality: A Fabian Study of Labour in Power, 1974–79* (London: Heinemann).

Bown, F. A. C. S. (1990) 'The Shops Bill', in Rush, M. (ed.) (1990) *Parliament and Pressure Politics* (Oxford: Oxford University Press).

Briggs, A. (1979) *The Age of Improvement 1783–1867* (London: Longman).

Brittan, S. (1969) *Steering The Economy: The Role of the Treasury* (London: Secker & Warburg).

Brittan, S. (1999) 'A Wrong Turning on the Third Way?' *New Statesman*, 1 January.

Brivati, B. and Bale, T. (eds) (1997) *New Labour in Power: Precedents and Prospects* (London: Routledge).

Brivati, B. (1997) 'Earthquake or Watershed? Conclusions on New Labour in Power' in Brivati, B. and Bale, T. (eds) (1997).

Brookes, R. H. (1959) 'Electoral Distortion in New Zealand', *Australian Journal of Politics and History*, Vol. 5, pp. 218–33.

Brookes, R. H. (1960) 'The Analysis of Distorted Representation in Two-Party, Single Member Systems', *Political Science*, Vol. 12, pp. 158–67.

Brown, C., Powell, L. and Wilcox, C. (1995) *Serious Money* (Cambridge: Cambridge University Press).

Brown, G. (1997) 'No Quick Fix On Jobs', *Financial Times*, 17 November.

Brown, G. (1998a) *Chancellor's Speech at the Mansion House 11 June 1998*.

Brown, G. (1998b) *Statement by the Chancellor of the Exchequer on the Comprehensive Spending Review 14 July 1998*.

Brown, G. (1998c) *Statement by the Chancellor of the Exchequer on the Pre-Budget Report on 3 November 1998*.

Brown, G. (1999) 'Equality – Then and Now', in Leonard, D. (ed.) (1999) *Crosland and New Labour* (London: Macmillan).

Browning, P. (1986) *The Treasury and Economic Policy, 1964–85* (London: Longman).

Bulpitt, J. (1988) 'Rational Politicians and Conservative Statecraft in the Open Polity', in Byrd, P. (ed.) *British Foreign Policy Under Thatcher* (Deddington: Philip Allan).

Burch, M. and Moran, M. (1985) 'The Changing British Political Elite 1945–83', *Parliamentary Affairs*, Vol. 38, No. 1.

Butler, D. and Kavanagh, D. (1997) *The British General Election of 1997* (London: Macmillan).

Butler, D. and King, A. (1965) *The British General Election of 1964* (London: Macmillan).

Butler, D. and King, A. (1966) *The British General Election of 1966* (London: Macmillan).

Butler, D. and Stokes, D. (1969) *Political Change In Britain: Forces Shaping Electoral Choice* (London: Macmillan).

Butler, D. Adonis, A. and Travers, T. (1994) *Failure In British Government: The Politics of the Poll Tax* (Oxford: Oxford University Press).

Byrd, P. (1991) 'Defence Policy: A Historical Overview and a Regime Analysis', in Byrd, P. (ed.) *Foreign Policy Under Thatcher* (Deddington: Philip Allan).

Cabinet Office (1997) *Guidance on the Working of the Government Information Service* (London: HMSO).

Cairncross, A. (1992) *The British Economy since 1945* (Oxford: Blackwell).

Callaghan, J. (1987) *Time and Chance* (London: Collins).
Campbell, A. (1992) 'Lying Makes News', *British Journalism Review*, Vol. 3, No. 3.
Campbell, A. (1999) *Beyond Spin: Government and the Media. Fabian Society Special Pamphlet 42* (London: Fabian Society).
Camps, M. (1972) 'Sources of Strain in Transatlantic Relations', *International Affairs*, Vol. 48, No. 4.
Carlson, I. and Ramphal, S. (1999) 'Might is not Right', *The Guardian*, 2 April.
Carvel, J. (1997) 'Blunkett Tries to End Panic over Tuition Fees', *The Guardian*, 29 July.
Castells, M. (1996) *The Rise of the Network Society* (Oxford: Blackwell).
Castle, B. (1980) *The Castle Diaries 1974–76* (London: Weidenfeld & Nicolson).
Chote, R. (1998) 'Passing the Pound', *Financial Times*, 4 April.
Clarke, H. D. and Stewart, M. C. (1995) 'Economic Evaluations, Prime Ministerial Approval and Governing Party Support: Rival Models Reconsidered', *British Journal of Political Science*, Vol. 25, pp. 145–70.
Clarke, H. D., Mishler, W. and Whiteley, P. (1990) 'Recapturing the Falklands: Models of Conservative Popularity, 1979–83', *British Journal of Political Science*, Vol. 20, pp. 63–81.
Clarke, H. D., Stewart, M. C. and Whiteley, P. F. (1998) 'New models for New Labour: the Political Economy of Labour Party Support, January 1992–April 1997', *American Political Science Review*, Vol. 92, pp. 559–75.
Cm 3861 (1998) *Defence Diversification: Getting the Most Out of Defence* (London: HMSO).
Cm 4310 (1999) *Modernising Government* (London: HMSO).
Coates, D. and Hillard, J. (1995) *UK Economic Decline: Key Texts* (Hemel Hempstead: Harvester Wheatsheaf).
Coates, D. (1975) *The Labour Party and the Struggle for Socialism* (Cambridge: Cambridge University Press).
Coates, D. (1980) *Labour in Power? A Study of the Labour Government 1974–1979* (London: Longman).
Coates, D. (1983) 'The Question of Trade Union Power', in Coates, D. and Johnston, G. (1983) *Socialist Arguments* (Oxford: Martin Robertson).
Coates, D. (1994) *The Question of UK Decline: The Economy, State and Society* (Hemel Hempstead: Harvester Wheatsheaf).
Coates, D. (1996) 'Labour Governments: Old Constraints and New Parameters', *New Left Review*, No. 219, 62–77.
Coates, K. (1998) 'Unemployed Europe and the Struggle for Alternatives', *New Left Review*, No. 227.
Coates, K. and Topham, T. (1986) *Trade Unions and Politics* (Oxford: Blackwell).
Coker, C. (1988) *Less Important Than Opulence: The Conservatives and Defence* (London: Institute for European Defence and Strategic Studies).
Commission on Social Justice (1994) *Social Justice, Strategies for National Renewal. The Report of the Commission on Social Justice* (London: Vintage).
Conservative Party (1997) *Our Vision for Britain* (London: Conservative Central Office).
Conservative Research Department/European Democratic Group Secretariat (1984) *Handbook for Europe 1984* (London: Conservative Central Office).
Coopey, R., Fielding, S. and Tiratsoo, N. (eds) (1993) *The Wilson Governments 1964–1970* (London: Pinter).

Corry, D. (1997) *Macroeconomic Policy and Stakeholder Capitalism*, in Kelly, Kelly and Gamble (eds) (1997).

Court, S. (1999) 'You've Forgotten Something, Santa', *The Guardian Education*, 19 January.

Cowley, P. (1997) 'The Conservative Party: Decline and Fall', in Geddes, A. and Tonge, J. (eds) (1997) *Labour's Landslide* (Manchester: Manchester University Press).

Cowley, P. (1999) 'The Absence of War? New Labour in Parliament', in Fisher, J., Cowley, P., Denver, D. and Russell, A. (eds.) (1999) *British Elections and Parties Review Volume 9* (London: Frank Cass).

Cowely, P. (1999) 'Blair's MPs: sheep who can bark', *New Statesman*, 22 November.

Cowley, P. and Norton, P. (1999) 'Rebels and Rebellions. Conservative MPs in the 1992 Parliament', *British Journal of Politics and International Relations*, Vol. 1, No. 1.

Cowley, P. and Norton, P. with Stuart, M. and Bailey, M. (1996), *Blair's Bastards: Discontent within the Parliamentary Labour Party*, Research Papers in Legislative Studies, January (University of Hull).

CPPBB (1997) *Promoting Prosperity: a Business Agenda for Britain* (London: Vintage).

Crewe, I. (1983) 'How Labour Was Trounced All Round', *The Guardian*, 14 June.

Crewe, I. (1986) 'On the Death and Resurrection of Class Voting: Some Comments on "How Britain Votes"' *Political Studies*, Vol. 34, pp. 620–38.

Crewe, I. (1988) 'Has the Electorate Become Thatcherite?', in Skidelsky, R. (ed.), *Thatcherism* (London: Chatto & Windus).

Crewe, I. (1991) 'Labor Force Changes, Working Class Decline, and the Labour Vote: Social and Economic trends in Postwar Britain' in Piven, F. F. (ed.) (1991).

Crewe, I. (1996) '1979–1996', in Seldon, A. (ed.), *How Tory Governments Fall* (London: Fontana).

Crewe, I., Gosshalk, B. and Bartle, J. (1998) *Political Communications: Why Labour Won the General Election of 1997* (London: Frank Cass).

Crewe, I. and King, A. (1994) 'Did Major Win? Did Kinnock Lose? Leadership Effects in the 1992 Election' in Heath, A., Jowell, R. and Curtice, J. (eds) (1994)

Crewe, I. and King, A. (1995) SDP: *The Birth, Life and Death of the Social Democratic Party* (Oxford: Oxford University Press).

Crewe, I. and Särlvik, B. (1983) *Decade of Dealignment: The Conservative Victory of 1979 and Electoral Trends* (Cambridge: Cambridge University Press).

Criddle, B. (1994) 'Members of Parliament', in Seldon, A. and Ball, S. (eds) (1994).

Criddle, B. (1997) 'MPs and Candidates', in D. Butler and D. Kavanagh (1997).

Crosland, A. (1956) *The Future of Socialism* (London: Cape).

Crosland, S. (1982) *Tony Crosland* (London: Coronet).

Crouch, C. (1998) 'A Third Way in Industrial Relations?', paper presented at the Conference 'Labour in Government: The Third Way and the Future of Social Democracy', Harvard University.

Crouch, C. (1999) 'The Parabola of Working Class Politics', in Gamble, A. and Wright, A. (eds), *The New Social Democracy* (Oxford: Blackwell).

Curtice, J. and Steed, M. (1997) 'The results Analysed', in Butler, D. and Kavanagh, D. (1997)

Cutler, P. (1997) 'Can Use of the PFI be Healthy?', *New Economy*, Vol. 4, No. 3.

Dalton, R. J. (1996) *Citizen Politics: Public Opinion and Political Parties in Advanced Industrial Democracies* (Chatham, NJ: Chatham House).

Daniel, C. (1997) 'May the Task-Force be With You', *New Statesman*, 1 August.

Daniels, P. (1998) 'From Hostility to "Constructive Engagement": The Europeanisation of the Labour Party', *West European Politics*, Vol. 21, No. 1.

Darling, A. (1997) 'A Political Perspective', in Kelly, G., Kelly, D. and Gamble, A. (eds) (1997).

Davies, B. (1997) Labour Party Shadow Further and Higher Education spokesperson, interview with author, Westminster, 3 September.

Deacon, D. and Golding, P. (1994) *Taxation and Representation: The Media, Political Communication and the Poll Tax* (London: John Libbey).

Deighton, A. (1987) 'The "Frozen Front": The Labour Government, the Division of Germany and the Origins of the Cold War, 1945–47', *International Affairs*, Vol. 63, No. 3.

Denver, D., Fisher, J., Cowley, P. and Pattie, C. (1998) *British Elections and Parties Review Volume 8: The 1997 General Election* (London: Frank Cass).

Denver, D. and Hands, G. (1992) *Issues and Controversies in British Electoral Behaviour* (Hemel Hempstead: Harvester Wheatsheaf).

Denver, D. and Hands, G. (1997) *Modern Constituency Electioneering: Local Campaigning in the 1992 General Election* (London: Frank Cass).

Denver, D., Hands, G. and Henig, S. (1998) 'Triumph of Targeting? Constituency Campaigning in the 1997 Election' in Denver, D., Fisher, J., Cowley, P. and Pattie, C. (eds) (1998).

Department of Trade and Industry (1998) *White Paper: Fairness at Work*. Cmnd 3968, May 1998 (London: HMSO).

DfEE (1992) *Choice and Diversity: A New Framework for Schools* (London: HMSO).

DfEE (1997a) *Education Act* (1997) (London: HMSO).

DfEE (1997b) *Framework for the organisation of schools*: Technical consultation paper (London: DfEE)

DfEE (1997c) *Teaching: High Status, High Standards* (London: DfEE Publications Centre).

DfEE (1997d) *Excellence in schools* (London: HMSO) July.

DfEE (1998a) *£776 Million Extra to Boost Standards and Access in Higher Education – Blunkett*, Press Release 570/98, 8 December.

DfEE (1998b) *£18 Billion Boost for Education*, PN: 360/98, 14 July.

DfEE (1998c) Invitation to Help Invent the Educational Future – Blunkett, Press Release 003/98, DfEE 6 January.

DfEE (1998d) *Teachers – Meeting the Challenge of Change*, Green Paper, DfEE, 4 December.

DfEE (1999a) *Prime Minister and David Blunkett Launch Action Plan for Inner City Education*, PN. 126/99, 22 March.

DfEE (1999b) *Blunkett Unveils Proposals for National Curriculum from 2000*, PN. 208/99, 13 May.

Dobson, A. (1988) *The Politics of the Anglo-American Special Economic Relationship* (Brighton: Wheatsheaf).

Donoughue, B. (1987) *Prime Minister* (London: Jonathan Cape).

Dorfman, G. (1979) *Government versus Trade Unionism in British Politics since 1968* (London: Macmillan).

Downs, A. (1957) *An Economic Theory of Democracy* (New York: Harper & Row).

Draper, D. (1997) *Blair's Hundred Days* (London: Faber & Faber).

Driver, S. and Martell, L. (1998) *New Labour: Politics after Thatcherism* (Cambridge: Polity).

Drucker, H. (1979) *Doctrine and Ethos in the Labour Party* (London: Allen & Unwin).

Drucker, P. (1986) 'The Changed World Economy, *Foreign Affairs*, Vol. 64, No. 4.

DSS (1998a) *New Ambitions for Our Country: A New Contract for Welfare*, Cm 3805 (London: HMSO).

DSS (1998b) *A New Contract For Welfare: Support for Disabled People*, Cm 4103 (London: HMSO).

DSS (1998c) *Beating Fraud Is Everyone's Business: Securing the Future*, Cm 4012 (London: HMSO).

DSS (1998d) *A New Contract for Welfare: Principles into Practice*, Cm 4101 (London: HMSO).

DSS (1998e) *A New Contract for Welfare: The Gateway to Work*, Cm 4102 (London: HMSO).

DSS (1998f) *A New Contract for Welfare: Partnership in Pensions*, Cm 4179 (London: HMSO).

DSS (1998g) *Households Below Average Income 1979–1996/7* (London: HMSO).

Dunleavy, P. (1979) 'The Urban Basis of Political Alignment: Social Class, Domestic Property Ownership, and State Intervention in Consumption Processes', *British Journal of Political Science*, Vol. 9.

Dunleavy, P. (1987) 'Class Dealignment in Britain Revisited', *West European Politics*, Vol. 10.

Eatwell, J. (1992) 'The Development of Labour Policy 1979–1992', in Michie, J. (ed.) (1992) *The Economic Legacy 1979–1992* (London: Academic Press).

Eccleshall, R. (2000) 'Party Ideology and National Decline' in English, R. and Kenny, M. (eds), *Rethinking British Decline* (London: Macmillan).

Ellison, N. (1997) 'From Welfare State to Post-Welfare Society: Labour's Social Policy in Historical and Contemporary Perspective', in Brivati, B. and Bale, T. (eds) (1997).

Emmanuelli, H. (1997) Interview with the author (10 December).

Epstein, L. (1966) *Political Parties in Western Democracies* (London: Pall Mall Press).

Esping-Andersen, G. (1990) *The Three Worlds of Welfare Capitalism* (Cambridge: Polity).

Evans, B. (1992) *The Politics of the Training Market: from Manpower Services Commission to Training and Enterprise Councils* (London: Routledge).

Evans, G (1998) 'Euroscepticism and Conservative Electoral Support: How an Asset Became a Liability', *British Journal of Political Science*, Vol. 28, pp. 573–90.

Evans, G., Curtice, J. and Norris, P. (1998) 'New Labour, New Tactical Voting? The Causes and Consequences of Tactical Voting in the 1997 General Election', in Denver, D., Fisher, J., Cowley, P. and Pattie, C. (eds) (1998).

Evans, G., Heath, A. and Lalljee, M. (1996) 'Measuring Left–Right and Libertarian–Authoritarian Values in the British Electorate', *British Journal of Sociology*, Vol. 47.

Evans, G. and Norris, P. (eds) (1999) *Critical Elections: British Parties and Voters in Historical Perspective* (London: Sage).

Ewing, K. (1987) *The Funding of Political Parties in Britain* (Cambridge: Cambridge University Press).

Fay, S and Young, H. (1978) 'The Day the Pound Nearly Died', *Sunday Times*, 21 May.

Fenley, A. (1980) 'Labour and the Trade Unions', in Cook, C. and Taylor, I. (eds) (1980) *The Labour Party: An Introduction to its History, Structure and Politics* (London: Longman).

Field, F. (1996) *Stakeholder Welfare* (London: IEA Health and Welfare Unit).

Field, F. (1998) 'A Hand-up or a Put-down for the Poor', *New Statesman*, 27 November, p. 8.

Fielding, S. (1997a) *The Labour Party: Socialism and Society since 1951* (Manchester: Manchester University Press).

Fielding, S. (1997b) 'Labour's Path to Power', in Tonge, J. and Geddes, A. (eds) (1997).

Fielding, S. (1999) 'The Penny-Farthing Machine Revisited: Labour Party Members and Participation in the 1950s and 1960s', paper to the Annual Meeting of the Political Studies Association, University of Nottingham.

Finer, S. (1956) 'The Individual Responsibility of Ministers', *Public Administration*, Vol. 34, pp. 377–96.

Finkelstein, D. (1998) 'Why the Conservatives lost', in Crewe, I, Gosschalk, B and Bartle, J. (eds) (1998).

Finlayson, A. (1999) 'Third Way Theory', *Political Quarterly*, Vol. 70, No. 3, pp. 271–9.

Flather, P. 'Education matters' in Jowell, R., Witherspoon, S. and Brook, L. (eds) (1988) *British Social Attitudes: the 5th Report*, Social and Community Planning Research, (Aldershot: Gower).

Flinders, M. and Smith, M. J. (1999) *Quangos, Accountability and Reform* (London: Macmillan).

Ford, R. (1998) 'Lone Mothers, Work and Welfare', *New Economy*, Vol. 5, No. 2.

Forrest, J. and Marks, G. N. (1999) 'The Mass Media, Election Campaigning and Voter Response: the Australian Experience', *Party Politics*, Vol. 5.

Fowler, N. (1991) *Ministers Decide* (London: Chapman).

Franklin, B. (1994) *Packaging Politics: Political Communications In Britain's Media Democracy* (London: Arnold).

Franklin, B. (1997) *Newszak and News Media* (London: Arnold).

Franklin, B. (1998) *Tough on Soundbites, Tough on the Causes of Soundbites: New Labour and News Management* (London: The Catalyst Trust).

Franklin, B. (ed.) (1999) *Misleading Messages: The Media, Misrepresentation and Social Policy* (London: Routledge).

Franklin, M. N. (1985) *The Decline of Class Voting in Britain: Changes in the Basis of Electoral Choice 1964–1983* (Oxford: Clarendon Press).

Freeden, M. (1999a) 'The Ideology of New Labour', *Political Quarterly*, Vol. 70, pp. 42–51.

Freeden, M. (1999b) 'True Blood or False Genealogy: New Labour and British Social Democratic Thought', *Political Quarterly*, Vol. 70, pp. 1–16.

Frieden, J. (1991) 'Invested Interests: The Politics of National Economic Policies in a World of Global Finance', *International Organization*, Vol. 45, No. 4.

Fry, G. K. (1985) *The Changing Civil Service* (London: Allen & Unwin).

Gaber, I. (1998) 'A World Of Dogs and Lamp-posts', *New Statesman*, 19 June.

Gaitskell, H. (1958) Letter to *The Times*, 5 July.

Gamble, A. (1988) *The Free Economy and the Strong State: The Politics of Thatcherism* (Basingstoke: Macmillan).

Gamble, A. (1992) 'Economic Policy', in Smith, M. J. and Spear, J. (eds) (1992).

Gamble, A. (1994) *Britain in Decline*, 4th edn (London: Macmillan).
Gamble, A. and Kelly, G. (1998) 'The British Labour Party and Monetary Union', Paper presented to the Conference on Social Democrats and Monetary Union, Oslo, May 30–31.
Gamble, A. and Kenny, M. (1999) 'Now we are two', *Fabian Review*, III, 10–11.
Gamble, A. and Kelly, G. (2000) 'The British Left and Monetary Union', *West European Politics*, Vol. 23, No. 1.
Gardiner, K. (1998) 'Getting Welfare to Work' *New Economy*, Vol. 5, No. 1.
Gardner, R. N. (1969) *Sterling-Dollar Diplomacy in Current Perspective* (New York: McGraw-Hill).
Garrett, G. (1994) 'Popular Capitalism: the Electoral Legacy of Thatcherism', in Heath, A., Jowell, R. and Curtice, J. (1994).
Geddes, A. (1995) 'The "Logic" of Positive Action?: Ethnic Minority Representation in Britain After the 1992 General Election', *Party Politics*, Vol. 1, No. 2.
Geddes, A. and Tonge, J. (eds) (1997) *Labour's Landslide: the British General Election 1997* (Manchester: Manchester University Press).
George, S. and Haythorne, D. (1996) 'The British Labour Party', in Gaffney, J. (ed.) (1996) *Political Parties and the European Union* (London: Routledge).
George, S. and Rosamond, B. (1992) 'The European Community', In Smith M. J. and Spear, J. (eds) (1992).
Giddens, A. (1998) *The Third Way: The Renewal of Social Democracy* (Cambridge: Polity).
Gilpin, R. (1987) *The Political Economy of International Relations* (Princeton: Princeton University Press).
Glyn, A. (1995) 'Social Democracy and Full Employment', *New Left Review*, Vol. 211.
Glynn, S. and Booth, A. (1996) *Modern Britain: An Economic and Social History* (London: Routledge).
Goldthorpe, J. H., Lockwood, D., Bechhofer, F. and Platt, J. (1968) *The Affluent Worker: Industrial Attitudes and Behaviour* (Cambridge: Cambridge University Press).
Goodman, G. (1979) *The Awkward Warrior. Frank Cousins: His Life and Times* (London: Davis-Poynter).
Gould, P. (1998a) *The Unfinished Revolution: How the Modernisers Saved the Labour Party* (London: Little, Brown).
Gould, P. (1998b) 'Why Labour Won', in Crewe, I., Gosschalk, B. and Bartle, J. (eds) (1998).
Grahl, J. (1997) *After Maastricht: A Guide to European Monetary Union* (London: Lawrence and Wishart).
Grant, W. and Marsh, D. (1977) *The CBI* (London: Hodder & Stoughton).
Gray, A. and Jenkins, B. (1998) 'New Labour, New Government? Change and Continuity in Public Administration and Government 1997', *Parliamentary Affairs*, Vol. 51, No. 2, pp. 111–30.
Green, D. (1993) 'Re-Energising Civil Society', In, *Reinventing Civil Society: The Rediscovery of Welfare Without Politics* (London: IEA Health and Welfare Unit), pp. 122–53.
Greenleaf, W. H. (1983) *The British Political Tradition* (London: Methuen).
Gregg, P. (1998) 'Comment', in *An Inclusive Society: Strategies for Tackling Poverty* (London: IPPR).

Gross and Thygesen (1998) *European Monetary Integration*, 2nd edn (London: Longman).

Gunter, R. (1963) Parliamentary speech, *Hansard*, 20 November, column 1016.

Hackett, G. and Thornton, K. (1998) 'Brown's Billions to Reduce Class Sizes', *Times Educational Supplement*, 17 July.

Hall, S. (1995) 'Parties on the Verge of a Nervous Breakdown', *Soundings*, Issue 1, Autumn 1995.

Hall, S. (1998) 'The Great Moving Nowhere Show', in *Wrong: Marxism Today Special Issue* (London: Marxism Today).

Hamnett, C. (1999) *Winners and Losers: Home Ownership in Modern Britain* (London: UCL Press).

Harmer, H. (1999) *The Longman Companion to the Labour Party, 1900–1998* (London: Longman).

Harrison, M. (1960) *Trade Unions and the Labour Party* (London: George Allen & Unwin).

Harrop, M. (1990) 'Political Marketing', *Parliamentary Affairs*, Vol. 43.

Hattersley, R. (1996) *Who Goes Home?* (London: Warner).

Hattersley, R. (1997a) 'Why I'm No Longer Loyal to Labour', *The Guardian*, 26 July.

Hattersley, R. (1997b) *Fifty Years On: a Prejudiced History of Britain since the War* (London: Little Brown).

Hattersley, R. (1998a). 'He has the Power but None of the Glory', *The Observer*, 18 January.

Hattersley, R. (1998b) 'Let's Hear It For Tony ... Or Else', *The Observer Review*, 22 February.

Hattersley, R. (1998c) 'Those great expectations', *The Guardian*, 28 April.

Haveman, R. (1997) 'Equity with Employment', *Renewal*, Vol. 5, Nos. 3 and 4.

Hay, C. (1994) 'Labour's Thatcherite Revisionism: Playing the Politics of Catch-Up', *Political Studies*, Vol. 42, No. 4.

Hay, C. (1998) 'Labouring Under False Pretences? The Revision of Economic Policy in the 'Modernisation' of the British Labour Party 1992–1997', *Contemporary Political Studies 1998*, Vol. 2.

Hay, C. (1999) *The Political Economy of New Labour: Labouring under False Pretences?* (Manchester: Manchester University Press).

Hazell, R. (1999) (ed.) *Constitutional Futures* (Oxford: Oxford University Press).

Hazell, R. and Cornes, R. (1999) 'Financing Devolution' in Hazell, R. (ed.) (1999).

Hazell, R. and Morris, B. (1999) 'Machinery of Government: Whitehall' in Hazell (ed.) (1999).

Hazell, R. and O'Leary, B. (1999) 'A Rolling Programme of Devolution: Slippery Slope or Safeguard of the Union?' in Hazell R. (ed.) (1999).

HC 100 II (1998) Foreign Affairs Committee, First report: Foreign Policy and Human Rights, Vol. II (London: HMSO).

Healey, D. (1990) *Time of My Life* (London: Penguin).

Heath, A. (1999) 'Social Change, Value Orientations and Voting Patterns since the 1980s', in Kastendiek, H., Stinshoff, R. and Sturm, R. (eds) (1999).

Heath, A., Jowell, R. and Curtice, J. (1985) *How Britain Votes* (Oxford: Pergamon Press).

Heath, A., Jowell, R. and Curtice, J. (1991) *Understanding Political Change: The British Voter 1964–1987* (Oxford: Pergamon Press).

Heath, A., Jowell, R. and Curtice, J. (1994) *Labour's Last Chance? The 1992 Election and Beyond* (Aldershot: Dartmouth).

Heery, E. (1998) 'The Relaunch of the Trades Union Congress', *British Journal of Industrial Relations*, Vol. 36, No. 3.

Heffer, E. (1986) *Labour's Future: Socialist or SDP Mark 2?* (London: Verso).

Heffernan, R. and Marqusee, M. (1992) *Defeat from the Jaws of Victory: Inside Kinnock's Labour Party* (London: Verso).

Heffernan, R. (1996) 'Accounting for New Labour: The Impact of Thatcherism, 1979–1995', in Hampsher-Monk, I. and Stayner, J. (1996) *Contemporary Political Studies 1996* (Exeter: Political Studies Association).

Heffernan, R. (1999) *New Labour and Thatcherism: Exploring Political Change* (Basingstoke: Macmillan).

Heikkila, M. *et al.* (1999) *Nordic Social Policy* (London: Routledge).

Held, D. (1998) 'Globalisation: The Timid Tendency', *Marxism Today*, Nov/Dec, pp. 24–7.

Held, D., McGrew, A., Goldblatt, D. and Perraton, J. (1999) *Global Transformations* (Cambridge: Polity).

Hennessy, P. (1992) *Never Again: Britain 1945–1951* (London: Jonathan Cape).

Hennessy, P. (1998) 'The Blair Style of Government', *Government and Opposition*, Vol. 33, pp. 3–20.

Hillman, J. (1998) 'The Labour Government and Lifelong Learning', *Renewal*, Vol. 6, No. 2, Spring.

Hills, J. (1998) *Thatcherism, New Labour and the Welfare State*, CASE paper 13 (London: CASE).

Hirsch, D. (1998) 'Who's Better Off Under Labour?', *New Statesman*, 25 September, pp. 18–20.

Hirst, P. (1997) *From Statism to Pluralism, Democracy, Civil Society and Global Politics* (London: UCL Press).

Hirst, P. and Thompson, G. (1996) *Globalisation In Question* (Cambridge: Polity).

HM Treasury (1997) *United Kingdom Employment Action Plan* http://www.hm-treasury.gov.uk

HM Treasury (1998) *Public Services for the Future – Modernisation, Reform and Accountability*, Cm 4181 (London: HMSO).

HMSO (1967) *Children and Their Primary Schools*, The Plowden Report.

HMSO (1997) The Education (Schools) Act 1997.

HMSO (1998) The School Standards and Frameworks Act 1998.

Hobsbawm, E. (1981) *The Forward March of Labour Halted?* (London: Verso).

Hobsbawm, E. (1998) 'The Death of Neo-Liberalism' in: *Marxism Today Special Issue* (London: Marxism Today).

Holbrook, T. M. (1996) *Do Campaigns Matter?* (London: Sage).

Holland, S. (1975) *The Socialist Challenge* (London: Quartet).

Hollins, T. (1981) *The Presentation of Politics: The Place of Party Publicity, Broadcasting and Film in British Politics 1918–39* (unpublished Ph.D. thesis, University of Leeds).

Home Office (1998) *Supporting Families* (London: Home Office).

Hood, C. (1999) *The Art of the State* (Oxford: Oxford University Press).

Howell, D. (1980) *British Social Democracy*, 2nd edn (London: Croom Helm).

Hughes, C. and Wintour, P. (1990) *Labour Rebuilt: The New Model Party* (London: Fourth Estate).

Hughes, K. and Smith, E. (1988) 'New Labour – New Europe', *International Affairs*, Vol. 74, No. 1.

Hutton, W. (1994) 'Reviving Bretton Woods', *New Economy*, Vol. 1, No. 4.

Hutton, W. (1995) *The State We're In* (London: Jonathan Cape).

Hutton, W. (1997) 'X Marks the Spot for the Start of the Euro Race', *The Observer*, 7 December.

Hutton, W. (1998a) 'Here Is A Programme That Allows New Labour To Face In Two Directions At Once, Its Favourite Posture', *The Observer*, 20 September.

Hutton, W. (1998b) 'How Big Money is Stitching up the NHS', *The Observer*, 13 December.

Ingham, B. (1991) *Kill the Messenger* (London: HarperCollins).

Jacques, M. (1998) 'Good to be Back', in *Marxism Today Special Issue* (London: Marxism Today).

Jaensch, D. (1989) *The Hawke–Keating Hijack* (Sydney: Allen & Unwin).

Jay, A. (ed.) (1996) *The Oxford Dictionary of Political Quotation* (Oxford: Oxford University Press).

Jay, D. (1985) *Sterling: Its Use and Misuse, a Plea for Moderation* (Oxford: Oxford University Press).

Jessup, G. (1991) *Outcomes: NVQs and the Emerging Model of Education and Training* (London: Falmer Press).

Johnson, R. W. (1974) 'The Political Elite', *New Society*, 24 January.

Johnston, R. J., Pattie, C. J. and Allsopp, J. G. (1988) *A Nation Dividing? The Electoral Map of Great Britain 1979–1987* (London: Longman).

Johnston, R. J., Pattie, C. J., Dorling, D. F. L., Rossiter, D. J., Tunstall, H. and MacAllister, I. (1998) 'New Labour landslide – same old electoral geography', in Denver, D., Fisher, J., Cowley, P. and Pattie, C. (eds) *British Elections and Parties Review Volume 8: the 1997 General Election* (London: Frank Cass).

Jones, B. (1977) *The Russia Complex: The British Labour Party and the Soviet Union* (Manchester: Manchester University Press).

Jones, J. (1986) *Union Man: an Autobiography* (London: Collins).

Jones, M. 'Keeper of the Skeleton Closet', *The Observer*, 4 January.

Jones, N. (1995) *Soundbites and Spindoctors* (London: Cassell).

Jones, N. (1999) *Sultans of Spin* (London: Victor Gollancz).

Jones, Peter M. (1987) 'British Defence Policy: The Breakdown of Inter-Party Consensus', *Review of International Studies*, Vol. 13, No. 2.

Jones, T. (1996) *Remaking the Labour Party: From Gaitskell to Blair* (London: Routledge).

Jordan, B. (1998) *The New Politics of Welfare: Social Justice in a Global Context* (London: Sage).

Joseph, K. (1976) *Stranded on the Middle Ground* (London: Centre for Policy Studies).

Judd, J. (1997) 'Blunkett Says "Naming and Shaming" Schools Works', *The Independent*, 11 November.

Judge, D. (1993) *The Parliamentary State* (London: Sage).

Kaldor, M., Smith, D. and Vines, S. (1979) *Democratic Socialism and the Cost of Defence* (London: Croom Helm).

Kane, I. (1997) interview with author, Manchester, 17 March.

Kastendiek, H., Stinshoff, R. and Sturm, R. (eds) (1999) *The Return of Labour – a Turning Point in British Politics?* (Berlin: Philo).

Katz, R. S. and Mair, P. (1995) 'Changing models of party organization and party democracy', *Party Politics*, Vol. 1, pp. 5–28.

Kaufman, G. (1997) *How to be a Minister* (London: Faber & Faber).

Kavanagh, D. (1995) *Election Campaigning: The New Marketing of Politics* (Oxford: Blackwell).

Kavanagh, D. (1997) 'The Labour Campaign', in Norris, P. and Gavin. N. (eds) *Britain Votes 1997* (Oxford: Oxford University Press).

Kavanagh, D. (1998) 'R. T. McKenzie and After' in Berrington, H. (ed.) *Britain in the Nineties* (London: Frank Cass).

Kavanagh, D. and Morris, P. (1989) *Consensus Politics from Attlee to Thatcher* (Oxford: Blackwell).

Kavanagh, D. and Seldon, A. (1999) *Inside Number Ten* (Oxford: Oxford University Press).

Keegan, W. (1984) *Mrs Thatcher's Economic Experiment* (London : Penguin).

Kellner, P. (1997) 'Why the Tories were Trounced', in Norris, P. and Gavin, N. T. (eds) (1997) *Britain Votes 1997* (Oxford: Oxford University Press).

Kellner, P. and Lord Crowther-Hunt (1980) *The Civil Servants* (London: Macmillan).

Kelly, G. (1997) 'Economic Policy', in Dunleavy, P., Gamble, M., Holliday, I. and Peele, G. (eds) (1997) *Developments in British Politics 5* (London: Macmillan).

Kelly, G., Kelly, D. and Gamble, A. (eds.) (1997) *Stakeholder Capitalism* (London: Macmillan).

Kelly, G. and Oppenheim, C. (1998) 'Working With New Labour', *Renewal*, Vol. 10.

Kennedy, P. (1981) *The Realities Behind Diplomacy* (London: Fontana).

Kenny, M. (1995) *The First New Left* (London: Lawrence and Wishart).

Kenny, M. and Smith, M. J. (1997a) '(Mis)understanding Blair', *Political Quarterly*, Vol. 68, pp. 220–30

Kenny, M. and Smith, M. J. (1997b) 'Reforming Clause Four: Hugh Gaitskell, Tony Blair and the Modernisation of the Labour Party' in D. Denver, J. Fisher, S. Ludlam and C. Pattie' (eds), *British Elections and Parties Review* (London: Frank Cass), pp. 110–26.

Keohane, D. (1993) *Labour Party Defence Policy Since 1945* (Leicester: Leicester University Press).

Kerr, P. (1999) 'The Postwar Consensus: a Woozle that Wasn't?', in Marsh, D., Buller, J., Hay, C., Johnston, J., Kerr, P., McAnula, S. and Watson, M. (1999) *Postwar British Politics in Perspective* (Cambridge: Polity).

King, A, (1992) 'The implications of one-party government', in King, A. (ed.), *Britain at the Polls 1992* (Chatham, NJ: Chatham House).

King, A. (ed.) (1998) *New Labour Triumphs: Britain at the Polls* (Chatham, NJ: Chatham House).

King, D. and Wickham-Jones, M. (1998) 'Training Without the State? New Labour and Labour Markets', *Policy and Politics*, Vol. 26, No 4,

Kinnock, N. (1994) 'Reforming the Labour Party', *Contemporary Record*, Vol. 8, No. 3.

Kirchheimer, O. (1966) 'The Transformation of the West European Party Systems', in La Palombara, J. and Weiner, M. (eds) *Political Parties and Political Development* (Princeton, NJ: Princeton University Press).

Kogan, D. and Kogan, K. (1982) *The Battle for the Labour Party* (Glasgow: Fontana).

Kooiman, J. (ed.) (1993) *Modern Governance: New Government – Society Institutions* (London: Sage).

Labour and British Social Democratic Thought', Political Quarterly,

Labour Party (1964) *Lets Go With Labour, The New Britain* (London: The Labour Party).

Labour Party (1989) *Meet the Challenge, Make the Change: a New Agenda for Britain* (London: The Labour Party).

Labour Party (1990a) *Democracy and Policy Making for the 1990s* (London: The Labour Party).

Labour Party (1990b) *Looking to the Future: a Dynamic Economy, a Decent Society, Strong in Europe* (London: The Labour Party).

Labour Party (1991) *Opportunity Britain* (London: The Labour Party).

Labour Party (1992a) *Report of the Annual Conference of the Labour Party 1992* (London: The Labour Party).

Labour Party (1994a) *Opening Doors to a Learning Society; a Policy Statement on Education*, delivered to the 1994 Labour Party Conference (London: The Labour Party).

Labour Party (1994b) Private Labour Party briefing memoranda from John Smith's Leader's Office.

Labour Party (1995) *Diversity and Excellence: a New Partnership for Schools* (London: The Labour Party).

Labour Party (1996a) *Excellence for Everyone* (London: The Labour Party).

Labour Party (1996b) *Lifelong Learning* (London: The Labour Party).

Labour Party (1996c) *Aiming Higher* (London: The Labour Party).

Labour Party (1997a) *Labour into Power: A Framework for Partnership* (London: The Labour Party).

Labour Party (1997b) *Partnership in Power* (London: The Labour Party).

Labour Party (1997c) *New Labour Because Britain Deserves Better* (London: The Labour Party).

Lafontaine, O. (1998) 'The Future of German Social Democracy', *New Left Review*, No. 227.

Le Grand, J. (1998) 'The Third Way Begins With Cora', *New Statesman*, 6 March.

Leadbeater, C. (1999) *Living on Think Air* (London: Viking Books).

Leadbetter, C. (1997) 'Woodhead strikes again', *New Statesman*, 19 September.

Lee, P. and Murie, A. (1998) 'Targeting Social Exclusion', *New Economy*, Vol. 5, No. 2.

Lees, C. (1998) 'The Art of Compromise : The SPD's Red-Green Route to Power', *Contemporary Political Studies* 1998, Vol. 2.

Lent, A. and Sowemimo, M. (1996) 'Remaking the Opposition?' in Ludlam, S. and Smith, M. J. (eds) (1996).

Leopold, J. (1997) 'Trade Unions, Political Fund Ballots and the Labour Party', *British Journal of Industrial Relations*, Vol. 35, No. 1.

Levitas, R. (1998) *The Inclusive Society? Social Exclusion and New Labour* (Basingstoke: Macmillan).

Lewis, D. (1997) *Hidden Agendas: Politics, Law and Disorder* (London: Hamish Hamilton).

Leys, C. and Panitch, L. (1997) *The End of Parliamentary Socialism: From New Left to New Labour* (London: Verso).

Lightfoot, S. (1997) 'An Employment Union for Europe?', *Politics*, Vol. 17, No. 2.

Lightfoot, S. (1999) 'Prospects for Euro-Socialism', *Renewal*, Vol. 7, No. 2.

Lindblam, C. E. (1977) *Politics and Markets* (New York: Basic Books).

Lipset, S. M. and Rokkan, S. (1967) 'Cleavage structures, party systems and voter alignment: an introduction', in Lipset, S. M. and Rokkan, S. (eds) *Party Systems and Voter Alignments* (New York: The Free Press).

Lister, R. (1997a) 'From Fractured Britain to One Nation? The Policy Options for Welfare Reform', *Renewal*, Vol. 5, No. 3/4, pp. 11–23.

Lister, R. (1997b) 'Social Inclusion and Exclusion', in Kelly, G., Kelly, D. and Gamble, A. (eds) (1997), pp. 99–107.

Lister, R. (1998) 'Fighting Social Exclusion... with one hand tied behind our back', *New Economy*, Vol. 5, No. 1.

Lloyd, J. (1997) 'A Dangerous Web They Spin', *New Statesman*, 24 October.

Lloyd, J. (1998) 'Third Way? They'll Do It Their Way', *New Statesman*, 4 December.

Lovenduski, J. (1997) 'Gender Politics: A Breakthrough for Women?', in Norris, P. and Gavin, N. T. (eds) (1997) *Britain Votes 1997* (Oxford: Oxford University Press).

Lowe, R. (1993) *The Welfare State in Britain Since 1945.* (Basingstoke: Macmillan).

Ludlam, S. (1992) 'The Gnomes of Washington: Four Myths of the 1976 IMF Crisis', *Political Studies*, Vol. 40, No. 4.

Ludlam, S. (1995) 'The Impact of Sectoral Cleavage and Spending Cuts on Labour Party/Trade Union Relations: the Social Contract Experience', in Broughton, D., Farrell, D., Denver, D. and Rallings, C. (eds) (1995) *British Elections and Parties Yearbook 1994* (London: Frank Cass).

Ludlam, S. (1996) 'The Spectre Haunting Conservatism: Europe and Backbench Rebellion', in Ludlam, S. and Smith, M. J. (eds) (1996).

Ludlam, S. (2000) 'Myths of the Winter of Discontent', *Politics Review*, Vol. 9, No. 3.

Ludlam, S. (ed.) (1998) *New Labour and the Labour Movement: Proceedings of a Conference held in Sheffield, June 1998* (Sheffield: University of Sheffield Political Economy Research Centre).

Ludlam, S. and Smith, M. J. (eds.) (1996) *Contemporary British Conservatism* (London: Macmillan).

Lynskey, J. J. (1970) 'The Role of British Backbenchers in the Modification of Government Policy', *Parliamentary Affairs*, Vol. 27, No. 1.

MacAskill, E. (1997) 'Cabinet Watch', *Red Pepper*, September.

MacIntyre, A. (1981) *After Virtue: A Study in Moral Theory* (London: Duckworth).

Mackintosh, J. (1962) *The British Cabinet* (London: Methuen).

Major, L. F. (1998) 'Blunkett Paves the Way for Poorest Students', *The Guardian*, 21 July.

Mandelson, P. and Liddle, R. (1996) *The Blair Revolution: Can New Labour Deliver?* (London: Faber & Faber).

Mandelson, P. (1997) 'Coordinating Government Policy', speech delivered to the conference on Modernising the Policy Process, at Regent's Park Hotel, 16 September.

Mandelson, P. (1998a) *Speech to European University Institute, Florence 30 January 1998* (London: The Labour Party).

Mandelson, P. (1998b) *Speech to the 1998 Annual Trades Union Congress* (London: Trades Union Congress).

Manser, W. A. P. (1971) *Britain in Balance: The Myth of Failure* (Harmondsworth: Penguin).

Marquand, D. (1988) *The Unprincipled Society* (London: Fontana).

Marquand, D. (1992) 'Halfway to Citizenship? The Labour Party and Constitutional Reform' in Smith, M. J. and Spear, J. (eds) (1992).

Marquand, D. (1997) *The New Reckoning* (Cambridge: Polity).

Marquand, D. (1998) 'The Blair Paradox', *Prospect*, May, pp. 19–24.

Marsh, D. and Rhodes, R. A. W (1992) *Implementing Thatcherite Policies* (Milton Keynes: Open University Press).

Martin, R. (1980) *TUC: the Growth of a Pressure Group 1868–1976* (Oxford: Clarendon Press).

MccGwire, S. (1997) 'Dance to the Music of Spin', *New Statesman*, 17 October.

McChesney, R. (1999) *Rich Media, Poor Democracy: Communicating Politics in Dubious Times* (Urbana and Chicago: University of Illinois Press).

McCormick, J. (1997) 'Mapping the Stakeholder Society', in Kelly, G., Kelly, D. and Gamble, A. (eds) (1997), pp. 108–21.

McDonald, O. (1992) *The Future of Whitehall* (London: Weidenfeld & Nicolson).

McIlroy, J. (1995) *Trade Unions in Britain Today* (Manchester: Manchester University Press).

McIlroy, J. (1998) 'The Enduring Alliance? Trade Unions and the Making of New Labour, 1994–1997', *British Journal of Industrial Relations*, Vol. 36, No. 4.

McInnes, C. (1998) 'Labour's Strategic Defence Review', *International Affairs*, Vol. 74, No. 4.

McKenzie, R. (1955) *British Political Parties* (London: Heinemann).

McKenzie, R. and Silver, A. (1968) *Angels in Marble: Working Class Conservatives in Urban England* (London: Heinemann).

McNair, B. (1995) *An Introduction To Political Communications* (London: Routledge).

McNair, B. (1998) 'Journalism, Politics and Public Relations: An Ethical Appraisal', in Kieran, M. (ed.) *Media Ethics* (London: Routledge).

McSmith, A. (1996) *Faces of Labour: The Inside Story* (London: Verso).

Mellors, C. (1978) *The British MP: A Socio-Economic Study of the House of Commons* (Farnborough: Saxon House).

Michels, R. (1962) *Political Parties: a sociological study of the oligarchical tendencies of modern democracy* (London: Collier-Macmillan).

Miliband, R. (1973) *Parliamentary Socialism*, 2nd edn (London: Merlin).

Miller, W. L., Clarke, H. D., Harrop, M., Leduc, L. and Whiteley, P. F. (1990) *How Voters Change: The 1987 British Election Campaign in Perspective* (Oxford: Clarendon Press).

Minkin, L. (1978a) 'The Party Connection: Divergence and Convergence in the British Labour Movement', *Government and Opposition*, Vol. 13, No. 4.

Minkin, L. (1978b) *The Labour Party Conference: A Study in Intra-Party Democracy* (London: Allen Lane).

Minkin, L. (1980) *The Labour Party Conference: A Study in Intra-Party Democracy*, 2nd edn (Manchester: Manchester University Press).

Minkin, L. (1991) *The Contentious Alliance: Trade Unions and the Labour Party* (Edinburgh: Edinburgh University Press).

Minkin, L. (1992) 2nd edn, *The Contentious Alliance: the Trade Unions and the Labour Party* (Edinburgh: Edinburgh University Press).

Mitchell, A. (1998) 'Why I am Sick of Women MPs', *Independent on Sunday*, 18 January.

Mitchell, J. (1998) 'The Evolution of Devolution: Labour's Home Rule Strategy in Opposition', *Government and Opposition*, Vol. 33, No. 4, pp. 479–96.

Mitchell, J. (1999) 'From Unitary State to Union State: Labour's Changing View of the United Kingdom and Its Implications', *Regional Policy and Politics*.

Monks, J. (1996) *New Unionism: Speech to 'Unions 96' Conference* (London: Trades Union Congress).

Monks, J. (1998a) *Into the Next Millennium – the Trade Unions' Next Steps. Text of a Lecture Delivered by TUC General Secretary John Monks at the Manchester Business School, June 18 1998* (London: Trades Union Congress).

Monks, J. (1998b) 'Government and Trade Unions', *British Journal of Industrial Relations*, Vol. 36, No. 1.

Morgan, K. O. (1984) *Labour In Power, 1945–51* (Oxford: Clarendon Press).

Morgan, K. O. (1997) *Callaghan: A Life* (Oxford: Oxford University Press).

MORI (1998) *Most Plus Other Important Issues, 1974–1998* (London: Market and Opinion Research International Ltd).

Mortimer, J. (1998) *A Life on the Left* (Lewes: The Book Guild).

Moscovici, P. (1997) *L'Urgence: Plaidoyer pour une autre politique* (Paris: Plon).

Mountfield, Lord (1997) *Report of the Working Group on the Government Information Service* (London: HMSO).

National Trade Union and Labour Party Liaison Committee (1998) *We did it* (London: The Labour Party).

Naylor, John F. (1969) *Labour's International Policy: The Labour Party in the 1930s* (London: Weidenfield & Nicolson).

Negrine, R. (1996) *The Communication of Politics* (London: Sage).

Nickell, S. and Layard, R. (1998) 'Labour Market Institutions and Economic Performance,' in Ashenfelter and Card (eds), *Handbook of Labour Economics*, North Holland.

Nicoll, A. (1998a) 'A Question of Credibility', *Financial Times*, 10 October.

Nicoll, A. (1998b) 'Arms Exports May Face Stricter Scrutiny By MPs', *Financial Times*, 2 July.

Nicoll, A. (1999) 'Seeking a Level Battlefield', *Financial Times*, 3 June.

Norris, P. and Lovenduski, J. (1995) *Political Recruitment: Gender, Race and Class in the British Parliament* (Cambridge: Cambridge University Press).

Norris, P. (1997a) 'The Battle for the Campaign Agenda', in King, A. (ed.) (1998).

Norris, P. (1997b) 'Anatomy of a Labour Landslide', in Norris, P. and Gavin. N. (eds), *Britain Votes 1997* (Oxford: Oxford University Press).

Norris, P. (1998) 'New Labour, New Politicians? Changes in the Political Attitudes of Labour MPs 1992–1997', in Dobson, A. and Stanyer, J. (eds) (1998) *Contemporary Political Studies 1998, Vol. 2* (Nottingham: Political Studies Association).

Norris, P. and Gavin, N. (eds) (1997) *Britain Votes 1997* (Oxford: Oxford University Press).

Norris, P., Curtice, J., Scammell, M. and Semetko, H. (1999) *On Message: Communicating The Campaign* (London: Sage).

Northern Ireland Office (1998) http://www.nio.gov.uk/apragee.htm.

Norton, P. (1975) *Dissension in the House of Commons 1945–74* (London: Macmillan).

Norton, P. (1980) *Dissension in the House of Commons 1974–1979* (Oxford: Clarendon Press).

O'Shaughnessy, N. (1996) 'Social Propaganda and Social Marketing: A Crucial Difference', *European Journal of Marketing*, Vol. 30, No. 10.

Oborne, P. (1999) *Alastair Campbell: New Labour and the Rise of the Media Class* (London: Aurum Press).

OECD (1999) *OECD Employment Outlook* (Paris: OECD).

OFSTED (1998) *Majority of Academic Educational Research is Second Rate, says Tooley*, press release *98–26*, 22 July.

Oppenheim, C. (1998) 'Welfare to Work: Taxes and Benefits', in McCormick, J. and Oppenheim, C. (eds), *Welfare in Working Order* (London: IPPR).

Owen, D. (1991) *Time to Declare* (Harmondsworth: Penguin).

Ozbudun, E. (1970) *Party Cohesion in Western Democracies: a Causal Analysis* (New York: Sage).

Padgett, S. and Paterson, W. (1991) *A History of Social Democracy in Post War Europe* (London: Longman).

Panebianco, A. (1988) *Political Parties: Organization and Power* (Cambridge: Cambridge University Press).

Panitch, L. (1976) *Social Democracy and Industrial Militancy: the Labour Party, Trade Unions and Incomes Policy, 1945–74* (Cambridge: Cambridge University Press).

Parkinson, M. (1970) *The Labour Party and the Organization of Secondary Education 1918–1965* (London: Routledge & Kegan Paul).

Parti Socialiste (PS) (1996) Final text of the National convention on *Mondialisation, Europe, France*, in *Vendredi*, No. 276.

Parti Socialiste (1997) *Changeons L'Avenir* (Paris: PS Presse).

Pattie, C. J., Whiteley, P. F., Johnston, R. J. and Seyd, P. (1994) 'Measuring Local Campaign Effects: Labour Party Constituency Campaigning at the 1987 General Election', *Political Studies*, Vol. 42, pp. 469–79.

Pattie, C. J. and Johnston, R. J. (1996a) 'The Conservative Party and the Electorate', in Ludlam, S. and Smith, M. J. (eds) (1996).

Pattie, C. J. and Johnston, R. J. (1995) 'It's Not Like That Round Here: Region, Economic Evaluations and Voting at the 1992 British General Election', *European Journal of Political Research*, Vol. 28, pp. 1–32.

Pattie, C. J. and Johnston, R. J. (1996b) 'Paying their Way: Local Associations, the Constituency Quota Scheme and Conservative Party Finance', *Political Studies*, Vol. 44, pp. 921–35.

Pattie, C. J., Dorling, D. and Johnston, R. J. (1995a) 'A Debt-owing Democracy: The Political Impact of Housing Market Recession at the British General Election of 1992', *Urban Studies*, Vol. 32, pp. 1293–315.

Pattie, C. J., Johnston, R. J. and Fieldhouse, E. A. (1995b) 'Winning the Local Vote: the Effectiveness of Constituency Campaign Spending in Great Britain', *American Political Science Review*, Vol. 89, pp. 969–83.

Pattie, C., Whiteley, P., Johnston, R. and Seyd, P. (1994) 'Measuring Local Campaign Effects: Labour Party Constituency Campaigning at the 1987 General Election', *Political Studies*, Vol. 42, No. 3.

Peacock, A. and Wiseman, J. (1961) *The Growth of Public Expenditure in the UK* (Princeton: Princeton University Press).

Peak, S. (1984) *Troops in Strikes: Military Intervention in Industrial Disputes* (London: Cobden Trust).

Pelling, H. and Reid, A. (1996) *A Short History of the Labour Party* (Basingstoke: Macmillan).

Perkins, B. (1986) 'Unequal Partners: the Truman Administration and Great Britain', in Roger Louis W. M. and Bull, H. (eds), *The Special Relationship* (Oxford: Clarendon Press).

Perrigo, S. (1995) 'Gender Struggles in the British Labour Party from 1979 to 1995', *Party Politics*, Vol. 1, No. 3.

Persson, G. (1998) 'Employment – New Skills for New Jobs', speech given at Bommersvik, 11 June.

Peterson, M. (1998) 'The View From Sweden', *Soundings*, No. 9.

Philpott, J. (1998) 'The Performance of the UK Labour Market', in Buxton T. *et al.* (eds), *Britain's Economic Performance* (London: Routledge).

Pierson, C. (1991) *Beyond the Welfare State* (Cambridge: Polity).

Pierson, C. (1996) 'Social Policy under Thatcher and Major', in *Contemporary British Conservatism in* Ludlam, J. S. and Smith, M. (eds). (1996).

Pimlott, B. (1992) *Harold Wilson* (London: HarperCollins).

Pinder, R. (1979) 'Traditional Skills and Progressive Education: Is there a Conflict?', in Rubenstein, D. (ed.) (1979) *Education and Equality* (Harmondsworth: Penguin Education).

Piper, J. R. (1974) 'Backbench Rebellion, Party Government and Consensus Politics: The Case of the Parliamentary Labour Party 1966–70', *Parliamentary Affairs*, Vol. 27, No. 4.

Piven, F. F. (ed.) (1991) *Labor Parties in Post-industrial Societies* (Cambridge: Polity).

Plant, R. (1998) 'So You Want to be a Citizen?', in *New Statesman*, 6 February.

Platt, S. (1998a) 'In and Out and Shaken All About', *Tribune*, 1 May.

Platt, S. (1998b) *Government by Task Force: a Review of the Reviews* (London: The Catalyst Trust).

Ponting, C. (1989) *Breach of Promise* (London: Hamish Hamilton).

Ponting, C. (1990) *Breach of Promise: Labour in Power 1964–70* (London: Penguin).

Poulantzas, N. (1976) *State, Power, Socialism* (London: Verso).

Porter, B. (1984) *The Lion's Share* (London: Longman).

Przeworski, A. (1985) *Capitalism and Social Democracy* (Cambridge, Cambridge University Press).

Pulzer, P. (1967) *Political Representation and Elections in Britain* (London: George Allen & Unwin).

Purves, L. (1997) 'Blair's Babes in the Wood', *The Times,* 2 December.

Rafferty, F. (1998a) 'Blunkett Delivers a Beefy Doorstep', *Times Educational Supplement,* 2 January.

Rafferty, F. (1998b) 'Education Bill; Three Defeats Leave Fences to Mend', *Times Educational Supplement*, 3 April.

Rafferty, F. (1998c) 'MP's fears over funding pledge', *Times Educational Supplement*, 3 July.

Recio, A. and Roca, J. (1998) 'The Spanish Socialists in Power : Thirteen Years of Economic Policy', *Oxford Review of Economic Policy*, Vol. 14, No. 1.

Reich, R. (1998) 'The Third Way Needs Courage', *The Guardian,* 21 September.

Reisman, D. (1997) *Crosland's Future: Opportunity and Outcome* (Basingstoke: Macmillan).

Rentoul, J. (1995) *Tony Blair* (London: Little Brown).

Reynolds, D. and Sullivan, M. with Murgatroyd, S. (1987) *The Comprehensive Experiment: a Comparison of the Selective and Non-selective System of School Organisation* (Lewes: The Falmer Press).

Reynolds, D. (1998a) interview with author, Newcastle, 17 March.

Reynolds, D. (1998b) *The Implementation of the National Numeracy Strategy: The Final Report of the Numeracy Task Force*, DfEE, June 1998.

Rhodes, R. A. W. (1997) *Understanding Governance* (Buckingham: Open University Press).

Richards, D. (1997) *The Civil Service under the Conservatives 1979–97: Whitehall's Political Poodles?* (Brighton: Sussex Academic Press).

Richards, D and Smith, M. J. (1997) 'How Departments Change: Windows of Opportunity and Critical Junctures in Three Departments', in *Public Policy and Adminstration*, Vol. 12, No. 2.

Richards, D. and Smith, M. J. (2000) 'Power and the Public Service Ethos', *West European Politics* (forthcoming).

Richards, H. (1997) *Times Higher Education Supplement*, 5 December.

Richards, H. (1998) 'Lords to Renew Fight Against Teaching Bill,' *Times Higher Education Supplement*, 12 June.

Richardson, W., Spours, K., Woolhouse, J. and Young, M. (1995) *Learning for the Future: Initial Report*, (London: Institute of Education, University of London, and Warwick: Centre for Education and Industry, University of Warwick), November.

Richter, I. (1973) *Political Purpose in Trade Unions* (London: George Allen & Unwin).

Riddell, P. (1998) *Parliament under Pressure* (London: Victor Gollancz).

Robbins, L. (1963) Report of the Committee on Higher Education appointed by the Prime Minister. Volume I: Report, *The Robbins Report*.

Robertson, D. (1997) 'Lifelong Learning: Can Labour Deliver the Unifying Strategy We Need?' *Renewal*, Vol. 5, Nos. 3/4, Autumn.

Robertson, D. (1996) *The Learning Bank and Individual Learning accounts-emerging policies for the funding of relationships in the tertiary learning market*, CVCP/SRHE seminar paper, 7/11/96 (not published).

Robertson, G. (1990) 'Britain in the New Europe', *International Affairs*, Vol. 66, No. 4.

Robinson, P. (1998a) 'Employment and Social Inclusion', in *An Inclusive Society: Strategies for Tackling Poverty* (London: IPPR).

Robinson, P. (1998b) *Literacy, Numeracy and Economic Performance* in *New Political Economy*, Vol. 3, No. 1.

Room, G. (ed.) (1995) *Beyond the Threshold: The Measurement and Analysis of Social Exclusion* (Bristol: Policy Press).

Rosamond, B. (1998) 'The Integration of Labour? British Trade Union Attitudes to European Integration', in Baker, D. and Seawright, D. (eds) (1998).

Rose, R. (1983), 'Still the Era of Party Government', *Parliamentary Affairs*, Vol. 36, No. 3.

Rose, R. and Davies, P. (1984) *Inheritance in Public Policy* (New Haven: Yale University Press).

Rose, R. and McAllister, I. (1990) *The Loyalties of Voters* (London: Sage).

Ross, J. F. S. (1955) *Elections and Electors* (London: Eyre & Spottiswoode).

Rossiter, D. J., Johnston, R. J. and Pattie, C. J. (1999) *The Boundary Commissions* (Manchester: Manchester University Press).

Rossiter, D. J., Johnston, R. J., Pattie, C. J., Dorling, D., MacAllister, I. and Tunstall, H. (1999) 'Changing Biases in the Operation of the UK's Electoral System, 1950–1997', *British Journal of Politics and International Relations*, Vol. 1, No. 1.

Roth, A. and Criddle, B. (1997) *New MPs of 1997 and Retreads* (London: Parliamentary Profiles Services Ltd).

Ruggie, J. (1982) 'International Regimes, Transactions and Change: Embedded Liberalism in the Post-War Economic Order', in *International Organization*, Vol. 36, No. 3.

Ryan, H. B. (1987) *The Vision of Anglo-America: the US–UK Alliance and the Emerging Cold War, 1943–46* (Cambridge: Cambridge University Press).

Sanders, D. (1991) 'Government Popularity and the Next General Election', *Political Quarterly*, Vol. 62, pp. 235–61.

Sanders, D. (1993) 'Foreign and Defence Policy', in Dunleavy, P. *et. al.*, *Developments in British Politics 4* (Basingstoke: Macmillan).

Sanders, D. (1995) 'Forecasting Political Preferences and Election Outcomes in the UK: Experiences, Problems and Prospects for the Next General Election', *Electoral Studies*, Vol. 14, pp. 251–72.

Sanders, D. (1996) 'Economic Performance, Management Competence, and the Outcome of the Next General Election', *Political Studies*, Vol. 44, pp. 203–31.

Sanders, D., Ward, H. and Marsh, D. (1987) 'Government popularity and the Falklands War: a Reassessment', *British Journal of Political Science*, Vol. 17, pp. 281–313.

Sassoon, D. (1993) 'The Union Link: the Case for a Friendly Divorce', *Renewal*, Vol. 1, No. 1.

Sassoon, D. (1996) *100 Years of Socialism* (London: I.B. Tauris).

Sassoon, D. (1997) *Looking Left: Socialism after the Cold War* (London: I.B. Tauris).

Sassoon, D. (1998) 'Fin-de-Siècle Socialism: The United, Modest Left', *New Left Review*, No. 227.

Saward, M. (1997) 'In Search of the Hollow Crown' in Weller, P., Bakvis, H. and Rhodes, R. A. W. (1997).

Scammell, M. (1995) *Designer Politics: How Elections are Won* (London: Macmillan).

Scammell, M. (1998) 'The Wisdom of the War Room: US Campaigning and Americanisation', *Media Culture and Society*, Vol. 20, No. 2.

Scharpf, F. (1991) *Crisis and Choice in European Social Democracy* (Ithaca: Cornell University Press).

Schonfield, A. (1958) *British Economic Policy since the War* (Harmondsworth: Penguin).

Schwarz, J. E. (1980) 'Exploring a New Role in Policy-Making: The British House of Commons in the 1970s', *American Political Science Review*, Vol. 74, No. 1.

Scott, R. (1996) *Report of the Inquiry into the Export of Defence Equipment and Dual Use Goods to Iraq* (London: HMSO).

Scottish Office (1998) *Social Exclusion in Scotland: A Consultation Paper* (London: HMSO).

Seldon, A. (1994) 'Conservative Century' in Seldon, A. and Ball, S. (eds), *Conservative Century: the Conservative Party Since 1900* (Oxford: Oxford University Press).

Select Committee on Public Administration (1998) *The Government Information and Communications Service: Report and Proceedings of the Select Committee together with Minutes of Evidence and Appendices. HC770* (London: HMSO).

Select Committee on Public Administration (1999) *Government Response to the Sixth Report From the Select Committee on Public Administrations (session 1997–98) On the Government Information and Communications Service, 19 January 1999* (London: HMSO).

Seyd, P. (1987) *The Rise and Fall of the Labour Left* (London: Macmillan).

Seyd, P. (1993) 'Labour: the Great Transformation', in King, A. (ed.) (1993).

Seyd, P. (1998) 'Tony Blair and New Labour', in King, A. (ed.) (1998).

Seyd, P. and Whiteley, P. (1992a) 'Labour's Renewal Strategy', in Smith, M. J. and Spear, J. (eds) (1992).

Seyd, P. and Whiteley, P. (1992b) *Labour's Grassroots: The Politics of Party Membership* (Oxford: Clarendon Press).

Seyd, P. and Whiteley, P. (forthcoming) *New Labour* (Basingstoke: Macmillan).

Sharpe, L. J. (1982) 'The Labour Party and the Geography of Inequality: A Puzzle, in D. Kavanagh (ed.) *The Politics of the Labour Party*, (London: Allen & Unwin).

Shaw, E. (1988) *Discipline and Discord in the Labour Party* (Manchester: Manchester University Press).

Shaw, E. (1994) *The Labour Party Since 1979: Crisis and Transformation* (London: Routledge).

Shaw, E. (1996) *The Labour Party Since 1945* (Oxford: Blackwell).

Shaw, E. (1999) 'Organisational Transformation in the Labour Party: The Case of Candidate Selection – Some Preliminary Findings', Paper to the Annual Meeting of the Political Studies Association, University of Nottingham.

Smith, D. (1987) *The Rise and Fall of Monetarism: The Theory and Politics of an Economic Experiment* (Harmondsworth: Penguin).

Smith, J. (1992) *New Paths to Victory* (London: The Labour Party).

Smith, M. (1988) 'Britain and the US: Beyond the "Special Relationship"', in Byrd, P. (ed.) *British Foreign Policy Under Thatcher* (Deddington: Phillip Allan).

Smith, M. J. (1992) 'A Return to Revisionism? The Labour Party's Policy Review', in Smith, M. J. and Spear, J. (eds) (1992).

Smith, M. J. (1994) 'Understanding the "Politics of Catch-Up": The Modernization of the Labour Party', *Political Studies*, Vol. 42, No. 4.

Smith, M. J. (1999) *The Core Executive in Britain* (London: Macmillan).

Smith, M. J. and Spear, J. (eds) (1992) *The Changing Labour Party* (London: Routledge).

Smith, P. 'Choice or Chaos?' in Tomlinson, H. (ed.) (1992) *The Search for Standards*, in association with The British Educational Management and Administration Society (Harlow: Longman).

Smith, S. (1991) 'Foreign Policy Analysis and the Study of British Foreign Policy', in Freedman, L. and Clarke, M. (eds) *Britain in the World* (Cambridge: Cambridge University Press).

Social Exclusion Unit (SEU) (1998) *Bringing Britain Together: A National Strategy for Neighbourhood Renewal*, Cm 4045 (London: HMSO).

Soskice, D. (1996) 'Stakeholding Yes; The German Model No', in Kelly, G., Kelly, D. and Gamble, A. (eds) (1997).

SPD (1998) SPD Manifesto for the 1998 General Election: *Work, Innovation and Justice* Resolution of the SPD Party Conference, Leipzig 17 April.

Spicker, P. (1997) 'The Welfare State and Social Protection in the United Kingdom', in Mullard, M. and Lee, S. (eds) *The Politics of Social Policy in Europe* (Cheltenham: Edward Elgar).

Stephens, P. (1997) 'A Foot in the Club', *Financial Times*, 15 December.

Stephens, P. (1998) 'The Blame Game', *Financial Times*, 18 May.

Stewart, M. (1978) *Politics and Economic Policy in the UK since 1964: The Jekyll and Hyde Years* (Oxford: Pergamon).

Stones, R. (1990) 'Government–Finance Relations in Britain 1964–7', *Economy and Society*, Vol. 19, pp. 32–55.

Strange, S. (1997) 'The British Labour Movement and EMU in Europe', *Capital and Class*, No. 63.

Svasand, L., Strom, K. and Rasch, B. (1996) 'Change and Adaptation in Party Organization' in Strom, K. and Svasand, L. (1996) *Challenges To Political Parties: The Case of Norway* (Ann Arbor: University of Michigan Press).

Svenska Arbetarpartiet (1998) *Election Manifesto 1998: With a View to the Future – the Policy of the Social Democrats for the 21st century* (Stockholm: SAP).

Tanner, D. (1990) *Political Change and the Labour Party 1900–1918* (Cambridge: Cambridge University Press).

Tant, A. P. (1993) *British Government: The Triumph of Elitism* (Aldershot: Dartmouth).

Tasker, M. (1997) 'Diversity, Choice and the Comprehensive', *Education Today and Tomorrow*, Vol. 49, No. 2, Summer.

Taylor, A. (1987) *The Trade Unions and the Labour Party* (London: Croom Helm).

Taylor, G. (1997) *Labour's Renewal? The Policy Review and Beyond* (Basingstoke: Macmillan).

Taylor, M. and Cruddas, J. (1998) *New Labour, New Links* (London: Unions 21).

Taylor, Peter J. (1990) *Britain and the Cold War: 1945 as Geopolitical Transition* (London: Pinter/ New York: Guilford).

Taylor, R. (1993) *The Trade Union Question in British Politics: Government and Unions since 1945* (Oxford: Blackwell).

Taylor, R. (1994) *The Future of the Trade Unions* (London: Andre Deutsch).

Taylor, R. (1998) 'The Fairness at Work White Paper', *Political Quarterly*, Vol. 69, No. 4.

Thatcher, M. (1993) *The Downing Street Years* (London: HarperCollins).

Theakston, K. (1992) *The Labour Party and Whitehall* (London: Routledge).

Theakston, K. (1997) 'New Labour, New Whitehall?', paper presented at PAC Conference, September.

THES (1997) Editorial, 'Swallowing Whole after Dizzying Spin', 25 July.

Thompson, A. (1998) 'Top group in top-up threat', *Times Higher Educational Supplement*, 20 February.

Thompson, H. (1996) *The British Conservative Government and the European Exchange Rate Mechanism* (London: Pinter).

Thompson, N. (1996) *Political Economy and the Labour Party: the Economics of Democratic Socialism 1884–1995* (London: UCL Press).

Timmins, N. (1997) 'Blair Aide Calls on Whitehall to Raise its PR Game', *Financial Times*, 9 October.

Timmins, N. (1999) 'The Death of Universalism', in *Financial Times*, 10 February.

Tindale, S. (1992) 'Learning to Love the Market: Labour and the European Community', *Political Quarterly*, Vol. 63, No. 3.

Tiratsoo, N. (ed.) (1991) *The Attlee Years* (London: Pinter).

Tomlinson, J. (1997) 'Economic Policy: Lessons from Past Labour Governments', in Brivati, B. and Bale, T. (eds) (1997).

Tomlinson, S (1997a) 'Sociological Perspectives on Failing Schools', in *International Journal of the Sociology of Education*, Vol. 7, No. 1.

Tomlinson, S (1997b) interview with author, Goldsmiths College, 18 March.

Tonge, J. and Geddes, A. (eds) (1997) *Labour's Landslide: The British General Election 1997* (Manchester: Manchester University Press).

Tooley, J. and Darby, D. (1998) *Educational Research: an OFSTED critique* (London: OFSTED Publications).

Tooley, J. (1997) interview with author, Derbyshire, 7 March.

Toolis, K. (1998) 'The Enforcer', *The Guardian Weekend*, 4 April.

Townsend, P. (1995) 'Persuasion and Conformity: An Assessment of the Borrie Report on Social Justice', *New Left Review*, No. 213.

Townsend, P. and Bosanquet, N. (eds) (1972) *Labour and Inequality* (London: Fabian Society).

Trades Union Congress (1991) *TUC Towards 2000* (London: Trades Union Congress).

Trades Union Congress (1994) *Campaigning for Change: a New Era for the TUC* (London: Trades Union Congress).

Trades Union Congress (1997a) *Trade Unionists Today* (London: Trades Union Congress).

Trades Union Congress (1997b) *Partners in Progress* (London: Trades Union Congress).

Trades Union Congress (1998) *Stakeholder Pensions: TUC Submission to DSS Consultation Document* (London: Trades Union Congress).

Travis, A. (1999) 'Straw to Target Burglars', *The Guardian*, 13 January.

Traynor, I. (1998) 'Peter's Passions', *The Guardian*, 16 March.

Treverton, Gregory, F. (1990) 'Britain's Role in the 1990s: an American View', *International Affairs*, Vol. 66, No. 4.

United States Senate (1977) *US Foreign Economic Policy Issues: the United Kingdom, France, and West Germany* (Washington: US Government Printing Office).

Vandenbroucke, F. (1998) *Globalisation, Inequality, and Social Democracy* (London: IPPR).

Vartiainen, J. (1998) 'Understanding Swedish Social Democracy: Victims of Success?', *Oxford Review of Economic Policy*, Vol. 14, No. 1.

Von Beyme, K. (1996) 'Party Leadership and Change in Party Systems: Towards a Post-modern Party State', *Government and Opposition*, Vol. 31, No. 2.

Walker, D. (1997) 'The Sir Humphreys Make Way for Blair Mandarins', *Independent on Sunday*, 14 September.

Walker, R. (1998) 'Promoting Positive Welfare', *New Economy*, Vol. 5, No. 2.

Ware, A. (1987) *Citizens, Parties and the State* (Cambridge: Polity Press).

Watkins, A. (1998) 'A Bloodthirsty Lot, the Women in the House', *Independent on Sunday*, 22 February.

Webb, P. (1995) 'Reforming the Labour Party-Trade Union Link: an Assessment', in Broughton, D., Farrell, D., Denver, D. and Rallings, C. (eds) (1995) *British Elections and Parties Yearbook 1994* (London: Frank Cass).

Weir, S. and Beetham, D. (1999) *Political Power and Democratic Control in Britain* (London: Routledge).

Weller, P. and Bakvis, H. (1997) 'The Hollow Crown: Coherence and Capacity in Central Government', in Weller, P., Bakvis, H. and Rhodes, R. A. W., *The Hollow Crown* (London: Macmillan).

Wheeler, N. J. and Dunne, T. (1998) 'Good International Citizenship: A Third Way for British Foreign Policy', *International Affairs*, Vol. 74, No. 4.

White, M. (1999) 'Want to Find Out What's Really Going On in British Politics? Read a Women's Magazine', *The Guardian*, 23 February.

White, S. (1998a) 'Interpreting the Third Way: Not One Road, But Many', *Renewal*, Vol. 6, No. 2.

White, S. (1998b) *The Economic Strategy of the 'New Centre-Left': A Contribution to the Nexus On-Line Discussion of the Economics of the Third Way* (London: Nexus).

Whitehead, P. (1986) *The Writing on the Wall: Britain in the 1970s* (London: Channel Four Books).

Whiteley, P. (1983) *The Labour Party in Crisis* (London: Methuen) (1997).

Whiteley, P. (1997) 'The Conservative campaign', in Norris, P. and Gavin, N. (eds).

Whiteley, P. and Seyd P. (1998) 'New Labour: New Grass Roots Party?', paper to the Annual Meeting of the Political Studies Association, University of Keele.

Whiteley, P. and Seyd, P. (forthcoming), *The Dynamics of Party Change* (Ann Arbor: University of Michigan Press).

Whiteley, P., Seyd, P. and Richardson, J. (1994) *True Blues: The Politics of Conservative Party Membership* (Oxford: Clarendon Press).

Wickham-Jones, M. (1995a) 'Recasting Social Democracy: a Comment on Hay and Smith', *Political Studies*, Vol. 43, No. 4.

Wickham-Jones, M. (1995b) 'Anticipating Social Democracy, Pre-empting Anticipations: Economic Policy-Making in the British Labour Party, 1987–1992', *Politics and Society*, Vol. 23, pp. 465–94.

Wickham-Jones, M. (1996) *Economic Strategy and the Labour Party: Politics and Policy-making, 1970–83* (London: Macmillan).

Williams, E. (1997) *Decide on the Architecture first, Times Higher Educational Supplement*, 21 November.

Williams, E. N. (1960) *The Eighteenth Century Constitution 1688–1815* (Cambridge; Cambridge University Press).

Williams, G. and Flynn, R. (1997) 'Beyond Simple NHS Models', *New Economy*, Vol. 4, No. 3.

Williams, G. L. and Williams, A. L. (1989) *Labour's Decline and the Social Democrats Fall* (Basingstoke: Macmillan).

Willsman, P. (1998) 'Insider's View of the Body Politic: Labour NEC briefing', *Tribune*, 11 December.

Wilson, H. (1974) *The Labour Government, 1964–70* (London: Weidenfeld & Nicolson).

Wilson, R. (1998) 'Modernising Central Government: the Role of the Civil Service', *Speech at Senior Civil Service Conference*, London, 13 October.

Wintour, P. (1998) 'New Blow for Cook in Ethics Battle', *The Observer*, 11 October.

Woolf, M. (1998) 'Brown's Blunders', *Financial Times*, 3 July.

Wring, D. (1997) 'Political Marketing and the Labour Party,' (unpublished PhD thesis, Cambridge University).

Young, H. (1997a) 'Not a Promised Land', *The Guardian*, 1 May.

Young, H. (1997b) 'Euro-X Marks the Spot of Incredulity', *The Guardian*, 11 December.

Young, H. (1998) 'Blair Needn't Be Afraid of the Bully: Sooner or Later He Will Call His Bluff', *The Guardian*, 25 June.

Index

Abbott, D., 100
Ad Hoc Committees, 151–4
Advertising, 24
Aiming Higher (1996), 194
Alford Index, 38, 39, 40
All Women Shortlists (AWS), 99–100, 107
Alternative Vote Plus, 160
Amnesty International, 230, 232
Amsterdam Summit, 67
Amsterdam Treaty, 226
Ancien Régime, 240
Anderson, P., 58
Annesley, C., 31, 259
Annual Conference, 73, 76, 80, 119, 122
Arms-to-Africa Affair, 232
Assisted Places Scheme, 193, 194
Atomic weapons, 4, 5, 113, 220, 221
Attlee, C., 4, 10, 33, 93, 104, 112–13, 169, 220–1
Austria, 55

Balls, E., 62, 63, 64, 66
Bank of England, 64, 123, 147, 149, 174, 178, 228, 253
Barber, M., 196
Bayley, S., 131
Beckett, M., 9, 77, 177, 178
Beetham, D., 89
Belgium, 55
Benn, T., 6, 8, 9, 14, 25, 28, 130
Bergounioux, A., 57
Best practice, 188
Bevan, A., 4, 5, 12, 130
Beveridge, W., 203, 207, 209, 251, 260
Bevin, E., 95, 250
Bevir, M., 250
Black Papers, 185, 187
Blair, T., 1, 9, 15, 27, 37, 44, 47, 60, 61, 65, 70, 73, 75, 76, 82, 86, 87, 92, 95, 96, 97, 100, 114–15, 117, 119, 120, 121, 124, 127, 128, 134,

136, 142, 144, 149, 151, 172, 184, 191, 192, 202, 231, 235, 236, 238, 243, 247, 256, 257, 259, 261, 262, 263, 264, 265, 266
Block Votes, 111–14, 118
Blunkett, 191, 197
Boateng, P., 100
Bondfield, M., 99
Boothroyd, B., 142
Boulton, A., 137
Boycott, R,, 136
Brandt, W., 250
Bretton Woods, 58, 170, 173, 220, 222, 261
British Education Study (BES), 39, 41, 43, 46, 47
British Representation Survey, 106, 108
Brittan, S., 251
Brown, George, 5, 12
Brown, Gordon, 9, 62, 64, 115, 136, 173, 174, 175, 180, 227, 243, 251, 259, 266
Buller, J., 31, 266
Bullock, Report, 242
Butler Education Act (1944), 184, 186
Butler, R., 153
Byers, S., 178

Cabinet Office, 150, 153
Callaghan, J., 5, 8, 14, 27, 35, 54, 73, 104, 119, 185, 199, 221, 223, 249, 252, 257, 261, 265
Campaign for Democratic Socialism, 5
Campbell, A., 132–7, 140–1
Capitalism, 55, 70, 168, 244
Centralization, 134, 150–1, 152
Central Office of Information (COI), 132, 144
Centre for Management and Policy Studies, 150
Charter 88, 240
Child benefit, 176, 230, 215

Childcare Tax Credit (CCTC), 211
Child Poverty Action Group (CPAG),
   214
China, 230, 231
Choice for England, A (1995), 158
Christian Democracy, 59, 214, 254
Citizens' income, 218
City Technology Colleges (CTCs),
   186, 192, 200
Civil society, 206, 214
Clarke, D., 150, 163
Clarke, H. D., 47
Clarke, K., 174
Class, 24, 38–40, 93, 185, 191, 192,
   245, 252
Clause IV, 5, 9, 12, 37, 77, 113, 128,
   172, 263, 264
Clift, B., 30, 266
Clinton, B., 57, 61, 213, 227, 231
Coates, D., 236
Cold War, 4, 11, 220–22, 224, 266
Cole, G. D. H., 250
Commission on Social Justice (CSJ), 9,
   29, 204–5, 208, 213, 218
Committee for Vice Chancellors and
   Principles (CVCP), 195
Communist Parties, 58
Company Law Review, 177
Cook, R., 230, 232
Comprehensive schools, 5, 185, 186,
   191, 192
Comprehensive Spending Review, 175,
   176, 196–7
Confederation of British Industry
   (CBI), 124, 175, 178, 242
Conservatives, 33–8, 44, 45, 50–2, 83,
   92, 96–9, 101–4, 116, 142,
   147–50, 154, 164, 167, 171, 172,
   178, 182, 185–7, 191 –3,
   197–201, 201–6, 211, 217, 229,
   237, 245, 253, 256–62, 266;
   spending plans, 11, 123, 154, 174,
   196, 212, 236
Conservatism, 251–2
Constitutional reform, 21–2, 145–66,
   244, 261
Control freakery, 141–3
Core executive, 148–54, 158, 161
Cousins, F., 95
Cowley, P., 30, 261, 264

Criddle, B, 96
Cripps, S., 4
Crosland, T., 4, 6, 14, 55, 170, 250;
   Future of Socialism, 4, 12, 186
Cunningham, J., 92, 150

Daily Express, 136
Darcy, D., 30, 261, 264
Dearing, R., 194
Dearing Report, 194
Decentralization, 3, 159
Decline, 10, 33, 220, 221
Defence policy, 23, 219–33
Deflation, 11–12
De Gaulle, C., 5
Delors, J., 57, 59, 66
Democracy, 41, 76, 132, 141–3
Demographic change, 93, 207, 245
Denmark, 55
Departmentalism, 149, 151
Détente, 222–4
'Devil eyes' campaign, 2
Devolution, 149, 155–9
Douglas-Home, A., 33, 34
Downs, A., 41
Drucker, H., 103

Education Action Zones (EAZs), 188,
   193, 196, 197, 200
Economic growth, 169, 175
Economic management, 4, 7–14,
   16–18, 46, 58, 60, 61, 167–83,
   228, 236, 245–6, 257
Economic policy, 168–73, 242–4, 267
Education policy, 4, 20–21, 184–201,
   235, 259–60
Education Reform Act (1988),
   196, 199
Electoral: campaigning, 47–9;
   constraints, 2, 15–16, 244–5;
   record, 3, 7, 32–7, 75, 262;
   reform, 159–61;
   strategy, 24–5, 246–7;
   system, 49–52
Electorate, 32–54; middle class, 5, 24,
   39, 186, 190, 217, 246, 254, 260,
   262; working class, 13, 15, 35,
   39–40, 44, 53, 244–6, 260, 262

England, 158, 195
Employability, 70–1, 167, 176,
    209–10
Employment Chapter, 67
Employment policy, 66–71, 226
Equal opportunities, 99, 210–11
Ethical: policy, 229–32;
    socialism, 252, 259
Ethnic minorities, 100–1
Euro-Keynsianism, 66, 72
Europe, 22–3, 36, 104
European Central Bank (ECB), 104,
    180, 227, 228
European Convention on Human
    Rights, 162
European Court of Human Rights, 157
European Economic Community
    (EEC), 5, 6, 15, 56–7, 171
European elections, 53, 160, 261
European Exchange Rate Mechanism
    (ERM), 37, 46, 228
Europeanization, 58–9, 207, 225–9,
    258, 266
European Monetary Union (EMU),
    104, 207
European social democracy, 2, 7,
    55–72, 171, 182, 214, 254
European Union (EU), 147, 148, 155,
    156, 159, 173, 180, 207, 214, 220,
    223, 225, 226, 227, 257, 266
European Works Councils, 127
Excellence for Everyone (1996), 192
Exchange Rate Mechanism (ERM),
    171, 172, 224

Fabian Society, 12, 216, 250
Fairness at Work (1998), 115, 116,
    120, 123, 124, 125, 177, 209
Falklands War, 8, 35
Families, 207
Family-friendly policies, 210–11
Field, F., 135, 180, 205, 211
Financial Times, 214
Finland, 55, 62
First-past-the-post, 49–52, 160
Flexibility, 68–71, 119, 206, 225, 237
Focus groups, 37, 47, 143
Foot, M., 4, 6, 8, 15, 46
Foreign policy, 219–33, 260
Foster, M., 107

France, 28, 55, 56, 57, 58, 62–70, 226,
    227, 259
Franklin, B., 31, 261
Freeden, M., 248, 250, 251
Freedom of information, 141, 162–4,
    261
Frieden, J., 58
Friedman, M., 63, 174
Full employment, 4, 13, 55, 67, 112,
    123, 169

Gaitskell, H., 4, 5, 12, 168, 170, 170,
    191, 204, 250, 263
Gamble, A., 31, 67, 259
George, D. L., 251
George, E., 174
George, S., 56
Germany, 55, 56, 58, 62, 63, 65, 68,
    69, 70, 120, 210, 222, 224, 226
Giddens, A., 215–16; Third Way,
    116, 216
Global economy, 171, 173, 179
Globalization, 58–9, 62–3, 207, 213,
    243–4
Gould, B., 247
Gould, P., 26, 28, 143, 190, 261
Government Information and
    Communications Service (GICS),
    132, 133, 136, 138–41, 144
Grammar schools, 184, 185, 191, 193
Gramsci, A., 237
Grant, B., 100
Grassroots Alliance, 188
Greece, 56, 57
Green Party, 58
Guardian, The, 133, 135, 137, 190,
    192, 264

Hague, W., 142
Hall, S., 238
Harman, H., 135, 137, 192
Hattersley, R., 8, 9, 15, 77
Hay, C., 1, 27, 238, 239
Haythorne, D., 56
Hazell, R., 153, 157, 158, 159, 164
Health Action Zones (HAZs), 212
Health and Safety Commission, 187
Healy, D., 6, 8
Heath, E., 5, 6, 116
Heffer, E., 8

Hegemony, 237–8
Hennesy, P., 153
Hewitt, P., 263
Higher education, 187, 189, 190,
    193–5; fees, 194–5
Higher Education Contribution Scheme
    (HECS), 194
Hill, D., 137
Hobhouse, L. T., 251
Holland, 55, 57, 62
Hood, C., 239
Humphreys, J., 137
Hutton, W., 59, 258
House of Lords, 160–1
Human rights, 127, 161–2, 230

Independent, 136
Independent learning accounts, 176
India, 220
Industrial policy, 12, 18, 177
Industrial relations, 112, 170, 226, 265
Industrial Training Boards, 186, 187
Industry and Society (1957), 4
Inflation, 6, 63, 64, 173–4, 179
Ingham, B., 134
In Place of Strife (1969), 5, 101, 102,
    113, 125
International Criminal Court, 230
International Monetary Fund (IMF), 6,
    11, 12, 13–14, 203
Iraq, 227, 231
Irvine, D., 150
Issue voting, 41, 44
Italy, 55, 58, 68, 69

Jackson, K., 128
Jacques, M., 212, 238
Jenkins, R., 5, 6, 8, 160
Johnson, A., 95
Joined-up government, 3, 149, 151,
    159, 208
Jordan, B., 213
Joseph, K., 59
Jospin, L., 67, 70
Journalists, 135–8

Kavanagh, D., 89
Keep Left (1947), 4
Kelly, G., 31, 67, 259
Kenny, M., 31, 259

Keynesian: demand management, 4, 7,
    10, 14, 34, 59, 62, 112, 114, 167,
    170, 187, 203, 259; welfare state,
    169, 256, 261
Keynes, J. M., 251
Kinnock, N., 6, 8, 9, 15, 25, 26, 27, 28,
    29, 30, 35, 46, 56, 57, 74, 75,
    76, 77, 78, 86, 87, 96, 114, 117,
    122, 124, 168, 171, 172, 177,
    181, 182, 190, 195, 203, 204,
    223, 225, 235, 238, 257, 261,
    262, 264, 265
Kohl, H., 67
Kok, W., 57
Kosovo, 227, 230

Labour alliance, 111
Labour's Programme (1973, 1976), 6
Lafontaine, O., 6, 63, 66
Laski, H., 250
League tables, 191
Leaks, 140, 161
Lewis, I., 107
Liberal Democrats, 90, 128
Liberalism, 55, 251, 252
Liberal Party, 32, 128, 154, 236
Lib-Lab Pact (1997), 6–7
Lifelong learning, 124, 193, 197,
    205–10
Lifelong Learning (1996), 193, 194
Lister, R., 210, 214–15
Livingstone, K., 83, 90, 118, 247
Lloyd, J., 2
Local Education Authorities (LEAs),
    187, 188, 191, 196, 199
Local policy forum, 79
London Mayor, 160, 161
Lovenduski, J., 93
Ludlam, S., 265

Maastricht convergence criteria, 59, 64,
    65, 72
Maastricht Treaty, 173, 214
MacDonald, R., 32, 236, 250
Macmillan, H., 33
MacMurray, J., 252
Macro-economic: policy, 62–8;
    stability, 173–6, 178, 182
Major, J., 2, 36, 46, 47, 132, 138–9,
    181, 199, 213, 225, 258

Mandelson, P., 8, 26, 44, 68, 114, 125, 131, 150, 178, 190, 261
Manifestos, 16–23, 78
Manpower Services Commission, 187, 247
marginal seats, 48–9
Marquand, D., 146, 250, 251
Marxism Today, 212, 213, 237, 238
McCaig, C., 31, 259
McDonnell, J., 106
McMahon Act (1946), 221
McNair, B., 133
Marr, A., 136
Means-testing, 205, 213, 215, 217, 260
Media machinery, 3, 8, 26, 35, 47–9, 74, 117
Meet the Challenge, Make the Change (1989), 8, 27
Mellors, C., 30, 261, 264
Membership, 15, 74–5, 82–9, 117
Michels, R., 201
Middle England, 2, 53, 213, 217, 246
Militant, 25
Millbank, 53, 117
Millbankization, 31, 133
Mill, J. S., 252
Minkin, L., 20, 21, 111, 117, 118, 123, 126, 127
Minimum wage, 116, 118, 121, 126, 172, 177, 251
Mitchell, J., 159
Mitterrand, F., 28, 59
Modernization, 3, 27–8, 176, 189–90, 203–6, 234–41, 254–7, 264
Monetarism, 3, 30, 34, 35, 59, 171, 174, 176, 178, 257
Monetary Policy Committee (MPC), 149, 174, 175, 180, 229
Monks, J., 115, 118, 124, 126
Morgan, R., 118
Morris, B., 199, 122, 125, 126, 153, 159, 164
Mountfield Report, 134
Mowlem, M., 150
Murdoch Press, 136, 228

NAIRU, 176, 178, 179
National Changeover Plan,. 173, 229
National Curriculum, 189, 192, 196, 199, 260

National Economic Development Council, 247
National Exectutive Committee (NEC), 9, 25, 73, 76, 78, 83, 84, 112, 135, 264
National Health Service (NHS), 4, 33, 42, 212
Nationalization, 4, 12, 15, 41, 118, 264
National Policy Forum, 9, 73, 79–82, 118
North Atlantic Treaty Organization (NATO), 4, 221, 226, 230, 258
Neo-liberalism, 11, 27, 59, 167, 181, 183, 212, 213, 237, 238
New Deal, 68, 172, 176, 186, 209, 211, 214, 215, 251
New Left, 237, 238, 240
'New realism', 25–6, 265
New Right, 59, 63, 188, 206, 207, 213, 214
News at Ten, 132
News management, 130–44, 261
Newsnight, 136
New Statesman, 103, 125
New Unionism, 123,
Next Step Agencies, 247
Norris, P., 108
North Atlantic Treaty Organization (NATO), 4
Northern Ireland, 50, 130, 139, 155, 156–8, 195, 208
Norway, 99
Nuffield election studies, 75
Number 10, 132, 133–5, 142, 144, 151,
Nursery Voucher Scheme, 188, 193

Old Labour, 2, 3, 167, 186–9, 204, 207, 256, 259, 261, 265
O'Leary, B., 157, 158
One member one vote (OMOV), 8, 9, 25, 26, 29, 77, 114
Opening Doors to a Learning Society (1994), 190–1
Open University, 5, 186
Opinion polls, 48
Ottawa Agreement, 230
Ozbudun, E., 102

Padgett, S., 55
Parliament, 92–110, 142–4, 145, 154

Parliamentary Labour Party (PLP), 92–110, 114,
Parliamentary sovereignty, 155–7, 162, 164
Parris, M., 132, 136
Partnership, 176, 214, 248
Partnership in Power (1996), 9, 79, 86, 118, 122
Partners in Progress (1997), 121
Party of European Socialists (PES), 66, 67
Party: funding, 75, 117–18; image, 24, 36, 44–7, 172; structure, 73–90
Pattie, C., 30
Paterson, W., 55
Pensions, 7, 118, 123, 203, 211–12, 260
Performance and Innovation Unit, 150
Pergau Dam affair, 229
Persson, I., 67, 70–1
Peterson, M., 69
Philips, M., 190
Plan Aubry, 68
Platell, A., 136
Plowden Report (1967), 185
Policy: commission, 79, 122; convergence, 41; making, 78–81, 258; modernization, 16–23; packaging, 131–3
Policy Review (1989), 16–23, 26, 28–9, 114, 151, 170–1, 187, 203, 238, 257
Political agency, 234–55
Portillo, M., 49
Portschach Summit, 67, 68, 226
Portugal, 57, 68
Powell, J., 135, 151
Power, 3, 81, 149
Press and Publicity Department, 130
Prescott, J., 9, 77, 160
Price Commission, 247
Prime Minister's Question Time, 142
Private Finance Initiative (PFI), 118, 121, 177, 212
Privatization, 36, 41, 121, 147, 148, 171
Proportional representaion, 160–1
Przeworski, A., 237

Qualified Majority Voting (QMV), 104
Quangos, 147, 148

Radical centre, 60–1
Rawnsley, A., 138
Reagan, R., 59
Rebellions, 101–10
Redistribution, 2, 9, 41, 61, 65, 68–9, 169, 170, 182, 203, 206, 214, 215
Reich, R., 60
Reynolds, D., 196
Regional Development Agencies (RDAs), 176, 177
Regional List System, 160
Review of Banking Competition, 177
Revisionism, 4, 5, 13–15
Rhetoric, 167, 168, 175, 182
Richards, D., 31
Richards, S., 103
Riddell, P., 148
Robbins, L., 186
Robertson, G., 226
Romer, P., 60
Rose, R., 257
Ross, E., 232
Ross, J. F. S., 93
Roth, A., 96
Routledge, P., 136
Royal Commission, 151
Russia, 230
Rutter, J., 139

Sassoon, D., 58
Save the Children, 230
Sawyer, T., 78
Scammell, M., 133
Scargill, A., 9, 28
Schäuble, W., 142
Schmidt, H., 250
School Standards and Framework Bill (1997), 195–6
Schröder, G., 67, 71, 226
Scotland, 50, 127, 155, 157–9, 195, 208
Scottish Parliament, 52, 82, 155–6, 159
Scott Report, 163, 229, 231
Secondary modern schools, 185
Sedgemore, B., 106

Select Committee on Public
  Administration, 138
Selection of candidates, 73, 77, 78
Seyd, P., 30, 263, 264
Shaw, E., 14, 24, 26
Sheffield, 53
Short, C., 75
Sierra Leone, 232
Single currency, 227–9
Skinner, D., 83
Smith, J., 8, 9, 28, 37, 57, 74–7, 96,
  114, 116, 118, 122, 124, 172, 177,
  181, 182, 190, 204, 235, 238,
  257, 265
Smith, M. J., 27, 31, 259
Social authoritarianism, 188, 252
Social citizenship, 202, 203, 210
Social communitarianism, 252
Social Contract, 13, 34, 113, 116
Social democracy, 2, 35, 55, 172, 177,
  181, 183, 216, 237, 243, 250, 252,
  254, 259
Social Democratic Party (SDP), 8, 15,
  29, 35; SDP / Liberal Alliance, 8,
  26, 35, 52
Social exclusion, 60, 180, 183, 202,
  207–8, 217
Social Exclusion Unit (SEU), 150, 208,
  214
Social fairness, 205, 217
Socialism, 1, 55, 168, 252
Socialist International, 56
Socialist Labour Party, 9, 127
Social justice, 62, 202, 204, 205, 213,
  217, 218, 236, 259
Social partnership, 116, 117, 125, 126,
  127, 177
Social Protocol, 116, 124, 127,
  209, 214
Solidarity Group, 8, 15
Sontag, S., 131
Soskice, D., 70
Soundbites, 130, 132
Spain, 55, 56, 64
Special advisers, 138–9
Spindoctors, 37, 47
Stakeholding, 69, 123, 205, 208
State Earnings-Related Pension
  Scheme (SERPS), 7, 211

state reform, 145–66
sterling crisis, 4, 6, 223
Strategic Arms Limitation Talks
  (SALT II), 222
Strategic Communications Unit, 132,
  134, 140, 144, 150
Straw, J., 160, 162, 163, 252
Suez crisis, 4, 5, 220–2
Sunday Express, 138
Sunday Times, 132
Supply-side economic policy, 171,
  176–8, 179, 180
Supporting Families (1998), 210
Sweden, 55, 57, 58, 62, 63, 65, 66, 68,
  70–1, 99, 231

Taskforces, 151–2, 196
Taxation, 2, 13, 17–18, 36, 64, 65, 67,
  156, 167, 172, 174, 175, 182,
  215, 258
Tax credits, 182, 213
Taylor, A., 190
Taylor, R., 126
Teaching and Higher Education Bill
  (1998), 194–5
Technical and Vocational Education
  Initiative (TVEI), 186
Thatcher, M., 2, 26, 34, 36, 40, 41, 42,
  46, 59, 110, 114, 125, 132, 144,
  181, 199, 203, 204, 213, 225, 229
Thatcherism, 13, 15, 24, 57, 129, 164,
  203, 204, 234–9, 241, 247–9, 251,
  252–9, 262, 266; influence on
  New Labour, 2, 27, 153, 198–200,
  212–13
'Third way', 2, 30, 55–72, 116, 119,
  216–17
Thirty-five-hour working week, 68–9
Times, The, 136
Today (R4), 137
Trade unions, 5, 6, 9, 19, 25–6, 28, 45,
  71, 74, 75–7, 111–29, 125, 168,
  172, 183, 187, 265
Trades Union Congress (TUC), 5, 111,
  112, 115–17, 124–7
Training and Enterprise Councils
  (TECs), 147, 148
Training policy, 186, 187, 196
Tribune Group, 5, 8, 15

Unemployment, 13, 63, 66, 69, 176,
    178–9, 206, 259
United States (US), 220, 221, 222, 224,
    227, 231
Universalism, 29, 203, 205, 214, 215,
    217, 243, 258, 260
University for Industry (UfI), 198

Vartiainen, J., 65
Vaz, K., 100
Voice for Wales (1997), 157
Von Beyme, K., 89

Wage policy, 111–13
Wales, 50, 155, 157–9, 195, 208
Walker, I, 136
Ware, A., 74
Weir, S., 89
Welfare: fraud, 215; policy, 19–20,
    64–5, 123, 202–18, 235, 259–60;
    reform, 118, 172, 180, 133;
    state, 55, 202, 206–12, 250–1, 258
Welfare-to-work, 124, 142, 176–8, 210
Welsh Assembly, 52, 82, 157, 159, 261
Western European Union (WEU), 226
Westminster, 3, 145, 156, 157, 160;
    model, 146–7, 154, 156, 160–1,
    163, 235, 244, 258

Whelan, C., 135, 139
Whiteley, P., 30, 263, 264
Whitty, L., 78
Wickhan-Jones, M., 30
Widdecombe, A., 107
Williams, Lord, 162
Wilson, H., 4, 5, 12, 27, 34, 56, 104,
    113, 191, 221, 223, 229, 235,
    240, 252
Wilson, R., 133, 151, 153
Wilson Report, 150
Windfall tax, 175, 215
Winter of Discontent, 7, 13, 14, 35, 45,
    111, 113
Wintour, P., 231
Woman's Hour (R4), 135
Women, 76–7, 99–100, 106–7, 206,
    210–11, 245
Woodhead, C., 197
Work-centred social policy, 69–71,
    172, 173, 180, 209–10
Working Families Tax Credit (WFTC),
    70, 176, 211, 213
World At One (R4), 135

Young, H., 135, 163
Your Right to Know (1997), 162–3

Zimbabwe, 232